T0347079

Justice versus Judiciary

Justice versus Judiciary

Justice Enthroned or Entangled in India?

Sudhanshu Ranjan

OXFORD
UNIVERSITY PRESS

OXFORD
UNIVERSITY PRESS

Oxford University Press is a department of the University of Oxford.
It furthers the University's objective of excellence in research, scholarship,
and education by publishing worldwide. Oxford is a registered trademark of
Oxford University Press in the UK and in certain other countries.

Published in India by
Oxford University Press
2/11 Ground Floor, Ansari Road, Daryaganj, New Delhi 110 002, India

ISBN-13 (print edition): 978-0-19-949049-3
ISBN-10 (print edition): 0-19-949049-X

ISBN-13 (eBook): 978-0-19-909626-8
ISBN-10 (eBook): 0-19-909626-0

Typeset in Adobe Garamond Pro 11/13
by Tranistics Data Technologies, Kolkata 700 091
Printed in India by Replika Press Pvt. Ltd

To the memory of my mother (*maiya*), Mithilesh Nandini,
who prized justice above everything else

Contents

Foreword

Sudhanshu Ranjan's book *Justice Versus Judiciary: Justice Enthroned or Entangled in India?* is a profound comment on the Indian justice delivery system. It is a comprehensive assessment of the social relevance and utility of the ways in which the system works in practice. It compels attention.

The author opens the debate with this statement:

> Authority and accountability go together. Authority bereft of accountability morphs into authoritarianism. So, every person or institution wielding power is held to account. It is the judiciary which holds every institution of the state to account. But ironically, for itself any idea of accountability is anathema in the name of its independence. This book grapples with the issue of the accountability of the judiciary.

In the next six chapters Sudhanshu Ranjan throws light on the actual working of the judicial machinery and its efficacy in the context of increasing civilizational complexities of the times. It is a resurrection of the old question—Who watches the watchmen?

A critic compared the power of judicial review and its increasing expansive sweep to a child which, given a hammer, believes that everything under the sun is worth pounding. In a non-trivial sense this may summarize the mood of self-righteousness and infallibility of the judicial system. Indeed, it is said that courts are not final because they are infallible; but they are infallible because they are final.

Law, it is said, is a notorious laggard. It does not reach out as science does. It follows social consensus which is itself behind the needs of times.

The pejorative remark is that the law is one generation behind the needs of the times; the courts are two generations behind and the judges three. Lord Denning identified two kinds amongst judges: the 'timorous Souls' and the 'Bold Spirits'. Lord Denning was himself known for his profoundly creative judicial mind. He set out to reform the law to make it irrelevant, meaningful to the times. But a recent assessment of the performance of the judicial department in England made by the Incorporated Law Reporting Society did not accord a pride of place to the judicial contribution of that great judge. The society in its 150th anniversary celebrated a couple of years ago, listed, what according to it, 15 cases that marked the developmental law in England for 150 years. Lord Denning's pronouncements were not accorded adequate recognition. The philosophy of judicial restraint—called the Thayer School named after James Bradley Thayer—and the philosophy of judicial activism seem to be the competing doctrines. Judicial law-making is now accepted. 'We do not believe in fairytales anymore,' declared Lord Reid. Chief Justice Earl Warren once said, 'Our judges are not monks or scientists, but participants in the living stream of our national life, steering the law between the dangers of rigidity on the one hand and of formlessness on the other. Our system faces no theoretical dilemma but a single continuous problem, how to apply the never-changing, principles of freedom to ever-changing conditions.'

It cannot be gain-said that despite all criticism the Supreme Court of India led a virtual judicial revolution. Social and economic justice became the watch-words of the new philosophy and the new jurisprudence. The distinguished lawyer the late Andhyarujina made some profound observations on this new judicial creed in an article published in the *Law Quarterly Review*. He said: 'the beneficial nature of this easy approach to courts by disregarding the conventional requirement of locus standi for the applicant, and the non-adversarial character of the court's intervention came to be widely appreciated by the public and even imitated by other common law jurisdiction.' Andhyarujina referred to Lord Woolf's acknowledgment: 'I soon realized that if that Court was to perform its essential role in Indian society, it had no option but to adopt the course it did and I congratulate it for the courage it has shown.' Justices Bhagvathi, Krishna Iyer, Chinappa Reddy and Desai—affectionately referred to as the 'Gang of Four'—led the charge. It's somewhat unfair to ignore that some of our great judges, to borrow Justice Holmes' phrase found the 'constitution paper and made it power'.

But then it is only a weak society that constantly appeals to judicial paternalism to solve all its problems. This will rob society of the excitement of democracy to fight issues out democratically. That is the hour of courts' temptation. Judicial activism can be a slippery slope. Generally Policy Issues are a difficult area for judicial penetration. Robert Borke in his *The Tempting of America* brings out how faint cracks appear in the foundations of the Constitution by judicial over-reach.

The twenty-first century will witness dramatic changes. The exploits of science and technology will be mind-blowing. In a recent book, *21 Questions for the 21st Century*, Yuval Noah Harari examines the impact of these new disruptive technologies. Many of our policies, practices, procedures, and systems have outlived their 'shelf-life'. Judicial practices and methods are no exception. Indeed, Sudhanshu Ranjan has a vision of the judiciary as an old man wearing, with attached fondness, the clothes of his youth unaware of the ridiculousness of the situation. The criticism may sound a bit strident but serves as a well-intentioned wake-up call.

Sudhanshu Ranjan's straightforward talk reminds us of Mark Twain's humour: 'It is by goodness of the God that in our country we have those three unspeakably precious things; freedom of speech, freedom of conscience, and the prudence, never to practice either of them.'

This book is a critical analysis of the judicial predicament and the problems which have become banal by reason of stereotyped speculation. The author's message is that the judiciary has to adopt new ways of thinking if it is to survive. Many share this view.

M.N. Venkatachaliah (Former Chief Justice of India)
Bengaluru
9 March 2019

Acknowledgements

On the occasion of the launch of my previous book *Justice, Judocracy and Democracy in India: Boundaries and Breaches* (2013), in New Delhi, former attorney general Soli J. Sorabjee had commented that I should put on a collar, a band, and a gown and join the bar to observe its functioning more closely as I was critical of the judiciary in the book. The then Chief Justice of India Altmas Kabir, while eulogizing my courage 'which few people have', to use his words, though disagreeing with me on many issues, agreed with Soli Sorabjee that I should join the bar. However, I did not join the bar but remained an onlooker observing developments in the judiciary keenly. The judiciary plays a crucial role in a democracy, and so it attracts public adulation as well as animadversion for whatever it does. But writing a book requires a lot of research. Being outside the field of law, the task was arduous. However, I got help from many friends, lawyers, former judges, and law professors who were generous enough to provide whatever help I needed.

My friend Lokendra Malik, advocate, was always a pillar of support who encouraged and inspired at every stage, provided books and introduced to some people who were quite helpful. I am greatly obliged to him. I am grateful to Poonam Saxena, vice-chancellor, National Law University, Jodhpur, India, and Sunil Gupta, Faculty of Law, University of Delhi, who helped me in research with valuable inputs and insight. M.P. Singh and B.B. Pandey, both former professors of Law, Delhi University, were helpful as they always have been and went through some of the chapters of the book and suggested improvements. Their endorsement gave me confidence. I am indebted to Justice B.P. Singh, former judge of the Supreme Court, and late Justice

G.C. Bharukha, former acting chief justice of the Karnataka High Court, who were always accessible and helpful. I don't have words to express my gratitude to Justice M N Vankatachaliah, former Chief Justice of India. At this old age, he was kind enough to write it. I am gratified to have a few words from a universally respected jurist.

My younger brother Shwetanshu Ranjan, advocate, Begusarai, Bihar, India, and Vinay Ranjan Prasad Verma, advocate, Begusarai, helped me research various provisions of the Civil Procedure Code and how these are misused to prolong litigations. K.K. Rai, senior advocate, and Chandrashekhar A. Chakalabbi, advocate, helped me with citations of many cases which saved my time. My friend Ambhoj Kumar Sinha, advocate, always gave support and encouragement. They are all part of my family and extended family, and I thank them profusely. Besides, I am grateful to Manoj Kumar Sinha, Director, Indian Law Institute, New Delhi; Ashok Malik, honorary advisor, Red Cross Society of India; Nitin Satija, Lexis Nexis; B. Mangalam, Department of English, Aryabhatta College, University of Delhi; and Rajesh Chauhan, Department of Hindi, Satyavati College, University of Delhi. They all helped me in different ways. I shall be failing in my duty if I do not thank the team at Oxford University Press. I am grateful to the Press for publishing this book.

The book would not have seen the light of the day without the support of my family which has to suffer as usual because I am not able to devote time to them. My wife Manjari, son Shwetabh, and daughter Shreya deserve special thanks for encouragement, support, and love they have given me. I also got encouragement from my brothers, sisters, in-laws, cousins, and friends. I thank them all. I miss my late parents who would have been delighted at its publication. I did not dedicate my books to them when they were alive. So, I am dedicating this book to my mother who personified justice. Alas, if I could do it when she was in this world.

1

Introduction

Authority and accountability go together. Authority bereft of accountability morphs into authoritarianism. So, every person or institution wielding power is held to account. It is the judiciary which holds every institution of the state to account. But ironically, for itself any idea of accountability is anathema in the name of its independence. This book grapples with the issue of the accountability of the judiciary. Its title *Justice versus Judiciary: Justice Enthroned or Entangled in India?* has been inspired by M.K. Gandhi for whom the profession of law became the means to enthrone justice, not 'entangle justice' in the net of law.[1] Unfortunately, it appears that justice is not being enthroned but entangled. Judges are more interested in flaunting their powers and status with little empathy for the victims who knock the door of the court. Perhaps, they are under a delusion that moving the court is a luxury for everyone, little realizing the sufferings the common man has to undergo. It leads many to bankruptcy, and still justice remains entangled in procedural rigmaroles. Lawyers are adept at entangling justice. Justice system is a prisoner in the hands of lawyers, judges, and the few moneyed litigants who can tweak the system in their favour. Thus, justice is entangled, not enthroned. Alas, we do not have another Gandhi.

The chapter 'Accountability of Judges' discusses why the accountability and independence of the judiciary are not antagonistic but mutually complementary. However, judging is a difficult job. The Bible says:

[1] Pyarelal Nayyar, *Mahatma Gandhi—The Early Phase*, vol. 1 (Ahmedabad: Navajivan Publishing House, 1965), p. 313.

Judge not, that ye be not judged (*Matthew* 7: 1)

Why beholdest thou the mote that is in thy brother's eye, but considerest not the beam that is in thine own eye. (*Matthew* 7: 3)

Judge not, and ye shall not be judged: condemn not, and ye shall not be condemned: forgive and ye shall be forgiven. (*Luke* 6: 37)

Bertrand Russell wrote:

You will remember that Christ said: 'Judge not lest ye be judged'. That principle I do not think you would find was popular in the law courts of Christian countries. I have known in my time quite a number of judges who were very earnest Christians, and they none of them [*sic*] felt that they were acting contrary to Christian principles in what they did.[2]

Judges are under a legal obligation to judge but while judging, they are themselves being judged; when they conduct trials, they are themselves on trial. In a sense, the job of judges is very easy because whatever they say is right. Since whatever they say is right, it becomes extremely difficult because they have to ascertain what is right. Thus, they are on trial while trying others. Alexander Hamilton, one of the founders of the United States Constitution and one of the authors of *The Federalist Papers*, famously commented that the judiciary 'has no influence over either the sword or the purse'. Its only power is its power of judgment, using which it can earn the respect of the people. Giordano Bruno was tried for heresy. Pope Clement VIII pronounced that he was a heretic, and the Inquisition issued the sentence of death. Bruno is said to have made threatening gestures towards the judges and to have told them: 'Maiori forsan cum timore sententiam in me fertis quam ego accipiam' (Perhaps you pronounce this sentence against me with greater fear than I receive it).[3]

The Legal Hearing of the Truth and Reconciliation Commission in South Africa put the law on trial; its purpose was to diagnose the malaise with law during apartheid and to erect an edifice of a democratic society. It was hoped that judges, lawyers, and law teachers would testify their roles and actions. However, judges refused to accept the invitation adducing the hackneyed logic of 'judicial independence'. David Dyzenhaus inveighs upon the role of judges:

---

[2] Bertrand Russell, 'Why I Am Not a Christian', in *The Basic Writings of Bertrand Russell* (London and New York: Routledge Classics, 2009), p. 573.

[3] Robert Hughes, *The Spectacle of Skill: Selected Writings of Robert Hughes*, with Introduction by Adam Gopnik (New York: Alfred A. Knopf), p. 463.

[J]udges for the most part failed in the role which independence protects because they confused government with the state, thus permitting the government to fail to live up to the responsibilities that attend a claim to be a democratic state. [*349] Having failed in their duty, judges could not claim the immunity from testifying that normally attaches to judicial role.[4]

Judges have been accused of the worst kind of dishonesty and prejudice as is found in the Biblical story of Daniel and Susanna. Two elders of the community, appointed as judges, saw Susanna bathing in her husband's garden, and were filled with lust for her. When she returned, they accosted her, threatening to claim that she was meeting a young man unless she agreed to have sex with them. She resisted and was arrested. As they were elders and also judges, people believed them and she was condemned to death for promiscuity. A young man called Daniel interrupted the proceedings and demanded that an inquiry be made into their allegations to prevent the execution of an innocent. After a careful cross-examination, the judges were proved to be liars.[5]

Judges can go horribly wrong. It may be inadvertent, and so no motive can be imputed except questioning their efficiency and competence. But many a time, justice is throttled under a design. So, judges must be held to account. Judges are held to account on various counts—their personal conduct as well as the decisions they hand down. Describing the role of a judge, the Supreme Court of India has rightly observed:

> The nature of judicial process, even at its tallest tower, is such that, to use Cordozo's elegant expressions 'a Judge even when he is free, is still not wholly free; he is not to innovate pleasure; he is not a knight-errant roaming at will in pursuit of his own ideal of beauty or of goodness; he is to draw inspiration from consecrated principles'. Where the Judges' values and those prevailing in society clash, the Judge must, in theory, give way to the 'objective right'.[6]

This is the problem in India that instead of giving way to the 'objective right' every judge has their own brilliant idea. It leads to uncertainty and, many a time, over-activism as well as abnegation of authority which is required to protect the common man's rights. All this leads to bench hunting as lawyers and litigants seek favourable benches. The erosion of judicial collectivism

---

[4] David Duzenhaus, *Judging the Judges, Judging Ourselves: Truth, Reconciliation and the Apartheid Legal Order* (Oxford: Hart Publishing, 2003), pp. 172–3.

[5] *The Apocrypha*.

[6] *Shiv Mohan Singh* v. *State* (*Delhi Administration*) 2 SCC 238, para 2.

has led to a chaos-like situation. Every division bench is expected to follow not only the decisions of larger benches but also of division benches. The Supreme Court has ruled:

> When there are binding decisions, judicial comity expects and requires the same to be followed. Judicial comity is an integral part of judicial discipline and judicial discipline the cornerstone of judicial integrity. No doubt, in case there are newer dimensions not in conflict with the ratio of the larger Bench decisions or where there is anything to be added to and explained, it is always permissible to do the same.[7]

In exceptional circumstances, the court may bypass or overlook some provision or procedure for the sake of justice. But it is a rarity. The Judicial Committee of the Privy Council upheld the violation of the principle of natural justice in *Nakkuda Ali* v. *Jayaratne*[8] on the ground that it was war time. In this case from Ceylon, the Privy Council held that the Controller of Textiles was not required to observe natural justice in deciding to revoke a license to engage in business as a fabric merchant. In revoking the license, the controller acted under the authority of the wartime-era Defence (Control of Textiles) Regulations, 1945, Regulation 62 of which empowered him to do so where he 'had reasonable grounds to believe that any dealer is unfit to be allowed to continue as a dealer'. It was alleged that Nakkuda Ali had fraudulently falsified his books, so as to be able to unlawfully claim credit from the bank. Ali's main contention was that he had been denied natural justice as he claimed that he was not allowed to see the affidavits on file with the controller, which had presumably been used to counter his own letter of explanation. But to get to the substantive stage of the case, he first had to show that the controller was amenable to the writ of certiorari—that is, that he was engaged in quasi-judicial decision-making and that he had the power to affect Ali's rights. It was on this point that Ali fell down. He argued that the inclusion of the requirement that the belief of unfitness be 'reasonable' in Regulation 62 enjoined the controller to act judicially. Ian Holloway has commented,

> This placed the Privy Council on the horns of a dilemma. On one hand, they were anxious to distance themselves from the highly criticized and disreputed judgement of the House of Lords in *Liversidge v. Anderson*. But on the other, they were concerned (since they were effectively deciding a question of English

[7] *Sunil Damodar Gaikwad* v. *State of Maharashtra* (2014) 1 SCC 129, para 20.
[8] (1951) AC 66.

law) not to unnecessarily deviate from the principles espoused by Atkin LJ and Lord Hewart. One cannot help but wonder what the Privy Council's position might have been had the alleged violation of Nakkuda Ali's procedural rights been more egregious (for the record shows that Nakkuda Ali actually knew the substance of the allegations made against him), but in the end, the Board found that the Controller of Textiles did not have a superadded duty to act judicially, hence the remedy of certiorari was not available to quash any departure from the obligation to observe natural justice.[9]

In reaching this conclusion, the Board pointed to the fact that the statutory regime did not lay down any procedure at all which the controller was supposed to observe while exercising his power. Nor did the regulations provide for a right of appeal or anything else which might have suggested that the controller was to engage in judicial-like deliberations when determining a license. However, the judgment was reversed once the war over.

Uncertainly is one thing that the law abhors. The Supreme Court has rightly said,

> Predictability and certainty is an important hallmark of judicial jurisprudence developed in this country in the last six decades and increase in the frequency of conflicting judgments of the superior judiciary will do incalculable harm to the system inasmuch as the courts at the grass root will not be able to decide as to which of the judgments lay down the correct law and which one should be followed.[10]

Again it held, 'judicial pronouncements unlike sand dunes are known for their stability and finality'.[11] Unfortunately, it is not happening. This chapter discusses in detail how divergent judgments are being delivered muddying the stream of law, and thus, adding to obscurity and confusion.

Another major issue is conflict of interest, and judges must recuse automatically if there be such a conflict, but this is not happening either. *R. v. Sussex Justices, Ex p Mc Carthy*[12] is a landmark case in which the King's Bench (UK) established the principle that mere appearance of bias is sufficient to overturn a judicial decision. Lord Hewart made a profound statement which got universal thumbs-up and is oft-quoted, 'it is not merely of some importance but is of fundamental importance that justice should not only

---

[9] Ian Holloway, 'Natural Justice and the New Property', http://www.austlii.edu.au/au/journals/MonashULawRw/1999/4.pdf (last accessed on 14 March 2015).

[10] *Official Liquidator* v. *Dayanand* (2008) 10 SCC 1, para 90.

[11] *Meghmala G. Narsimha Reddy* (2010) 8 SCC 383, para 2.

[12] (1924) 1 KB 256 (1923) All ER Rep 233.

be done, but should manifestly and undoubtedly be seen to be done'. In 1923, McCarthy, a motorcyclist, was involved in an accident and was prosecuted before a magistrate's court, and charged with dangerous driving. The magistrate's clerk belonged to a firm of solicitors acting in a civil claim for the other party to the accident. McCarthy was convicted. As he came to know of the clerk's provenance, he appealed for the quashing of the conviction. Chief Justice Hewart of the King's Bench said that though the clerk did not influence the judgment at all, nothing is to be done which creates even a suspicion that there has been an improper interference with the course of justice. Thus, the conviction was quashed.

The only job of judges is to do justice and it should be visible. However, of late, judges do not appear to be keen to ensure that justice also seems to be done. Even the open court system is being discarded in the sense that except lawyers and litigants, nobody else is allowed in higher courts. The Supreme Court of India has become a fortress, and so have become most of the high courts which were accessible to the common man earlier. I saw at Begusarai in January 2018 that even in the district and sessions courts, only advocates and witnesses are allowed. This gnaws at the credibility of the judiciary which boasts of having open courts where anyone can walk in. In *Home Office* v. *Harman*,[13] Lord Scarman elucidated in his dissenting judgement (joined by Lord Simon) that 'there is also another public interest involved in justice done openly, namely that the evidence and argument should be publicly known, so that society may judge for itself the quality of justice administered in its name, and whether the law requires notification'. Lord Shaw, in *Scott* v. *Scott*,[14] elucidated the principle of open justice by referring to Bentham: 'Publicity is the very soul of justice. It is the keenest spur to exertion and the surest of all guards against improbity. It keeps the judge himself while trying under trial: Where there is no publicity there is no justice.'[15] There are exceptions to it in rare circumstances where in camera proceedings become necessary to ensure justice, but as Lord Diplock summarized beautifully in *Attorney-General* v. *Leveller Magazine Limited*[16] that departure must be '... justified to the extent and to no more than the extent that the court reasonably believes it to be necessary in order to serve the ends of justice ... if the way that courts behave cannot be hidden from the public ear and eye, this provides

---

[13] (1983) 1 AC 280.
[14] (1913) AC 417.
[15] (1913) AC 417, p. 477.
[16] (1979) AC 440.

a safeguard against judicial arbitrariness or idiosyncrasy and maintains the public confidence in the administration of justice'.[17]

The principle was restated by the Court of Appeal of England and Wales in *Guardian News and Media Ltd. V. R & Erol Incedal*.[18] In this case, the issue of derogating from open justice was linked with that of national security. Defendant Incedal had been charged with several offences relating to terrorism. The Court reiterated that open justice could only be departed from in unusual or exceptional circumstances.

The lack of accountability sometimes reaches heights of preposterousness. In July 1997, the Patna High Court triggered off storm when its division bench monitoring the fodder scam cases gave verbal order to the CBI to requisition the army's help to arrest Lalu Prasad (Yadav), then chief minister of Bihar. The division bench consisted of Justices S.N. Jha and S.J. Mukhopadhyay. A Central Bureau of Investigation (CBI) official approached Justice Jha telephonically to complain that they were not getting cooperation from the administration to serve warrant of arrest on Lalu issued by the CBI court, Patna, in a fodder scam case and arrest him. Throwing norms to wind, the judge asked him to seek the help of the army. The particular official also called CBI judge Sudhanshu Kumar Lal and complained. Lal was more dignified and judicious, asking him to file a petition in the court next day. Perhaps, the CBI approached the High Court judge after not getting the desired reply from the CBI judge. The joint director of the CBI (East) in charge of fodder scam investigation, U.N. Biswas asked the SP, CBI, Patna, to requisition the services of the army who did it, but the army did not comply with the request. It is inscrutable why the CBI was in such a great hurry to arrest Lalu on the night of 29 July 1997 itself and not at all worried about arresting other ministers of the state government against whom the same warrant was pending. The ineluctable legal position is that judges cannot give any verbal orders. Justice Jha later clarified that he did not give any direction but told the CBI that it could take the army's help if it so desired. Howbeit, it was not the business of the monitoring court to advise or direct the CBI on how to execute the warrant issued by a subordinate court. Judges do not discuss anything regarding any pending case with anyone, much less with any party to the case. Even an advice of the court may be taken as directive as the concerned official could quote that the judge had advised the CBI to requisition the service of the army.

[17] 1979) AC 440, pp. 449–50.
[18] (2016) WLR (D) 67.

Further, Article 144 of the Constitution is very explicit that all authorities, civil or judicial, in the territory of India shall act in the aid of the Supreme Court. One cannot gloss over the fact that there is no mention of military or defence personnel. Thus, even the Supreme Court has no authority to direct the army, leave alone the high courts. Ruling of the Privy Council given in *Nazir Ahmed* v. *King Emperor*[19] is very clear that if a power is bequeathed, it must be exercised in the particular mode prescribed or not at all. Even senior army officials minced no word in condemning it which would have set a dangerous precedent.[20]

If the State government did not cooperate with the CBI, it could be taken to task for the dereliction of duty later on. But how can a judge foresee the fall-out of the arrest of a topnotch leader on public peace? The essence of the administration lies in anticipating the unanticipated. The administration would have been held responsible if his arrest would have caused the breach of peace. True, nobody is above the law and the warrant must be executed irrespective of the stature and might of the accused, but heaven would not have fallen by the delay of a day or two. The administration has to be tactful also that no such untoward incident takes place. Moreover, judicial methods are not always adequate to secure justice as has been sharply demonstrated by *Zacharia* v. *Republic of Cyprus*.[21] The Fugitive Offenders Act, 1881, provides that a fugitive must be repatriated if there is a prima facie case, unless the superior court, on a habeas corpus, considers, inter alia, that it would be improper to do so. Zacharia averred that his life would be in jeopardy if he was returned to Cyprus. Lord Radcliffe, in his dissent, upheld his contention, but Lord Simonds and Lord Devlin differed. Nevertheless, Lord Simonds added that the appellant had recourse to the Secretary of State who could refuse to return him if it was unjust to do so, for he '... may have access to information more reliable than that supplied by the conflicting affidavits upon which the court must come to a judicial decision'. Lord Devlin said that if the court gave concurrent jurisdiction of the Secretary of State it was 'because there may be considerations of a political or administrative character which go to the justice of fugitive's return and are better inquired into by the executives'. Zacharia applied to the secretary of State and he declined to order Zacharia's return to Cyprus.

---

[19]   AIR (1936) PC 253.

[20]   Sudhanshu Ranjan, 'Judges Are Not above Law', *The Sunday, Times of India*, 7 September 1997.

[21]   (1963) AC 634.

Departmental inquiry was initiated against Biswas for his adventurism in seeking the army's help and a charge sheet was issued. However, the Calcutta High Court quashed the charge sheet and exonerated him on 29 April 1998.[22]

Apart from judicial misconduct, the credibility of the judiciary has been badly dented by reports of bribery and indiscretion. Still, no judge has been impeached so far, though the process was initiated many a time. It calls for formulating some new mechanisms to rein in such errant judges. Some judges were forced to resign but there are many who refused to do so.

Another chapter 'Lawyer, Heal Thyself' discusses the role of lawyers. Like judges, bar is another pillar of the judiciary. However, instead of acting as officers of court to arrive at justice, lawyers are seen as the ones throttling justice by using dirtiest shenanigans. They are mercenary out and out having little regard for justice. They have no qualms giving wrong advice to clients to encourage litigation. They have the unmatched skill of prolonging litigations if their cases lack merit, something like filibustering. Many lawyers even lie in the court to save their clients who are in the wrong. In *Harishankar Rastogi* v. *Girdhari Sharma*,[23] the Supreme Court through Justice V.R. Krishna Iyer said, 'the bar is an extension of the system of justice; an advocate is an officer of court. He is master of an expertise but more than that, accountable to the court and governed by a high ethic. The success of the judicial process often depends on the services of the legal profession.'

Earlier, Justice Krishna Iyer ruled,

The vital role of the lawyer depends upon his probity and professional lifestyle. Be it remembered that the central function of the legal profession is to promote the administration of justice. If the practice of law is thus a public utility of great implications and a monopoly is statutorily granted by the nation, it obligates the lawyer to observe scrupulously those norms which make him worthy of the confidence of the community in him as a vehicle of justice-social justice.[24]

In *Afzal* v. *State of Haryana*,[25] the Court also held: 'A responsible advocate, if he speaks with the same voice two diametrically opposite statements, and is accepted to be correct the conduct not only is unbecoming of responsible advocate but also needs deprecation in strongest terms.'

Fee structure of lawyers in high courts and the Supreme Court is mind-boggling. Obviously the poor are priced out of the legal system. The poor

---

[22] *Dr U.N. Biswas* v. *Union of India and Ors* (1998) 2 CALLT 194 HC.
[23] (1978) 2 SCC 165, para 3.
[24] *Bar Council of Maharashtra* v. *M.V. Dabholkar* (1976) 2 SCC 291, para 15.
[25] (1995) Supp. 2 SCC 388, para 8.

cannot afford to fight even in the lower court. Advocates can work for anyone irrespective of their crime under the facetious logic of right of defence. Thus, Fali S. Nariman had no compunction defending Warren Anderson, the CEO of the Union Carbide Corporation. Thousands of people died and hundreds of thousands were maimed and injured when gas leaked from the Union Carbide Corporation's (UCC) plant in Bhopal in December 1984. It was nothing short of genocide as the accident was waiting to happen amidst clear indications of the plant being in a ramshackle condition. The top management including Anderson was in the know of the impending disaster but turned a Nelson's eye as if the people of Bhopal deserved nemesis. Anyway, Nariman brazened it out and accepted Anderson's brief. Obviously, the remittance was huge and he became the highest tax payer of the country in the individual category that year, courtesy Anderson.

Where is justice if it is to be purchased? Is justice reserved for the highest bidder? Lost in the labyrinth of merit, it is the meritorious who make fortune and spend fortune on meritorious lawyers to launder their taint!

Another chapter is 'Judicial Delays'. As the heading suggests, it deals with the problem of interminable court processes and how delays defeat justice. The problem of judicial delays has been a cause of concern for almost a century, and so, in 1924, Rankin Committee was set up to explore reasons and suggest remedies, as civil cases were not being disposed of in six months. Imagine, a period of over six months was a matter of worry. Justice Rankin, in his report, attributed it to adjournments and delay in serving summons which is still the order of the day. After independence, the matter was raised in Parliament that cases were not being disposed of expeditiously. Prime Minister Jawaharlal Nehru conceded it and the Law Commission was set up by an executive order, and the then Attorney General M.C. Setalvad was appointed the first chairman of the Commission. The Commission traversed the whole country, and in its 14th report, suggested measures so that cases are disposed of within six months. What is the result? Even criminal cases like murder and rape keep pending for decades and civil cases for generations, a few cases for centuries.

The court is duty bound to protect the people's rights, adjudicate dispute between two parties, and pronounce its verdict on the innocence or the guilt of the person concerned. The way cases drag on for decades mostly at the behest of the parties likely to lose on merit with the courts showing indulgence to them, expensive lawyers work wonders for their clients who have committed the most revolting crimes, the process of law is abused by the moneyed, influential litigants or accused, and cases are decided in the most unpredictable manner, applying different yardsticks for the privileged and the unprivileged, one cannot but get convinced that the judiciary is not the refuge of the poor nor an impartial arbitrator. However, everyone is under a legal mandate to proclaim that they have full faith in the judiciary. But is it really so? The then chief justice of India, Justice R.M. Lodha, in an interview to the author on the last day of his office for DD News, said that two institutions of India which command maximum respectability and credibility worldwide are the Supreme Court and the Election Commission, and that people have faith in these two institutions. I countered him that such public perceptions are formed by the court's activism which creates tremor by its judgements in high-profile cases like CWG, 2-G, Coal Blocks, and so on, and it appears that the judiciary is the only savior of democracy in India, but any common man who has had the bad luck of going to court may not have that faith in the judiciary as is bandied about.[26]

It is only the smugglers, scamsters and bigwigs, politicos, and bureaucrats, accused in big cases, who proclaim their faith in the judiciary from housetops. But a common man, running after seeking justice and getting insulted in the process every day, with justice eluding him even after decades, does not hold this opinion, though he may not have the courage to say so publicly. This is borne out by what Neelam and Sanjay Krishnamoorthy, who lost both their children in the Uphaar Cinema fire tragedy on 13 June 1997, have written,

> Nineteen years ago, I lost faith in god. Now, I have lost faith in the Indian judiciary. I have always had the greatest respect for the courts, but I am compelled to say I am devastated by the Supreme Court judgment, which has given the Ansals (owners of the Uphaar Cinema) the luxury of buying their freedom for a paltry (at least to them) sum of Rs. 60 crore. Had it been the lives of the children of politicians or judges that were lost, justice would have been served within a year. But the judiciary could not understand the plight of a mother who has stood for nineteen years before the courts, only to face immense disappointment. Nobody cares about ordinary people, but the rich and powerful get away.
>
> I regret having pursued the Uphaar case so vigorously for nineteen years. I should have just shot those responsible for the deaths of my children and the fifty-seven others. I would have pleaded insanity, exactly what the Ansal's counsel accuse me of. By now, I would have finished my sentence as well.[27]

By not deciding cases expeditiously, the court not only helps the criminals and wrong-doers but, in fact, confers legitimacy on the illegalities being

---

[26] Telecast on DD News on 27 September 2014.

[27] Neelam Krishnamoorthy and Sanjay Krishnamoorthy, *Trial by Fire* (Gurgaon: Penguin Random House, 2016), p. 188.

perpetrated. Not only private litigants and criminals, even the government, which has unfortunately become the biggest litigant, uses the forum of the court to justify its illegalities. Even in simple promotion cases of its employees, the government after losing in the Central Administrative tribunal (CAT), files appeal in the high court, and then again in the Supreme Court after losing in the high court. Not only this, it uses the most reprehensible tricks to protract and seeks adjournments ad nauseam which are most surprisingly granted. And then, if the question is raised in the Parliament, the government replies that the matter is in the court. This is half-truth which is more dangerous than white lies. The reply is misleading as the government is the appellant.

So 'The matter is sub judice' is a wonderful tool to justify the most heinous acts. Once a matter becomes sub-judice, the sufferer loses all rights as the government would not do anything, and the court would keep granting adjournments to help the government which raises question about its independence. Service laws are well-settled, but even service cases run into decades, Supreme Court grants leave when the government has lost in CAT and then in the high court. Then the apex court would complain that the judiciary is over-burdened. Will the employees, not getting a single promotion in their entire career, or the kin of a rape victim who was murdered after rape, who keep running for justice for decades, have any faith in the system? But no one can say anything as the matter is in the court. Influential and affluent individuals also use the forum of the court to justify their wrongdoings as the matter is in the court. Can the court not see through the design that its forum is being misused to deny justice to the sufferers? But willy-nilly it helps the wrong-doers by granting adjournments.

The irritant of the unending delay can be compared with the fable of boiling frog. It suggests that if a frog is put into boiling water, it will jump out immediately, but if it is put into tepid water which is then heated slowly, the frog will be cooked to death as it will not be able to perceive the danger. Scientists have made claims and counter-claims about its veracity. Nineteenth-century experiments bear out that if the heating is sufficiently gradual, the frog will not jump out, but recent experiments suggest that the premise is false. German physiologist Friedrich Goltz, while carrying out experiments searching for the soul, showed that while a frog whose brain was removed will not escape if the heating is slow, an intact frog attempted to jump out of the water when the temperature reached 25° C. Other nineteenth-century experiments by Heinzmann[28] and Fratscher,[29] show that frogs did not try to escape

[28] A. Heinzmann, C. Fratscher, and William Thompson Sedgwick (1872).
[29] A. Heinzmann, C. Fratscher, and William Thompson Sedgwick (1875).

if the water was heated gradually. In 1888, Sedgwick[30] tried to reconcile the diametrically opposite results by explaining that the apparent contradiction was due to different heating rates. He concluded that if the heating be sufficiently gradual, no reflex action will be produced even in normal frogs. In 1995, Professor Douglas Melton of the Harvard University said the opposite that the frog would not jump out if put into boiling water and would die, but escape from the cold water before it gets hot. In 2002, Victor H. Hutchinson, Professor Emeritus of Zoology at the University of Oklahoma, dismissed the legend as entirely incorrect. However, the moral of the story is that people are not circumspect to react to threats that arise gradually and thus make way for their own perdition.

Indian courts give dates after dates. So, parties come on each date which is generally after a few months only to hear that the hearing is adjourned and then they again wait for a few months for the next date. Again the matter is adjourned. The process goes on for decades, but it is not done in one go, that is, the court will not give another date after a decade or two as it may lead to violence. So, like the slow heating of water, dates are given in installments and carried on for decades. The sufferer has to die but not at once. S/he will be emaciated to death in a long drawn process stretched into decades. Hindi satirist Hari Shankar Parsai, has portrayed the angst beautifully:

> Till now I thought that Arjuna did not want to fight the war, but Krishna prevailed upon him. It was not good. What would Arjuna do if not fight? He would go to the court, file a case of land ownership. But if the Pandavas, who returned from the forest, could somehow manage the court fee, how would they have paid lawyers, witnesses? And what would have happened to the Dharamaraja in the court? He would have been blown off at the first question in the cross-examination. Can the truthful ever fight any case! Even Bheema would lose fat in the litigation in court. The war decided it in 18 days; it would have taken 18 years in the court. And Duryodhana was sure to win because he had money. Truth is invisible; money is visible. Money is visible to the God of justice, not the truth. Perhaps the Pandavas would have died fighting the case because Duryodhana would have gone on seeking adjournments. After the Pandavas their sons would have fought and then their sons. It was so nice of Krishna that he got a decision in 18 days by making Arjuna fight. Otherwise, today scions of Kauravas-Pandavas would have been fighting the case in a civil court.[31]

[30] https://ipfs.io/ipfs/QmXoypizjW3WknFiJnKLwHCnL72vedxjQkDDP 1mXWo6uco/wiki/Boiling_frog.html, accessed on 11 March 2019.
[31] 'Kachahari jane wala janwar', *Parsai Rachnavali*, 3, Fifth Edition (Delhi: Rajkamal Prakashan, 2012), p. 206.

In the chapter 'Supreme Court's Power to Do Complete Justice', an attempt is made to explore the extent and limitations of the power of the apex court under Article 142, which gives the sweeping power to give any decision or order to do complete justice in any matter or cause pending before it. This is an exceptional power not to be found in any other Constitutions of the world. Since it is an exceptional power, decisions given under it do not have any binding force as is with Article 141, nor are they cited as precedents.

In the initial years after the enforcement of the Constitution, the Supreme Court rarely invoked this power. But since 1990s, there is a growing tendency to exercise its jurisdiction under Article 142, which is worrisome. The Supreme Court took suo moto cognizance of the case pertaining to Triple Talaq on 16 October 2015, when a two-judge bench of the Court comprising Justices Anil R. Dave and Adarsh Kumar Goel, ruled in *Prakash and Ors* v. *Phulvati and Ors*,[32] that the Hindu Succession Act, 1956, amended in 2005, could not apply retrospectively. In the second part of the judgement, the Court talked about injustices faced by Muslim women and questioned the Muslim personal law practices of marriage and divorce, and registered a suo motu public interest litigation (PIL) to examine whether the practices of arbitrary divorce (Triple Talaq), polygamy, and nikah halala violated women's dignity.

> An important issue of gender discrimination which though not directly involved in this appeal, has been raised by some of the learned counsel for the parties which concerns rights to Muslim women.... It was pointed out that in spite of guarantee of the Constitution, Muslim women are subjected to discrimination. There is no safeguard against arbitrary divorce and second marriage by her husband during currency of the first marriage, resulting in denial of dignity and security to her. Although the issue was raised before this Court in Ahmedabad Women Action Group (AWAG) vs. Union of India, (1997) 3 SCC 573, this Court did not go into the merits of the discrimination with the observation that the issue involved state policy to be dealt with by the legislature. It was observed that challenge to the Muslim Women (Protection of Rights on Divorce) Act, 1986 was pending before the Constitution Bench and there was no reason to multiply proceedings on such an issue.
>
> It is pointed out that the matter needs consideration by this Court as the issue relates not merely to a policy matter but to fundamental rights of women under Articles 14, 15 and 21 and international conventions and covenants. One of the reasons for the court having not gone into the matter was pendency

[32]   (2016) 2 SCC 36.

of an issue before the Constitution Bench which has since been decided by this Court in *Danial Latifi vs. Union of India*, (2001) 7 SCC 740.[33]

The Court clarified that though the Constitution Bench did not address the said issue, it nevertheless held that Article 21 included the right to live with dignity which means that a Muslim woman could invoke fundamental rights in such cases. The division bench of the Court also asked the chief justice of India (CJI) to set up an appropriate bench to examine if Muslim women face gender discrimination in cases of divorce. Several organizations including the AIMPLB and Muslim women impleaded themselves in the case. Subsequently, on 29 June 2016, the Court observed that Triple Talaq among Muslims would be tested on 'touchstone of constitutional framework'. Thus, a five-judge Constitution Bench comprising Chief Justice J.S. Khehar, and Justices Kurian Joseph, Rohinton Fali Nariman, Uday Umesh Lalit, and S. Abdul Nazeer, all from five different faiths, was constituted which declared the practice of Triple Talaq as unconstitutional by a majority of 3:2.[34]

Chief Justice J.S. Kheahr, writing for himself and Justice Abdul Nazeer, held that 'Triple Talaq' is an integral part of the Muslim religious practice, but added that this is a case which presents a situation where this Court should exercise its discretion to issue appropriate directions under Article 142 of the Constitution, and directed the Union of India to consider appropriate legislation, particularly with reference to 'talaq-e-biddat' expressing hope that the contemplated legislation will also take into consideration advances in Muslim 'personal law—Shariat', as have been corrected by legislation the world over, even by theocratic Islamic States.

The CJI issued an injunction against pronouncement of 'talaq-e-biddat' by Muslim husbands for a period of six months, and if the process of legislation commences within the said period, if it is decided that the practice of 'talaq-e-biddat' be done away with altogether, the injunction would continue, till legislation is finally enacted, failing which, the injunction shall cease to operate.

It is baffling that the two judges took recourse to Article 142 of the Constitution which confers an extra-ordinary power to do complete justice despite holding the Triple Talaq as an integral part of the religious practice of

[33] (2016) 2 SCC 36, paras 27–8.

[34] *Shayara Bano* v. *Union of India and Ors*, with Suo Motu Writ (C) No. 2 of 2015, 'Muslim Women's Quest For Equality', In *Re* v. *Jamiat Ulma-I-Hind* (2017) 9 SCC 1.

Muslims. Justice Kurian Joseph, in his separate judgment disagreed with the CJI that it is integral to Islam. He wrote that a practice does not become valid merely because it has continued for long. He ruled:

> I also have serious doubts as to whether, even under Article 142, the exercise of a Fundamental Right can be injuncted. When issues of such nature come to the forefront, the discourse often takes the form of pitting religion against other constitutional rights. I believe that a reconciliation between the same is possible, but the process of harmonizing different interests is within the powers of the legislature ... However, it is not for the Courts to direct for any legislation.[35]

The third judgement is written by Justice Rohinton Fali Nariman, with Justice Uday Umesh Lalit concurring. Disagreeing with Justice Khehar, Justice Nariman struck down Triple Talaq as violative of the right to equality and the equal protection of law under Article 14.

It is a matter of great satisfaction that Justice Kurian Joseph took exception to taking recourse to directing the legislature for making a law in this regard. Justice Nariman did not invoke the extra-ordinary jurisdiction of Article 142 either and decided the case on the touchstone of Article 14. Even the division bench which took the cognizance of the matter suo moto spoke of the violation of Articles 14, 15, and 16. If Court invokes Article 142 after taking the cognizance of any matter suo moto, it means freewheeling for the apex court which does in two stages what it cannot do in one. Article 142 can be invoked only if the matter is pending before the Court. But if the Court first takes suo moto cognizance and then uses its power under Article 142, it means bypassing the limitations it has under the Constitution and usurping the role of the legislature as well that of the executive. In *Kesavananda Bharati* v. *State of Kerala*,[36] the Court accepted the argument of Nani A. Palkhiwala that the Parliament cannot do in two stages what it cannot do in one stroke. Thus, it could not lift limitations on its own amending power and then amend what was impermissible under those limitations. Fortunately the CJI was overruled by his colleagues.

The apex court has still not decided whether it can supplant a substantive law under Article 142 or it is only to supplement. Though judgements given under are not cited as precedents, it does not mean freewheeling as if Article 142 provides a carte blanche to do whatever the Supreme Court feels like. There must be a simulacrum of consistency in different judgements

---

[35] Paras 24 and 25.
[36] AIR (1973) SC 1461.

pronounced under it even if they are not binding. Many judgements given under it have been subjected to searing criticism. Its direction in *State of Tamil Nadu* v. *K. Balu*,[37] to ban sale of liquor within 500 metres of national state high ways evoked severe reactions from different classes that it is a policy matter falling within the domain of the executive and the subject matter of liquor is within the exclusive jurisdiction of state legislatures. It was also argued that it would lead to loss of millions of jobs and loss of rankings for five-star hotels. However, I feel that banning the sale of liquor along highways is not wrong, keeping in view the fatalities involved, it should be done under the right to life (Article 21).

On 19 April 2017, in a significant verdict with huge political ramifications, the Supreme Court restored criminal conspiracy charges against senior BJP leaders L.K. Advani, Murli Manohar Joshi, Union Minister Uma Bharati, Kalyan Singh, and others in the 25-year-old Babri Masjid demolition case.[38] Allowing the appeal of the CBI, the Division Bench of Justices Pinaki Chandra Ghose and R.F. Nariman ordered the transfer of proceedings from the Court of Special Judicial Magistrate, Rai Bareilly, to the court of Additional Sessions Judge (Ayodhya Matters) at Lucknow, with the direction to frame an additional charge under Section 120-B against Advani and others. Kalyan Singh was given immunity under Article 361 of the Constitution for being the governor, but the Court directed to frame charge against him as soon as he ceases to be one. It further directed to conclude the trial within two years with a specific direction to conduct day to day hearing with no adjournment on any grounds except when the Sessions Court finds it impossible to conduct trial on a particular day for which reasons will have to be recorded, and there will be no transfer of the judge during this period.

25 years is a pretty long period for a criminal trial to conclude finally. But in such an important case, the trial begins after 25 years. The Court has invoked Article 142 to transfer the proceeding from Rai Bareilly to Lucknow. K.K. Venugopal contested vehemently the invocation of extraordinary jurisdiction under Article 142 on the ground that the Court's power is circumscribed by Section 406 of the CrPC that authorizes transfer only from one criminal court subordinate to one high court to another criminal court of equal or superior jurisdiction subordinate to another high court. The Court ruled that Section 406 does not apply as the transfer is

---

[37] (2017) 2 SCC 281.

[38] *State (through Central Bureau of Investigation* v. *Kalyan Singh and Others* (2017) 7 SCC 444, Criminal Appeal No. 751 of 2017, SLP, Cr. 2275 of 2011.

from one criminal court to another criminal court subordinate to the same high court. Venugopal further contested that this transfer can be effected by the high court under Section 407 only, but the Court did not accept this contention holding:

> Again the fact that the High court has been given a certain power under the Code of Criminal Procedure does not detract from the Supreme Court using a constitutional power under Article 142 to achieve the same end to do complete justice in the matter before it. In the present case, there is no substantive mandatory provision which is infracted by using Article 142.[39]

This is a welcome clarification that no substantive mandatory provision is being infracted. Thus, the Court admits that this special power under Article 142 is not to supplant any substantive law. This case has been meandering in the corridors of different courts for 16 long years. On 12 February 2001, the Lucknow bench of the Allahabad high Court decided that the insertion of the separate FIR 198 of 1992 against Advani, Joshi, and six others in the original notification of the State government directing the cases to be tried by a special court at Lucknow was procedurally flawed. The flaw was that there had been no consultation with the High Court which, it held, was curable. On 16 June 2001, the CBI petitioned the State government to cure the defect which was rejected on 28 September 2002. The CBI did not challenge the rejection. The apex court reacted differently at different times. Raju Ramchandran has written:

> It is also worth looking at the varying judicial reactions in the Supreme Court in the same case over a span of four years. Last week's judgment (the instant judgement delivered by Justices Ghose and Nariman) had no hesitation in recording that the case with which it was concerned pertained to crimes affecting the secular fabric of the Constitution. But in 2013 the reaction of the bench headed by Justice H.L. Dattu ... was different. At that time the much respected senior counsel P.P. Rao, was appearing for the CBI.... In support of his plea for early hearing he referred to the incident as a crime and described it as a matter of national imporrtance ... he was sharply pulled up ... the bench reportedly said, Do not say it is a national crime or matter of national importance. We are yet to decide it. Unless we or the trial court decide this way or that way you cannot make such a statement.[40]

---

[39] *State (through Central Bureau of Investigation* v. *Kalyan Singh and Others*, para 26.

[40] Raju Ramachandran, 'Towards Complete Justice at Last', *The Hindu*, 24 April 2017.

It is clear that there is no consistency in the invocation of Article 142 by different benches.

The chapter 'The Binary Application of laws' deals with discrimination faced by the underdogs while those with power and pelf are given differential and deferential treatment. The highfalutin injunctions of law that it is no respecter of person are golden words to be read in books only. There are instances galore to be found in everyday life. A.V. Dicey defined the rule of law as the absence of arbitrary power, equality before the law, or the equal subjection of all classes to the ordinary law of the land administered by ordinary law courts and that the Constitution is not the source but the consequence of the rights of individuals, as defined and enforced by the courts. In *Indira Gandhi* v. *Raj Narain*,[41] the Supreme Court of India has quoted it with approval but disagreed with the third part that the Constitution is not the source but the consequence of the rights of individuals. The Court further elucidated:

> United Nations, held its Congress in Delhi in 1959 where lawyers, judges and law teachers representing fifty-three countries affirmed that the rule of law is a dynamic concept which should be employed to safeguard and advance the political and civil rights of the individual in a free society. One of the committees of that Congress emphasised that no law should subject any individual to discriminatory treatment. These principles must vary from country to country depending upon the provisions of its Constitution and indeed upon whether there exists a written Constitution. As it has been said in a lighter vein, to show the supremacy of the Parliament, the charm of the English Constitution is that 'it does not exist'. Our Constitution exists and must continue to exist. It guarantees equality before law and the equal protection of laws to everyone. The denial of such equality, as modified by the judicially evolved theory of classification, is the very negation of rule of law.[42]

Justice Y.V. Chandrachud went to the extent of warning, 'A Constitution which, without a true nexus, denies equality before the law to its citizens may in a form thinly disguised, contain reprisals directed against private individuals in matters of private rights and wrongs.'

However, the constitutional guarantee of equality before law appears to be a hollow slogan. No wonder, the extremism is on the rise vindicating Justice Chandrachud. Privileged and powerful people get special treatment in jails too.

---

[41] (1975) Supp. SCC 1, p. 258.
[42] (1975) Supp. SCC 1, p. 258.

V.K. Sasikala, interim general secretary of the AIADMK, allegedly got VIP treatment in the jail after being convicted in a disproportionate assets case. Karnataka Chief Minister Siddaramaiah, ordered a high-level probe into allegations made by the then deputy inspector general against Prison Department officials, including providing VIP treatment to her for a bribe of Rs 2 crore.[43] Later, video footage surfaced showing her walking into the main entry area of the Parappana Agrahara Central Prison in Bengaluru in civilian clothes. It suggested that she had gone out of prison.[44] When Lalu Prasad was arrested after conviction in a fodder scam case in January 2018 in Ranchi, two of his aides surrendered in an allegedly false case on the same day their boss was convicted and sent to prison. They did so to serve Lalu in jail.[45]

The Supreme Court has been singing paeans to the right of equality. In *Mani Ram* v. *State of MP*,[46] Justice V.R. Krishna Iyer wrote, 'If mason and millionaire were treated alike, egregious inequality is an inevitability. Likewise, geographic allergy at the judicial level makes mockery of equal protection of the laws *within the territory of India*. India is one and not a conglomeration of districts, untouchably apart'.

'My Lord and Your Excellency' is a chapter of general nature which highlights the deformity of human nature which loves to be seen as superior to others. All invocation to equality is nothing but hollow incantation when people are forced to use honorifics for the select dignitaries. It punches holes into the fabric of democracy which is based on the concept of equality. However, the concept of equality is notional. Even in a democracy, some are more equal than others. No wonder, Alexis de Tocqueville was flummoxed at how equals were ruling equals in a democracy. The hangover of the feudal system is most pronounced in the judiciary which is not prepared to adapt to democratic mores. The kind of subordination witnessed in the judiciary is not seen even in the army. A district judge cannot sit before a high court judge. Many judges of the subordinate judiciary, including district judges touch the feet of high court judges.

I may conclude that justice is an endangered species, especially for the have-nots. Justice Gajendra Gadhkar has narrated an interesting anecdote.

[43] 'VIP Treatment for Saikal: Karnataka CM Orders Probe', *Indian Express*, 14 July 2017.

[44] 'Did Sasikala Go out of Bengaluru Prison?', *The Hindu*, 24 August 2017.

[45] '2 Lalu Aides Got Arrested to Serve Him in Jail, Claim Cops', *Times of India*, 10 January 2018.

[46] (1978) 4 SCC 47, para 2.

When Viceroy Lord Reading went to Patna to inaugurate the new building of the Patna High Court, a layman asked him at the garden party, 'Why do you call your courts, courts of law rather than courts of justice?' Lord Reading gave a witty reply, 'Governments do not believe in using satire in determining the nomenclature of their institution'.[47]

---

[47] Justice P.B. Gajendragadhkar, p. 36. See Godbole, pp. 15–16.

2

Accountability of Judges

King James I presumptuously claimed that he could judge whatever cause he pleased in his own person, against which no appeal would lie. He solicited the opinion of Archbishop Bancroft who approbated that the scriptures gave the king the power to try cases. He even told the judges that they were simply delegates of the king and what could be done by the agent could be done by the principal. But Justice Lord Edward Coke, Chief Justice of the Court of Common Pleas, told the king that he had no right to pass judgment in legal causes which James called 'a traitorous speech'.[1] Coke had obtained a prior consent of the judges and responded to Bancroft in the *Case of Prohibitions del Roy*[2] in 1608, asserting that 'the king cannot adjudge any case, either criminal, as treason, felony, and so on, or betwixt party and party ... but these matters ought to be determined and adjudged in some court of justice according to the law and custom of England'.[3] The king retorted that he always thought and often heard the boast that the English law was founded upon reason and if that be so, why did he and others not have reason like the judges. The Lord chief justice replied that whilst:

> God has endowed Your Majesty with excellent science as well as great gifts of nature, you are not learned in the laws of this your Realm of England. The legal causes which concern the life or inheritance, or goods or fortunes, of your

[1] John Hostettler, *Sir Edward Coke*, First Indian reprint (Delhi: Universal law Publishing Co. Pvt. Ltd), 2006, p. 69.
[2] 12 Reports 65, Hostettler, *Sir Edward Coke*, p. 69.
[3] Hostettler, *Sir Edward Coke*, pp. 69–70.

subjects are not to be decided by natural reason but by the artificial reason and judgment of law, which is an art which requires long study and experience before a man can attain to the cognizance of it.[4]

He added that the law is the golden meet-wand and measure to try the causes of His Majesty's subjects and it is by that law that His Majesty is protected in safety and peace. King James flew into a rage: 'Then I am to be under law—which it is treason to affirm'. The chief justice replied, 'Thus wrote Bracton "the King is under no man, save under God and the law" (non-sub homine sed sub deo et lege)'.[5]

The irony is too glaring to be glossed over. Lord Coke might have fearlessly, though humbly, reminded the king that no one was above the law, but it seems that this sententia does not apply to judges any longer. Lord Acton's oft-quoted statement—'Power tends to corrupt and absolute power corrupts absolutely.... Great men are always bad men',[6]—may be quoted by those dealing in trite aphorisms but simply quoting it does not act as a check against corruption. Therefore, some mechanism must be created so that power is accompanied by accountability without which it leads to autocracy. Every institution or individual has to be accountable to the people at large. Charity begins at home, but ironically, though everyone else has been made accountable with the over-activism of the judiciary, the only institution which is not accountable to anyone is the judiciary itself. Though judges of the lower court are accountable to their respective high courts which are empowered to supervise and discipline them under Articles 227 and 235 of the Constitution of India, the judges of the higher judiciary, that is, the Supreme Court of India and high courts are accountable to none. Several disturbing reports have appeared in the media in recent decades highlighting the misconduct of judges. However, any attempt to make judges accountable is resisted by them on the facetious ground that it will impinge on the independence of the judiciary. David Pannick remarked that judicial independence was not designed as, and should not be allowed to become, a shield for judicial misbehaviour or incompetence or a barrier to examination of complaints about injudicious conduct on apolitical criteria:

> Unless and until we treat judges as fallible human beings whose official conduct is subject to the same critical analysis as that of other organs of the government,

---

[4]   Hostettler, *Sir Edward Coke*, p. 70.

[5]   Quoted by A.K. Sen, in the Lala Lajpat Rai Memorial Lecture, 1963, on the topic: Justice for the Common Man, see *Justice for the Common Man* (Lucknow-Delhi: Eastern Book Company, 1964), p. 25.

[6]   Letter to Bishop Mandell Creighton, April 1887.

judges will remain members of a priesthood who have great powers over the rest of the community, but who are otherwise isolated from them and misunderstood by them, by their mutual disadvantage.

Some politicians, and a few jurists, urge that it is unwise or even dangerous to tell the truth about the judiciary. Judge Jerome Frank of the US Court of Appeals sensibly explained that he had little patience with, or respect for, that suggestion. I am unable to conceive … that, in a democracy, it can ever be unwise to acquaint the public with the truth about the workings of any branch of government. It is wholly undemocratic to treat the public as children who are unable to accept the inescapable shortcomings of man-made institutions…. The best way to bring about the elimination of those shortcomings of our judicial system which are capable of being eliminated is to have all our citizens informed as to how that system now functions. It is a mistake, therefore, to try to establish and maintain, through ignorance, public esteem for our court.[7]

Judicial Accountability in Other Countries

The US made a law, titled as Judicial Councils Reforms and Judicial Conduct and Disability Act, 1980, to deal with this canker, the provision of impeachment notwithstanding. Under the Act, there is a Judicial Council for each Circuit and a National Judicial Conference at the apex. They have been given power to censure a judge, request him to seek retirement, or direct that no cases be assigned to the judge for a limited period. However, till date only one Supreme Court judge has been successfully impeached in the year 1805, though under the 1980 Act, complaints are investigated by a committee of judges and actions were taken.

In Germany, there is a Judges Disciplinary Committee comprising heads of all five concurrent divisions of courts and the president of the Constitutional Court. Judges are tried by the committee if charges are raised against them.

Canada has a Judicial Council since 1971. Its disposal is quite fast—66 per cent of the complaints are concluded within three months and 94 per cent within six months. Australia too has such a commission since 1987 which receives a large number of complaints and several judicial officers accused of corruption resigned either before the conduct division began the inquiry process or before it concluded its deliberation.

[7] David Pannick, *Judges* (New York: Oxford University Press, 1988), p. 205.

The UN Basic Principles on the Independence of the judiciary have provisions relating to discipline, suspension, and removal of judges as follows:

Discipline, Suspension, and Removal

17. A charge or complaint made against a judge in his/her judicial and professional capacity shall be processed expeditiously and fairly under an appropriate procedure. The judge shall have the right to a fair hearing. The examination of the matter at its initial stage shall be kept confidential, unless otherwise requested by the judge.

18. Judges shall be subject to suspension or removal only for reasons of incapacity or behaviour that renders them unfit to discharge their duties.

19. All disciplinary, suspension or removal proceedings shall be determined in accordance with established standards of judicial conduct.

20. Decisions in disciplinary, suspension, or removal proceedings should be subject to an independent review. This principle may not apply to the decisions of the highest court and those of the legislature in impeachment or similar proceedings.[8]

Judicial Over-Reach and Under-Reach

There can be no dispute that the judges of the high courts and the Supreme Court of India do wield tremendous powers. However, power comes with a price which bestows huge responsibility and calls for strict adherence to dos and don'ts. Therefore, they must be made accountable not only in respect of their personal conduct and integrity, but also in regard to the judicial verdicts that they deliver, which befuddle many a time and are thus incomprehensible, to say the least. The need for judicial accountability has increased all the more as the judiciary is, nowadays, performing not only judicial functions, but virtually executive functions as well, for which the government is accountable to the people. Articles 141, 142, and 144 make the Supreme Court the most powerful institution in the country, and Articles 32 and 136 also confer wide powers on it. But such unbounded powers without any concomitant accountability tend to make it an autocratic and narcissistic institution. Unmindful of the

---

[8] Adopted by the Seventh United Nations Congress on the Prevention of Crime and the Treatment of Offenders held at Milan from 26 August to 6 September 1985 and endorsed by General Assembly resolutions 40/32 of 29 November and 40/146 of 13 December 1985, http://www.ohchr.org/EN/ProfessionalInterest/Pages/IndependenceJudiciary.aspx (last accessed on 13 October 2018).

budgetary and other vital implications, it passes orders which are simply not implementable, such as the one for the interlinking of rivers, a policy decision which falls clearly in the domain of the executive.[9] It is able to do all this because it is not held to account for all such acts.

Today, the judiciary is often doing with impunity what the executive could not or can never do, since it is answerable to the people. Courts, instead of protecting the rights of the insulted and the injured, are pushing them further into the margins by handing out decisions such as demolishing slums and removing pavement dwellers,[10] banning cycle rickshaw in certain areas of Delhi,[11] removing hawkers from the streets of Delhi and Mumbai,[12] thereby violating the fundamental right to shelter and to carry on any occupation or trade conferred by the Constitution of India. The Supreme Court has not hesitated to interfere even with the military operations which are considered sacrosanct. In 1993, when the military was carrying out its operations to flush out militants from the Hazratbal shrine in Srinagar, it restricted the food supplies to hostages as a matter of strategy. The Court ordered that the provision of food of 1,200 calorie value should be supplied to hostages. Reacting to this, an army General wrote: 'For the first time in history, a Court of law was asked to pronounce judgment on the conduct of an ongoing military operation. Its verdict materially affected the course of operation.'[13]

The Supreme Court went overboard to mitigate the sufferings of people reeling under severe drought and directed the Centre to set up a National Disaster Management Fund (NDMF) within three months under Section 47 of the Disaster Management Act, 2005, which provides for it.[14] Though the Court's concern for the drought-affected is laudable, its direction was *per incuriam* (through lack of care, without the basis of law) as Section 47 had not been notified then. Led by Finance Minister Arun Jaitley, the

---

[9] *In Re: Networking of Rivers*, Writ Petition (Civil) No. 512/2002, Supreme Court of India, 1 November 2002.

[10] *M. C. Mehta* v. *UOI*, AIR (2006) SC 1325 (2006) 3 SCC 399.

[11] *Hem Raj and another* v. *Commissioner of Police*, WP (C) 3419 (1999), Delhi High Court, decided 26 July 2006.

[12] *Sodan Singh and Ors.* v. *New Delhi Municipal Committee and others* (1989) 4 SCC 155; *Bombay Hawkers' Union and others* v. *Bombay Municipal Corporation and others*, AIR (1985) SC 1206 (1985) 3 SCC 528; *Ekta Hawkers' Union and Anr.* v. *Municipal Corporation, Greater Bombay and others* (2004) 1 SCC 625.

[13] T.R. Andhyarujina, 'Disturbing Trends in Judicial Activism', *The Hindu*, 6th August 2012.

[14] *Swaraj Abhiyan-I* v. *Union of India* (2016) 7 SCC 498, decided on 11 May 2016.

government accused the judiciary of wanton interference in the executive's exclusive domain of earmarking funds for various purposes under the budgetary exercise. Mr Jaitley said: 'Step by step, brick by brick, the edifice of India's legislature is being destroyed.'[15]

On 27 January 2016, the Supreme Court ordered Arunachal Pradesh Governor J.P. Rajkhowa to respond as to why he recommended president's rule in the sensitive border state, little realizing that governors enjoy 'complete immunity' and are not answerable to courts for acts done in their official capacity. On 1 February, a five-judge bench, headed by Justice J.S. Khehar, graciously accepted its slip-up, saying it would only be 'just and appropriate' to take back the notice issued to Mr Rajkhowa: 'If we have made a mistake, we will recall our order ... there is no problem.'[16] The acknowledgement of the mistake is praiseworthy.

In 2007, when Prime Minister Dr Manmohan Singh spoke of judicial overreach it created a national hubbub that the executive and the judiciary were headed for a face-off.[17] Dr Singh's comment was incontrovertible but incomplete, as it presented only one side of the coin. It is not only a problem of overreach, where the judiciary oversteps, breaching its boundary but also a problem of under-reach where courts shirk their responsibilities, despite having the jurisdiction, resulting in monstrous injustice. All this is also taking place because judges are not made accountable under our constitutional framework.

The habeas corpus case[18] is the most glaring example of this judicial abnegation, wherein the conduct of judges reflected that their sole concern was to get elevated as the next chief justice of India (CJI) rather than discharging their judicial functions properly. In the *Narmada Bachao Andolan* case[19] the Supreme Court stayed the construction of the Sardar Sarovar dam on the plea of the Narmada Bachao Andolan that several legal formalities including environmental clearance were not observed and that no plans had been made for the rehabilitation of the displaced people whose lands had been submerged. The question was not whether the dam should be constructed. The Court was only asked not to allow the respondents to raise the height of

[15] 'SC Erred in Disaster Relief Order?', *Times of India*, 26 May 2016.

[16] 'Supreme Court Recall Notice to Governor', *The Hindu*, 2 February 2016.

[17] The prime minister's inaugural address at the Conference of chief ministers and chief justices of high courts on 'Administration of Justice on Fast Track' held in New Delhi on 8 April 2007, *Times of India*, 9 April 2007, and also other newspapers.

[18] *ADM, Jabalpur* v. *Shivkant Shukla*, AIR (1976) SC 1207.

[19] *N. B. A.* v. *Union of India* (1998) 8 SCC 308.

the dam till the people displaced were properly rehabilitated. But the Court's verdict that came after seven long years said that the construction of the dam could proceed simultaneously with the environmental impact studies. This simply nullified the very purpose of laying down the requirement of getting the environmental impact assessment or cost benefit analysis of the project done, which was a mandatory legal requirement. Taking the affidavits filed by the state governments regarding the promise of rehabilitation in future at its face value, it permitted the height of the dam to be raised.

There are other instances wherein the rights of the people have been whittled down and justice denied. It is a common knowledge and experience of all those who are aware of the day to day proceedings in the Supreme Court that more than 90 per cent of the petitions/appeals filed before it under Article 136 of the Constitution of India are dismissed, and the Supreme Court does not even write a single sentence in its orders explaining the reasons for such dismissal. And once a petition is dismissed, the petitioner cannot move the court again. D.C. Pandey has rightly pointed out:

> The current practice of disposing of matters has hardened against re-opening matters in the interests of justice even when non-speaking orders have been passed. To this extent the rule (laid down) in *Daryao* v. *State of Uttar Pradesh*, AIR 1961 SC 1457, has become almost a dead letter. Under the rule, a petition 'dismissed *in limine* without a speaking order ... cannot be treated as creating a bar of *res judicata*'. The courts have been treating a non-speaking order as raising a bar analogous to *res judicata*. Sometimes an order passed without any application of mind has been hardened into *res judicata* due to lack of vigilance on the part of the counsel or obduracy on the part of the judge.[20]

The Supreme Court returned the reference sent by the president under Article 143 of the Constitution with respect to the Rama Janmabhhomi-Babri Masjid dispute on the issue as to whether a temple was in existence at the site in Ayodhya where the Babri Masjid stood later on. A majority of three judges held that the reference could not be taken as an effective 'alternate dispute settlement mechanism'.[21] So, it could not be permitted to substitute for the pending suits and legal proceedings. The Court felt that the reference

---

[20] D.C. Pandey, 'Justice in Absentia', *Journal of Indian Law Institute*, vol. 29, 1987.

[21] Madhav Godbole, *The Judiciary and Governance in India* (New Delhi: Rupa and Co., 2009), p. 39.

had become 'superfluous and unnecessary'.[22] The two judges (in minority) opined that the Court was entitled to decline to answer a reference, but then it must give reasons for doing so. The grounds given by the Court for declining to answer the reference were, (a) it favoured one religious community over another, (b) the Union Government did not propose to resolve the dispute according to the court's opinion but just wanted to use it as a springboard for negotiations, (c) the main protagonists on both sides of the dispute had not appeared before the Court to lead evidence or for cross-examination, and finally, the process would invite criticism from either or both sides.

The reasoning adduced by the Court for returning the reference is baffling as it did so after obtaining an undertaking from the Union Government that it (government) shall abide by the opinion of the Court, though the opinion given under presidential reference is not binding per se. Furthermore, why should the apex court fight shy of giving an opinion just because it may favour one religious community or may be subject to criticism which it could brave out. After all, the appeal against the verdict of the Allahabad High Court[23] which created brouhaha, is pending before it.

Sheela Barse Case

In *Sheela Barse* v. *Union of India*,[24] the manner in which the Supreme Court dealt with the things can aptly be described as irresponsible and pathetic, to say the least. The petitioner prayed for the release of 1,400 boys and girls who were illegally detained in several states. Notices were issued to the Union and about 24 states. Some of the states did not file their respective counter affidavits in the matter even after six months of having received notices thereof. After several adjournments, the Court fixed 2 December 1986 for the final hearing of the matter. On the said date also, the final hearing did not take place and the Court kept adjourning the matter fixing 8 dates subsequently for it. This was done notwithstanding the fact that the children were admittedly in illegal detentions. As if it were not enough, again 24 adjournments were granted, sometimes on flimsiest grounds, and thus three years elapsed but the petition could not be heard finally. On 21 July 1988, a distraught and desperate Barse, at a press conference, revealed as to how the apex court was handling a sensitive case like this in such a casual manner. She also stated that

[22] Godbole, *The Judiciary and Governance in India*.
[23] *Gopal Singh Visharad* v. *Jahor Ahmad* (2011) 86 ALR 646 (2011) ILR 1 All 387.
[24] (1988) A. SC 2221.

when she tried to speak, Justice Misra threatened to haul her up for contempt of court if she did not sit down. She divulged her intention to withdraw the case, because even if the petition was heard and an order passed, there was no guarantee that the orders would be complied with, as its earlier directions were flagrantly violated. On 27 July 1988, Sheela filed an application seeking court's permission to withdraw her petition. Justice Misra quipped that she was given a privilege by the Court which was being withdrawn. The statement displayed lack of basic understanding of the Constitutional provision and scheme that right to move the Supreme Court under Article 32 in case of a violation of a fundamental right is itself a fundamental right, and not a privilege. Obviously, it was subjected to ridicule in the media. Realizing the blunder, Justice Venkatachaliah passed an order on 29 August 1988 removing Sheela Barse from the petition, but, nevertheless, recorded in the order that Article 32 conferred a fundamental right to move the Supreme Court for the enforcement of fundamental rights. H.M. Seervai has rightly described this order as 'a travesty of justice'.[25] He also endorsed Barse's retort to the bench that the Supreme Court had become dysfunctional.[26] It is pertinent to mention here that earlier the same Supreme Court had showered applause on her for bringing the matter before the Court.

Directions Regarding the Interlinking of Rivers and Raising the Height of Dams

The Supreme Court directly forayed into the domain of the executive when it issued a writ of mandamus to the Union Government as well as concerned State Governments for the inter-linking of rivers (ILR).[27] The background behind the genesis of this petition is very curious as the Court directed to convert an interim application (I.A. No. 27) filed in another case pertaining to Yamuna into an independent PIL. A bench in Supreme Court took *suo motu* cognizance of a write-up published in *Hindustan Times*, dated 18 July 1994, titled 'And quiet flows the maili Yamuna' and served notices to the concerned authorities. Since then, the writ petition is being monitored by the Court itself. During the pendency of the case, I. A. No. 27 came to be filed wherein the *amicus curiae* appointed in that case referred to the

---

[25] H.M. Seervai, *Constitutional Law of India*, vol. II (Bombay: N.M. Tripathi Private Ltd., 1993), pp. viii–x, viii.

[26] Seervai, *Constitutional Law of India*, vol. II, p. ix.

[27] *In Re: Networking of River* (2012) 4 SCC 51 (2012) 3 SCALE 74 [writ petition (Civil) No. 512 of 2002].

address of the then president of India, A.P.J. Abdul Kalam, on the eve of the Independence Day in 2004 which, inter alia, related to creating a network between different rivers in the country to deal with the paradoxical situation of floods in one part of the country and drought in other parts. The Court realized its limitations in the following words:

> We would recommend, with all the judicial authority at our command, that these projects are in the national interest, as is the unanimous view of all experts, most State Governments and particularly, the Central Government. But this Court may not be a very appropriate forum for planning and implementation of such a programme having wide national dimensions and ramifications. It will not only be desirable, but also inevitable that an appropriate body should be created to plan, construct and implement this inter linking of rivers program for the benefit of the nation as a whole.[28]

However, the Court did not fight shy of giving directions despite realizing its limitations and asked the Union Government, particularly the Ministry of Water Resources, to forthwith constitute a committee to be called a 'Special Committee for inter-linking of rivers'. It further spelled out as to who shall be its members and that the committee would meet once in two months and it would be entitled to constitute sub-committees and would submit bi-annual report to the Union cabinet which would take final and appropriate decisions as expeditiously as possible and preferably within 30 days from the date the matters are first placed before it for consideration.

Surprisingly, on 31 October 2002, a bench headed by then Chief Justice, B.N. Kirpal had given similar directions. He retired the next day. Later, he was asked at the National Law School University of India, Bangalore, as to how he could pass such an order when the judiciary does not have the mandate to direct the executive to take up certain projects. He replied that it was only a suggestion and not a direction.[29]

The Supreme Court, however, repeated its act nearly a decade later. Himanshu Thakkar has rightly faulted the judgment in the following words:

> The Supreme Court order asks the government to implement the interlinking of rivers, when there is no existing scheme to do so. In case of 14 of the

[28] *Re: Networking of River*, para 63.
[29] Himanshu Thakkar, 'Can We Laugh Away the SC Order on ILR as a Comedy or Tragedy?', http://www.rediff.com/news/column/why-inter-linking-of-rivers-is-not-possible/20120309.htm (last accessed on 25 March 2016).

30 schemes, there is no existing feasibility report. The pre-feasibility and feasibility studies that exist are also all outdated, the water use pattern today has far outstripped availability in almost all basins.

In any case, none of the water balance studies or pre-feasibility studies are in the public domain. The quality of the studies is so bad that National Water Development Agency is afraid to put them out in the public domain.... Moreover, for none of the schemes is there a detailed project report or environment clearance or any other statutory clearances. How can the apex court ask for implementation of a scheme for which neither a feasibility report nor a DPR exists, and the available studies are not only outdated but they have not passed independent scrutiny? ... Each of the 30 schemes of the ILR is supposed to get through several statutory, legal and procedural steps. None of the schemes have [sic] gone through any of it. How can the SC ask for implementation of a scheme where such legal steps are necessary?

In each such legal step, the answer could actually be no. Now with the SC order, will the concerned sanctioning authorities be forced to say yes when law seeks their judgement on whether the scheme is viable or acceptable? If they were to say no, will they be prosecuted under contempt of court cases? If not, how can the scheme be implemented? ... if you take up ILR before the entire basin wide options are assessed and implemented, it is likely that you may end up finalising a project that will have no water, making the whole construction and costs incurred useless.[30]

Further, water is a state subject and the Centre cannot ride roughshod over it. Such a project has huge ramifications that may cause severe law and order problem as it may spawn internecine wars between states. In about 10 years of the pendency of the matter before the Supreme Court, only nine states replied to the Court's notice: three states (Assam, Sikkim, and Kerala) said a flat 'no' to the proposal, and three (Punjab, Bihar, and Odisha) gave their conditional assent, but the conditions are such that they cannot be carried out, and only three states (Tamil Nadu, Rajasthan, and Gujarat) said 'yes' and out of these three, Rajasthan and Gujarat have refused to share their waters so far with other states. Moreover, the judgment has some international ramifications also, as it will have an impact over countries like Nepal, Bhutan, and Bangladesh. This is puzzling considering the fact that the Supreme Court does not have any jurisdiction over other nations. The Court gave liberty to the *amicus curiae* appointed in the case, Ranjit Kumar, to file a case of contempt if its directions are not complied with. However, no such case has been

---

[30] Thakkar, 'Can We Laugh Away the SC Order on ILR as a Comedy or Tragedy?'.

filed even though there is hardly any effort by the government to implement the Court's directives.

Again, it was baffling to see the Supreme Court badgering the state of Karnataka to release the Cauvery water for Tamil Nadu, and the state government consistently flouting the directions calling them not implementable. Between 5 and 20 September 2016, the SC gave three directions to the state of Karnataka asking it to release water and continuously revised its order after non-compliance by the state government.[31] Thereafter, it reduced the volume to 12,000 cusec on 12 September and finally to 6,000 cusecs on 20 September.[32]

Surprisingly, the third direction was issued after the Supervisory Committee on Cauvery Water Disputes Tribunal (CWDT) directed the state of Karnataka to release 3,000 cusecs per day for ten days. These directions spawned widespread ethnic riots in the state and Chief Minister Siddaramaiah, flatly refused to implement the directions. The state government convened a special session of the legislative assembly which passed a unanimous resolution against sharing its water with Tamil Nadu during the lean season. Leaders cutting across party lines pooh-poohed these directions and emphatically said that they were not afraid of being hauled up for the contempt of court when people were dying. However, the apex court again issued the same directions.

It raises a serious question regarding the enforceability of the order of the apex court. Why did the Supreme Court not haul up the state government for its contempt if its orders were legally impeccable? And why was the state government being so audacious to have proclaimed from the house tops that the court's orders would not be implemented. Perhaps there was a catch; the SC seems to have overstepped. The Water Disputes Act, 1956, enacted under Article 262 of the Constitution of India, empowers the Union Government to set up a tribunal for the adjudication of water disputes between two or more states. The CWDT, set up on 2 June 1990, gave its final award in the year 2007. It directed for constitution of a Cauvery Management Board (CMB) to regulate the flow of water during the lean season. Though the award is called 'final', it is not final as the aggrieved

---

[31] On 5 September, it asked to release 15,000 cusecs of water per day till 16 September (I.A. No. 10/2016 in Civil Appeal No. 2456/2007 *State of T. Nadu* v. *State Karnataka and Ors*).

[32] I.A. No. 12/2016 in I.A.NO. 10 in Civil Appeal No. 2456/2007 *State of Karnataka and Ors.* v. *State of T. Nadu*.

parties can seek clarifications. After this, the last and final award comes, which cannot be challenged before any court. In the instant case, Karnataka, Tamil Nadu, and the Union Government have filed clarification petitions before the tribunal which are yet to be disposed of. The state of Karnataka and Tamil Nadu also filed their respective Special Leave Petitions (SLP) before the Supreme Court which were admitted but are yet to be disposed of—a typical case of judicial delays. However, the Court has been time and again giving interim directions.

The question is: on what basis did the SC decide the volume of water to be released? When the Supervisory Committee, a body of experts, asked Karnataka to release 3,000 cusecs of water per day, how could the Court ignore its findings and order to release 6,000 cusecs? The Court has no expertise to ascertain how much water should be released. The Supervisory Committee was set up on the directions of the apex court itself as the CMB had not been constituted. Karnataka made its stand clear that it has only potable water and as per the national water policy, water is to be used first for the purpose of drinking.

The Supreme Court was spared of embarrassment as Karnataka released water after a long delay but only when the water level of Cauvery welled up because of rains. The non-compliance of the directions of the court, especially the apex court, would lead to social anomie and the breakdown of the rule of law. It will be a dangerous situation. But many a time, the directions are either non-implementable or are simply given without jurisdiction.[33]

In another case of water dispute, the Supreme Court in *State of Tamil Nadu* v. *State of Kerala*[34] declared as unconstitutional the Kerala Irrigation and Water Conservation (Amendment) Act, 2006, constituting the Dam Safety Authority to prevent the State from raising the water level in the Mullaperiyar dam from 136 ft to 142 ft. A Constitution Bench of five judges held that the Court in its 2006 judgment had given a determination on a fact in dispute between the two states and none of the parties could enact a law that was in conflict with that determination. The Court emphasized that the doctrine of separation of powers between the executive, judiciary, and legislature must be respected and that the independence of the judiciary alone would ensure Rule of Law. The issue was whether it was safe to raise the level of water to the height as desired by the state of Tamil Nadu. Ramaswamy R. Iyer, former

---

[33] See Sudhanshu Ranjan, 'Bridge over Cuavery Waters: Ball Isn't in the Court', *Economic Times*, 8 October 2016.

[34] Original Suit No. 3 of 2006, decided on 7 May 2014.

Union secretary, Water Resources, questioned the competence of the court to decide the issue of safety. He observed as follows:

> The dam will not become safe because the learned judges say so, and it will not become unsafe if the learned judges consider it unsafe. (One is reminded of the English legend of King Canute and the sea.) This is clearly a matter for expert determination. If all experts agree, then there is no need for a judicial determination. If there is a difference among the experts, then it is surely not for a judge to say which view is right.[35]

It may be mentioned that late Mr Iyer was himself from the state of Tamil Nadu and yet, he criticized the judgment that upheld Tamil Nadu's plea. If the dam is breached, it will hamper severely the state of Kerala and not Tamil Nadu. Kerala was ready to give an equal amount of water to Tamil Nadu and was prepared to construct another dam for this purpose at its own cost. However, the apex court found merit in the plea of Tamil Nadu and struck down Kerala's law. High dams are always under threat. The 2017 Oroville crisis is a reminder of threats posed by high dams. Oroville Dam is the tallest dam in the US. Storms in early February 2017 caused heavy damage to its spillways which obstructed the safe release of floodwater. Consequently, over 1,80,000 people living downstream had to be evacuated. Thus, nobody knows when a dam will be damaged and havoc will be wreaked.

Use of Diesel Cars and Trucks and Imposition of Pollution Tax

In recent decades, the Supreme Court has issued a number of directions in order to keep the pollution in the National Capital Territory of Delhi in check. On 16 December 2015, it banned registration of luxury cars and SUVs with engine capacity of 2,000 cc or more till 31 March 2016, banned trucks older than 10 years from plying in Delhi and ordered that Light Commercial Vehicles (LCVs) would have to pay a pollution tax of Rs 1,400 and trucks Rs 2,600 while entering the city. It further directed that new diesel cars with engines smaller than 2,000 cc would be required to pay one time pollution tax.[36] Article 265 of the Constitution reads: 'No tax shall be levied or collected except with the authority of law.' Courts do not have the power to make law. Thus, the tax imposed by the Supreme Court is

---

[35] Ramaswamy R. Iyer, 'Mullaperiyar: A Matter of Judicial Overreach', *The Hindu*, 16 May 2014.

[36] *M. C. Mehta* v. *Union of India*, Writ petition (Civil) No. 817 of 2015 and others.

ultra vires of Article 265. The Supreme Court has ruled that when the tax is held to be void as being unconstitutional or illegal, the tax collected would have to be refunded.[37] However, on 10 May 2016, the Court allowed diesel cabs running on all India Tourist Permits to ply in National Capital Region (NCR) until the expiry of these permits. It modified its earlier orders which barred diesel taxis from plying in NCR which led to protests by cab owners and drivers.[38] This sent a somewhat disturbing signal that the Court is empowered to modify its order in the face of protests.

Criminalization of Politics and Judicial Pills

In a landmark judgment rendered on 10 July 2013, the Supreme Court declared Section 8(4) of the Representation of People Act, 1951 (hereinafter 'R. P. Act, 1951' in short), as *ultra vires* of the right to equality and equal protection of all laws guaranteed by Article 14 of the Constitution of India.[39] It disqualifies a sitting MP/MLA instantly upon conviction in a criminal case. Many MPs, including Mr Lalu Prasad, were thus disqualified and barred from contesting elections. Clauses (1), (2), and (3) of Sections 8 of the R. P. Act, 1951 lays down the crimes and punishments which shall disqualify a candidate from contesting elections but Section 8(4) created an exception in favour of sitting MPs/MLAs as they are given three months' time to file an appeal against the judgement convicting them and can thus continue to hold their position till the pendency of the appeal. The judgment was widely hailed by the civil society which is solicitous about the canker of criminalization afflicting the body politic of the country.

It is true that the Parliament refused to take cognisance of the malaise and did not come forward with a law to contain it, and so the activism of the court got accolades and public support bequeathed legitimacy to its overstepping. The two-judge bench conveniently overlooked the judgment of the five-judge Constitution Bench in *K. Prabhakaran* v. *P. Jayarajan*[40] which clearly ruled that the Parliament by enacting Section 8(3) and Section 8(4) has chosen to distinguish between two categories—one, a person who is an MP or MLA on the date of conviction, and two, a person who is not—which

---

[37] *U.P. Pollution Control Board* v. *Kanoria Industrial Ltd.*, AIR (2001) SC 87 (2001) 2 SCC 549.

[38] *M.C. Mehta* v. *Union of India*, Writ petition (Civil) No. 817 of 2015 and others, dated 10 May 2016.

[39] *Lily Thomas* v. *Union of India* (2013) 7 SCC 653.

[40] (2005) 1 SCC 754.

is a reasonable classification as 'it is based on a well laid down differentia and has nexus with a public purpose sought to be achieved'. The question is: can a division bench overrule a decision of a Constitution Bench? Articles 102(1) and 191(1) of the Constitution of India have laid down provisions regarding disqualification from the membership of either Houses of Parliament and State Legislative Assembly and Council respectively, and also empowers the Parliament to make laws regarding disqualification. However, there is no mention as to when the disqualification becomes effective. So, it is for the Parliament to make provision regarding the same. Instead of relying on Prabhakaran's case, the Court relied on the decision of the Constitution Bench in *Election Commission, India* v. *Saka Venkata Rao*[41] which held that Article 191 lays down the same set of disqualifications for election as well as for continuing as a member. If there was any confusion, the best course of action for the division bench would have been to refer the matter to a larger Constitution Bench. The Supreme Court, in *Government of Andhra Pradesh and Ors.* v. *P. Laxmi Devi,*[42] clearly held that striking down of a statute by the court is a grave step. The court should declare a law as *ultra vires* not merely because it is possible to take such a view, but only when the unconstitutionality is beyond question and no other interpretation is possible. The Supreme Court also dismissed the review petition filed by the Union of India on 4 September 2013.[43]

The apprehension of conviction by the lower court and subsequent exoneration by the higher court is not unfounded as was evident in the case of J. Jayalalithaa who had to resign as the chief minister of Tamil Nadu and go to jail after she was convicted by a special court (Bengaluru) in a case regarding her disproportionate assets and was sentenced to four years in jail and the Court also imposed a fine of Rs 100 crore on 27 September 2014. However, on 11 May 2015, the Karnataka High Court acquitted her and she returned as the chief minister of the state. She passed away in harness, but the Supreme Court, reversing the HC's judgment, upheld the decision of the trial court.[44]

In another decision delivered in *Chief Election Commissioner* v. *Jan Chowkidar,*[45] the Court disqualified persons behind bar from contesting elections. Relying on Section 62(5) of the R. P. Act, 1951, which debars a person who is in police custody from exercising their franchise in elections,

[41]   AIR (1953) SC 210.

[42]   (2008) 4 SCC 720, AIR (2008) SC 1640.

[43]   *The Hindu*, New Delhi; *The Times of India*, New Delhi, 5 September 2013.

[44]   *State of Karnataka* v. *Selvi J. Jayalalitha and Ors.,* 2017 SCC OnLine SC 134, decided on 14 February 2017.

[45]   (2013) 7 SCC 507, on 10 July 2013.

the Court said that Sections 3, 4, and 5 entitle only an elector to contest, and so a person who is not an elector cannot contest elections. This is stretching logic too far to reach a desired conclusion. Section 2(e) defines an elector as a person who is entered in the voters' list and is not disqualified under Section 16 of the Act. It is important to note that there is no mention of Section 62(5) in Section 2(e). It is heartening to note that the Parliament amended Section 62(5), clarifying that those behind bars are eligible to contest elections though they would not be eligible to vote. On the basis of this amendment, the Supreme Court allowed the review petition filed by the government. Had it not been done, it would have opened up floodgates for misuse.

Directions Regarding the Constitution of the Information Commission

In *Union of India* v. *Namit Sharma*,[46] the Supreme Court recalled its earlier directions that the Information Commissions being quasi-judicial bodies must be manned by people from legal background.[47] Breaching the doctrine of separation of powers themselves, the Court held that these Commissions are tribunals whose functioning is quasi-judicial and akin to the court system, and so the entire administration of justice has to be independent and managed by persons of legal acumen, expertise, and experience to inspire full faith in the justice delivery system. It went on to direct that since it is judicial tribunal having the essential trappings of a court, the appointments to the Information Commission must be made in consultation with the judiciary. The Court further observed that in the event, the government desires to appoint not only judicial members but also experts from other fields, then it would be necessary that the Commission works in benches comprising one judicial member and one other member from the specified fields as mentioned in sections 12(5) and 15(5) of the RTI Act. Laying down the procedure of appointment, the Court said that appointments have to be made in consultation with the CJI in case of Chief Information Commissioner and judicial members of the Central Information Commission and the chief justices of the high courts of the respective States, in the case of State Chief Information Commissioner and judicial members of that State Commission. It also directed that the Chief Information Commissioner of the Central Information Commission must only be a former judge of the Supreme Court or a retired chief justice of the high court and other judicial members must be amongst the former judges of the high courts.

[46] (2013) 1 SCC 745.
[47] (WP (C) No. 210 of 2012.

This was a clear intrusion into the domain of legislature by way of judicial directions. However, the Court took cognisance of the severe public criticism that it was creating sanctuaries for the retired judges and allowed the review petition filed by the Union Government admitting that giving such directions was tantamount to encroachment on the domain of the legislature. However, the Court rightly ruled that the committees while making recommendations to the president or the governor, as the case may be, for appointment of Chief Information Commissioner and Information Commissioners must give justification as to why a particular name is being recommended by mentioning against his/her name the facts to indicate his/her eminence in public life which must be accessible to citizens as part of their right to information. It further ruled that whenever Chief Information Commissioner is of the opinion that intricate questions of law are to be decided in some matter, s/he will ensure that it is heard by an Information Commissioner who has the knowledge and experience in the field of law.

Sahara Case: Jail without FIR

Subrata Roy, head of Sahara India group, languished in jail between 4 March 2014 and 6 May 2016 without knowing under which law he had been incarcerated and for what crime.[48] I do not support his irregularities, but the Cr.PC is very clear that the court cannot send a person to judicial custody unless there is an inquiry or trial pending. In his case, there was not even an FIR. It has been decided by the Supreme Court in Lalu Prasad's case when the CBI court, Patna, was unable to take cognizance in the absence of a sanction for prosecution. So, the judge referred the matter to the Patna High Court which ruled that if there is no sanction, there can be no cognizance, and so no judicial custody.[49] The same was upheld by the Supreme Court. So, what is Subrata Roy's crime? Was it contempt of court for not abiding by the Court's order of 2010 requiring Sahara Group to pay over Rs 20,000 crores to the Securities and Exchange Board of India (SEBI)? But then the maximum punishment under the law could only be six months' jail term. However, he remained behind bars for over two years, and then also he was released on parole because of his mother's death, and his bail was subsequently extended. Further, even charges under the contempt of court were not framed. The

---

[48] *Sahara India Real Estate Corporation Limited and Ors* v. *Securities and Exchange Board of India and Anr.* (2013) 1 SCC 1 (Civil Appeal No. 9813 of 2011).

[49] *S.K. Lal, Special Judge, CBI, Patna* v. *Lalu Prasad*, Pat HC (1998) 1 PLJR 782, decided on 28 November 1997.

criminal law is based on the proof of facts beyond reasonable doubt whereas the civil law works on the test of balance of probabilities. There is a long distance to be covered between what may be true and what is actually true. In the Sahara case, the party wanted Justice J.S. Khehar to recuse, but he refused. On 6 May 2014, he delivered a judgment running into 207 pages in which he reiterated his 4 March order and rejected Subrata Roy's bail petition.[50] Reacting to the prayer for recusal, the judge thundered that the Court would not succumb to mind games played by litigants and their eminent counsel, and asserted that not hearing the matter would constitute an act in breach of the oath of office which judges take, which mandates them to perform the duties of their office to the best of their ability, without fear or favour, affection or ill-will.

Surprisingly, within hours after it, he recused. He also told the Registry of the Supreme Court that in future, no matter pertaining to any Sahara Group company should be placed before a bench of which he is a part.[51] This is inscrutable. With another judge on the bench, Justice K.S. Radhankrishnana, having retired, the bench had to be constituted afresh. It is curious to note that Justice Radhakrishnan claimed that he faced 'pressure, tension and strain' while hearing the case involving Sahara Group chief Subrata Roy and two other directors with a contempt case for non-refund of inverstors' money.[52]

President's Rule Lifted for Three Hours Like Curfew

In the Uttarakhand case,[53] adjudicating on the legality of President's Rule, the Supreme Court created a constitutional void for three hours by asking the Union Government to lift it for three hours on 10 May 2016 for conducting the floor test as to whether the unseated Harish Rawat's government enjoyed confidence of the House or not. On 6 May, it ordered to conduct the floor test but debarred the Speaker from presiding over the proceedings. Instead it appointed Principal Secretary, Legislative Assembly, for the purpose. When it was brought to the Court's notice that there was no such post, and instead

[50] *Subrata Roy Sahara* v. *Union of India and Ors.* (2014) 8 SCC 470: Writ Petition (Crl) No. 57 of 2014.

[51] 'Sahara: Amid Allegations of "Pressure", SC Judge Opts Out', *Indian Express*, 2 May 2014.

[52] 'Unimaginable Pressure, Tension: SC Judge Who Heard Sahara Case', *Indian Express*, 11 May 2014.

[53] *Union of India* v. *Harish Chandra Singh Rawat* (2016) 16 SCC 744, SLP No. 11567 of 2016.

it was Secretary, Legislative Assembly, or Principal Secretary, Legislative and Parliamentary Affairs, State of Uttarakhand, it modified its order on 9 May and appointed both to oversee:

> This Court, being the sentinel on the qui vive of the Constitution, is under the obligation to see that the democracy prevails and not gets hollowed by individuals. The directions which have been given on the last occasion, was [*sic*] singularly for the purpose of strengthening the democratic values and the constitutional norms. The collective trust in the legislature is founded on the bedrock of the constitutional trust. This is a case where one side even in the floor test does not trust the other and the other claims that there is no reason not to have the trust. Hence, there is the need and there is the necessity to have a neutral perceptionist to see that absolute objectivity is maintained when the voting takes place. Solely for the aforesaid purpose, we intend to modify the order by directing that the Principal Secretary, Legislative and Parliamentary Affairs who belongs to the cadre of the District Judge shall remain present to conduct the affairs with perceptible objectivity and singularity of purpose of neutrality along with the Secretary Legislative Assembly. The order is modified accordingly.[54]

It may be noted that the principal secretary, Legislative and Parliamentary Affairs, was not entitled to enter the premises of the Legislative Assembly without the Speaker's permission. There was no government for this period in the state as there was neither state government nor Central rule. Only God knows who was holding the reins of governance in the state. Thus, the President's Rule was converted into a curfew which was lifted for some time so that people are able to buy essential items. It is also inscrutable as to whose trial of strength it was when the chief minister had not been reinstated.

The Court also decimated the institution of the Speaker by keeping him away from the floor test, replacing him with officers. It is in flagrant violation of Article 212 of the Constitution of India which reads:

1. The validity of any proceedings in the legislature of a state shall not be called in question on the ground of any alleged irregularity of procedure.
2. No officer or member of the legislature of a state in whom powers are vested by or under this Constitution for regulating procedure or the conduct of business, or for maintaining order, in the Legislature shall be subject to the jurisdiction of any court in respect of the exercise by him of those powers.

[54] *Union of India* v. *Harish Chandra Singh Rawat*, dated 9 May 2016.

The Court surpassed its earlier directions passed in *Jagdambika Pal* v. *Union of India and Ors.*,[55] when it passed the unprecedented order to hold a composite floor test not provided in the Constitution to ascertain as to who enjoyed the majority support—Kalyan Singh or Jagdambika Pal, and also elaborate directions given in the Jharkhand case[56] for conducting the floor test. Even in these judgments, which were subjected to searing criticisms, the Court did not prevent the Speaker from presiding over the proceedings of the House. An institution should not be thrown into a state of disuse just because some irregularities were allegedly committed or some people say that they do not have faith in it. Reforms may be an urgent desideratum but emasculating a body in the name of reforms is worse and thus undesirable. The Supreme Court got international opprobrium for its infamous judgment in the habeas corpus case,[57] which upheld the suspension of the right to life during the Emergency as constitutionally valid. Does it mean that the SC should have been disbanded?

Contradictory Judgments on Transgender and Homosexuality

Two important judgments of the Supreme Court—one pertaining to gay rights and the other to transgenders—having wide ramifications are in sharp conflict with each other, reaffirming once again the erosion of judicial collectivism. In *Suresh Kumar Kaushal* v. *NAZ Foundation*,[58] decided on 11 December 2013, the Court reversed the historic judgment of the Delhi High Court in *Naz Foundation* v. *Government of NCT of Delhi*[59] that held Section 377 of the Indian Penal Code (IPC), 1860 to be unconstitutional to the extent that it criminalized sexual acts between two consenting adults of the same sex. Section 377 of the IPC criminalizes 'carnal intercourse against the order of nature with any man, woman or animal'. Since the IPC does not define 'carnal intercourse against the order of nature', the courts have interpreted that any non-procreative carnal intercourse is against the order of nature since the purpose of 'carnal intercourse' is procreation. In common parlance, it was interpreted as an anti-sodomy law.

The Delhi High Court, with its cogent reasonings, declared Section 377 to be unconstitutional as it criminalizes a person's core identity solely on

---

[55] (1999) 9 SCC 95.

[56] *Anil Kumar Jha* v. *Union of India and Anr.* (2005) SCC 150.

[57] *ADM, Jabalpur* v. *Shivkant Shukla*, AIR (1976) SC 1207.

[58] (2014) 1 SCC 1.

[59] (2009) 160 DLT 277 (2009) 111 GRJ 1 (2009) 3 JCC 1787.

the basis of their sexual orientation, and, thus, is violative of Article 21 of the Constitution of India. It said that the Constitution guarantees the right to privacy and the right to dignity and the right of full personhood under Article 21. It added that the very existence of the section in the statute book impacts homosexuals adversely even when the provisions are not enforced as they are treated as 'unapprehended felons'. It also rejected the argument of moral indignation to curtail the right to privacy and dignity. The High Court decided that Section 377 violates the right to equality guaranteed by Article 14 and right to non-discrimination on the ground of sex under Article 15, and the right to privacy and dignity under Article 21. It said that Article 14 is the genus, while Articles 15 and 16 are the species.

The State did not go in appeal but a group of religious leaders and astrologers challenged the validity of judgment before the apex court. Showing self-restraint the Court left it to the legislature to decide whether to retain, delete, or amend this law, observing that laws are presumed to be constitutional, based on the premise that the legislature, being a representative body of the people and accountable to them, is aware of their needs and acts in their best interests within the confines of the Constitution. Justice G.S. Singhvi, who authored this judgment, took a diametrically opposite view in *Satyawati Sharma (Dead) by LRS v. Union of India*[60] that legislation which may be reasonable at the time of its enactment may with the passage of time and/or due to change in circumstances become arbitrary, unreasonable, and violative of the doctrine of equality. On this ground, he struck down Section 14(1)(e) of the Delhi Rent Control Act as violative of Article 14 of the Constitution of India.

However, giving a short shrift to Article 14, the Court ruled in the gay rights case that those who indulge in 'carnal intercourse in the ordinary course' and those who indulge in it against the 'order of nature' constitute different classes of people and can be classified separately under Article 14 of the Constitution of India, glossing over the main issue whether there is any order of nature. The Court said that there was insufficient evidence to prove that homosexuals were being discriminated against. The most disturbing observation of the Court is that the lesbian, gay, bisexual, transgender (LGBT) community forms a 'miniscule fraction of the country's population'. It stares in the face of Supreme Court's jurisprudence in many decisions that the number of people impacted by the law should not be a consideration in examining the constitutionality of a statute. The observation is deeply shocking as the

---

[60] (2008) 5 SCC 287 (decided on 16 April 2008).

miniscule fraction cannot mobilize support in terms of numbers to pressure the legislature to delete the provision. This is exactly what the US Supreme Court ruled in *United States* v. *Carole Products Company*.[61] The judgment is often quoted for its historic 'Footnote Four'. The Court laid down the system of heightened scrutiny for laws targeting 'discrete and insular minorities', which lacked the normal protection of the political process, compared with the lower scrutiny applied in this case for economic regulations.

The Supreme Court of India has not adduced reasons as to how does it differ with the Delhi High Court on its interpretation of right to privacy and dignity under Article 21 of the Constitution of India. Leaving the issue to the legislature is inscrutable when the attorney-general of India clearly told the Court that the government supported the Delhi High Court's judgment on Section 377 of the IPC. It specifically mentioned a 2013 legislation amending the law dealing with sexual assault to drive home the point that the Parliament decided not to repeal or revisit it. Surprisingly, the Court referred to the attorney-general as '*amicus*' (friend of the court) in its judgment which forced him to publicly clarify that he had very much represented the government's official position.[62]

Though it is true that the judiciary should observe self-restraint and leave legislation to the legislature, the track record of the apex court suggests otherwise. It did not hesitate in striking down the Constitution (Ninety-Ninth Amendment) Act, 2014, which was passed unanimously by both Houses of Parliament, with just one walk out in Rajya Sabha by Ram Jethmalani, and 20 State Legislative Assemblies.[63] Though it is true that the apex court failed to protect the liberty and dignity of a 'miniscule fraction of population', it is not proper to let the Parliament go unscathed. Critics of the judgment should also build up pressure on legislators to repeal the discriminatory law.

However, the Supreme Court, in *National Legal Services Authority* v. *Union of India*[64] on 15 April 2014, that is, barely four months later, delivered a landmark judgment to abolish the gender discrimination in the society by treating transgenders as a third gender category. It is in sharp contrast to the gay rights judgment. The Court accepted the prayer of the Transgender Community (TG) that non-recognition of their gender identity violates Articles 14 and 21

[61] 304 U.S. 144 (1938).

[62] Tarunabh Khaitan, 'The Legislative Court', *The Hindu*, 24 December 2013.

[63] *Supreme Court Advocates-on-Record Association and Anr.* v. *Union of India* (2016) 5 SCC 1 (decided on 15 October 2015).

[64] (2014) 5 SCC 438.

of the Constitution of India. Justice K.S. Radhakrishnan, with Justice A.K. Sikri concurring, empathizes with them in the opening paragraph itself:

> Seldom, our society realizes or cares to realize the trauma, agony and pain which the members of Transgender community undergo, nor appreciates innate feelings of the members of the Transgender community, especially of those whose mind and body disown their biological sex. Our society often ridicules and abuses the Transgender community and in public places … they are sidelined and treated as untouchables, forgetting the fact that the moral failure lies in the society's unwillingness to contain or embrace different gender identities and expressions, a mindset which we have to change.

The Court's reasoning is based on strong constitutional foundations and give TGs the protection of no less than five fundamental rights. They are entitled to equality before law and the equal protection of laws available to every person, not only men and women under Article 14. Article 15(1) prohibits discrimination on grounds of sex by the state, while Article 15(2) prohibits such discrimination even by private citizens with regard to access to public spaces. Article 16 prohibits discrimination on the grounds of sex in matters of public employment. The Court laid down that the term 'sex' does not only mean biological sexes of male and female, but included people who consider themselves neither male nor female. Unlike in *Suresh Kumar Kaushal*, the Court clearly held that everyone, regardless of sexual orientation or gender identity, is entitled to the enjoyment of privacy without arbitrary or unlawful interference. The Court not only recognized TGs, but also gave the directions to treat them as socially and educationally backward class of citizens and give reservation in educational institutions and government jobs. It may sound like a legislative court but the Court has gone by the mandate of international law and human rights conventions, encouraging legislators to incorporate the same into the municipal law. The Court has ratiocinated that an affirmative action policy that keeps in mind only historical injustice, would certainly result in under-protection of the most deserving backward class of citizens, which is constitutionally mandated. The logic is impeccable.

The judgment was hailed by the national and international press but it also lamented that the LGBT community was left high and dry by the same court. The Court reiterated its stand to extend the benefits of reservation to TGs in *Ram Singh* v. *Union of India*.[65]

---

[65] (2015) 4 SCC 697 (decided on 17 March 2015).

Such conflicts can easily be resolved if the Supreme Court forms Constitution Benches on issues of such vital ramifications as mandated by Article 145(3). Since there is no accountability, nor is the principle of *stare decisis* being followed, many a judge comes up with a brilliant idea defying the precedent. Even a historic case like *Lily Thoma* v. *Union of India*[66] which set aside section 8(4) of the R. P. Act, 1951, as unconstitutional, leading to instant disqualification of MP/MLAs immediately after conviction by the lower court, was decided by a division bench of two judges. The judgement has serious legal, constitutional, and political implications.

Judiciary's Brazen Attempt to Escape Accountability under the RTI Act

Judges generally take the plea that the functioning of the judiciary is most transparent as proceedings take place in the open court and every judgment is a public document which is subject to ruthless criticism. Thus, the courts are under a constant public scanner which no other functionary of the state is subject to. This logic, doubtless, holds water but only partially. Now, after the enforcement of the Right to Information (RTI) Act in 2005, all decisions of other functionaries too can be questioned, resulting in government employees having sleepless nights. But here also the judiciary has illegally kept itself away from the purview of this law and consequently from the public scrutiny of even its administrative matters. In fact, the RTI Act is getting attenuated as there is hardly any relief to appellants from higher judiciary when they are frustrated by the supine Information Commissions mostly manned by bureaucrats. Earlier, high courts and the Supreme Court rushed to the rescue of those seeking transparency in government functioning, but then they changed their tack having realized that the same yardstick is being applied to them to question opacity. Most of the high courts did not even appoint Public Information Officers (PIOs) as required under the law, for a long time, and those which appointed PIOs, framed their own rules arbitrarily, which clearly prohibited the disclosure of information on administrative matters relating to expenditure of judges, procedure followed in appointments of Class III and IV employees of the high court by the judges, and so on. Thus, the Delhi High Court Rules provided, '5. Exemption from disclosure of information— The information specified under Section 8 of the Act shall not be disclosed and made available and in particular the following information shall not be

[66] (2013) 7 SCC 653.

disclosed: '(a) Such information which is not in the public domain or does not relate to judicial functions and duties of the Court and matters incidental and ancillary thereto.'

On the basis of this self-acquired power, it initially refused to give any information regarding the appointment of Class III and IV employees by the high court who were reportedly appointed without any public advertisement or selection and also the expenditure of its budget when Prashant Bhushan, an activist lawyer, sought it under the RTI Act. This information was subsequently provided after the Chief Information Commission (CIC) directed the disclosure and also asked the chief justice of the Delhi High Court to amend the rules, which was subsequently done by the Delhi High Court.

Several other high courts, however, still have rules prohibiting the disclosure of administrative or financial information. This is a flagrant violation of the Act as exemptions from disclosures are permissible only on certain grounds specified under Section 8 of the Act. Further, giving another body blow to the very spirit of the Act, the Delhi High Court rules arbitrarily enhanced the application fees from the nominal Rs 10 to up to Rs 500 and the penalty for non-disclosure was reduced from Rs 25,000 to a meagre Rs 500, which can hardly act as a deterrent. When Justice A.P. Shah took over as the chief justice of the Delhi High Court in May 2010, he reversed all the retrograde rules prohibiting information, hike in application fees, and reduction in fines. Justice Shah's acts to ensure transparency are laudable.

The Supreme Court even formally asked the government to amend the RTI Act to bring it out of the purview of the CIC, an autonomous body, and also to provide that the CJI can interdict any release of information which will not be questioned. Prashant Bhushan has written:

> After having loudly announced that the citizens have a right to know everything that goes on in public institutions, the Supreme Court asks the government to effectively exempt it from the purview of the Act by removing the jurisdiction of the independent appellate authority, the Central Information Commission, over the registrar of the court. It was also recommended [by the Supreme Court] that the Chief Justice should be the final word in deciding whether any information about the court should be given out or not.... All this has ensured that the judiciary becomes a law unto itself, totally non-transparent, and accountable to none.[67]

---

[67] Prashant Bhushan, 'Reclaiming the Judicial System in India', *Background Paper for the National Convention on Restructuring of Judicial System*, held in Delhi, March 2007. See Madhav Godbole, 'Judicial Reforms Nowhere in Sight', in *The Judiciary and Governance in India*, pp. 408–9.

Reluctance to Declare Assets

Judges of the Supreme Court finally declared their assets on 2 November 2009 on the Court's website (www.supremecourtofindia.nic.in).[68] In fact, this declaration follows a long-drawn legal battle between the Supreme Court and the CIC and a sustained campaign by the people demanding transparency in the judiciary.

It all started when Subhash Chandra Agrawal filed an application on 10 November 2007 before the Central Public Information Officer (CPIO), Supreme Court of India, asking him to furnish a copy of the resolution dated 7 May 1997 of the Full Court of the Supreme Court ('the 1997 Resolution') which requires every judge to make a declaration of all assets. He further sought information relating to the declaration of assets furnished by the respective chief justices of the high courts. By order dated 30 November 2007, the CPIO informed the applicant that information relating to the declaration of the judges' assets was not held by or under the control of the Registry of the Supreme Court and, therefore, it could not be furnished. Not satisfied, the applicant challenged this order before the appellate authority. The petitioner contended that if the CPIO did not hold the information, he should have disclosed the authority holding it, and should have referred the application to that authority, invoking Section 6(3) of the RTI Act. It was also contended that assuming that the CPIO did not have the information, since the applicant had sought information regarding the declaration of assets made by the various chief justices of the high courts, the CPIO should have transferred the matter to the respective CPIOs. Accepting the argument, the appellate authority remanded the matter for reconsideration to the CPIO.

After remission, the CPIO rejected the application with following observations:

> In the case at hand, you yourself knew that the information sought by you is related to various High Court(s) in the country and instead of applying to those Public Authorities you have taken a short circuit procedure by approaching the CPIO, Supreme Court of India remitting the fee of Rs. 10/-payable to one authority and getting it referred to all the public authorities at the expense of one Central Public Information Officer. In view of this, the relief sought by you cannot be appreciated and is against the spirit of Section 6(3) of the Right to Information Act, 2005.

[68] 'SC Judges List Their Assets for the People', *Indian Express*, 3 November 2009; 'SC Judges Declare Their Paltry Assets', *Times of India*, 3 November 2009.

You may, if so advised approach the concerned public authorities for desired information.[69]

The applicant approached the CIC contending that the CPIO's order maintained a studied silence about the disclosure of information on the declaration of assets by the judges of the Supreme Court to the CJI in accordance with the 1997 Resolution. The CPIO submitted that the registrar of the Supreme Court did not hold the information and that the 1997 Resolution was an in-house exercise; and the declarations regarding the judges' assets were voluntary. Further, the resolution itself describes the submission of such declarations as 'confidential', and, therefore, any disclosure of the information regarding such declarations would be in breach of a fiduciary relationship as the declarations were submitted to the CJI in his personal capacity, not his official one. The CPIO also averred that the disclosure would be contrary to the provisions of Section 8(1) of the Act.

The CIC gave the reasoning that since the Supreme Court was established by the Constitution of India and is a public authority within the meaning of Section 2(h) of the Act. Section 2(e)(i) was referred to contend that the CJI was a competent authority, under the Act, empowered to frame Rules under Section 28 of the Act to carry out provisions of the Act. It was held that rule making power is conferred by the provisions of the Act on the chief justice and the Supreme Court who cannot disclaim being public authorities. The appeal was allowed on the following reasoning:

The rule making power has been explicitly given for the purpose of carrying out the provisions of the RTI Act. The Act, therefore, empowers the Supreme Court and the other competent authorities under the act and entrusts upon them an additional responsibility of ensuring that the RTI Act is implemented in letter and spirit. In view of this, the contention of the respondent public authority that the provisions of Right to Information act are not applicable in case of Supreme Court cannot be accepted.

The learned counsel appearing on behalf of the Supreme Court during the course of hearing argued that the information concerning the declaration of assets by the judges is provided to the Chief Justice of India in his personal capacity and it is 'voluntary' and 'confidential'. From what was presented before us, it can be inferred that the declaration of assets are filed with the Chief Justice of India and the office of the Chief Justice of India is the custodian of this information. The information is maintained in a confidential manner and

[69] Quoted by the Delhi High Court in *The CPIO, Supreme Court of India* v. *Subhash Chandra Agrawal and Anr.*, W. P. (C) 288/2009, para 3.

like any other official information it is available for perusal and inspection to every succeeding Chief Justice of India. The information, therefore, cannot be categorized as 'personal information' available with the Chief Justices in their personal capacity.

The only issue that needs to be determined is as to whether the Chief Justice of India and the Supreme Court of India are two distinct Public Authorities or one Public Authority. In this context, it would be pertinent to refer again to the provisions of section 2 (h) of the Right to Information Act, the relevant part of which reads as under:

2(h) 'Public authority' means any authority or body or institution of self-government established or constituted...[70]

The Supreme Court challenged the order of the CIC in the Delhi High Court. The High Court requested eminent constitutional expert, Fali S. Nariman, to become *amicus curiae* in the case. However, Nariman declined saying he was 'biased' because he was of the firm opinion that judges must declare their assets.[71] He wrote, 'Judges of the highest court who have powers to life and death over us citizens, judges who can (and do) send people to jail for contempt of its order must—I repeat must—show that they are amenable to good practice.'[72] He also recalled his visit to the US under the auspices of the Indo-US Legal Forum, and wrote that he came across a US law that mandated each Supreme Court judge, not only to make public his assets each year, but about every gift which was worth more than $50. He remembered reading a catchy news item: 'Clarence Thomas discloses box of 50 cigars', which told the public how a US Supreme Court judge had to declare this gift as its value exceeded $50.[73]

The High Court upheld the order of the CIC. Justice Ravindra Bhatt, in his eloquent judgement, wrote:

This court is of the opinion that the volitional nature of the resolutions should be seen as the higher judiciary's commitment to essential ethical behaviour, and its resolve to abide by it. Therefore, that such need to declare assets is not mandated by Parliamentary law, or any statutory instrument, becomes of secondary importance. The mere fact that Supreme Court

[70] *The CPIO, Supreme Court of India* v. *Subhash Chandra Agrawal and Anr.*, para 5.

[71] 'Nariman: I Am Biased, Can't Be Friend of the Court', *Times of India*, 21 January 2009.

[72] 'Nariman'.

[73] 'Nariman'.

judges (through the 1997 Resolution) and members of the higher judiciary (through the Judicial Conference Resolution) recognize these as normative, and governing their conduct, is sufficient to bind them. They formed a set of conventions of the Constitution. To conclude otherwise would *endanger credibility* of the institution, which prides—by its adherence to the doctrines of precedent, and *stare decisis* (in the discharge of its constitutional obligation in judging)—in consistency, and by meaning what it says, and saying what it means. This aspect is summed up aptly by an Australian Judge in the following manner:

Some standards can be prescribed by law, but the spirit of, and the quality of the service rendered by, a profession depends far more on its observance of ethical standards. These are far more rigorous than legal standards.... They are learnt not by precept but by the example and influence of respected peers. Judicial standards are acquired, so to speak, by professional osmosis. They are enforced immediately by conscience'.[74]

There is yet, perhaps one more powerful reason to hold that the 1997 Resolution binds members of the higher judiciary. In its interpretation of non-statutory instruments—be they orders, circulars, or policies—by state, or agencies (as understood under Article 12 of the Constitution of India), the Supreme Court has ruled on several occasions[75] that such executive determinations are binding on the authority, making it (*executive authority must be rigorously held to the standards by which it professes*).[76] While there cannot be any dispute that the 1997 Resolution was made by a body—Full Court of the Supreme Court, and the 1999 Resolution, through a chief justices' conference—which is not accorded constitutional status, and granted that high courts are not 'subordinate' to the Supreme Court in the sense that the latter has no powers of superintendence, yet, those bodies (the conference) are undeniably collegial, consisting of the highest judicial authorities of each high court, and the Supreme Court. The decisions taken, and resolutions adopted during their deliberations are aimed at arriving at common solutions to grapple problems that beset the legal system of the country as a whole. The resolutions and decisions are taken seriously, and with the intention of implementation. To put it otherwise, the resolutions were made (and similar resolutions, are made) to be followed and adhered to. In these circumstances, it would be robbing the

---

[74] Justice J.B. Thomas, *Judicial Ethics in Australia*, 2nd ed. (Sydney: LBC Information Services, 1997).

[75] *Ramana Dayaram Shetty* v. *International Airport Authority of India* (1979) 3 SCC 489; *H.V. Nirmala* v. *Karnataka State Financial Corpn.* (2008) 7 SCC 639; *G.J. Fernandez* v. *State of Karnataka* (1990) 2 SCC 488; and *Union of India* v. *Rajpal Singh* (2009) 1 SCC 216.

[76] *Ramana Dayaram Shetty* v. *International Airport Authority of India*.

solemnity of the Resolutions adopted in 1997, to say that they were made with the expectation of not being implemented.

This court is also mindful that the law declared in the Supreme Court, based on the existence of conventions of the Constitution, in the Supreme Court Advocates on Record Association case, ushered a new chapter in the annals of our constitutional history, whereby the function of recommending appointments to the higher judiciary was left almost exclusively to the senior most echelons of the High Court and Supreme Court (for High Courts') and for the Supreme Court, exclusively to a defined collegial body of its five senior most judges. One (perhaps) implied and inarticulate premise of the judgement was the emergence of professionally better equipped judges, with the required degree of independence, insulated from potential conflicts and capable of handling complex legal issues for the years to come. The 1997 Resolution, and the Judicial Conference Resolution of 1999 have to be placed in perspective, and this historical contest, where the higher judiciary—in the wake of the 1993 judgement, committed itself, for the first time, to a declared set of codified standards. In view of the above discussion, the court finds that the 1997 Resolution binds all those covered by it.[77]

The Court also rejected the argument of fiduciary relationship between the CJI and other judges in the context of declaration of assets:

... a fiduciary relationship is one whereby a person places complete confidence in another in regard to a particular transaction or his general affairs or business. The relationship need not be 'formally' or 'legally' ordained, or established, like in the case of a written trust; but can be one of moral or personal responsibility, due to the better or superior knowledge or training, or superior status of the fiduciary as compared to the one whose affairs he handles. If viewed from this perspective, it is immediately apparent that the CJI cannot be a fiduciary vis-à-vis Judges of the Supreme Court; he cannot be said to have superior knowledge, or be better trained, to aid or control their affairs or conduct. Judges of the Supreme Court hold independent office, and there is no hierarchy, in their judicial functions, which places them at a different plane than the CJI. In these circumstances, it cannot be held that asset information shared with the CJI, by the judges of the Supreme Court, are held by him in the capacity of a fiduciary, which if directed to be revealed, would result in breach of such duty. So far as the argument that the 1997 Resolution had imposed a confidentiality obligation on the CJI to ensure non-disclosure of the asset declarations, is

---

[77]   *The CPIO, Supreme Court of India* v. *Subhash Chandra Agrawal* (2009) SCC Online Del 27 14 (2009) 162 DLT 135 (2010) 1 Kant LJ 383 (2009) 82 AIC (Sum 13) 8, paras 49–51. [W.P. (C) 288/2008].

concerned, the court is of opinion that with the advent of the Act, and the provision in Section 22—which overrides all other laws, etc. (even overriding the Official Secrets Act) the argument about such a confidentiality condition is on a weak foundation. The mere marking of a document, as 'confidential', in this case, does not undermine the overbearing nature of Section 22. Concededly, the confidentiality clause (in the 1997 Resolution) operated, and many might have *bona fide* believed that it would ensure immunity from access. Yet the advent of the Act changed all that; all classes of information became its subject matter. Section 8(1) (f) affords protection to one such class, i.e. fiduciaries. The content of such provision may include certain kinds of relationships of public officials, such as doctor-patient relations; teacher-pupil relationships, in government schools and colleges; agents of governments; even attorneys and lawyers who appear and advise public authorities covered by the Act. However, it does not cover asset declarations made by Judges of the Supreme Court, and held by the CJI.[78]

The Court pronounced that the CJI is a public authority under the RTI Act, and the CJI holds the information pertaining to asset declarations in his capacity as chief justice; that office is a 'public authority' under the Act and is covered by its provisions. It further ruled that the declaration of the assets by the Supreme Court judges is 'information' within the meaning of the expression, under Section 2(f) of the Act and that the contents of the declarations, pursuant to the 1997 Resolution—and the 1999 Conference Resolution—are entitled to be treated as personal information, and may be accessed in accordance with the procedure prescribed under Section 8(1)(j); they are not otherwise subject to disclosure. It clarified that as far as the information sought by the applicant in this case was concerned (that is, whether the declarations were made pursuant to the 1997 Resolution) the procedure under Section 8(1)(j) is inapplicable. On the issue of whether lack of clarity about the details of the declaration of assets and their details, as well as lack of security renders such declarations and their disclosure unworkable, Justice Bhatt made the following suggestion:

> These are not insurmountable obstacles; the CJI, if he deems it appropriate, may in consultation with the Supreme Court judges, evolve uniform standards, devising the nature of information, relevant formats, and if required, the periodicity of the declarations to be made. The forms evolved, as well as the procedures followed in the United States—including the redaction norms—under the Ethics in Government Act, 1978, reports of the US Judicial Conference,

---

[78] *The CPIO, Supreme Court of India* v. *Subhash Chandra Agrawal*, para 58.

as well as the Judicial Disclosure Responsibility Act, 2007, which amends the Ethics in Government Act of 1978 to: (1) restrict disclosure of personal information about family members of judges whose revelation might endanger them; and (2) extend the authority of the Judicial Conference to redact certain personal information of judges from financial disclosure reports may be considered.[79]

The Supreme Court challenged the decision of the single judge before a division bench of the High Court. In the appeal it was questioned as to why Justice Bhatt delved into 'irrelevant' issues such as the 'role of judges in society ... role of courts and the scheme of power-sharing ... duties of judges' which constitute no legal basis for invoking RTI against Supreme Court Judges. It further said: 'The learned single judge has undertaken an exercise of elucidation of the concepts of essential ethical behaviour of judges which are not relevant for determining whether the RTI applicant had the right to information.'[80]

A full bench of the High Court, comprising A.P. Shah, CJ, Vikramjit Sen and S. Muralidhar, JJ, upheld the single-judge decision and strongly advocated for transparency in the judiciary:

> It was Edmund Burke who observed that 'All persons possessing a portion of power ought to be strongly and awfully impressed with an idea that they act in trust and that they are to account for their conduct in that trust'. Accountability of the Judiciary cannot be seen in isolation. It must be viewed in the context of a general trend to render governors answerable to the people in ways that are transparent, accessible and effective. Behind this notion is a concept that the wielders of power—legislative, executive and judicial—are entrusted to perform their functions on condition that they account for their stewardship to the people who authorize them to exercise such power. Well defined and publicly known standards and procedures complement, rather than diminish, the notion of judicial independence. Democracy expects openness and openness is concomitant of free society. Sunlight is the best disinfectant.[81]

The Supreme Court filed an appeal against this judgement of the division bench of the Delhi High Court in its own Court, where it was pending since

---

[79] *The CPIO, Supreme Court of India* v. *Subhash Chandra Agrawal*, para 84.

[80] *Secretary General, Supreme Court of India* v. *Subhash Chandra Agrawal*, LPA 501 of 2009, Delhi High Court: 'SC slams Delhi HC Judge Who Said the CJI Comes under RTI', *Indian Express*, 6 October 2009.

[81] *Secretary General, Supreme Court of India* v. *Subhash Chandra Agrawal*, para 121.

then. However, during the pendency of the case before the Delhi High Court, the Union Government, on 3 August 2009, tried to introduce the judges (Declaration of Assets and Liabilities) Bill in the Rajya Sabha that sought to make it mandatory for judges to declare their assets but insulated them from any questioning by the public. Section 6(1) of the Bill read, 'the declaration made by a Judge to the competent authority shall not be made public or disclosed, and shall not be called for, put into question by any citizen, court or authority, and no judge shall be subjected to any inquiry or query in relation to the contents of the declaration by any person'.

The opposition to the bill came from parties as varied as the BJP to the Left parties who criticized the government in seeking to treat judges as a separate category different from other public servants as well as the common man, and forced the Law minister, Veerappa Moily, to withdraw the Bill.[82] A strident opposition alleged that this not only violated the Right to equality granted under Article 14, but also the Right to freedom of speech and expression granted under Article 19(1)(a) which, as interpreted by the Supreme Court, also included the right to information. The Bill provided that the declaration would be known only to the president and the CJI. Thus, the Bill was a fine example of linguistic distortion where a declaration was meant for concealment, not for disclosure. It not only embarrassed the government but also brought down the image of judges to a substantial degree.

Further, open dissent by a few sitting high court judges against the CJI for his staunch opposition to make the judges' assets public made the then Chief Justice, K.G. Balakrishnan, defensive and left him, to some extent, alienated. Justice D.V. Shylendra Kumar of the Karnataka High Court hit the nail on the head by questioning the authority of the CJI to speak on behalf of all judges.[83] In an article published in *New Indian Express* on 20 August 2009, he wrote that the 'most damaging and uncalled for impression (has been) created in the minds of the public' that the judges of the superior courts, who enjoy constitutional protection and immunity, 'are wary of disclosing their assets' and would like to keep this information 'well-guarded ... and also cover up a possible misdeed or a possible improper acquisition'.[84] Another

[82] 'Left and Right, MPs for Tougher Judges' Assets Law, Force Govt to Defer Bill', *Indian Express*, 4 August 2009, also see *Times of India*, *The Hindu*, and *Hindustan Times* of the same date.

[83] 'Want to Disclose Assets ... CJI can't Speak for All of Us: Karnataka High Court judge', *Indian Express*, 21 August 2009.

[84] 'Want to Disclose Assets'.

judge of the Punjab and Haryana High Court, Justice K. Kannan, declared his assets on 22 August 2009.[85] He wrote that though he held the view that judges are not in the same league as politicians and did not agree in principle with demands to keep the details of their assets in the public domain, yet he wanted to prove a point that they had nothing to hide. Subsequently, the Kerala High Court took the lead in making the assets of all 33 judges public by placing the declarations on the website http://highcourtofkerala.nic.in/assets.html.[86]

All this, and a campaign by the public in the media forced the Supreme Court judges to make their disclosures public. The declaration of the assets by the judges of the Supreme Court was a step in the right direction, though it was too late. By challenging the direction of the CIC in the High Court, and then going in appeal against its single-judge decision, the CJI gave an impression that instead of being a paladin of the values of impartiality and transparency, he was more interested in protecting his peers. This voluntary move appeared less voluntary, and more forced, a step taken under the pressure of civil society. The CJI consistently took the stand that if the Parliament makes a law to declare the judges' assets, they would do so.[87] Inadvertently, he invited the legislature to control the judges, which any government would only be too happy to do, but which no right-minded person would like. Thus, the Supreme Court missed a rare opportunity to establish its moral authority which is a *sine qua non* for its independence. Though this disclosure is welcome, it leaves much to be desired. Since it is voluntary, the declaration is not an annual routine process, and some have not declared again after doing it once. It is the people's right to know the financial backgrounds of judges of this poor country.

Challenging the Order of the CIC Directly in the Supreme Court, Bypassing the High Court

The Supreme Court has not been able to reconcile itself to the idea of transparency. Embarrassed and upset by a spate of CIC orders that the judiciary divulge details on sensitive issues such as the appointment of judges,

---

[85] *India Express*, New Delhi, 23 August 2009.

[86] 'Kerala HC First to Make Assets of Judges Public', *Indian Express*, 6 October 2009.

[87] CJI K.G. Balakrishnan's interview to the author, telecast on DD News on 19 January 2009.

in November 2009, the CJI, K.G. Balakrishnan wrote to Prime Minister Manmohan Singh seeking his intervention in exempting matters relating to the administration of justice from the purview of the RTI Act.[88] The letter emphasized that the process of appointment to the higher judiciary was based on a 1993 judgement of the Supreme Court, and that the collegium meetings seldom put its views on people rejected for the post of judge in black and white. He further pointed out that there were other sensitive matters relating to the administration of justice, which if divulged, could create division within the judiciary and ultimately tell on its independence. The CJI's argument that members of the collegium do not record their opinion in writing, and so, no information or reason could be provided for one's selection, rejection, or elevation as judge, is not tenable. If it is not recorded, it only violates the law laid down in that judgement that consultations would be recorded in black and white.[89]

Further, in an unusual move, the Supreme Court filed appeals before itself directly against two orders of the CIC. One was against the order in which the CIC directed that file notings regarding the appointment of three judges to the Supreme Court in 2008, which had bypassed three senior chief justices of different high courts, namely, A.P. Shah of Delhi, A.K. Patnaik of Madhya Pradesh, and V.K. Gupta of Jharkhand, be made public.[90] The petitioner sought to know why their seniority had been ignored. Another appeal filed on 30 November 2009 was against the order which directed it to disclose the correspondence between the CJI and Justice R. Reghupathi of the Madras High Court on the pressure allegedly put on the judge by a union minister.[91] Perhaps, the Supreme Court was wary of the fact that earlier the Delhi High Court decided against it in the assets declaration case, and so, not taking any chance, it moved itself. The appeal regurgitated the same logic that the CJI held such information in a fiduciary capacity, and hence it should be exempted from being made public under Section 8(1)(e) of the RTI Act. The Supreme Court might have avoided the route of moving the High Court first, with a view to settling law in this regard. But moving the apex court against the order of the CIC is certainly not proper. The Supreme Court had itself

[88] 'Curb RTI Ambit in Judiciary, CJI asks PM', *Times of India*, 27 November 2009.

[89] *Supreme Court Advocates on Record Association* v. *Union of India* (1993) 4 SCC 441, AIR (1994) SC 268.

[90] *CPIO of the Supreme Court* v. *Subhah Chandra Agrawal*, SLP (C) No. 32865/09.

[91] *CPIO of the Supreme Court* v. *Subhah Chandra Agrawal*, SLP (C) No. 32866/09.

struck down Articles 323-A and 323-B to the extent that they precluded the jurisdiction of the high courts under Articles 226 and 227 pertaining to the appeal against decisions of Central Administrative Tribunals which were filed directly before the Supreme Court. It laid down that the Supreme Court could be moved under Article 136 only after exhausting the remedy before the high courts.[92] It reasoned that the writ jurisdiction of the high court is a basic feature of the Constitution, and bypassing it would be unconstitutional. Still, since Article 136 bequeaths wide amplitude to the Supreme Court to grant special leave to appeal against any judgement, decree, determination, sentence, or order in any case passed by any court or tribunal in the territory of India, the appeal against the order of the CIC may stand scrutiny on the touchstone of legality, but not of propriety. What was the urgency to bypass the High Court? Did the apex court not want to take any chances after its experience in the assets declaration case? It also appears preposterous that the Supreme Court is examining the applicability of a law vis-à-vis itself. Technically speaking, the doctrine of necessity will apply, but again, the question of propriety comes up.

On 21 November 2017, the Delhi High Court again rejected the right of citizens to get information from the Supreme Court. An ex-school teacher R.S. Misra filed an RTI application with the Supreme Court Registry, and it wanted to redress his grievances in a case which he had already lost. Earlier, he had written two letters to different judges for this purpose. Rejecting his application, the Registry asked him to apply under the Supreme Court rules. Misra challenged the decision before the CIC. Additional Registrar Smita Sharma, who represented the Supreme Court before the Commission, objected only to the use of the RTI but did not question Misra's request per se. She contended that he could access the information sought only under the Supreme Court rules. Arguing further, she averred that the rules were in consonance with the RTI, and urged the Commission to reinstate the primacy of the Supreme Court rules over the RTI following the precedents set by the Commission. Rejecting these contentions, Commissioner Shailesh Gandhi decided that the Supreme Court rules undermined the RTI in four key ways. The rules do not provide for a time frame for furnishing information, nor does it provide for an appeal mechanism and penalties for delays or wrongful denial of information, as has been laid down in the RTI Act. What is more, the rules make disclosure of information to citizens contingent upon 'good cause shown'. Thus, he pronounced that the rules are not in consonance

---

[92] *L. Chandra Kumar* v. *Union of India* (1997) 3 SCC 261, AIR (1997) SC 1125.

with the RTI Act and held that it was mandatory for the Registry to respond to applications within the RTI framework alone.[93]

Peeved, the apex court moved the Delhi High Court against the order. Justice S. Muralidhar stayed the Commission's decision. Since Section 23 of the RTI Act does not allow any appeal against the orders of the Information Commission in any court, the aggrieved parties move the High Court under its writ jurisdiction. So, the Supreme Court also invoked this constitutional provision, but it was obligatory for the High court to justify its exercise of power under the writ jurisdiction in the particular case. High courts entertaining petitions against the commission's orders is quite welcome as in most of the cases, the commission favours the state leaving the appellants high and dry. So, the aggrieved parties have an option. But the apex court invoking the writ jurisdiction of the high court which grants a favourable order is deeply disturbing.

Supreme Court's Stress on Transparency and RTI in Earlier Cases

The Supreme Court has conveniently forgotten how it sang paeans in its various judgements about the people's right to information to strengthen democracy. In *Union* v. *Association for Democratic Reforms*,[94] it directed the Election Commission to make it mandatory for candidates contesting elections for Parliament or State Legislative Assemblies or Councils to disclose their criminal antecedents, assets and liabilities, and educational qualifications. The Court held that freedom of voting was part of the freedom of expression, a fundamental right, which could not be exercised effectively if voters did not have such information about contesting candidates. Thus, it trod the virgin ground to bring the RTI of the voter within the sweep of Article 19(1)(a) of the Constitution which guarantees Right to freedom of expression. It refused to buy the argument that the Right to vote was not a fundamental right; it is a statutory right under Article 326 of the Constitution. How then could the freedom to exercise this right be a fundamental right? Though the Court conceded that it was not empowered to give directions to amend the Act or the statutory rules, it, nonetheless, held that 'in case when the Act or Rules are silent on a particular subject and the authority implementing the same has constitutional or statutory power to implement it, the Court can necessarily

---

[93] Aniket Aga, 'Information at the Court's Discretion', *The Hindu*, 13 December 2017.

[94] (2002) 5 SCC 294.

issue directions or orders on the said subject to fill the vacuum or void till the suitable law is enacted'. When the Parliament overturned this judgement by adding Section 33(B) to the Representation of the People Act, 1951 requiring candidates to give information only about criminal cases pending against them, and not the other information, the Supreme Court set aside this section as unconstitutional,[95] and ruled that the right to vote is a constitutional right though not a fundamental right; however, the right to make a choice by means of ballot is part of the freedom of expression.

Earlier, in several cases, it stressed on transparency. It flatly rejected the government's claim of privilege on the Blue Book, containing security instructions for the prime minister in Indira Gandhi's case:

> In a government of responsibility like ours, where all the agents of the public must be responsible for their conduct, there can be but few secrets. The people of this country have a right to know every public act, everything, that is done in a public way, by their public functionaries. They are entitled to know the particulars of every public transaction in all its bearing.... The responsibility of officials to explain and to justify their acts is the chief safeguard against oppression and corruption.[96]

What an irony! Judges wax eloquent about the rights of the people when it concerns other wings of the government, but all these pontifications come to naught when applied against them. In the Judges' case, it was the judges who insisted on the disclosure of the correspondence between the Union Law minister and the CJI regarding the appointment and transfer of judges on the grounds that the government was performing a constitutional function and it was a matter of public interest why a particular judge was dropped or allowed to continue. The Union Law minister, in a letter dated 18 March 1981, addressed to several chief ministers had asked them to inquire whether additional judges in the high courts of their states were agreeable to their transfers outside their states. The Court again rejected the government's claim of privilege on the correspondence:

> Where a society has chosen to accept democracy as its creedal faith, it is elementary that the citizens ought to know what their government is doing. The citizens have a right to decide by whom and by what rules they shall be governed and they are entitled to call on their behalf to account for their conduct.

---

[95] *PUCL* v. *Union* (2003) 4 SCC 399.
[96] *State of Uttar Pradesh* v. *Raj Narain*, AIR (1975) SC 865 at 884, per J. Mathew.

No democratic government can survive without accountability and the basic postulate of accountability is that the people should have information about the functioning of the government. It is only if people know how government is functioning that they can fulfil the role which democracy assigns to them and make democracy a really effective participatory democracy. 'Knowledge', said James Madison, 'will for ever govern ignorance and a people who mean to be their own governors must arm themselves with the power knowledge gives. A popular government without popular information or the means of obtaining it is but a prologue to a farce or tragedy or perhaps both'. The citizens' right to know the facts, the true facts, about the administration of the country is thus one of the pillars of the democratic State.... It has been truly said that an open government is clean government and a powerful safeguard against political and administrative aberration and inefficiency.[97]

A Constitution Bench of seven judges, in this case, with only Fazal Ali, J. dissenting, decided the Indian law of crown privilege, now known as public interest immunity, in the light of *Conway* v. *Rimmer*.[98] In Conway, the Court had to strike a balance when privilege was claimed for some particular documents, which would be crucial to Conway in his action. So, the Law Lords ordered their disclosure after perusing the documents in private. Similarly, in the Judges' case, the Supreme Court clearly ruled that the harm that would be caused to the public interest by non-disclosure would far outweigh any harm that would be caused by disclosure. Justice Bhagwati added:

it may be noted that the discontinuance of an additional Judge by the Central Government is a serious matter and if such discontinuance is *mala fide* or based on irrelevant grounds, it would tend to affect the independence of the judiciary and it is, therefore, necessary in order to maintain public confidence in the independent functioning of the judiciary that the people should know whether the constitutional requirements were complied with before the decision was taken not to continue the additional judge and whether any oblique motivations or irrelevant considerations influenced the Central Government in reaching that decision.[99]

In this case, the judges invoked the right to know when they found their own interests in jeopardy. But why should the same right not be invoked on the same grounds when the apex court annexed the power of appointment

---

[97] *S. P. Gupta* v. *Union of India*, AIR (1982) SC 149 at 232–3.
[98] (1968) A.C. 910.
[99] *S.P. Gupta* v. *Union of India*, AIR (1982) SC 149 at 249–50.

and transfer of judges from the executive in the Second Judges' case.[100] The collegium of the Supreme Court rejects several names recommended by the collegiums of high courts for appointments as judges, and in some cases, even the entire panel is rejected. Is it not a matter of public interest, and are people not entitled to know why a particular name was selected or rejected? How can there be two standards? Now the Supreme Court is claiming the privilege which it rejected in the name of public interest when the government claimed it. Now some judges argue that disclosure of reasons for non-selection of a lawyer recommended for elevation as judge would adversely affect his practice. If transparency is demanded of the government why should it not apply to the judiciary? If democracy has been accepted as the creedal faith, people must know how independently the judiciary is functioning. The independence of the judiciary is the hallmark of democracy and the threat to it is not only from without, but also from within.

The reluctance of the superior judiciary to be accountable under the RTI Act is not difficult to understand. It will have no answers if questions are asked in respect of appointments and transfer of judges. It is an open secret that the collegium system never worked satisfactorily, and instead of improving the quality of judges, it protected the interests of its members by accommodating their wards. In the Third Judges' case,[101] the Supreme Court expanded the number of collegium members from three to five for the appointment of judges to the Supreme Court. For appointments to the high courts, it also provided for consultations with those judges who had been elevated from the high court for which the appointment was being made. And these judges, who are not members of the collegium, *are playing havoc*, to use the words of a former CJI, and vetoing recommendations of the collegiums of the high courts.[102] They question why their candidates are not accommodated. Obviously, the Supreme Court will have no reply if questions with respect to appointments are asked. The Supreme Court struck down the Constitution (99th Amendment) Act, 2014, which replaced the collegium system with the National Judicial Appointments Commission, and thus, revived the collegium system.[103] There must be proper reasons for selection

---

[100] *Supreme Court Advocates on Record Association* v. *Union of India* (1993) 4 SCC 441, AIR (1994) SC 268.

[101] *In re Art 143 of the Constitution, Presidential Reference 1998* (1998) SCC 739, AIR (1999) SC 1.

[102] In a personal chat with the author.

[103] *Supreme Court Advocates-on-Record* v. *Union of India* (2016) 5 SCC 1 (decided on 15 October 2015).

or rejection. Clearly, transparency will expose the gaping holes in the appointment process. No wonder, the Delhi High Court stayed the direction of the
CIC to the Union Law Ministry to make the file related to the appointment
of judges public. In fact, most such orders of the CIC are being stayed by the
courts which had once championed the cause of openness.

The same is true regarding the transfers of judges. No one knows on what
grounds judges are transferred. In the Judges' case[104] the then CJI, Y.V.
Chandrachud, J., filed a counter affidavit before the Constitution Bench
headed by Justice P.N. Bhagwati, clarifying that the transfer of Justice K.B.N.
Singh, the then chief justice of the Patna High Court, to the Madras High
Court was not because of any personal prejudice. If the CJI has to file a counter affidavit in the Court to make his stand clear, why can information not be
sought from the courts? Between 1950 and 1975, only 25 High Court judges
were transferred, but during the emergency, this power of transfer was used
by the government to punish independent judges and sixteen judges were
transferred in May-June 1976. Now, it is routine process under the policy of
having one-third of judges in each high court from outside and it is done by
the Supreme Court collegium.

In fact, the RTI Act does not permit any appeals to be entertained by any
court. Section 23 says, 'No court shall entertain any suit, application or other
proceeding in respect of any order made under this Act and no such order
shall be called in question otherwise than by way of an appeal under this Act'.
Nevertheless, the Supreme Court and high courts are vested with some constitutional powers that override any statute, though certain limitations have
been placed on high courts by the Constitution and further enunciated by the
Supreme Court. Research, assessment, and analysis Group (RaaG), New Delhi,
Satark Nagrik Sangathan (SNS), New Delhi have rightly raised the question:

> [A]nother important issue that emerges is how the courts interpret their powers
> and obligations as public authorities and competent authorities. There is also
> the question: does the fact that the high court is a 'Constitutional body' imply
> that all its dictums, especially those manifested through the rules formulated
> by it, have constitutional status and are outside the jurisdiction of Section 22
> of the RTI Act, even if they are inconsistent with the RTI Act [sic]? Similarly,
> are all the statutory obligations that other PAs have under the RTI Act, also
> binding on the courts?

The Supreme Court has held on a number of occasions that the jurisdiction of high courts under Article 226 of the Constitution is a supervisory

---

[104] *S. P. Gupta* v. *Union of India* (1981) Supp. SCC 97, AIR (1982) SC 1858.

one and not an appellate one. In *Sub-Divisional Officer, Konch* v. *Maharaj Singh*,[105] the Court ruled that the High Court cannot examine the evidence and re-appreciate it while exercising its powers under Article 226. Similarly, in *Sadhana Lodh* v. *National Insurance Company Ltd.*,[106] the Court emphatically laid down that the supervisory jurisdiction conferred on the high courts under Article 227 of the Constitution is confined only to see whether an inferior court or Tribunal has proceeded within its parameters and not to correct an error apparent on the face of the record, much less of an error of law. It clarified that in exercising the supervisory power under Article 227 of the Constitution, the high court does not act as an Appellate Court or the Tribunal. It is also not permissible for a high court on a petition filed under Article 227 of the Constitution to review or re-weigh the evidence upon which the court below or Tribunal purports to have passed the order or to correct errors of law in the decision. Many high courts have also taken a similar view.

However, several high courts decide cases going beyond the writ jurisdiction and re-appreciate the evidence, categorical pronouncements of the apex court in this regard notwithstanding. RaaG, New Delhi, and SNS, New Delhi, have found how the verdicts of the apex court are being flouted by none other than the high courts:

> Despite these judicial pronouncements, at least some HC orders seem to go beyond the writ jurisdiction and actually look at and re-appreciate the evidence. Two typical examples are described below.
>
> In *HC-DEL Central Information Commission 2011*, the Delhi High Court seemingly examined and took a view on the evidence and then struck down the ICs assessment, holding that the time taken was reasonable, contrary to what was held by the CIC:
>
> '10. Be it noted that information was supplied in respect of (i), (ii) and (iii) within the requisite period. As far information pertaining to other items are concerned, there is some delay. On a perusal of the information sought and the time consumed, we find that reasonable period has been spent and hence, that would tantamount to an explanation for delay caused by the officer concerned.
>
> 11. In view of the aforesaid, the reduction of the penalty by the learned single Judge is justified...'
>
> In *HC-P&H Vimal Kumar Setia 2014*, the Punjab and Haryana High Court similarly evaluated the evidence and imposed its own appreciation

---

[105]   (2003) 9 SCC 191.
[106]   (2003) AIR 1561 (2003) 1 SCR 567 (2003) 4 SCC 524.

over that of the Information Commissioner (IC), even quoting the lack of mala fide 'intention' as a justification for reducing penalty for delay, even though the RTI Act only prescribes lack of mala fide as a mitigation for illegitimate refusal.

1. Challenge in the present writ petition is to the show cause notice dated 24.07.2008 (Annexure P5) and the order dated 26.09.2008 (Annexure P8), passed by the State Information Commissioner, Punjab, whereby it had directed the petitioner to deposit ₹ 25,000/-, as penalty, under the Right to Information Act, 2005 (for short, the 'Act'), on account of delay in supplying the information.

7. Section 20 of the Act provides that where the Public Information Officer, without any reasonable cause, does not furnish the information within the time specified or mala fidely denies the request for information, penalty is to be imposed @ ₹ 250/- per day, from the date the application is received till the date the information is furnished and the total amount of such penalty shall not exceed ₹ 25,000/-. That the amount of maximum penalty had been imposed under the Act, this Court is, thus, of the opinion that it would suffice, in the interest of justice, that amount of penalty is reduced to a sum of ₹ 15,000/-, in the facts and circumstances of the present case as in the present case, no mala fide intention, as such, is there and the petitioner has shown reasonable cause.

8. Accordingly, the present writ petition is partly allowed and the impugned order of the Commission is modified. The petitioner is directed to deposit a sum of ₹ 15,000/-, within a period of 4 weeks from today, failing which, the amount will be recovered from his salary/pay. Clearly there is a need for a much wider public debate on what is the legitimate role of high courts, relating to the RTI Act, under Articles 226 and 227 of the Constitution.[107]

Judges may be reminded that when in trouble, they have gone public about their distress to protect themselves. On 14 July 1997, the then CJI J.S. Verma shocked the whole country when he disclosed in the open court that judges were being pressured in the Writ Petition No. 340–3 of 1993, in The Matter of *Vineet Narain and Ors.* v. *Union of India and Ors.*, popularly known as the *Jain Hawala* case. Justice Verma thundered with anger and anguish that he and his brother judges on the Hawala bench had come under

---

[107] *Tilting the Balance of Power: Adjudicating the RTI Act*, Research Team: Amrita Johri, Anjali Bhardwaj, and Shekhar Singh, RaaG, New Delhi, SNS (New Delhi: Rajpal and Sons, 2017 [2016]), pp. 33–4.

'persistent pressure' not to hear the matter.[108] Justice Verma told this author that first Justice Bharucha complained to him that he got such a call and then Justice S.C. Sen made a similar complaint. When I asked him why he did not initiate contempt proceedings against them, he replied that he asked the Union Home Secretary and the Director, Intelligence Bureau, to trace the calls, but after a few days they informed him that the call could not be traced. He added that he then decided to disclose it in the court so that those trying to exert pressure must know that it would not work. He did so because he knew that those involved must be present in the court and the people would also know.[109] Thus, he also appealed to the people's constituency when he did not get support from the government in detecting the caller. Unfortunately, the same people are treated shabbily when they invoke their right to know.

Since judges are not accountable to any one, some of them rarely deliver judgements and keep them reserved. They even retire conveniently before bothering to deliver their judgements and those cases have to be reopened. There are judges who seldom write judgements in their entire career except writing 'I agree'. Obviously, if someone wants to know how many judgements are kept reserved and for how long, or how many judgements a particular judge had delivered over a specific period or his/her entire tenure, the higher judiciary will be in an embarrassing position. So, it has adopted the best way, by placing an insulating cover over itself in the name of the independence of the judiciary, to keep the light of the RTI at bay so that the truth can never be known. Judicial processes comprise hearings and decision-making only, the rest being administrative matters are not covered by any immunity which clearly fall under the purview of the RTI.

Besides, the judgments or proceedings of the courts may be open to all, but the problem is that people do not have any option beyond criticism, which too is generally quite veiled, mild, and diplomatic for the fear of contempt. They cannot set things right even in cases of gross illegalities, even though technically the decisions may be right, since what the Supreme Court says becomes the law of the land. The Supreme Court refuses to entertain a petition against violation of fundamental rights under Article 32 and directs the petitioner to approach the high court first. When it happened for the first time, it created a commotion in the legal fraternity but the petitioner did not receive any remedy.[110] The Court, instead of learning from the criticism, has

---

[108] *Times of India*, 15 July 1997, *Indian Express*, 15 July 1997.

[109] Interview of Justice J.S. Verma, ex-CJI, to the author in the programme '*Tête-à-tête*' telecast on DD News on 29 May 2010 at 10 pm.

[110] *P. N. Kumar* v. *Municipal Corpn. of Delhi* (1987) 4 SCC 609.

now made it almost a rule that the petitioner must go to the high court first in cases of violation of fundamental rights. Here lies the difference between the judiciary and other wings of government, whose illegal decisions can be rectified by the courts.

The Supreme Court must realize that rights are like technologies which cannot be withdrawn once given. Before the late 1990s, people had not even heard of a mobile or the Internet but today, no government can dare to withdraw these because people have tasted their fruits. Similarly, rights cannot be revoked after being conferred, as people get used to them.

Judicial Statistics Not Available

The biggest roadblock to the judicial reforms is the complete non-availability of vital judicial statistics. The courts stonewalled any queries or information sought prior to the enforcement of the RTI Act despite pontificating on the virtues of transparency. The attitude has not changed even after the coming into force of the transparency law.

V.K.S. Chaudhary, former advocate general of UP, has narrated an interesting incident as to how the judiciary dodges accountability and refuses to give information. The chief minister of the state asked him to study the impact of huge pendency of criminal cases on law and order. He has written:

> He (chief minister) had also desired me to get statistics of cases filed, decided and pending for the last year, for which statistics were available, to enable us to apply our minds to the problem. Accordingly *I, as the Advocate General*, wrote a letter to the Registrar of the High Court to give us whatever statistics were available. A Deputy Registrar replied, 'The High Court does not consider it in public interest to disclose this information to you (meaning the Advocate General).'[111]

So, even the information sought by the advocate general at the behest of the chief minister, to study the law and order situation is not considered in the public interest! Fali S. Nariman has cited an instance when the Delhi High Court refused to give information to the Union Government on the time taken to deliver judgments after the conclusion of hearings. The Law Ministry needed the information to reply to a question asked by a member of

---

[111] V.K.S. Chaudhary, *The Ivory Tower: 51 Years of the Supreme Court* (New Delhi: Universal Publishing Company, 2002), p. 237. See Godbole, *The Judiciary and Governance in India*, p. 403.

Parliament. The High Court reportedly reasoned that it would compromise judicial independence. Anyone, not talking through their hat, will vouch that such information is not to be sneezed at if some effective step is to be taken to clean the cobweb. Nariaman has commented: 'Judicial independence means deciding cases without being influenced by anybody. But disseminating information about how many cases get decided in the courts will not compromise judicial independence at all. This is a wrong impression that the judiciary, among all organs of the government, must remain totally secretive, and nobody must know anything that is happening in the judiciary.'[112]

Fall in the Quality of Judgements

There has recently been a considerable erosion of judicial collectivism with different benches giving divergent and conflicting decisions. Reservation for the weaker sections in government jobs and educational institutions is one such area where the Supreme Court has created maximum confusion. Which is why Justice Felix Frankfurter of the US Supreme Court suggested to B.N. Rau, the Constitutional adviser to the Constituent Assembly, when he visited the US for discussions with eminent persons regarding the Indian Constitution, that the jurisdiction exercisable by the Supreme Court should be exercised by the full court: the highest court of appeal should not sit in divisions because that may make the law uncertain.[113] The precipitate fall in the quality of judgements is directly proportional to the atrophy in the personal integrity and rectitude of judges. Seervai's comment is apposite:

> This fall in the conduct and character of judges is reflected in the falling standard of their judgements. It is submitted that apart from cases of bribery and corruption, of repaying debts of gratitude which judges owed to their seniors or friends at the Bar, and apart from settling old scores with some Counsel, whom the judges disliked at the Bar, another factor has emerged which has not been generally noticed. It is that in cases involving the Union or the State Governments on matters to which those Governments attach great importance, consciously or unconsciously, judges have allowed their judgements to be deflected by the thought that their chances of promotion in the High Courts and their chances of elevation to the Supreme Court would be prejudiced if

[112] *Frontline*, 27 August 2004. See Godbole, *The Judiciary and Governance in India*, p. 403.

[113] *The Framing of India's Constitution: A Study* (New Delhi: Indian Institute of Public Administration, 1968), p. 487.

their judgements went against the Union or the State. In admitting the charges of corruption brought against him, Lord Chancellor Bacon pleaded in mitigation that 'his offences were offences of the times'. In his Introduction to Mr. Cecil's book, 'Tipping the Scales' a distinguished judge of our own day, Lord Delvin, brought out the full implication of Lord Bacon's plea when he said that the lesson to be learned from Mr. Cecil's book was that 'judges are not now, neither they have been in the past, much better or much worse than other public servants'.[114]

Several judgements, instead of bringing about clarity, have added to the confusion. The right to establish and administer educational institutions under Article 30 of the Constitution is one contentious issue which has provoked considerable litigation. The amplitude of this right and permissible regulations were the subject matter of more than 35 leading decisions by the Supreme Court up to 2005.[115] The 11-judge Constitution Bench of the Supreme Court in *T.M.A. Pai Foundation* v. *State of Karnataka*,[116] overruled its earlier decision in *J.P. Unnikrishnan* v. *State of AP*,[117] which allowed the government or other state agencies to interfere in admission practices of private unaided professional colleges, including fixing a government quota, controlling the admission procedure, and regulating fee structure. It held that these restrictions are not permissible under Article 19(6) of the Constitution in respect of the fundamental right of all citizens to run educational institutions as an occupation under Article 19(1)(g). Thus, the Court allowed even majority communities to establish and run educational institutions under the right to carry on any occupation.

Subsequently, in an unprecedented move, the Supreme Court constituted a five-judge bench in *Islamic Academy of Education* v. *State of Karnataka*,[118] to explore the true import of the 11-judge bench's verdict in the Pai Foundation case. Actually, some state governments tried to fix a quota of up to 75 per cent for admissions in unaided professional colleges (both minority and majority) and also a strict fee structure, the categorical ruling by a bench of 11 judges to the contrary notwithstanding. This led to the Islamic Academy case. In a bizarre manner, the five-judge bench overruled the 11-judge bench in the

---

[114] Seervai, *Constitutional Law of India*, vol. II, pp. viii–x, v–vi.
[115] See Dr M.P. Raju, *Education: A Mission in Jeopardy* (Delhi: Media House, 2005), p. 24.
[116] (2002) 8 SCC 481.
[117] (1993) 1 SCC 645.
[118] (2003) 6 SCC 697.

name of interpretation and brought those regulations back. It created government quotas even in unaided minority institutions. In order to legitimize
their patently unconstitutional act, the judges took recourse to Article 142
which bequeaths extraordinary power for doing complete justice. But it is
inscrutable how Article 142 gives a smaller bench the power to overrule a
larger one. They drew their own conclusions, ignoring the express directions
stating that these did not constitute *ratio decidendi*.

However, the five-judge bench failed to dispel all ambiguities, and then
another Constitution Bench of seven judges was set up in *P.A. Inamdar* v.
State of Maharashtra.[119] Overruling Islamic Academy, it restored the ruling of
the *T.M.A. Pai Foundation* v. *State of Karnataka* case,[120] and held that neither
can the policy of reservation be enforced by the state nor can any quota or
percentage of admissions be carved out for appropriation by the state in an
unaided educational institution.

There are several instances where smaller benches have overruled larger
ones. That is why, initially, the SC sat as a full court in constitutional cases.
B. Sen has written:

> In the early fifties, the Supreme Court sat a full court in all constitutional cases
> and in not more than two divisions where other matters were concerned. The
> judges also read out their opinions in open court in the fashion of the House
> of Lords, which at times could take the entire day. This invariably meant that
> whenever the Court was hearing an appeal or a petition of some importance,
> such as the *Delhi Laws Act* cases (1951 SCR 747) or *Gopalan's* case there was
> hardly any work even for a small resident Bar.[121]

Besides, many judges do not deliver judgements and get transferred or
elevated or retire. This is atrocious as it causes untold hardships to the parties
concerned. There are judges who have hardly written any judgments and are
elevated even to the apex court. All this happens because they are not accountable. The Bombay High Court had developed the tradition of handing out
judgements in the court immediately after the hearing concluded. It has
many advantages as the judges are attentive and they remember everything.
Once the judgement is reserved, they are likely to forget many vital facts
and arguments adduced. India should learn from the International Court of

---

[119] (2005) 6 SCC 537.
[120] (2002) 8 SCC 481.
[121] B. Sen, *Six Decade of Law, Politics & Diplomacy: Some Reminescences and Reflections* (New Delhi: Universal Law Publishing Co., 2010), p. 57.

Justice (ICJ), The Hague. It has 15 judges and the full court sits; the quorum is 11. After the hearing concludes, all judges write judgements. A committee of five judges is formed which studies all judgements and then the ratio is derived. So, the judges of the ICJ do not have the luxury to sit idle and not write judgments; further, there is no confusion about the ratio.

Unpredictability of the Justice System and Bench-Hunting

The erosion of judicial collectivism has created unpredictability which leads to bench-hunting as justice is subject to the vagaries of the bench, not the Constitution and the law. In November 2017, this malaise came to the fore in the medical admission scam case. On 8 November 2017, Justice J. Chelameshwar, the senior most judge in the Supreme Court after the CJI, admitted a petition filed by the Campaign for Judicial Accountability and Reforms (CJAR)[122] asking it to set up a Special Investigation Team (SIT) headed by a former CJI to investigate into the allegations of corruption and bribery in the case, and listed for hearing within two days. Sometime after the order was passed, the Supreme Court Registry informed Prashant Bhushan, the counsel for the CJAR, that the CJI had moved it to a different bench, comprising Justices A.K. Sikri and Ashok Bhushan. The next day, that is, on 9 November, advocate Kamini Jaiswal filed an identical new petition with similar prayers, and Dushyant Dave, senior advocate, mentioned before the bench headed by Justice Chelameshwar the same day for its urgent hearing.[123] It was averred in the petition that the CBI had registered an FIR against Lucknow-based Prasad Education Trust. The medical college run by the Trust was debarred by the government from admitting students for the years 2017–18 and 2018–19. The FIR named a retired judge of the Orissa High Court, I.M. Quddusi as an accused who had allegedly been negotiating through a middleman to get a favourable order in the petition pending before the Supreme Court. The bench issued notice to the Union Government and the CBI and recorded that the FIR contained allegations which were disturbing and that these pertained to functioning of this Court. It directed that the matter be heard by the Constitution Bench of first five judges in the order of seniority. The matter was finally listed for 13 November.

On 10 November, the bench, headed by Justice A.K. Sikri directed that the petition filed by the CJAR be placed before the CJI for listing the matter.

---

[122]   *CJAR* v. *Union of India*, Writ Petition (Criminal) No.169 of 2017.
[123]   *Kamini Jaiswal* v. *Union of India*, Writ Petition (Criminal) No.176 of 2017.

The CJI, Justice Dipak Misra, exercising his administrative power, constituted a five-judge Constitution Bench which he himself presided over. The bench said that a piquant situation had arisen as there was conflict between the orders passed by the two benches. The Constitution Bench held that the CJI was the master of the roster. Prashant Bhushan took exception to the CJI being part of the bench, as he was hearing the case of the medical college, and alleged in the open court room that the allegation was directly against him to which Justice Misra reacted that his statement was contemptuous for which he could be hauled up.[124]

Finally, Jaiswal's petition was disposed of on 14 November by a bench comprising Justices R.K. Agrawal, Arun Mishra, and A.M. Khanwilkar.[125] The Court castigated the filing of an identical petition when another petition filed by the CJAR was coming up for hearing before another bench the next day, and objurgated it as 'forum hunting'. The Court dwelt upon the canker of forum shopping in depth and referred to *Union of India & Ors.* v. *M/s CIPLA lt. and Anr.*,[126] in which it was held that even making allegations of a per se conflict of interest require the matter could be transferred to another bench is another form of forum hunting. Cipla was held guilty of forum shopping as it had filed petitions in the Bombay High Court, the Karnataka High Court, and also an affidavit in the Delhi High Court as a member of the Bulk Drug Manufactureres Association for a relief, and then it also moved the Allahabad High Court. The CJAR's petition was also dismissed subsequently by the same bench which also imposed a heavy cost of Rs 25 lakh on it.

Judges in the People's Court

The whole controversy surrounding it reached the climax on 12 January 2018 when four senior most judges of the Supreme Court after the CJI, namely, Justices J. Chelameshwar, Ranjan Gogoi, Madan B. Lokur, and Kurian Joseph, created history by blowing the whistle on CJI Dipak Misra. In an unprecedented move, the four judges held a news conference and alleged that everything was not well with the apex court, and that the democracy would be in jeopardy if issues were not addressed immediately. In a letter addressed to the CJI, they questioned the arbitrary manner in which cases were being

---

[124] http://www.caravanmagazine.in/vantage/corruption-allegations-courtroom-drama-the-chief-justices-court (last accessed on 14 January 2018).

[125] *Kamini Jaiswal* v. *Union of India* (2018) 1 SCC 156.

[126] (2017) 5 SCC 262.

allocated to different benches and alleged that cases having far-reaching consequences had been assigned by the chief justices of this court selectively to
the benches 'of their preference' without any rational basis.[127]

The basic question is why a particular bench or judge is preferred? The law
is the same; then how much latitude does a judge enjoy by way of interpretation? It is evident that Justice Chelameshwar acted contrary to well-established
procedure of law. However, the fact that he gave the order as prayed by the
petitioner, justifies why bench-hunting is done. Since it was an extra-ordinary
case implicating judges of the apex court including the CJI, the malaise of
forum shopping was exposed, otherwise it would have remained under the
carpet. It is not a new phenomenon; lawyers and litigants want and wait
for favourable benches. It is because there is not one Supreme Court but
as many as the number of judges or at least the number of benches, which
is 13 at the moment. Judgments or orders passed by different benches are
divergent lacking even a simulacrum of uniformity based on law. There is a
total erosion of judicial collectivism and consequently of judicial discipline as
every judge has his/her own brilliant ideas which s/he enforces irrespective of
well-settled laws.

Most of the time, the Supreme Court is sitting in divisions of two or three
judges. As mentioned above, in the initial years of its formation, Constitution
Benches of the full Court usually decided cases. The largest Constitution
Bench so far was of 13 judges in Kesavananda Bharati (1973), when the total
strength of the Supreme Court was 14. Now, Constitution Benches are a rarity, and when formed, these comprise generally five or seven judges. Division
benches overrule decisions of Constitution Benches in the name of interpretation. All this causes utter confusion and leads to multiplication of litigation as
everyone feels like taking a chance. Even high courts and subordinate courts
are confused as the law is not clear.

The apex court took note of this bench-hunting long back in *Sarguja
Transport Service* v. *State Transport Appellate Tribunal, MP*[128] and held:

> The point for consideration is whether a petitioner after withdrawing a writ
> petition filed by him in the High Court under Article 226 of the Constitution
> of India without the permission to institute a fresh petition can file a fresh
> writ petition in the High Court under that Article … we are of the view that
> the principle underlying Rule 1 of Order XXIII of the Code (CPC) should be

---

[127] *Times of India*, New Delhi, 13 January 2018; *Indian Express*, New Delhi,
13 January 2018; *The Hindu*, New Delhi, 13 January 2018.
[128] (1987) 1 SCC 5.

extended in the interests of administration of justice to cases of withdrawal of writ petition also, not on the ground of *res judicata* but on the ground of public policy…. It would also discourage the litigant from indulging in bench-hunting tactics.

Advocate Mohit Chaudhary was barred from practicing for one month by the Supreme Court as he accused the Registry of the Court of favouring the opposite party by posting the case as the supplementary matter before the special bench despite the matter not being part-heard. He alleged that it was done with the objective of 'Bench Hunt'.[129]

The apex court was meant to decide issues of grave legal or constitutional importance but now it has become a court of appeal and thousands of special leave petitions keep pending which do not involve any major legal or constitutional issues. Even service matters are admitted by the Supreme Court in which the government has lost in the Central Administrative Tribunal and again in the high court in appeal. That is why Justice, Felix Frankfurter of the US Supreme court had suggested to Rau that the Supreme Court should exercise its jurisdiction through the full court and that the highest court of appeal should not sit in divisions.

The presser by the four judges naturally touched off storm as the world watched stupefied and flustered, as bits of mortar went flying. Unprecedented in the whole world, it was described variously as rebellion, anarchy, mutiny, trade unionism, judges stooping a new low, and so on. The immediate provocation was the marking of a petition, asking for probe into the death of CBI judge, B.H. Loya in December 2014 who was presiding over the trial into the alleged fake encounter of Sohrabuddin Sheikh case in which Amit Shah, the BJP president, was an accused who has since been discharged, to a division bench headed by Justice Arun Mishra. Questioning the intent of the CJI, the four judges alleged that sensitive cases were being assigned to junior judges insinuating that pliant judges were handpicked. So, the allegation was loud and clear that judgements were being fixed. Though they did not name Justice Arun Mishra, but it was clear who the target was. In the letter addressed to the CJI, they questioned his role as arbitrary calling him only the first among equals. Thus, there was a glaring contradiction in the letter as all judges are equal according to them, and yet they presumptuously think in terms of senior and junior judges. Besides, every bench is presided

---

[129] In *Re: Mohit Chaudhary* (2017) SCC OnLine SC 939, decided on 17 August 2017.

over by a senior judge. Thus, judge no. 2 may be sitting with judge no. 18 in order of seniority, or judge no. 7 may be sitting with judge no. 15. So, how does a bench become junior when a senior judge is presiding? Justice Mishra cried in the next meeting of judges that his image had been tarnished.[130] He asserted that earlier CJIs like T.S. Thakur and J.S. Khehar also assigned him tough cases.

Moreover, seniority is no guarantee to ensure justice as happened in the *Habeas Corpus* case[131] during the emergency. In this case, a Constitution Bench of five senior most judges was formed as the senior members of the SC Bar such as V.M. Tarkunde and others prevailed upon the CJI not to handpick but to go by seniority. This proved catastrophic as all the four judges after the CJI were to become CJI in succession. The fear of supersession made them prostrate before the executive, upholding its right to suspend the right to life during the emergency. Justice H.R. Khanna stood erect and dissented and paid its price as he was superseded by Justice M.H. Beg as the CJI. The remaining two judges, Justices Y.V. Chandrachud and P.N. Bhagwati also adorned the post. Perhaps a junior judge might have displayed more muscle.

Justice Chelameshwar's blood might be up for missing the top slot (CJI) by a whisker as he took oath as a Supreme Court judge minutes after Justice Dipak Misra, though he was senior even to Justice J.S. Khehar, who became the CJI on 4 January 2017 as Chelameshwar was elevated as an additional high court judge in May 1997, that is, two years before Khehar was elevated as a high court judge in 1999 when Justice Chelameshwar was confirmed. Besides, he was made chief justice of a high court in 2007, again two years before Justices Khehar and Misra were appointed high court chief justices in November and December 2009 respectively. However, Chelameshwar is not the only example whose seniority was overlooked. There are instances galore when judges appointed earlier are superseded by later appointees. Conflicts between senior judges are not unusual which often surface in the form of ego tussle. There was a lot of bad blood between then CJI Y.V. Chandrachud and the next in line, Justice P.N. Bhagwati who were reportedly not on talking terms because the latter wanted to be elevated to the apex court before Justice Chandrachud, which would have given him a tenure of over eight years as the CJI. Bhagwati was practicing at the Bombay High Court but

---

[130] http://www.news18.com/news/india/supreme-court-judge-in-loya-case-breaks-down-during-meeting-with-cji-1633181.html (last accessed on 17 February 2018).

[131] *A.D.M., Jabalpur* v. *Shivkant Shukla* (1976) 2 SCC 521, AIR (1976) SC 1207.

when the Gujarat High Court was established in 1960, he was elevated and sent there. Since it was a small High Court, he became its chief justice before Chandrachud became chief justice of the Bombay High Court, though he was elevated as a judge earlier. But Justice Bhagwati claimed seniority over him as he became chief justice of the High Court before him.

Judges seem to have been smitten by the virus of ambition which is but the last infirmity of a noble mind according to John Milton. Instead of gaining credibility and immortality by the incisiveness of their judgements they want sensitive cases and elevation to the top slot. Justice Chelameshwar boycotted the meetings of the collegium for long accusing the system as opaque and he was the only one to have dissented in the Fourth Judges' Case.[132] He animadverted the collegium system by likening to a club where favourites were played and favours exchanged, and used words like 'sycophancy', 'tradeoff', and 'lobbying' for appointment of judges. He quoted from this author's book *Justice, Judocracy and democracy in India: Boundaries and Breaches*:

> ... even party men can be fiercely independent after being appointed judges, as has been proved by some judges who were active in politics. Justice K. S. Hegde served as a member of Rajya Sabha from 1952 to 1957 and he was elevated as a High Court judge directly from Rajya Sabha. Though he was a Congress MP, he proved to be so independent that he was superseded in 1973 in the appointment of the CJI by his own party's government. Justice Tek Chand was also member of Rajya Sabha before becoming a judge. He was appointed when he was a sitting MP. But he proved to be a fine judge whose report on prohibition is a landmark. Another prominent example is Justice V. R. Krishna Iyer who was made a judge of the Kerala High Court in 1968, though he had not only been an MLA but also a minister in the Namboodiripad government (1957–59) in Kerala. In 1973, Justice S. M. Sikri, the CJI, was opposed to the elevation of justice Iyer to the apex court on the ground that he had been a politician who had held the office of a cabinet minister in Kerala. It was A. N. ray who cleared his elevation, and Justice Iyer proved to be a luminous example of what a judge ought to be. He was one of the finest judges who ever sat on the bench of the Supreme Court who tried to bridge the gap between the Supreme Court and the common people. There is also the example of Justice Bahrul Islam who served as a member of Rajya Sabha for 10 years before being appointed a High Court judge. He was subsequently eleved to the Supreme Court. He absolved Jagannath Mishra, the Chief Minister of Bihar, in the urban cooperative bank scandal and immediately thereafter resigned to contest the Lok Sabha election

---

[132] *Supreme Court Advocates-on-Record Association* v. *Union of India* (2016) 5 SCC 1.

as a Congress (I) candidate from Barpeta—he never enjoyed a clean reputation. So, it is not proper to make any generalization.[133]

The issue of roster is sensitive and the CJI may manipulate justice by handpicking judges of his choice. It punches holes into the credibility of the judiciary. The same system obtains in high courts. But over a period of time majority of sensitive cases has gone to junior judges. *Times of India* tracked 15 'super sensitive cases of national importance' in the last two decades like the ones relating to Bofors, Rajiv Gandhi's assassination, L.K. Advani's trial in Babri Masjid demolition, Sheikh fake encounter, best bakery, and the case pertaining to the The Board of Control for Cricket (BCCI), and found that all these were assigned by respective CJIs to 'select benches' headed by junior judges.[134]

If the CJI, or the CJ of the high court is not honest, judgements will be fixed. Under Article 145(1) of the Constitution, subject to the provisions of any law made by Parliament, the Supreme Court may from time to time, with the approval of the president, make rules for regulating generally the practice and procedure of the Court. Under Article 246 read with Entry 77 of the Union List, the Parliament can make laws in regard to the Constitution, organization, jurisdiction, and powers of the Supreme Court. However, the Parliament has not enacted any such law as to how benches should be formed or cases should be assigned. So, the Supreme Court has been making rules for conducting its own business, and the latest is the Supreme Court Rules, 2013. Order VI of these rules deals with 'Constitution of Division Courts and Powers of Single Judges', it is silent in respect of roster. The practice is that cases are allotted to different benches subject wise as it is not physically possible for any chief justice either in the Supreme Court or in high courts to allocate each case personally to different benches. Howbeit, s/he may assign sensitive cases to benches of his/her choice whose capabilities s/he trusts. But it is expected of the CJI and chief justices at high courts to discharge their administrative powers of allocating cases judiciously. The Supreme Court has itself admonished various authorities several times to exercise their powers in a transparent and judicious manner.

---

[133] *Supreme Court Advocates-on-Record Association* v. *Union of India*, p. 55. See also, Sudhanshu Ranjan, *Justice, Judocracy and democracy in India: Boundaries and Breaches* (New Delhi, London, New York: Routledge, 2012), pp. 185–6.

[134] https://timesofindia.indiatimes.com/india/super-sensitive-cases-being-given-to-junior-sc-judges-for-last-20-years/articleshow/62501674.cms (last accessed on 24 February 2018).

Though the issues raised may be genuine, it does not concern the common man very much, who is afraid of going to the court for the fear of inordinate delays and exorbitant expenses. The four judges were very agitated over important cases not being assigned to them, but were they hurt by the denial of justice to the common man? One of the parties, who is in the wrong but is affluent enough to tweak the system, is invariably interested in delaying the case. Judges become parties to their design by granting adjournments ad nauseam. A poor litigant from Kerala or Nagaland, coming to attend the hearing in the Supreme Court comes only to hear that the matter is adjourned. Such things do not agitate them. I have heard judges telling government employees on the verge of retirement but not getting a single promotion, 'Okay, you will get arrears if you win the case after retirement'. This shows how insensitive they are to common man's sufferings.

The four judges cut off their noses to spite their faces as they virtually robbed the highest court of its moral authority. They impeached not only CJI Dipak Misra, but also Justice Arun Mishra, who was painted as the lackey of the government. The insinuation was very clear that the CJI was fixing benches to favour the government but they pulled punches. Any other person making such allegation would have invited the sword of contempt and landed in jail in no time. Nevertheless, there are people who defend these judges for bringing the stench of the rotting system out, portraying it warts, and thus saving the institution. What had been happening was an open secret, but the voices from within lent credence to the general belief.

Anyway, these judges certainly breached the unwritten golden rule of remaining inured to self-restraint and keeping aloof from publicity. Judges are considered faceless who speak through their judgements only. Howbeit, of late, they have acquired faces, thanks to internet, as their photos are downloaded from the court's website and published in newspapers or telecast on TV. Lord Widgery, Lord chief justice of England (1971–80) was categorical that 'the best judge [is] the man who [is] least known to the readers of the *Daily Mail*', and advised, 'judges should not court publicity and certainly should not do their work in such a way as to "catch the eye of the newsman"'.[135] Actually, he was quoting an aphorism of Lord Justice MacKinnon in *On Circuit* (1940), p. 27: 'He is the best judge whose name is known to the fewest readers of *The Daily Mail*.[136] Lord Atkinson (Law Lord from 1905 to 1928) was an extreme example of keeping himself secluded from the world, who perhaps

---

[135]   See David Pannick, 'Publicity', in *Judges*, p. 169.
[136]   Pannick, 'Publicity', p. 242.

wrote nothing outside his judicial pronouncements. He would be mostly reticent in the House of Lords. He had no children or friends. Since he left no information about himself, it is said that the Lord Chancellor's office faced difficulty in tracing his wife to pay pensions.[137]

In January 1986, Lord Chancellor Hailsham of the UK advised judges, who were approached by the BBC, against appearing on a BBC Radio programme about barristers. He opined that the 'independeence of the judiciary' might be threatened by judicial participation in such a programme. However, two judges ignored the advice and appeared on the programme. Lord Hailsham clarified that he was merely 'representing the collective view of the judges on keeping the rules in place'.[138] These rules were formulated by Lord Chancellor Kilmuir in December 1955, when Lieutenant-General Sir Ian Jacob, the director general of the BBC, sent a request for a number of judges to be granted permission to participate in a series of radio lectures about great judges of the past. These rules are contained in a letter that he wrote in response to Jacob's request. These are known as Kilmuir rules which he formulated after consulting the Lord chief justice, the master of Rolls and the president of the Probate, Divorce and Admiralty Division. It was an academic programme, but he advised them not to participate as 'the overriding consideration was the importance of keeping the judiciary of the country insulated from the controversy of the day'.[139] However, ignoring the advice, two judges appeared on the programme, perhaps displaying the true independence of the judiciary.

There are instances of Law lords having written letters to newspapers in response to criticism of their judgements. Lord Atkin suffered personal attack for his historic dissent in *Liversidge* v. *Anderson*[140] in the interpretation of Regulation 18B of the Defence (General) Regulations 1939. Its emergency powers gave liberty to the home secretary to intern people without trial if he had *reasonable cause* to believe that they had *hostile associations*. Sir John Anderson used this emergency power to detain Jack Perlzweig who used the name Robert Liversidge without giving any reason. In appeal, the Appellate Committee of the House of Lords had to decide whether the Court could

[137] Lord Stevens, *Law and Politics: The House of Lords as a Judicial Body 1800–1976* (Littlehampton Book Services Limited, 1979), p. 259.

[138] Letter from Lord Hailsham to *The Guardian* 27 January 1986. See Pannick, *Judges*, p. 173.

[139] Pannick, *Judges*, p. 174.

[140] (1941) 3 All ER 338.

examine the home secretary's actions on an objective yardstick. The home secretary refused to disclose certain documents on grounds of national security.
The plaintiff sought damages for false incarceration. Lord Atkin dissented,
holding that the defendant was obliged to give further and better particulars in his defence, asserting that he had reasonable cause to believe that the
claimant was a person of hostile associations. He elucidated that one of the
pillars of liberty in English law is the principle that every imprisonment is
prima facie unlawful and that it is for a person directing imprisonment to
justify his act, and held that the only exception is in respect of imprisonment ordered by a judge, who from the nature of his office cannot be sued,
and the validity of whose judicial decisions cannot in such proceedings
be questioned. Describing the majority judgement as fantastic, he wrote
that he had listened to the arguments which might have been addressed
acceptably to the Court of king's bench in the time of Charles I. He censured the judges as more executive minded that the executive. The Leftist
Q.C.D.N. Pritt, who had appeared for Bhagat Singh in the Privy Council,
appeared for detainee Liversidge. So infuriated were some of his brother
judges that Lord Maugham who had presided at the hearing wrote a letter
to *The Times* excoriating Atkin's language.[141] It is said that Lord Atkin could
never recover from this shock and he passed away in 1944. Now, his dissent
has been accepted as the legally correct interpretation. Some other judges
also wrote letters to newspapers as dis Viscount Dilhorne in 1975 and the
same year Justice Bridge wrote to *The Times* in response to criticism of one
of his decisions.[142]

The presser gave an opportunity to some Opposition parties to contem-
plate initiating the impeachment motion against CJI Dipak Misra.[143] Some
leaders alleged that Justice Misra was partial to the government and referred
to the allegations made by the four judges.

Judicial Indiscipline

Judicial indiscipline is visible in full glare with different benches speaking in
different voices, leading to utter confusion and uncertainty. Law is enacted to
give finality to the subject concerned. Nevertheless, confusion persists which
is removed by the court, and the ultimate finality comes from the Supreme

---

[141] Stevens, *Law and Politics*, p. 259.
[142] See Pannick, *Judges*, pp. 178–9.
[143] *The Hindu, Times of India, Indian Express*, New Delhi, 28 March 2018.

Court which lays down the law by way of interpretation and filling in the gaps, if any. If the apex court falters by not acting in unison, it is a sure recipe for disaster. Unfortunately, this is what is happening as different benches of the Court are taking contradictory stands, sometimes diametrically opposed.

On 21 February 2018, a three-judge bench of the Supreme Court headed by Justice Madan B. Lokur refused to follow the decision of another three-judge bench headed by Justice Arun Mishra, and requested the other Supreme Court benches and the high courts not to deal with cases pertaining to the interpretation of or concerning Section 24 of the Right to Fair Compensation and Transparency in Land Acquisition, Rehabilitation and resettlement Act, 2013. On 8 February 2018, the bench led by Justice. Mishra, with a majority of 2:1 in *Indore Development Authority (dead) Through LRS*,[144] overruled a 2014 verdict given by another three-judge bench headed by Justice R.M. Lodha in *Pune Municipal Corporation* v. *Harakchand Misrimal Solanki*,[145] terming it as *per incuriam* (decided carelessly in ignorance of law). Justice Lokur was part of the three-judge bench in this case. It appears as if the two judges gave the pip to each other and it influenced their decisions. Justice Lokur was among the four judges who censured CJI Dipak Misra for allocating sensitive cases to Justice Arun Mishra. As confusion ruled the roost, on 22 February, two two-judge benches referred the matter to the CJI for constituting a larger bench to give it finality, who did constitute a Constitution Bench of five judges on 24 February.

A decision cannot be overturned at the drop of a hat. In *Keshav Mills Ltd.* v. *Commissioner of Income Tax, Bombay*,[146] the Supreme Court clarified that barring considerations of a substantial and compelling nature, it would be reluctant to overrule its own decisions. Again, in *Bengal Immunity Co. Ltd.* v. *State of Bihar and Ors.*,[147] it admitted that it has the power to revise its previous decisions, but nevertheless stressed that it must be done sparingly and with circumspection.

The court cannot be the Theatre of the Absurd where all communication breaks down, and the logical construction and reasoning gives way to illogical speech and ultimately to silence. The term refers to dramatic works of some European and American writers of the 1950s and 1960s who agreed with Albert Camus's anxiety expressed in his essay 'The Myth of Sisyphus'

---

[144] Civil Appeal No. 20982 of 2017.
[145] (2014) 3 SCC 183.
[146] (1953) SCR 950, AIR (1953) SC 187 (1953) 23 ITR 230.
[147] (1955) 2 SCR 603, AIR (1955) SC 661 (1955) 6 STC 446.

$(1942)^{148}$ that human situation is essentially absurd and devoid of purpose. Courts remove absurdity by injecting purpose and bringing in clarity.

It is not only that coordinate benches of equal strength are not abiding by the decisions delivered by another bench, but sometimes division benches defy Constitution Benches which is nothing short of sacrilege. In *Dr Subramanian Swamy* v. *Director, CBI*,[149] a five-judge Constitution Bench of the Supreme Court struck down Section 6-A of the Delhi Special Police Establishment Act, 1946, which requires the prior sanction of the central government to conduct any inquiry or investigation into any offence alleged to have been committed under the Prevention of Corruption Act, 1988 if the allegation relates to the employees of the Central government of the level of joint secretary or above. When the British government enacted the Criminal Procedure Code (Cr. P.C.), government servants were given protection, as Section 197 provides that prosecution against them cannot be launched without prior sanction of the government. The British had come to rule; so they wanted to protect their officers. They did not have such a provision in their own country. After independence, the Government of India not only refrained from fine-tuning these laws enacted by colonial rulers, but also provided for similar protections while legislating other laws. Thus, Section 19 of the Prevention of Corruption Act added one more protection requiring the investigating agency to obtain prior sanction from the government for prosecution. The Supreme Court raised a valid question, namely, 'How can two public servants against whom there are allegations of corruption or graft or bribe taking or criminal misconduct under the P.C. Act, 1988 be made to be treated differently because one happens to be a junior officer and the other, a senior decision maker?' Calling it a breach of rule of law, the Court held that it amounted to negation of equality under Article 14. However, in *L. Narayana Swamy* v. *State of Karnataka* (2016),[150] a division bench of the Supreme Court took a contrary view that further investigation of a public servant under Section 156(3) of the Cr. P.C. cannot be ordered without prior approval.

Article 145(3) of the Constitution mandates that 'any case involving a substantial question of law as to the interpretation of the Constitution' must be decided by a Constitution Bench of at least five judges. Howbeit, this principle has not been observed in many cases as issues of grave legal

[148]   Albert Camu, 'The Myth of Sisyphus', in French (Paris: Éditions Gallimard, 1942), in English (London: Hamish Hamilton, 1955).

[149]   (2014) 8 SCC 682.

[150]   (2016) 8 SCALE 560 (2016) SCC OnLine SC 908.

implications were decided by division benches. In *Selvi and Others* v. *State of Karnataka and Anr.*,[151] a bench of three judges decided the constitutionality of narco-analysis.

Judgements are supposed to be crisp and clear leaving no scope for any ambiguity. However, many a time, it has been difficult to derive the *ratio decidendi* (principles underlying a decision) from the judgement. As discussed above, we have seen how two Constitution Benches were set up, one after another, to derive the ratio of *T.M.A. Pai Foundation* v. *State of Karnataka.*[152]

Sometimes, judgements are *per incuriam*, and even death sentences have been awarded wrongly. In *Santosh Kumar Satishbhushan Bariyar* v. *Maharashtra,*[153] the Supreme Court pointed out that *Ravji* v. *State of Rajasthan*[154] and six subsequent cases in which Ravji was followed were decided *per incuriam*, as the law laid down therein is at variance with the one laid down in *Bachan Singh* v. *Punjab,*[155] and clarified that before giving death sentence, the court should not confine its consideration principally or merely to the circumstances connected with the particular crime, but must also give due consideration to the circumstances of the criminal. These cases are: (a) *Shivaji @ Dadya Shankar Alhat* v. *State of Maharashtra,*[156] (b) *Mohan Anna Chavan* v. *State of Maharashtra,*[157] (c) *Bantu* v. *State of Uttar Pradesh,*[158] (d) *Surja Ram* v. *State of Rajasthan,*[159] (e) *Dayanidhi Bisoi* v. *State of Orissa,*[160] and (f) *State of Uttar Pradesh* v. *Sattan @ Satyendra and Others.*[161]

However, these judgements are not the result of judicial indiscipline, but of oversight. The Court added that the Bachan Singh threshold of 'the rarest of rare cases' has been most variedly and inconsistently applied by the various high courts, as also the Supreme Court. Judgements must be precise and pellucid, free from convolution and circumlocution, based objectively on law and facts.

[151]   (2010) 7 SCC 263 (5 May 2010).
[152]   (2002) 8 SCC 481.
[153]   (2009) 6 SCC 498.
[154]   (1996) 2 SCC 175.
[155]   AIR (1980) SC 898 (1980) CriLJ 636 (1982) (1) SCALE 713 (1980) 2 SCC 684 (1983) 1 SCR 145.
[156]   (2008) 15 SCC 269.
[157]   (2008) 7 SCC 561.
[158]   (2008) 11 SCC 113.
[159]   (1996) 6 SCC 271.
[160]   (2003) 9 SCC 310.
[161]   (2009) 4 SCC 736.

Another ugly instance of judicial indiscipline was the unseemly behaviour of the then judge of the Calcutta High Court Justice C.S. Karnan, who was transferred from the Madras High Court because of his obstreperous and obnoxious behaviour. A seven-judge Constitution Bench of the Supreme Court sentenced him to six months of imprisonment for the contempt of Court on 9 May 2017 taking suo moto cognizance of his behaviour.[162] CJI J.S. Khehar lamented in the opening paragraph:

> The task at our hands is unpleasant. It concerns actions of a Judge of a High Court. The instant proceedings pertain to alleged actions of criminal contempt, committed by Shri Justice C.S. Karnan. The initiation of the present proceedings suo-motu, is unfortunate. In case this Court has to take the next step, leading to his conviction and sentencing, the Court would have undoubtedly travelled into virgin territory. This has never happened. This should never happen. But then, in the process of administration of justice, the individual's identity, is clearly inconsequential. This Court is tasked to evaluate the merits of controversies placed before it, based on the facts of the case. It is expected to record its conclusions, without fear or favour, affection or ill-will.[163]

He terrorized his colleagues in the Madras High Court so much that many successive chief justices of the Madras High Court wrote to the CJIs seeking his transfer. Twenty sitting judges of the same High Court, through a joint representation, also sought his transfer. During this period, the Registrar General of the Madras High Court informed the Supreme Court that Justice Karnan had initiated suo moto proceedings and stayed administrative orders passed by the chief justice of the Madras High Court. A division bench of the Supreme Court, after hearing the matter, restrained Justice Karnan from either hearing or issuing any directions in said petition and other matters connected therewith but granted him the permission to file special leave petition.[164]

The directions of the apex court failed to rein him in who continued to besmirch his colleagues at the High Court with his vituperative words by addressing communications to the highest executive and judicial authorities. He wrote to the chief justice of the High Court dated 21 May 2015, complaining against the roster that he was not assigned important cases and alleged that a particular judge of the high court did not have the requisite qualifications and that his certificates were forged. He concluded the letter

---

[162] *In Re: Hon'ble justice C. S. Karnan* (2017) 7 SCC 1.
[163] *In Re: Hon'ble justice C. S. Karnan*, para 1.
[164] *In Re: Hon'ble justice C. S. Karnan*, para 3.

alleging that the chief justice of the Madras High Court had committed offences under the provisions of the Scheduled Castes and Scheduled Tribes (Prevention of Atrocities) Act, 1989. He wrote another letter dated 5 February 2016, to the home secretary, Tamil Nadu, asking him to extend protection to a lawyer—Peter Ramesh Kumar—who had made serious allegations against a few judges, and what is interesting is that he asked the home secretary to treat his letter as a 'suo-motu judicial order'. In the above letter, Justice Karnan had directed the Registry of the Madras High Court, to assign the *suo-moto* writ petition a number. He wrote another letter to the CJ making wild casteist allegations and also kept sending letters to other authorities. In another letter written on 26 October 2016, he asked the city police commissioner to register criminal cases as he claimed to be a victim of social and caste discrimination, and added that he had been subjected to agony on account of ragging and demeaning actions of judges of the Madras High Court.

Ultimately, he was transferred to the Calcutta High Court by the CJI on 12 February 2016. However, three days later, in a *suo moto* order, Justice Karnan stayed his transfer order himself defying the principle of natural justice that nobody can be a judge in his own case. He also directed the Chennai Police commissioner to file an FIR under the SC/ST (Prevention of Atrocities) Act against two Supreme Court judges, namely, Justices J.S. Kheahr and R. Bhanumathi, who read out the transfer order cleared by CJI T.S. Thakur.[165] He sent the copy of his order to the president, the prime minister, the Union law minister, and other political leaders including Sonia Gandhi, Ram Vilas Paswan, and Mayawati. He also asked the CJI to submit a written statement on the issue through his subordinates, explaining reasons for his transfer by 29 February. Within a few hours, the Supreme Court quashed his order and asked the Madras High Court to stop allocating work to him.[166] Justice Karnan was forced to join the Calcutta High Court but he continued with his misbehaviour and the Supreme Court initiated *suo moto* contempt proceedings against him for denigrating the judicial institution. On 10 March 2017, creating a history of sorts, a seven-judge bench comprising CJI J.S. Khehar and Justices Dipak Misra, J. Chelameshwar, Ranjan Gogoi, Madan B. Lokur, P.C. Ghose, and Kurian Joseph issued a bailable warrant against him, and asked the director general of Police, West Bengal,

---

[165] https://www.telegraphindia.com/1160216/jsp/nation/story_69595.jsp   (last accessed on 4 March 2018).

[166] www.thehindu.com/news/.../supreme-court...justice-karnanjustice.../ article8240425.ec... (last accessed on 4 March 2018).

to personally serve the warrant on him. Later, addressing a press conference at his residence in Kolkata, Justice Karnan reacted like this, 'It is a motivated, ridiculous and illegal order'.[167] He urged the president to recall the warrant, and directed secretaries-general of both Houses of Parliament to place the facts before presiding officers for a thorough probe. He again alleged that he was being targeted because of his caste. However, he appeared before the Supreme Court on 31 March but remained defiant and insolent and refused to apologize. He also demanded that he should be restored the judicial work of which he had been divested. When the seven-judge bench asked him to furnish a proper reply within four weeks, he audaciously told them that he would not appear in the Court again and dared them to arrest and put him in jail.[168] Undeterred, he went on creating history by passing orders against the CJI and other judges of the apex court. On 14 April, he summoned all the seven judges of the Constitution Bench which had issued bailable warrant against him to his residential court in Kolkata. On 8 May, he convicted them (CJI and six other judges) for various offences under SC/ST (Prevention of Atrocities) Act and sentenced them to five years of imprisonment. He held them guilty of insulting him and not allowing him to carry on his duty as a judge and issued warrants of arrest against them.

Finally on 9 May 2017, the same seven-judge Constitution Bench convicted him for the contempt of court.[169] The Court ruled:

> On merits, we are of the considered view, that Sri Justice C.S. Karnan, has committed contempt of the judiciary. His actions constitute contempt of this Court, and of the judiciary of the gravest nature. Having found him guilty of committing contempt, we convict him accordingly. We are satisfied to punish him by sentencing him to imprisonment for six months. As a consequence, the contemnor shall not perform any administrative or judicial functions.[170]

Attorney-general, K.K. Venugopal suggested to the Court to wait for his retirement before proceeding against him, but the CJI thundered that in contempt, the Court does not distinguish and that Justice Karnan was wrong if he thought that he would not be punished for being a sitting judge.

---

[167] 'SC Issues Bailable Warrant against Justice C.S. Karnana', *The Hindu*, 11 March 2017.

[168] 'Karnan Defies SC, Dares Judges to Put Him in Jail', *The Asian Age*, 1 April 2017.

[169] In *Re: Hon'ble Justice C.S. Karnan* (2017) 7 SCC 1.

[170] In *Re: Hon'ble Justice C.S. Karnan*, para 2.

The Court also restrained the media from publishing his statements. Justice Karnan proved to be utterly pusillanimous and went into hiding to evade arrest. He retired on 12 June while on the run, and was arrested from a resort at Malumichampatti near Coimbatore on 21 June.[171]

The fact that he absconded after being sentenced, speaks volumes about his character. He questioned the impartiality of the higher judiciary projecting himself as a victim and calumniating the whole institution. Thus, he played revolutionary discarding conventional mores and refusing to accept that the judiciary is a holy cow. He spoke up but misused his power to protect himself and finally went into hiding like a coward. Those fighting the system, embrace the punishment to further reinforce their point: how unjust the system is. Mahatma Gandhi pleaded guilty in the court many a time saying that he would break the law again as he considered it unjust and invited punishment, so did Bhagat Singh who refused to hire even a lawyer.

Further, the behaviour of Justice Karnan raises many disturbing questions. If a judge acts so whimsically to settle score with the people he has differences with and misuses his power like this, he can ruin them for no fault of theirs. CJI and other judges could save themselves as the apex court can overturn the orders/judgements of the high court. But what about the common man? Like a knight errant, he would send anyone to jail to satisfy his ego. It came to light as the abuse of power was too brazen and he targeted judges of the high court and also the apex court including the CJI. The misuse of power by judges is not unusual and victims are doomed to suffer.

The Problem of Corruption

Corruption in the Judiciary from Ancient Times

It is true that corruption in the judiciary existed from the earliest times. It is evident from the system that obtained in ancient Athens at the time of Plato when 'the Dikasteria, or Supreme Court, consisted of over a thousand members (to make bribery expensive), selected by alphabetical rote from the roll of all the citizens'.[172] There were over one thousand judges, while there were 400,000 inhabitants in the city, of whom 250,000 were slaves without any political rights. Francis Bacon (1561–1626) was given important offices and

---

[171] http://www.thehindu.com/news/national/justice-karnan-arrives-in-kolkata/article19114346.ece (last accessed on 11 March 2018).

[172] Will Durant, *The Story of Philosophy* (New York: Washington Square Press, Inc., 1962), p. 4.

high honours by Queen Elizabeth I and King James I. He was made Baron Verulam and Viscount St. Albans, and became Lord Chancellor. In 1620, he was accused of accepting gifts in his official capacity as a judge. First, he accepted 100 Pounds in Aubrey's case.[173] Aubrey sued Sir William Brooker, but the case never got listed for hearing. When Aubrey complained of delay, he was advised by someone that 100 pounds might help. He went with Sir George Hastings and Jenkins to Lord Chancellor's residence in Gray's Inn. These two made over the money to Bacon. Still the case did not come up for hearing. Aubrey wrote letters to Bacon to which he did not reply. Finally, the Lord Chancellor told him, 'If you importune me any more, I will lay you by the heels'.[174]

After some time, the case was heard, and 'a very prejudicial and murdering order was made against Aubrey in his cause'. Sir George Hastings protested to Bacon, and asked him to change the order and undo the injustice. The Lord Chancellor promised to rectify but did not. When Sir Hasings threatened to expose him, Bacon warned, 'You are not to do so. If you do, George, I must deny it upon my honour.'[175]

The next to accuse Bacon was Edward Egerton who brought proceedings against his brother Sir Rowland Egerton. He paid as bribe a basin and ewer worth 50 pounds or more and subsequently a bag full of 400 pounds in gold sovereigns. However, he again decided the case against Edward Egerton. It is not known whether he accepted gratification from the winning parties also.

Aubrey and Edward Egerton complained against the Lord Chancellor. The House of Commons constituted a committee to inquire into the allegations. In the course of investigation, the committee came to know of other cases in which bribes were paid to him. The Commons forwarded these complaints to the Lords along with the supporting evidence. The Lords appointed a Select Committee of the House which examined witnesses. They framed 28 separate Articles of Charges against Lord Chancellor Bacon.

He admitted to his guilt but denied that it had influenced his decisions. He added, 'After this example, it is like that judges will fly from any thing that is in the likeness of Corruption (though it were a great distance) as from a serpent.'[176]

---

[173] (1620) 2 State Tr 1087.

[174] Rt. Hon. Lord Denning, *Landmarks in the Law* (New Delhi: Aditya Books Private Limited, 1993), p. 45.

[175] Denning, *Landmarks in the Law*, p. 45.

[176] Denning, *Landmarks in the Law*, p. 48.

He was found guilty; the Lord chief justice ordered like this:

That the lord Viscount St Albans, Lord Chancellor of England, shall undergo a fine and ransom of 40,000 pounds. That he shall be imprisoned in the tower during the king's pleasure—that he shall for ever be incapable of any office, place, or employment, in the state or commonwealth. That he shall never sit in parliament, nor come within the verge of the Court.[177]

He was removed from office, and on 31 May 1620, he was taken to the Tower as a prisoner sentenced to jail. But the king granted him a pardon and he retired to private life. However, this is not the first instance of judges' corruption. 70 years before, old Bishop Hugh Latimer deplored the reprehensible practice: *Omnes diligent munera* (They all love bribes. Bribery is a princely kind of thieving).[178]

Thus, in all ages, the judiciary has been infested with corruption, but there were mechanisms to keep a check on this, and also to remove depraved and dissolute judges. In India also, the judiciary was the first to be infected by the virus of corruption. From the earliest days, when courts were formally set up, court clerks' palms had to be greased, without which dates could not be obtained. This was when other functionaries of the government were almost free from the taint of corruption. But in India, no serious effort was made to extirpate it.

According to Transparency International's Global Corruption Report 2007, a whopping Rs 2,630 crores was paid every year as bribe to court officials of the lower judiciary.[179] The only saving grace for India in the report is a one line statement, 'The upper judiciary is relatively clean'. But this also came with a rider: 'there are obvious exceptions'. The report further says that 77 per cent of respondents in a survey in India believe the judiciary is corrupt. It adds that the perception of corruption is higher in India and Pakistan than in Hong Kong, Malaysia, Singapore, and Thailand. In Pakistan, 55 per cent of the respondents said the judiciary was corrupt. It also says, 'The degree of delays and corruption has led to cynicism about the justice system. People seek short cuts through bribery and favours, leading to further unlawful behaviour. A prime example is the unauthorized buildings in Indian cities. Construction and safety laws are flouted in connivance with persons in authority.'[180]

---

[177] Denning, *Landmarks in the Law*, pp. 48–9.
[178] Denning, *Landmarks in the Law*, p. 49.
[179] *Times of India*, 25 May 2007.
[180] *Hindustan Times*, 26 May 2007.

Opinions of Some Erstwhile Chief Justices of India and Judges

Corruption in the higher judiciary is now a confirmed fact, though there may be differences of opinion on the degree. Justice J.S. Verma, admitted it immediately after demitting the office of the CJI in an interview to *Indian Express*, 'There is no point in saying that there is no corruption in the judiciary. No one is going to say it, much less accept it. One cannot go on sweeping it under the carpet and not expect it to show. It is showing now.... Therefore, the time has come to enact a law to hold judges accountable ... when moral sanction doesn't work, then legal sanction is required.'[181] He regretted that 'traditions and conventions' were not good enough as guarantees for judicial accountability any longer. He said, 'If after making a reasonable inquiry, you find that there is something wrong and you tell the judge concerned, he will say who are you to ask me to resign ... I have taken the oath. That is the attitude. Social sanctions don't work and therefore legal sanctions are required.'[182] Another sitting CJI, S.P. Bharucha, admitted in 2001 that '80 per cent judges of the country were honest and incorruptible and the smaller percentage was bringing the entire judiciary into disrepute'.[183] It was an admission that 20 per cent of the judges were corrupt. Thus, the prevalence of corruption in the higher judiciary was acknowledged, though the percentage of corrupt judges may be more or less, because the CJI has no instrument to measure it. Yet another chief justice, V.N. Khare also admitted to it just before his retirement, 'Of course, corruption is there but mostly in subordinate judiciary. It is shaking the faith of the people in the judiciary.... The degree varies in the high courts but there is no corruption in the Supreme Court.'[184] CJI Designate, Justice P. Sathasivam was quite candid, 'I should fairly admit that the judiciary is not untouched by corruption. When we take the oath as judge, we swear to be fair and impartial in all our judicial functions. However, on some occasions in the past, few judges have wilfully dishonoured the oath by adopting to corrupt practices.'[185]

A former judge of the Supreme Court lamented that 'everything was rotten about the Indian judiciary'. On being asked why he did not make this remark

[181] *Indian Express*, 22 January 1998.

[182] *Indian Express*, 22 January 1998.

[183] See T.R. Andhyarujina, 'Judging Judges, Credibly', *Indian Express*, 14 June 2005.

[184] expressindia.com, 1 May 2004.

[185] J. Venkatesan, 'Judiciary not Untouched by Corruption', interview with Justice P. Sathasivam, *The Hindu*, 1 July 2013.

when he was in office, he replied, 'I was afraid of the safety of my wife and children.'[186] Another judge, Shivraj Patil, rued that 'there was some amount of degradation in the judiciary'.[187] Yet another judge, Justice Saldhana stated that there must be qualitative changes in the judiciary.[188]

Impeachment Motion Impracticable

Justice Ramaswami's Case

This reinforces the need to evolve some kind of mechanism to make the judges of the higher courts accountable, especially because their impeachment is well-nigh impossible. The Constitution does not use the word 'impeachment' in case of judges in Articles 124 and 217, but is used in the context of judges also as the procedure for removing them is similar to that of president, where the word has been used in Article 61. A judge of the Supreme Court can be impeached only the ground of 'proved misbehaviour or incapacity' [Article 124(4)] and so can be a high court judge [Article 217(1)]. The Judges (Inquiry) Act, 1968, prescribes the procedure for investigation and proof of misbehaviour. The issue of corruption in the superior judiciary became a theme of open public discourse when, in 1990, Justice V. Ramaswami of the Supreme Court was accused of serious misdemeanour, though people did talk about it even earlier. The CJI Sabyasachi Mukherjee, refused to allocate him any work, but he insisted on sitting on the bench. The three-member judges' committee, in its report to the chief justice, recommended against withholding work from Justice Ramaswami. The recommendation was questionable because even the three-judge sub-committee had not exculpated him from the charge of irregularities and misuse of funds mentioned by the auditor-general's report. Legal luminaries, as well as common people were aghast that a judge facing an inquiry by a properly constituted committee was sitting on the bench. There was a precedent in America not to allocate work to a judge facing an inquiry. A judge of the Federal Court was not given any work by the chief justice as his conduct was being probed. The accused judge challenged it in the Supreme Court but his plea was rejected.

Finally the committee of three judges, in a cutting indictment, recorded its clear findings that Ramaswami had misused his office, was guilty of 11 out

---

[186] *Times of India*, 18 December 1998, cf., 'Judicial Accountability', *Journal of Indian Law Institute*, January–March 2006, p. 94.

[187] *The Hindu*, 15 June 2003.

[188] *The Hindu*, 12 January 2003.

of the 14 charges and did not deserve to adorn the apex court. The accused judge, from the beginning, behaved like a defiant litigant, uncooperative with the inquiry, raising technical defences and casting aspersions against the three inquiring judges. As the Inquiry Committee began its work, M. Krishnamani, Congress MP, challenged the functioning of the Committee in the Supreme Court on the ground that Justice Ramaswami was not given a fair hearing and that he was entitled to a copy of the report. The Court dismissed the petition saying that the petitioner had no *locus standi*, and if Justice Ramaswami wanted a copy of the report, he would have to file a petition himself.[189] Subsequently, Ramaswami's wife moved the Court on behalf of her husband with the prayer that a copy of the report of the Inquiry Committee be made over to her husband before it was submitted to the Speaker of the Lok Sabha so that he may go in for judicial review in case the Committee found him guilty. A Constitution Bench of five judges by majority of 3:2 decided that if the Inquiry Committee absolves the judge either unanimously or by majority, the matter ends there and the Parliament is not required to deliberate on it. It implies that there can be no judicial review in either of its finding. But if the Committee finds the judge guilty, the matter goes to the Parliament which will consider the report on merit on the basis of materials available before it and whether the finding is correct. So, the Parliament can still reject those charges and disapprove of the impeachment motion.

Something of the sort happened as the impeachment motion brought against him failed, because some Tamil MPs made it a North versus South issue and Prime Minister P.V. Narasimha Rao, issued an oral whip to his party members to abstain from voting. The failure of the impeachment motion proved that it was a political, not a legal, remedy which did not work. Reportedly, it was Congress MP, Mani Shankar Aiyar who manipulated his party in favour of Justice Ramaswami as there were a large number of voters of Ramaswami's caste in his constituency. It was the first ever impeachment motion brought in the Parliament in the history of independent India and it was the quasi-judicial function of the Parliament to decide on it. But, the Parliament did not act, abnegating its role. Technically, the motion failed, but some legal experts felt that the charges remained, as these were not rejected by the Parliament. A writ petition was filed in the Supreme Court asking it to declare the motion of impeachment passed, arguing that a member abstaining from vote should be deemed to have voted for it. Rejecting the argument, the Court ruled that the requirement of 'not less than two-thirds present

---

[189] *M. Krishnaswami v. Union of India* (1992) 4 SCC 605.

and voting' in Article 124(4) means that the requisite number of members support the motion by casting their votes.[190]

It was also rumoured that under some tacit agreement, the accused judge promised to resign if the motion was not passed. But he did not. Though he wanted to sit again as a judge after the failure of the impeachment motion, Chief Justice Venkatachalaiah refused to give him any judicial work and he had to stay at home, drawing his salary till he retired a year later.

However, it is also true that if judges are removed on the charges on which Justice Ramaswami was sought to be impeached, a large number of judges would face removal. The charges included spending public money on decorating chief justice's bungalow at Chandigarh imprudently and excessively and also keeping for himself some pieces of furniture bought at the office cost. Atal Bihari Vajpayee had likened it to the theft of hen.[191] But three eminent judges found him guilty of corruption and indiscretion. This shows the level of integrity honest judges themselves expect of their peer.

First Impeachment Proceeding

Before this, the first impeachment proceeding sought to be started in the Parliament was also against a Supreme Court judge, Justice J.C. Shah, revered for his probity and rectitude. Ironically, he was sought to be punished for his integrity, and the process was initiated by a dishonest civil servant against whom Justice Shah had decided a case in the Supreme Court. The aggrieved bureaucrat, through chicanery, obtained signatures of as many as 199 MPs for an appeal to the Speaker of the Lok Sabha to commence impeachment proceedings against him. However, it proved a non-starter as the Speaker of the Lok Sabha, G.S. Dhillon, successfully convinced a majority of the signatories of the irresponsibility of their act.[192]

Impeachment of Justice Soumitra Sen by Rajya Sabha

A history of sort was created when Justice Soumitra Sen earned the dubious distinction of being the only judge of the higher judiciary so far to be impeached by any House of Parliament. Rajya Sabha impeached him on

[190] *Lily Thomas* v. *Speaker, Lok Sabha* (1993) 4 SCC 234.

[191] Fali S. Nariman, 'We Need Fearless Judges', *Indian Express*, 8 March 2011.

[192] See Nani A. Palkhivala, 'The Supreme Court's Judgement in the Judges' Case', in *We, the People* (Bombay: Strand Book Stall, 1986), p. 234.

18 August 2011. The process began when 58 Rajya Sabha MPs, cutting across party lines, submitted a petition to Chairperson Mohammad Hamid Ansari seeking the removal of the Calcutta High Court Judge Soumitra Sen on grounds of financial impropriety.[193] Earlier, then CJI K.G. Balakrishnan, in a letter to the prime minister, dated 4 August 2008, recommended his impeachment. The letter was sent after an in-house committee of the Supreme Court found him involved in financial misappropriation before he was appointed judge. In 1984, while Sen was practicing as a lawyer, he was made the receiver in a dispute concerning the Steel Authority of India. Moreover, that he chose to retain the money even after being elevated to the High Court in 2003, and parted with it only after the High Court ordered him in April 2006 to return it, also weighed heavily on the panel while arriving at the recommendation. The CJI wrote:

> Soumitra Sen was also appointed as a Special Officer by Calcutta High Court in another case (an Appeal arising out of C.P. No. 226 of 1996). In that case (C.P. No. 226 of 1996), the High Court had directed payment of Rs. 70,00,000 to the workers of Calcutta Fans, a company in liquidation and Mr. Justice Soumitra Sen, then a practising Advocate, was appointed as a Special Officer to disburse that amount to the workers. S.B. Account No. 01SLP0013400 was opened by him for that purpose and the amount of Rs. 70,00,000/- meant for disbursement for workers was deposited in that account on February 7, 1997. A sum of Rs. 25,00,000 from Special Officer's account was invested by Justice Soumitra Sen with a company M/s. Lynx India Ltd., which, later on went into liquidation.
>
> On March 7, 2002, Steel Authority of India Limited (Plaintiff) wrote a letter to the Receiver asking him to furnish information and detailed particulars about the sale proceeds received by him and the amount of interest which had accrued thereon. The Receiver did not supply the information sought by the Plaintiff. Thereupon, the Plaintiffs filed an application (GA No. 875/2003) for direction to the Receiver to handover the sale proceeds and render true and faithful account of all the moneys held by him. No affidavit was, however, filed by the Receiver in spite of the notice being served on him. When the application came-up for hearing before a Single Judge of the Calcutta High Court, the Receiver, who had, by that time been elevated to the Calcutta High Court, did not come forward to assist the Court either by filing an affidavit or by giving information through any lawyer or recognized agent, despite service of the copy of the application on him ...

[193] '58 RS MPs for HC Judge's Impeachment', *Times of India*, 21 February 2009; 'Impeaching HC Judge: MPs Take the First Step', *Indian Express*, 21 February 2009.

The entire amount in the bank accounts was gradually withdrawn by the Receiver so as to reduce the balance to Rs. 811.56 in S.B. A/c No. O1SLPO813400 and Rs. 2,340.08 in S.B. A/c No. O1SLPO632800 as on May 31, 1999. Both the Accounts were closed on March 22, 2000 and May 21, 2002 respectively ...[194]

When the matter was brought to the notice of the High Court, the single judge bench of Justice Kalyan Jyoti Sengupta of Calcutta High Court concluded that the receiver had converted and appropriated, *prima facie*, the said amount, lying in his custody, without the authority of the Court and the act and conduct of the erstwhile receiver was nothing short of criminal misappropriation, In April 2006, the Court asked him to return the money with interest accrued from 1993. Sen had to deposit Rs 52.46 lakh with the Court.

Thus, Sen's misconduct continued even after being appointed a judge. The CJI then constituted a three member Committee, comprising Justice A.P. Shah (then chief justice, Madras High Court), Justice A.K. Patnaik (then chief justice, High Court of Madhya Pradesh), and Justice R.M. Lodha (then judge, Rajasthan High Court) to conduct a fact-finding inquiry. The Committee submitted its report on 1 February 2008, after calling for relevant records and considering the submission made by Justice Soumitra Sen, who appeared in person before the Committee. The Committee concluded that Soumitra Sen did not have honest intentions right from the year 1993, since he mixed the money received as a receiver and his personal money, and converted the receiver's money to his own use.

The prime minister sent the letter to the Ministry of Law and Justice, but it kept hanging fire, and when the government did not take any action, the CPI(M) took the initiative to impeach him. It was supported by some other parties including the BJP. The motion signed by 57 MPs was admitted in Rajya Sabha on 27 February 2009. CPI(M) MP Sita Ram Yechury took the lead. The Chairman, Rajya Sabha, constituted a committee under sub-section (2) of section 3 of the Judges (Inquiry) Act, 1968, to inquire into the allegations. The Committee initially comprised Justice D.K. Jain, then judge, Supreme Court, Justice T.S. Thakur, the CJ, Punjab and Haryana High Court, and Fali S. Nariman, distinguished jurist and senior advocate. However, Justice Jain resigned subsequently and Justice B. Sudarshan Reddy, judge, Supreme Court, was nominated in his place on 25 June 2009. The committee was again reconstituted on 16 December 2009 due to the elevation of Justice Thakur to the Supreme Court, and he was replaced by Justice Mukul Mudgal,

[194] www.hindu.com.

then CJ, of the same high court. The committee unanimously arrived at the conclusion that the allegations were true.[195]

The motion for removal of Justice Soumitra Sen finally came up before Rajya Sabha on 17 August 2011 and Sen defended himself. He trained his guns on former CJI K.G. Balakrishnan over charges of misappropriation of funds and misconduct alleging that it was his pre-determined move to hold him guilty. In his defence lasting nearly two hours in the Upper House which converted into a court for the first time, Justice Sen said, 'I have exhausted my remedies in accordance with the law. I have come here to seek justice. If you impeach me, it will be gravest injustice done ever. Kindly apply your mind before deciding on the judgment, as it is a question of my life.'[196] He further said that a division bench of the Calcutta High Court had exonerated him. Sen tried to play the victim card, equating his impeachment with the 1894 trial of Captain Alfred Dreyfus in France for selling military secrets to Germany. It was Emile Zola who later raised the issue of unfair trial of Dreyfus and called it an exercise in 'anti-Semitism'. But Yechury rightly reminded Sen that it was an era in France when the process of separation of Church from the State was going on and could hardly be equated with his misappropriation case. The House heard him with rapt attention. The author was listening to the debate from the press gallery. Arun Jaitley, leader of the Opposition, tore into his argument saying that the judgment of the division bench was obtained on the basis of some concession. There was pin drop silence in the House. Finally, on 18 August 2011, Rajya Sabha passed the motion for his removal with an overwhelming majority of 189 votes in favour and 17 against.[197] Before the motion could be taken up in Lok Sabha, Justice Sen resigned on 1 September.

After the letter written by CJI Balakrishnan against Justice Soumitra Sen became public, J.S. Verma, who held the office of the CJI from March 1997 to January 1998, revealed that he had also recommended action against a high court judge when he was in office, but the government turned a deaf ear.[198] He said that the recommendation was sent after a proper inquiry in

---

[195] http://rajyasabha.nic.in/rsnew/Soumitra_Sen_Judge.pdf (last accessed on 25 May 2013).

[196] http://www.rediff.com/news/slide-show/slide-show-1-justice-soumitra-sen-impeachment-rajya-sabha/20110817.htm (last accessed on 4 August 2013).

[197] *Times of India, The Hindu, Indian Express, Dainik Hindustan, Dainik Jagran, Jansatta*, 19 August 2011.

[198] 'I Wanted Action Against a Judge but PMO Sat on It: CJI Can't Do More Than This. Executive should have Acted. - J.S. Verma, Former Chief Justice of India', *Mail Today*, 9 September 2008.

which the judge was given a chance to defend himself. However, the government did not act.

Other Attempts at Impeachment

Even before the Parliament could decide on Sen's impeachment, 75 opposition MPs served a notice to the Chairman of the Rajya Sabha to move a motion to impeach the chief justice of the Karnataka High Court, P.D. Dinakaran.[199] The Congress again kept itself aloof. Justice Dinakaran was in the eye of storm after his name was recommended for elevation to the Supreme Court by its collegium. The Forum for Judicial Accountability charged him with acquiring 700 acres of land which far exceeds Tamil Nadu's land ceiling law. In fact, he was accused of encroaching on public land. Besides, there were also various allegations of corruption against him. The Forum sent a letter to the CJI detailing the charges against Justice Dinakaran. Eminent jurists including Fali S. Nariman, Ram Jethmalani, Shanti Bhushan, and Anil Divan had, in the letter, urged the CJI 'not to appoint' Justice Dinakaran as a Judge of the Supreme Court, to 'initiate a thorough enquiry into all the allegations' against him and 'take appropriate action thereafter'.[200] They even wrote to Prime Minister Manmohan Singh and President Pratibha Patil, seeking intervention and calling for a probe into the allegations before notifying the appointment of Justice Dinakaran to the Supreme Court. The Collector of Tiruvallur corroborated the allegations against him.

Significantly, on 16 December 2009, the Karnataka High Court registrar general issued a notification that the CJ would not be presiding over judicial work till further notice.[201] Immediately thereafter, Justice D.V. Shylendra Kumar of the Karnataka High Court questioned the continuance of Justice Dinakaran as the administrative head of the Court despite withdrawing from judicial duties following the initiation of the impeachment process.[202]

However, the matter got embroiled in politics even before reaching a logical conclusion. Several Dalit MPs rallied behind Dinakaran and criticized the

[199] 'V-P Accepts Impeachment Notice, Justice Dinakaran Says won't Quit', *Indian Express*, 13 December 2009.

[200] 'Leave Me out of Australia Trip: Justice Dinakaran, at the Centre of Row, Tells CJI', *Indian Express*, 17 September 2009.

[201] 'Dinakaran Not to Hold Court Till Further Notice', *Times of India*, 18 December 2009.

[202] 'HC Judge: Dinakaran Should Keep Off All Work', *Indian Express*, 20 December 2009.

move as anti-Dalit.[203] UP Chief Minister Mayawati also wrote to the prime minister that the principle of natural justice was not observed in Dinakaran's case, and that he should be given adequate opportunity to present his side.[204] Ultimately, after much acrimony and controversy, Dinakaran was transferred to the Sikkim High Court. In a unique development, the Karnataka High Court went to the Supreme Court against one of its own judges, D.V. Shylendra Kumar, who denounced Dinakaran on his blog, and the apex court reprimanded Justice Kumar admonishing him to remain silent.[205]

Justice Dinakaran was subsequently transferred to the Sikkim High Court. Before the motion for his removal could be taken up in Rajya Sabha, he resigned on 29 July 2011. In his resignation letter addressed to the president, he wrote that he was being targeted because he happened to be a Dalit:

> I have a sinking suspicion that my misfortune was because of my circumstances of my birth in the socially oppressed and under privileged society. Integrity of members of these communities who attain high office is always baselessly questioned through innuendo, smearing and spreading of false rumours while the privileged are treated by the vested interests as embodiment of all virtues.
>
> In order to maintain the dignity of my office and to prove that I do not have any lust for the office, position and power, I do not want to adopt any dilatory tactics. I am submitting my resignations.[206]

On 30 January 2018, CJI Dipak Misra wrote to president and the prime minister for the impeachment of Justice S.N. Shukla of the Allahabad High Court, who was accused of misconduct in the medical admissions scam. The move came following adverse remarks from an in-house committee headed by the Madras High Court Chief Justice Indira Banerjee, set up by the CJI that examined his role. Justice Shukla was advised to step down but he declined. Chief Justice D.B. Bhosale of the Allahabad High Court withdrew judicial work from him from 23 January 2018. CJI Misra had expressed 'shock' at an

---

[203] 'Cong MPs See Dalit Angle, Rally behind Dinakaran', *Indian Express*, 19 December 2009, 'MPs: Dinakaran being Hounded for being a Dalit', *Times of India*, 19 February 2009.

[204] 'Dinakaran ke bahane Dalit Rajniti', *Dainik Jagaran*, 20 December 2009.

[205] 'HC Goes to SC against Own "Blogger Judge" for "Berating" Dinakran', *Indian Express*, 15 June 2010.

[206] http://www.thehindu.com/news/national/justice-dinakaran-resigns/article2305932.ece.

order passed by a division bench led by Justice Shukla on 1 September 2017, allowing the Lucknow-based G.C.R.G. Memorial Trust in defiance of a 'graphically clear' restraining direction from the Supreme Court on August 28 to stop admissions for the academic session 2017–18.[207] The Supreme Court noted with dismay how Justice Shukla, on 4 September, even made some corrections to the 1 September order by hand. On 23 November, CJI Misra, in a 14-page judgment, held that the division bench, led by Justice Shukla, had abandoned 'the concept of judicial propriety' and transgressed judicial rules to 'proceed on a path where it was not required to'. The CJI noted that such transgressions caused 'institutional problems'. The CJI constituted the in-house committee shortly after this judgment on 8 December.[208]

Justice Shukla was also presiding over a division bench that passed an order on 25 August 2017 in the case of another banned medical college of the Lucknow-based Prasad Education Trust, which led to a scandal and the CJI had to intervene and reverse it. In an interim order, Justice Shukla restrained the Medical Council of India from de-listing the Prasad Education Trust's medical college. The CBI has mentioned this order in its FIR that alleges a criminal conspiracy hatched by officials of the Prasad Education Trust along with several persons, including I.M. Quddusi, retired judge of the Orissa High Court, to lift the ban on the college from admitting students for the couple of years.

First Impeachment Motion against the CJI

An impeachment motion was brought against the CJI, Justice Dipak Misra, on 20 April 2018 by seven Opposition parties led by Congress. It was for the first time that a motion was brought for the removal of the CJI. A petition signed by 64 MPs—total 71 signatures but seven had retired—was submitted to M. Venkaiah Naidu, chairman of Rajya Sabha.[209] Though Justice Misra was under cloud, the allegations were tentative which contained surmises couched in innuendos like 'may have been', 'likely to fall', 'appears to have', far from being 'proved misbehaviour' as required by the Constitution for the removal of a judge of the higher judiciary. The first charge in the removal

[207] http://www.thehindu.com/news/national/allahabad-high-court-judge-shukla-to-be-impeached/article22598457.ece (last accessed on 29 March 2018).

[208] http://www.thehindu.com/news/national/allahabad-high-court-judge-shukla-to-be-impeached/article22598457.ece (last accessed on 29 March 2018).

[209] 'In a First, Seven Parties Submit Motion to Remove CJI to V-P', *Times of India*, 21 April 2018.

motion pertained to alleged medical admission scam in Prasad Education Trust case which said that prima facie evidence suggested that 'CJI Misra may have been involved in the conspiracy of paying illegal gratification in the case.[210] The second charge pointed out that the CJI dealt with the case in which 'he too was likely to fall within the scope of investigation', both on administrative as well as judicial side, thus attracting 'the first principle of the code of conduct for judges'.[211] It further alleged (third charge) that Justice Misra 'appears to have' antedated an administrative order dated 6 November 2017, which amounted to a serious act of forgery/fabrication. The fourth charge referred to a four-decade-old land deal in which Misra, then a lawyer, had allegedly given a false affidavit to acquire land which was cancelled by the local additional district magistrate but Justice Misra surrendered the land after being elevated to the apex court. The fifth charge reiterated the allegations levelled by four most senior judges in their presser on 12 January 2018, as discussed in detail earlier, that he abused his administrative authority to assign 'important politically sensitive cases to select benches in order to achieve pre-determined outcome'.[212]

The motion divided the Congress as former Prime Minister Manmohan Singh, former Home Minister P. Chidambaram, and former Law Minister Ashwini Kumar and Salman Khurshid opposed it and Singh and Kumar as PMs did not sign the petition. Khurshid said, 'Removal is too serious a matter to be played with frivolously on the grounds of disagreement with any judgment or with any point of view of the court.'[213] It was not only the first removal motion against any CJI, but it was for the first time that it was brought on the ground of political bias in favour of the ruling party mortgaging the independence of the judiciary. The fourth allegation of buying land through a false affidavit raises questions about the efficiency of the Congress government as he was elevated as a high court judge in January 1996 when P.V. Narsimha Rao was the prime minister, and again elevated to the Supreme Court in October 2011 during the UPA Government headed by Manmohan Singh. How was his misdemeanour glossed over? It is clear from day one when one is appointed to apex court whether s/he would become CJI unless there is supersession. This is kept in mind while elevating someone to the Supreme Court.

It is clear that the Opposition led by the Congress wanted to gain political dividends by traducing the CJI and thus arranging the government as

[210] 'Chief Justice in Eye of Political Storm', *Times of India*, 21 April 2018.

[211] 'Chief Justice in Eye of Political Storm'.

[212] 'Chief Justice in Eye of Political Storm'.

[213] 'Chief Justice in Eye of Political Storm'.

it was a non-starter from the beginning. It lacked the number and it also knew full well that petition was likely to be rejected as it had threatened to move the Supreme Court in case of rejection. Besides, the cumbersome process could not have been complete before 2 October 2018, when Justice Misra was to retire. Chairman M. Venkaiah Naidu rejected the motion. The Opposition cried foul that the chairman usurped the judicial role of the inquiry committee in appreciating evidence. Section 3(I)(b) of Judges (Inquiry) Act, 1968, reads:

[I]n the case of a notice given in the Council of States, by not less than fifty members of that Council; then, the Speaker or, as the case may be, the Chairman may, after consulting such persons, if any, as he thinks fit and after considering such materials, if any, as may be available to him, either admit the motion or admit the same.

So, the discretion of the presiding officer cannot be questioned, though every discretion is to be used judiciously. Earlier, G.S. Dhillon, then Speaker, Lok Sabha, rejected such a motion which was brought against Justice J.C. Shah in May 1970. It has been discussed above. The petition was submitted following a campaign by O.P. Gupta, a former official, charging Shah with dishonesty after the judge censured him orally during a hearing. The notice was, however, turned down by the Speaker after stating it as 'frivolous'.[214] The discretion was given to the presiding officer after due deliberation. When the Judges (Inquiry) Bill was introduced in 1964, it was referred to a Joint Committee of the Parliament. Then attorney general for India, C.K. Daphtary, eminent lawyers, M.C. Setalvad, L.M. Singhvi, and N.C. Chatterjee, Gopal Swarup Pathak, a former high court judge who became vice-president India later on, Prakash Narain Sapru, a former high court judge, and K.K. Shah and M.N. Kaul, former secretary-general, Lok Sabha, appeared before the Committee. Kaul was very categorical that the Speaker/Chairman must be conferred power to examine whether any prima facie case is made out. He cited an example that eminent scientist Meghnath Saha had lodged a complaint against a judge which was the first case of this kind after the enforcement of the Constitution. According to Kaul, Speaker G. Mavalankar told the complainant, 'Look here ... it is my duty as Speaker,

[214] http://www.newindianexpress.com/nation/2018/apr/24/rejection-of-impeachment-notice-against-cji-had-precedent-five-decades-ago-1805494.html (last accessed on 26 May 2018).

to satisfy myself ... initially it is my power and responsibility to admit it or not to admit it. I think I should view it with an extremely critical eye; that is to say if I have no recourse left, then in those circumstances alone I will place this on the order paper.'[215] Kaul added that the prime minister, the home minister, and the CJI supported Mavalanakar.

As the Congress had already announced, some two Congress MPs, Pratap Singh Bajwa and Amee Harshaday Yajnik, challenged the chairman's decision in the Supreme Court. However, on 8 May 2018, it was 'dismissed as withdrawn' by a five-judge Constitution Bench after petitioners' counsel Kapil Sibal said he was withdrawing the petition as the Constitution Bench refused to provide the petitioners details of the administrative order by which the bench was constituted. Sibal argued that the CJI did not have the power to constitute the Constitution Bench by an administrative order nor could the Registrar place it directly before the Constitution Bench.[216]

Make the Process Simpler

Thus, it is clear that it is not only a failure of the judiciary in self-regulation, but the executive and the legislature have also failed miserably. Therefore, some other less cumbersome mechanism is needed. The Supreme Court can help by its judicial order. For example, it can rule that further inquiry by the Parliament is not required once it has been conducted by the Supreme Court's in-house committee and the judge is found guilty. After all, in the Second Judges' case,[217] it did lay down that the collegium of the Supreme Court would have the final say in the appointment of judges, though there is no such provision in the Constitution. Further, judges against whom impeachment proceedings have been initiated should not be allowed to resign. The resignation of a government servant is not accepted without vigilance clearance. The same yardstick, if not a more stringent standard, should be applied to the holder of a constitutional position, especially judges who are virtually immune from any accountability.

[215] A. Surya Prakash, 'Impeachment: The Chairman was Right, *The Pioneer*, 8 May 2018, http://www.dailypioneer.com/columnists/edit/impeachment-the-chairman-was-right.html (last accessed on 26 may 2018).

[216] https://www.financialexpress.com/india-news/cji-impeachment-congress-withdraws-plea-challenging-vennkaiah-naidus-decision-lawyers-question-sc-decision-on-bench/1159355/ (last accessed on 27 May 2018).

[217] *Supreme Court Advocates-on-Record Association* v. *Union of India* (1993) 4 SCC 187.

Instances of Judges' Corruption

Instances of judges' corruption are not few and far between. There have been cases when judges themselves have levelled serious allegations against brother judges. In 1990, Justice Kenia of the Bombay High Court had to withdraw from the division bench that was hearing the case, *Mehta* v. *Mehta*.[218] The other judge on the bench was Justice S.K. Desai. Kenia disclosed that he received threats from Thelma Menezes, a close friend of Justice Desai. It was also a matter of record that Desai had taken keen interest in her personal litigation pending in the civil court. She also visited Raj Bhavan frequently when Desai was the acting governor of Maharashtra. Kenia even sat on fast in protest against this. There was vociferous protest from lawyers. Then Desai was transferred to the Kerala High Court and he put in his papers.[219] Later, in an interview, Desai condemned the system whereby he was censured without being heard, but he admitted to his friendship with Thelma.[220] Ironically, a few months after this controversy, Kenia himself came under a cloud with reports of Rs 1.5 lakh found in the toilet attached to his chamber. The city Bar Association passed a no-confidence motion against him and three other judges, Sharad Manohar, V.S. Kotwal, and Guttal, JJ.

In 1995, charges of corruption rocked the same High Court again and Justice Vijay Bahuguna had to resign in the face of grave charges against him (later, he became an MP, and in 2012, chief minister of Uttarakhand). Sometime later, Chief Justice, A.M. Bhattacharjee was forced to quit following an admission that he accepted US$80,000 as royalty for the overseas publication of his book *Muslim Law in India*. Lawyers alleged that the money paid was not by way of royalty but was a cover for illegal considerations and passed a resolution of no confidence against him.[221]

After the turn of the millennium, cases of ignoble conduct by judges swelled. The year 2002 proved to be a year of calumny for the higher judiciary. Three judges of the Karnataka High Court were caught with women lawyers, but not even an FIR was lodged. A Committee of chief justices was set up to

---

[218] M.A. Rane, 'The Judiciary—A Crisis of Credibility', in *Good Times, Bad Times, Sad Times: Selected Writings of M. A. Rane*, published by M.A. Rane 75th Birthday Felicitation Committee, Mumbai, 2001, p. 111.

[219] M.A. Rane, 'The Judiciary: A Crisis of Credibility', *The Radical Humanist*, August 1990. *Selected Writings of M. A. Rane*, published by M.A. Rane 75th Birthday felicitation Committee, Mumbai, 2001, pp. 111–12.

[220] *The Illustrated Weekly of India*, 24–30 June 1990.

[221] *C. Ravichandran Iyer* v. *Justice A.M. Bhattacharjee* (1995) 5 SCC 457.

probe the matter but ironically the Karnataka High Court also started hearing a parallel contempt petition against the newspapers and the journalists who reported this. Surprisingly, the Committee cleared the tainted judges, but its report was never brought into the public domain. The Supreme Court rejected the petition to make it public.[222] Is it conceivable that anyone would dare to depose before the Committee and tell the truth?

Similarly, Justice Arun Madan of the Rajasthan High Court was charged with promising to give a favourable judgement to a lady litigant if she obliged him sexually. The charge against Justice Madan was found to be *prima facie* true but no action was taken initially on the grounds that the committee had discovered other serious charges against him in the course of the inquiry. One charge was that he marked a case in which he wanted to favour one of the parties as 'part-heard', though it was not so. It was said that action would be taken when the inquiry was complete and till then the tainted judge would discharge his duties. Ultimately, Madan resigned when the Committee found the allegations true. But is this sufficient? Madan continued to function as a judge even after it became evident that he was a moral wreck. After resigning, he started practicing in the Supreme Court. Interestingly, before becoming a judge of the high court, Madan was caught stating that he had to tender a written apology. Another judge of the same high court was transferred as he allegedly sexually molested a male constable.[223] A Kerala High Court judge reportedly assaulted a young motorcyclist for not allowing his car to overtake him on a busy road in Kochi.[224]

In the same year, three judges of the Punjab and Haryana High Court were at the centre of a controversy surrounding the Punjab Public Service Commission (PPSC) scandal. Agents of the PPSC chairman alleged that these judges had pulled strings to get their kin selected in the examinations conducted by the Commission.[225] The then chief justice of the High Court, Arun B. Saharya, in his inquiry, found clinching evidence establishing the complicity of the three judges in the scam. He withdrew work from them but a few hours before retiring he restored the work, as he could do nothing more. He sent his report to then CJI B.N. Kirpal, who conveniently sat on the file

[222] *Indira Jaising* v. *Registrar, the Supreme Court* (2003) 4 SCALE 643.
[223] *Outlook*, 25 November 2002. Godbole, *The Judiciary and Governance in India*, p. 555.
[224] *Times of India*, 5 December 2002. Godbole, *The Judiciary and Governance in India*, p. 555.
[225] See Bipin Pubby, 'Judges above All', *The Indian Express*, 17 July 2002.

and retired without taking any action. Later, they were virtually absolved with only a rap on the wrist. One judge was spared because he was to retire shortly. Another was transferred with a minor stricture and the third said that he would not resume his duties and would be on leave till retirement, and so no action was deemed necessary. One wonders why politicians, officials, and others have to face trial even after they relinquish their offices. An Hon'ble judge of a high court, held his court on the railway platform and threated the station master to haul up for contempt asking him to explain why a coupe in the air-conditioned first class had not been reserved for him.[226] It is a question mark on the judicial process that such people can be appointed judges of the high court.

The credibility of the judiciary took another body blow when *Indian Express*, in a series of reports published from 2 August 2002, exposed the petrol pump scam showing how members of the ruling party at the Centre and their friends and relatives were allotted a large number of petrol pumps and gas agencies. It not only discredited the government, but also retired judges of high courts and district courts, who as chairmen of dealer selection boards, carried out the diktat of the Petroleum minister.[227]

In 2004, judges of the Punjab and Haryana High Court yet again made national news when the then chief justice of the High Court, Justice B.K. Rai, sought explanation from them as to how they accept membership of an expensive club offered to them free of cost. It was during the hearing of a PIL, in the infamous *Forest Hill Golf and Country Club* case, that the club management informed the court that it had given honorary membership to two judges—Justice Varinder Singh and Justice Viney Mittal. When Justice Roy issued notices to them, it united all the other judges against him and led to an unprecedented strike on 19 April 2004.[228] And when he indicted the judiciary severely in his hard-hitting judgement, it antagonized his fellow judges further. Actually, these judges were nursing a grouse against Justice Roy, as he had issued an administrative order earlier barring the kin of judges to appear before them. His directive identified 12 judges whose relatives were advocates and forbade them from appearing before any of these 12. This ensured that a judge could not help even a

[226] Chaudhary, *The Ivory Towers*, p. 205. Godbole, *The Judiciary and Governance in India*, p. 554.

[227] See Manoj Mitta, 'Judges Face a Credibility Crisis', *Indian Express*, 8 August 2002.

[228] See Manoj Mitta, 'Roll-Back of Judicial Code?', *Indian Express*, 24 June 2004.

fellow judge's kin. The two sides traded charges of 'bias and mala fides' in their correspondence preceding the strike.[229] Then CJI, V.N. Khare admitted that the strike by judges of the High Court had dented the image of the higher judiciary. However, when Justice R.C. Lahoti took over as the CJI, he declared that no action would be taken against the 25 Judges of the Punjab and Haryana High Court who went on strike. Surprisingly it was Justice Roy who was moved out to Guwahati and then to Sikkim. Justice Lahoti publicly excoriated Justice Roy, 'I have an X-ray-like view of the case pertaining to Justice Roy. He pinpricks his colleague judges and paints them black in his attempt to emerge hero (sic).'[230] This statement is a clear example of contempt of court by a sitting CJI as it shakes people's faith in the chief justice of a high court.

Justice Shamit Mukherjee of the Delhi Court had to quit after his involvement in the Delhi Development Authority scam became public. He was forced to resign by the then CJI, V.N. Khare. Justice Khare was approached by the Union home secretary and the CBI director late one evening with clinching evidence and tapes of Justice Mukherjee's misconduct, and requested his permission to arrest him. Justice Khare sought some time and called Justice Mukherjee the next morning, asking him to resign. He not only refused to do so, but also gave a veiled intimidation that he could get anyone impeached as he enjoyed considerable political influence and connections. He resigned only when Justice Khare told him outright that he had got foolproof evidence of his corruption and would sanction his arrest.[231] Justice Mukherjee resigned, but withdrew his resignation within three hours, realizing that with his resignation he would lose his immunity. However, by then it had already been accepted. Investigations have revealed that wine and women were supplied to him.

Justice J.A. Sethna of the Gujarat High Court beat up Justice P.B. Majumdar of the same court. Sethna alleged that Majumdar was favouring his son and other friends while Majumdar made other serious allegations against him.[232] Either both of them were correct or at least one of them must be correct but no action was taken against either, except that Sethna was transferred to Sikkim, upon which he resigned. He dared the CJI to take action against him and threatened to expose him.

[229] Mitta, 'Roll-Back of Judicial Code?'.
[230] See A.G. Noorani, 'Order, Order', *Hindustan Times*, 6 December 2005.
[231] As told by V.N. Khare to the author.
[232] *Hindustan Times*, 12 January 2007.

In another case, a large amount of money was recovered from a judge's house, but the judge comfortably explained that his wife ran a dairy business. Over the years she had accumulated the cash, and did not put it into a bank.

Even the conduct of the judges of the Supreme Court, including a few chief justices, has marred the reputation of the judiciary. In 1997, the Committee on Judicial Accountability led by former justices such as Tarkunde and Tewatia and noted lawyers like Shanti Bhushan and Anil Divan exposed the judicial misdemeanours of a sitting Supreme Court Judge, Justice M.M. Punchhi. The Committee found him guilty of seven charges, some of which were quite serious. He gave relief to Kashinath Tapuria (son-in-law of Haridas Mundhra, notorious for the Mundhra scandal in the 1950s, which cost T.T. Krishnamachari's job as the union finance minister), illegally without a full hearing. His two daughters, then unmarried, were allotted two plots of land from the discretionary quota of the chief minister of Haryana. This was on the same day that he passed an order on an appeal against a judgement of the high court in a case where the vice-chancellor of a university in Rohtak was allegedly suspended at the instance of the chief minister. When he was high court judge, Justice Punchhi allegedly had an adverse remark recorded against a sub-judge by his immediate superior, because the judge had shown the courage to decide a case against Kulwant Rai, the husband of Mrs Punchhi's sister. The case was decided in 1981 but the adverse comments were recorded much later, when Justice Punchhi became the inspecting judge. Curiously, the sub-judge was condemned without being heard.

While on the Constitution Bench of the Supreme Court, which was hearing the writ petition challenging the inquiry committee constituted to probe Justice Ramaswami's conduct, he was present at the house of the accused judge. He tried to assist him while the list of properties owned by the judge was being checked. Further, Justice Punchhi also tried to frighten the court officers to ensure that a specific comment was interpolated. He had to withdraw from the bench after his nefarious role came to light. He had reportedly insisted on being appointed to the bench. There were several other charges as well.[233] The Committee sent its representation to the CJI but no cognizance was taken, and Punchhi himself later became the CJI.

Serious allegations of corruption were levelled against A.S. Anand, former CJI. The charges pertain to the period when he was a judge and later chief justice of the Jammu and Kashmir High Court. Some of these allegations

[233] C.R. Irani, 'My Lord, Let Right Be Seen to Be Done!', *The Statesman*, 29 September 1997.

are that he passed orders to favour the person who gave an expensive plot of land to his daughter, Shabnam Anand, at a throw-away price; filed a false affidavit before the government of Jammu and Kashmir that he did not own any house or land in the state and received land at a concessional rate from the state government; and passed several illegal orders to benefit his family.[234] Allegations of favouritism were levelled against Y.K. Sabharwal, former CJI, that he delivered several orders as the CJI on the sealing operations in Delhi against the principle of natural justice. As commercial shops were sealed, prices of shops in malls rose exponentially which benefited his sons who had investments in some malls. In an unprecedented move, Sabharwal wrote an apologia running into over half a page in *Times of India*. He wrote, 'Allotments made in 1999 and 2000 are being used at this stage after his retirement to impute motives for judgements and orders of sealing passed in 2006. The plot allotted in 2006 is not a commercial plot as insinuated. It is an industrial plot allotted in view of my sons' growth in export business as per the scheme. The allotment has no link, direct or indirect, with orders regarding sealing of properties in Delhi'.[235]

On 15 March 2005, Justice S.N. Variava grimaced with disgust and shouted in the court that there was pressure on him from the Patna High Court regarding a change of the special judge, CBI, Patna, hearing the disproportionate assets (DA) case against Lalu Prasad, former chief minister. Variava headed a division bench that was hearing an appeal against the constitution of a division bench of the Patna High Court by the Supreme Court, set up to decide a particular aspect of the DA case which also involved a change of the trial judge. But instead of initiating contempt proceedings against the concerned person the very next day, he recanted saying that it was an academic query. It is alleged that as consideration for recantation a close friend of his was appointed additional solicitor-general, and for this the advocate concerned was designated senior overnight by the Patna High Court where he rarely appeared.

On 16 March 2007, Justice A.R. Lakshmanan of the Supreme Court broke down in the open court before a scheduled hearing of a petition filed by Akhilesh Yadav, MP and son of the then UP Chief Minister Mulayam Singh Yadav, seeking a review of the Court's order of 1 March directing a CBI probe into their alleged DA. Justice Lakshmanan declined to hear the

[234] Allegations against Justice A.S. Anand, www.judicial reforms.org.
[235] 'A Former Chief Justice of India Defends His Honour', *The Sunday, Times of India*, 2 July 2007.

matter after dropping a bombshell that he had received an anonymous letter in the morning. He did not divulge its contents except saying, 'The contents are heinous.'[236] Senior counsel, including Soli J. Sorabjee, former attorney-general, present at Court urged him not to recuse himself from the case as it would amount to putting a premium on the letter. But Justice Lakshmanan did not relent. The letter was received at his residence by fax which did not contain the number from where it was sent. It reportedly threatened to expose him if any relief was given to Yadav, and also levelled several allegations against him. The case was sensitive since any order was likely to affect Yadav's political prospects as UP was in the midst of Legislative Assembly elections. It is not difficult to understand that no ordinary person can dare to write such a letter to a Supreme Court judge and send it by fax, when the number can be discovered easily. The whole matter needed to be investigated, but surprisingly it was Lakshmanan who backed out of any probe the very next day, 'I don't want any probe. I don't want to comment on yesterday's incident…. The chapter is closed once and for all.'[237] Now it is anyone's guess as to why a person against whom serious accusations have been made should oppose a probe. It is understandable if the person levelling the charges does so. Anyway, irrespective of what the judge desired, the government or an in-house committee of the Supreme Court should have investigated it thoroughly.

A former Judge of the Supreme Court, S.N. Phukan, used an Indian Air Force aircraft while he was the head of a commission of inquiry constituted to inquire into the Tehelka scam, though he was not entitled to this. The *Outlook* magazine of 9 May 2005 exposed this, and on 4 May 2005 Defence Minister, Pranab Mukherjee, told the Rajya Sabha that the former Defence Minister, George Fernandes, approved the use of the aircraft in December 2003. He stated that Phukan also visited Ajanta and Ellora in Maharashtra on 25 December 2003 during his official visits to the state, but it was not known who actually paid for the trips to these two places. He added, 'Normally, for a visit of a commission (of inquiry), IAF aircraft are not provided.'[238] I have personal knowledge that many judges of the Supreme Court and chief justices of high courts use chartered planes, provided by industrialists, for their personal travels; more often than not, cases of such industrialists are pending before these courts.

[236] *The Hindu*, 17 March 2007.
[237] *The Hindu*, 18 March 2007.
[238] *Asian Age*, 5 May 2005.

It is equally disturbing to know that in the name of 'better relations and good will with the Supreme Court', Mahanagar Telephone Nigam Limited (MTNL), in 2002, gave cell phones with all the facilities to the CJI and other judges of the apex court. The judges not only accepted them, but also demanded extra phones for their registrars. What is more appalling is that the allurements were sought to be justified by the registrar-general, 'Private companies are also after us with discounts. We have opted for a government company'. The fact that the MTNL was a party in a case pending before the Court is irrelevant, 'What conflict of interest? The government is giving us funds in the form of our salaries. That does not mean we cannot hear any cases against the government.'

What an unmistakable sense of justice—a salary, which is given to discharge a particular duty, has been equated with allurements, which are never offered without a consideration! People with a logical bent of mind can always adduce several arguments to justify wrongs. But such arguments debunk more and protect less. Will the logical culmination of this position not be that accepting bribes from a party does not amount to corruption if the judgement is legally sound and not influenced by pecuniary gratification? However, the Supreme Court decided to pay for the phones after the commotion created by the media.

A sensational cash-at-judge-door scam was another ignominious chapter in the history of the higher judiciary. A bribe of Rs 15 lakhs was delivered at the residence of Justice Nirmaljit Kaur of the Punjab and Haryana High Court in Chandigarh on 13 August 2008, though it was allegedly meant for her namesake, Justice Nirmal Yadav. As soon as Justice Kaur found the money in a sack, she informed the High Court chief justice and the police registered an FIR against three people.[239] The money was delivered by Prakash Raj, clerk of Sanjeev Bansal, then additional advocate general of Haryana. Bansal was allegedly paid a huge amount by one Ravinder Singh, a Delhi-based businessman, to settle a criminal case pending in the High Court. Reportedly, it was a case of mistaken delivery. The CJI constituted an in-house three-judge committee to probe the case.

S.F. Rodrigues, the governor of Punjab, who was also Chandigarh's administrator general, recommended a CBI probe into the scam after consultations with the then High Court Chief Justice, Tirath Singh Thakur. The CJI allowed the CBI to question the two judges. The in-house committee comprising Justice H.L. Gokhale, then chief justice of the Allahabad High

---

[239] *Times of India*, 18 August 2008.

Court, Justice K.S. Radhakrishnan, chief justice of the Gujarat High Court and subsequently elevated to the Supreme Court, and Justice Madan Lokur of the Delhi High Court, concluded in December 2008 that the cash payment made at Justice Kaur's door was actually meant for Justice Yadav.

The controversy got murkier as Justice Yadav, in a letter to then CJI, K.G. Balakrishnan, cast personal aspersions against the other judge under suspicion. After receiving notice from the CJI, Justice Yadav replied that Justice Kaur was given a clean chit as she was close to a Supreme Court judge who was present in her house when the cash was delivered at her doorstep. She even alleged that the Supreme Court judge had an illicit relationship with Justice Kaur which was the reason the Supreme Court probe committee absolved her. 'The almost two-decade old liaison between the Judge of the Supreme Court and the Judge at whose residence cash was delivered, has been talk of the town for all these years. It is on this ground that the SC Judge's wife sought divorce,' said the letter. She added, 'The committee itself records that a Judge of the SC and a senior Judge of the High Court may have been present in the house at the time of delivery of the cash.'[240] According to Yadav, the committee's finding on the presence of two other judges on the spot was borne out by call records from their mobile phones. Following the cash delivery, the Supreme Court judge's son, for instance, made five calls to lawyer Sanjeev Bansal, who is alleged to have sent the money at the instance of the businessman Ravinder Singh.

In her second reply to the CJI dated 27 January 2009, she refused to depose before the committee, 'I have a right to reject the report as the same has been conducted in a lopsided manner. Unless an enquiry is ordered into all allegations against all judges concerned, I refuse to submit to such informal procedure … The proposal of in-house procedure was rejected by the Full Court of Punjab and Haryana High Court. Therefore, it does not have any binding force.'[241] She said that Prakash, who delivered the money, told the committee that he knew Kaur and it was not a mistaken delivery, but his statement was conveniently ignored.

Ultimately, after about 15 months, Justice Yadav was cleared by the Supreme Court collegium headed by CJI K.G. Balakrishnan.[242] The collegium

[240] 'Justice Yadav Casts Personal Aspersions on Fellow Judge', *Deccan Herald*, 13 January 2009.

[241] 'Justice Yadav Denies Involvement in Cash Delivered at Justice Kaur's Residence', *The Hindu*, 31 January 2009.

[242] 'Nirmal Yadav Gets a Clean Chit', *The Hindu*, 7 November 2009.

accepted the Union Law Ministry's report which said that no case was made out to prosecute her and there was 'insufficient evidence' of the involvement of the judge in the scam. The CBI sent its preliminary report to then Attorney General Milon Banerjee, who stated that there was insufficient evidence to initiate prosecution against Justice Yadav. The Law Ministry concurred with the attorney general's opinion. It dropped the move to prosecute her and conveyed this to the CJI. The CBI's volte face in the case to petition to the Court to close the case was based on the opinion of not just the law minister, Veerappa Moily, but also the CJI, K.G. Balakrishnan. Citing the discussion on the matter with Moily and Justice Balakrishnan, the CBI filed the closure report.[243] The decision to close the first-ever case of judicial graft involving a huge cash recovery flew in the face of the breakthroughs achieved by the Chandigarh police which originally investigated the case in August 2008 and Justice Yadav's indictment in December 2008 by the in-house committee appointed by the CJI himself.

The collegium then took the decision to transfer her to the Uttarakhand High Court. The question then arose: for whom was the cash meant. The judges committee exculpated Justice Kaur and no evidence was found against Justice Yadav. But Yadav herself levelled serious allegations against Kaur. Then was she guilty of perjury? Besides, why was Justice Yadav transferred if she was not guilty? Then all of a sudden, the new CJI, Justice S.H. Kapadia, reviewed the decision of his predecessor Justice Balakrishnan and okayed the prosecution of Justice Yadav, and President Pratibha Patil granted the sanction for her prosecution on 28 February 2011, the day she was to retire. Thus, she became the first judge of the higher judiciary against whom sanction of prosecution was granted. She challenged the sanction on the ground that Justice Kapadia had no power to review the decision of his predecessor, and sought the quashing of the proceedings against her, but the Supreme Court refused to entertain her plea saying that Justice Balakrishnan had not denied sanction but had only commented that no action was required at the moment. A bench of Justices H.L. Dattu and Dipak Misra said the matter should not linger in the top court anymore.[244] Earlier, two judges recused themselves from hearing her case. First, it was Justice Khehar who recused on 13 April 2012, and then Justice S.S. Nijjar bowed out of the hearing on 2 July 2012.[245]

[243] 'CBI Cites CJI to Close Graft Case', *Times of India*, 26 December 2009.

[244] 6 July 2013, http://starlive24.in/news/politics/cash-at-judge-door--sc-rejects-nirmal-yadav-plea-to-block-probe/26606.html (last accessed on 13 October 2018).

[245] 'Cash-at-Judge Door: SC Judge Recuses from Hearing Plea', *Indian Express*, 3 July 2012.

On 13 September 2013, the Punjab and Haryana High Court stayed the framing of charges against Yadav. Anupam Gupta, special public prosecutor for the CBI in the case, tore into the order in a written statement:

I am deeply distressed by the High Court's order passed today. It betrays an insensitivity to judicial corruption that cannot be viewed with equanimity. The High Court cannot have a dual approach or standard—one for judges and another for all other accused. Would the High Court have passed this order if the principal accused had not been a former High Court Judge?[246]

Speaking to *The Hindu*, he said:

Justice Sanghi failed to observe the elementary precaution and propriety of issuing notice to the CBI and hearing it before passing the September 13 order. By requisitioning the trial court's record, the Judge has, for all practical intents and purposes, disabled the Special Judge, CBI, from proceeding any further with Justice Nirmal Yadav's trial for a virtually indefinite period of time. Given the practice in the High Court and the volume of litigation before it, the prospect of Justice Yadav's petition being finally decided by the High Court within three months is far too remote to be believed. A cynic would not be wrong in assuming that, despite its gravity, the case has been put in the cold storage.[247]

However, the CBI court framed charges against her after the apex court, on 3 January 2014, dismissed her plea for a stay on proceedings of the trial court and pulled her up for adopting delaying tactics. Charges were framed under Section 11 of the Prevention of Corruption Act.[248]

Another scam that shook the foundations of judicial credibility was the Ghaziabad provident fund scam in which 36 judges, including one Supreme Court and 11 high court judges, were beneficiaries of a multi-crore scam. Money belonging to the employees of the Ghaziabad court was allegedly secreted by Ashutosh Asthana, the accountant. The scam broke out in 2008 and the Supreme Court ordered the CBI to investigate it and allowed it to

---

[246] *The Hindu*, 14 October 2013, http://www.thehindu.com/todays-paper/tp-opinion/getting-its-own-off-the-hook/article5232482.ece (last accessed on 6 January 2016).

[247] *The Hindu*, 14 October 2013, http://www.thehindu.com/todays-paper/tp-opinion/getting-its-own-off-the-hook/article5232482.ece (last accessed on 6 January 2016).

[248] http://www.news18.com/news/india/corruption-charges-framed-against-former-hc-judge-nirmal-yadav-662673.html (last accessed on 4 March 2017).

interrogate even its sitting judge, Justice Tarun Chatterjee. The scam acquired a hideous dimension when the main accused, Asthana, died under mysterious circumstances on 18 October 2009 in jail, amidst the suspicion that he was poisoned. Though his family cried foul, the police said the autopsy was inconclusive.[249]

It was alleged that a serving judge of the Allahabad High Court pressured Asthana to retract his confessional statement.[250] It is a curious tale of two affidavits that create suspicion. On 20 August 2009, Asthana filed an affidavit in the Ghaziabad special court saying that he was forced to include the name of the judge 'after he was tortured in police custody along with his wife and daughter. This judge had nothing to do with the scam and his rivals wanted the name to be included.'[251] However, hours within filing this affidavit, his lawyer filed another which read, 'I have been pressurized at various levels by some judges to withdraw their names, and in future also, if any document is filed in my name absolving any one from the scam, it should be checked with me.'[252]

His sudden death after this affidavit speaks volumes about the conspiracy and the pressure that was exerted on the poor employee. The situation became uglier when Attorney General, G.E. Vahanvati complained to the Supreme Court that the Ghaziabad judge dealing with the provident fund scam case was not cooperating and not even recording the statements of witnesses.[253]

Besides these, there are plenty of incidents of judicial corruption. In 2009, the Punjab vigilance department gave the High Court of the state a damning report about judicial malpractices such as fixing and organizing favourable hearings. Despite a very clear recommendation from the chief justice of the Punjab and Haryana High Court to transfer Justice Mehtab Singh Gill, one of the two judges mentioned, no action was taken.[254] On 13 November 2011, lawyer daughter of an ex-judge of the Bombay High Court, S.B. Mhase, was arrested by the anti-corruption wing of the CBI for allegedly demanding a

---

[249] 'Death of Ghaziabad PF Scam Accused: No Clues in Autopsy', *The Indian Express*, 19 October 2009.

[250] 'Was Asthana Being Pressured by an HC Judge?', *Hindustan Times*, 5 November 2009.

[251] 'Was Asthana Being Pressured by an HC Judge?'.

[252] 'Was Asthana Being Pressured by an HC Judge?'.

[253] 'Ghaziabad PF Scam: Judge Not Cooperating, Says Vahanvati', www.topnews.in/Ghaziabad-pf-scam (last accessed on 13 November 2009).

[254] 'Judiciary Opaque, Court Trouble: Punjab High Court Malpractices Are the Result of a Larger Trouble', *Hindustan Times*, 5 June 2009.

bribe of Rs 30 lakh from a complainant at the Maharashtra State Commission for consumer Disputes Redressal of which he was chairman.

There are also instances when courts have found judges guilty of using their judicial powers to benefit themselves. One such example is that of Justice B.P. Banerjee who stayed the allotment of land by the state government in Salt Lake, Kolkata ruling that no allotment would be made during the pendency of the case. He then applied for land and vacated the stay, whereupon, he was allotted a large plot on which he got constructed a palatial house. The Supreme Court cancelled his allotment and described it as erosion of the judicial system.[255]

In February 2017, the surfacing of a 60-page suicide note by former Arunachal Pradesh Chief Minister, Khaliko Pul jolted the nation. Pul made sensational allegations against many top notch politicians including the then Preisdent Pranab Mukherjee, and sitting and retired judges of the apex court including the then CJI J.S. Khehar and past CJIs H.L. Dattu and Altmas Kabir, and sitting judge Justice Dipak Misra of receiving huge gratification.[256] Pul was the chief minister of Arunachal Pradesh who was unseated because of the judgement of the Supreme Court which quashed the imposition of the President's Rule in Arunachal Pradesh. He committed suicide on 9 August 2016 and immediately thereafter his suicide note was discovered. The note typed in Hindi, bears his signature on all pages. In the note, he alleged how heavy amount was given to judges to get favourable judgments, and how he was approached by the son of the CJI Khehar for not declaring the President's Rule illegal in lieu of Rs 86 crore. He got an adverse judgement as he could/did not pay the money. He has also written that he lost his faith in the judiciary.

Pul's first wife Dangwimsai Pul wrote a letter to CJI J.S. Khehar demanding registration of FIR and probe into the allegations. The CJI converted her letter into a criminal writ petition and ordered grant of open court hearing.[257] Angered, she withdrew her petition before the Court was to hear it. Senior counsel Dushyant Dave, appearing for her, objected to the Court taking up the matter on the judicial side though it was filed on the administrative side and also opposed the listing of the issue before a bench

---

[255] *Tarak Singh and Others* v. *Jyoti Basu and Ors* (2005) 1 SCC 201.

[256] http://judicialreforms.org/wp-content/uploads/2017/02/pul-s-suicide-note.pdf (last accessed on 4 March 2017).

[257] 'CJI Orders Hearing of Plea by Pul's Wife on Note He Left before Suicide', *Indian Express*, 23 February 2017.

of Justices A.K. Goel and U.U. Lalit, saying that Justice Goel could never hear the matter as he was a colleague of the CJI in the Punjab and Haryana High Court.

The publication of the note with redacted names raises questions about the integrity of the polity as well as the independence and accountability of the judiciary. Allegations are quite specific. Later, Dangwimsai met Vice-President Hamid Ansari on 28 February seeking registration of an FIR and investigation into allegations of corruption against then CJI Khehar and sitting Supreme Court judge Dipak Misra who succeeded Justice Khehar as the CJI. She did not meet the president as his name also figured in it.

Even in an internationally publicized case like the Bhopal Gas Leakage disaster was allegedly fixed and the compensation awarded by the Supreme Court was a pittance. The Union Carbide Corporation wanted the case to be fought in India as the US court would have awarded an astronomical amount that would have been a death knell to the company. However, even in India, it wanted a settlement as it was aware of the judgment in *M.C. Mehta* v. *Union of India*[258] in which a Constitution Bench headed by Chief Justice P.N. Bhagwati laid down that the principle of absolute liability must be applied in cases of such accidents where the owners of the plant and suppliers of the technology are supposed to have the special knowledge of the design and the technology of the plant. B. Sen has written:

> In fact whilst hearing *M. C. Mehta's* case the Bench was quite conscious of the issues involved in the Bhopal Gas disaster case. So it came somewhat of a surprise when a Court assisted settlement was reached at a figure of $ 470 million which was no more than a flea bite (sic) where the Union Carboide was concerned. That amount was ordered to be paid to the Government without ensuring that whatever paltry sum the victims were likely to get was in fact given to them and not be frittered away in bureaucratic bungling. A few months later I was In Washington where, I happened to meet one of the lawyers of Union Carbide at the Cosmos Club. When I congratulated him on his victory, he smiled and said, 'We were fortunate to get a good fixer' and walked away without entering into any further conversation.[259]

In this context, it would be relevant to quote what Neelam and Sanjay Krishnamoorthy, who lost both children in the Uphar fire tragedy, which

---

[258] (1987) 1 SCR 819.

[259] B. Sen, 'The Supreme Court Revisited', in *Six Decades of Law, Politics and Diplomacy* (New Delhi: Universal Law Publishing Co., 2010), pp. 289–90.

claimed 59 lives in all, have written about how the Supreme Court was sought to be pressured when it was to pronounce its verdict:

[A] day before the judgment of our civil appeal was pronounced, that is on 12 October 2011, I received a telephone call from a journalist whose identity I am unable to share. He informed me that the judgment would be delivered the next day. He also informed me that while he had been in the court, a legal luminary appearing on behalf of Sushil Ansal (main accused) in the criminal appeal chose to be present in the courtroom of the presiding judge who had heard our civil appeal, and informed him that he should be careful in delivering the judgment in our case, as it would have major repercussions on other ongoing criminal appeals.[260]

It is appalling that a renowned advocate directly seeks to influence the Court and it is not taken as contempt.

In some cases, the courts have gone completely out of jurisdiction to benefit private parties. In one case, the Supreme Court was constrained to make swingeing indictment of the Allahabad High Court:

We are sorry to say but a lot of complaints are coming against certain Judges of the Allahabad High Court relating to their integrity. Some Judges have their kith and kin practising in the same Court, and within a few years of starting practice the sons or relations of the Judge become multi-millionaires, have huge bank balances, luxurious cars, huge houses and are enjoying a luxurious life. This is a far cry from the days when the sons and other relatives of judges could derive no benefit from their relationship and had to struggle to the bar like any other lawyer.[261]

The Court clearly remarked that something is rotten in the Allahabad High Court.

The facts of the case are that there is a *dargah* (shrine) called 'Dargah Hazrat Syed Salar Masood Ghazi R.A.' in the Bahraich district of UP. It is managed by a committee of management. The petitioner, a proprietor of circuses, claimed that he ran circuses and *jhoola* (swing) in fairs and other places of public gathering. He claimed that he held 'Jeth Mela' in the aforesaid dargah in the month of Jeth for a period of 40 days every year,

[260] Neelam and Sanjay Krishnamoorthy, *Trial By Fire* (Gurgaon: Penguin Random House India, 2016), p. 90.

[261] *Raja Khan* v. *UP Sunni Central Waqf Board and Anr.* (2011) 2 SCC 741, pp. 8–9.

and the *waqf*[262] had been allotting him land for it. However, in 2010, the waqf refused to allot him land. He filed writ petitions against it in the Lucknow bench of the Allahabad High Court twice which were dismissed. Then he filed a suit in district Hamirpur and when an objection was raised about territorial jurisdiction as the dargah is in Bahraich, he filed a writ petition in the Allahabad High Court, on which the single judge passed ex-parte interim orders directing the waqf to allot him land within three days. The district magistrate and the superintendent of Police were directed to pass appropriate order in the compliance of this order. The Supreme Court was shocked to see the order as the property in question is in Bahraich which falls within the territorial jurisdiction of the Lucknow bench and so the Allahabad bench had no jurisdiction to entertain it. Further, writ petition was not maintainable as it does not lie against a private party.

After all, what is their accountability—flout the law with impunity? There is an interesting conversation between Justice Learned Hand and his clerk:

> Sonny ... to whom am I responsible? No one can fire me. No one can dock my pay. Even those nine bozos [judges of the Supreme Court] in Washington, who sometimes reverse me, can't make me decide as they wish. Everyone should be responsible to someone. To whom am I responsible? Then the judge turned and pointed to the shelves of his library: 'To these books about us. That's to whom I am responsible.[263]

The Allahabad High Court moved the Supreme Court for expunging its vitriolic remark against it but the Court refused to do so.[264]

Ruma Paul, former judge of the Supreme Court, has very boldly pointed out seven sins of the judiciary:

> [J]udges have to be above corruption in the monetary sense. But it needs restating just as needed stating in 1988 when judges of 37 countries gathered in Bangalore and formulated what have come to be known as the Banglaore Principles ... Detailed guidelines have been classified under 6 heads termed

---

[262] Habous or mortmain property is an inalienable charitable endowment under Islamic law, which typically involves donating a building, plot of land, or other assets for Muslim religious or charitable purposes with no intention of reclaiming the assets

[263] The Hon. Judge Robert H. Alsdorf, 'Judicial Accountability: An Elected Judge's Perspective', in *Judges and Judicial Accountability*, edited by Cyrus Das and K. Chandra, pp. 203–4. Godbole, *The Judiciary and Governance in India*, p. 510.

[264] I. A. NO. 2 in SLP (C) No. 31797 of 2010.

'values': Independence, Integrity, Impartiality, Propriety, Equality, Competence and Dligence. In fact all six values are facets of the first and cardinal one of 'independence'. Judges are fierce in using the word as a sword to take action in contempt against critics. But the word is also used as a shield to cover a multitude of sins some venial and others not so venial … I have chosen seven.

The first is the sin of 'brushing under the carpet' or turning a Nelsonian eye. Many judges are aware of injudicious conduct of a colleague but have either ignored it or refused to confront the judge concerned and suppressed any public discussion on the issue often through the great silencer- The Law of Contempt.

The second sin is that of 'hypocrisy'. A favourite rather pompous phrase is 'Be you ever so high, the law is above you' or words to similar effect. Yet judges who enforce the law for others often break that law with impunity. This includes traffic regulation and other regulation to which the 'ordinary' citizens are subject. Some in fact get offended if their cars are held up by the police at all while controlling the flow of traffic—the feeling of offence sometimes being translated into action by issuance of a rule of contempt against the hapless police constable—all in the name of judicial independence.

The third sin is that of secrecy. The normal response of Courts to any enquiry as to its functioning is to temporize, stonewall and prevaricate …

If 'independence' is taken to mean 'capable of thinking for oneself' then the fourth sin is plagiarism and prolixity. I club the two together because the root cause is often the same namely the prolific and often unnecessary use of passages from text-books and decisions of other judges—without acknowledgment in the first case and with acknowledgment in the latter. Many judgements are in fact mere compendia or digests of decisions on a particular issue with very little original reasoning in support of the conclusion.

Often judges misconstrue judicial independence as judicial and administrative indiscipline. Both of these in fact stem from judicial arrogance as to one's intellectual ability and status…. The Supreme Court has laid down standards of judicial behaviour for the subordinate judiciary such as 'He should be conscientious, studious, thorough, patient, punctual, just, impartial, and fearless of public clamour, regardless of public praise but sadly some members of the higher judiciary exempt themselves from the need to comply with these standards.

Intellectual arrogance or what some may call intellectual dishonesty is manifest when judges decide without being bound by principles of stare decisis or precedent …

This brings me to the seventh and final sin of nepotism or what the oath of office calls 'favour and affection'.[265]

---

[265] Ruma Paul, 5th V.M. Tarkunde Memorial Lecture: An Independent Judiciary, New Delhi, 10 November 2011.

On the issue of plagiarism, it may be pertinent to quote George H. Gadbois, JR, who has written that very few judges can be rated as learned:

> Few of the judges could fairly be labelled as scholars and very little of their writings can be considered important contributions. There are exceptions, of course, the most notable one being B. K. Mukherjea's *The Hindu Law of religious and Charitable Trusts*, still regarded, more than a half century later, as a definitive work on the subject. Another likely to stand up the test of time is O. Chinappa Reddy's recent *The Court and the Constitution of India: Summits and Shadows.*[266]

Allegations of Sexual Harassment

In 2013–14, serious allegations of sexual harassment levelled against two former judges of the apex court, namely, Justices A.K. Ganguly and Swatanter Kumar, shook the entire judiciary. In both cases, it was female law interns who worked with them levelled the charge. In case of Ganguly, the complainant alleged that the former judge called her to his hotel in Delhi on the pretext of finishing some report and asked her to share the room and kissed her.[267] A committee of three judges of the Supreme Court comprising Justices R.M. Lodha, H.L. Dattu, and Ranjana Prakash Desai, after investigation, found the allegations true.[268] Ganguly vehemently denied allegations that his verdicts led to conspiracy.[269] He was heading the West Bengal State Human Rights Commission and had refused to resign on moral grounds. But then he resigned when the Union Government hinted that it might intervene if Ganguly did not step down. Then Union Law Minister Kapil Sibal said, 'There is a procedure where the government can step in on proved misbehaviour.... We will take a position on it, but I hope such a situation will not arise.'[270] Under Article 317 of the Constitution, the president is empowered to remove chairman or a member of a Public Service Commission on the

[266] George H. Gadbois, JR, *Judges of the Supreme Court of India*: 1950–1989 (Oxford University Press, 2011), p. 374.

[267] Indira Jaising, '"When I Tried to Move Away, He Kissed My Arm, Repeated He Loved Me ... Asked Me to Share Room"', *Indian Express*, 16 December 2013.

[268] 'Panel Finds Merit in Intern's Charge against Ganguly', *Times of India*, 5 December 2013.

[269] 'Ganguly Writes to CJI, Says Being Targeted by Those His Orders Hurt', *Indian Express*, 29 December 2013.

[270] 'Govt Can Act against Ganguly: Sibal', *Hindustan Times*, 17 December 2013.

ground of misbehaviour after the Supreme Court, on a reference made to it by the president, has, on inquiry held that s/he ought to be removed. The same process applies to the chairman of Human rights Commission also. He resigned and the matter ended there; the case never went to the court.

While the dust was yet to settle in Ganguly's episode, another law intern came out with similar allegations against Justice Swatanter Kumar. In her affidavit filed in the Supreme Court, she named Kumar as her tormentor and the incident dated back to May 2011 when he was a sitting judge of the apex court. But the Supreme Court did not act on her complaint asserting that it would not entertain any such allegations against retired judges.[271] He once asked her if she could travel with him and stay in a hotel and on another occasion kissed her on her left shoulder. The Supreme Court issued notice to Kumar on a writ petition filed by the law intern. Kumar also filed defamation cases against the complainant and some media houses. She moved the Supreme Court with a prayer to transfer the defamation case out of Delhi in view of the 'institutional bias operating in his favour'.[272] Kumar, in the meanwhile, obtained a gag order from the Delhi High Court and so the matter was not reported.

In another sensation case, a female additional sessions judge, posted in Gwalior, alleged that Justice S.K. Gangele of the Madhya Pradesh High Court made sexually explicit comments and sexual advances towards her. He even asked her to dance as an item girl in a party thrown by him on the occasion of his 25th marriage anniversary. When she did not succumb to his overtures, she was transferred to Sidhi though she had requested that she should not be disturbed till the exam of her daughter. Having no other way, she resigned. A probe panel set up by CJI consisting of then Allahabad High Court Chief Justice Dhananjay Chandrachud, then Delhi High Court Chief Justice G. Rohini, and Rajasthan High Court judge Ajay Rastogi gave a clean chit to Gangele. The inquiry panel asked the complainant whether she should have filed a complaint had she not been transferred, and she replied 'probably not'. However, the report stopped short of indicting Gangele for hosting a lavish party, 'Whether such a public event to mark a wedding anniversary would fit in with the norms of propriety and dignity which a high court judge is expected to follow is not a matter on which this committee needs to

[271] 'Another SC Judge, Another Intern, Same Charge', *The Pioneer*, 11 January 2014.
[272] 'Woman Who Accused SC Judge of Harassment Wants Case Out of Delhi', *Indian Express*, 14 May 2014.

hazard a guess.'[273] The fact that she resigned lends credence to her charge and reflects on her helplessness. However, the clean chit given by the in-house committee of the Supreme Court could not convince parliamentarians who took up the matter in Rajya Sabha which started investigating the allegations under the Judges (Inquiry) Act, 1968. The complainant and Gangele made their submissions before the Upper House.[274] Gangele also obtained a gag order from the Delhi High Court, and so, the media was not able to report.

The gag orders issued by the Delhi High Court in the cases of two judges defy logic and fair play. If gag orders are to be passed, it should be universal in all criminal cases and the identity of the accused must not be divulged unless convicted by the court.

Conflict of Interest

The issue of conflict of interest rocked the legal fraternity in the last quarter of 2009 when several judges recused themselves from various cases on this ground. It came to the fore prominently when Justice Kapadia decided a PIL which challenged the award of mining right in the Niyamgiri hill of south Orissa, home to Dongria Kondh, to Vedanta, a company which flagrantly violated environmental norms. Justice Kapadia substituted Vedanta with Sterlite Industries which is a subsidiary of Vedanta, and interestingly, he himself has shares in it. It touched off a storm when Prashant Bhushan, an activist lawyer, gave an interview to an English weekly taking exception to this. Justice Kapadia fumed in open court and clarified that he went ahead after making disclosures.[275] However, his explanation that he made the disclosure in the court and that none of the parties objected to his being on the bench glosses over the fact that it was not a general adversarial case, but a PIL. Further, none of the three original petitioners—Biswajit Mohanty, Prafulla Samantra, and Academy of Mountain Environics—was given a chance to be heard.

---

[273] '"Clean Chit" to MP HC Judge in Sexual Harassment Case', *Times of India*, 3 August 2015.

[274] 'Sexual Harassment Accused HC-Judge Gangele Faces Rajya Sabha Heat', http://www.legallyindia.com/the-bench-and-the-bar/sexual-harrasment-accused-hc-judge-sk-gangele-feels-rajya-sabha-heat-20151204-6932 (last accessed on 27 February 2017).

[275] 'Justice Kapadia Fumes over Sterlite Shares Allegation', *Times of India*, 6 October 2009.

The Supreme Court's clearance to Sterlite to go ahead with mining came as a surprise, as its own Central Empowered Committee had recommended denying permission, as mining would bring about an environmental calamity besides depriving thousands of tribals of their livelihood. Besides, Justice Kapadia gave this clearance without rejecting or overruling the report of the Court's own committee.[276] Moreover, he made the disclosure on 26 October 2007, though the case had been dragging on since 3 May 2005.

Justice R.V. Raveendran went ahead with the hearing of a case involving Mukesh Ambani's Reliance Group and Anil Ambani's Reliance Natural Resources Limited (RNRL) on the grounds that he had shares in both groups and none of the parties had objected to his presence after his disclosure. He however recused himself soon thereafter, when the matter of judges hearing cases of companies in which they hold shares became a major public issue. Even before the controversies veering around Justices Kapadia and Raveendran could die down, another revelation about then Karnataka High Court Chief Justice P.D. Dinakaran, already under a cloud, jolted the nation when he passed orders in favour of a family whose hospitality he had enjoyed in Canada.[277]

The controversies over conflict of interest and the declaration of assets by judges coincided. Disclosures by Judges of the Supreme Court made a significant revelation that most of them have invested in shares and mutual funds. This has raised another issue: whether judges should be allowed to invest in shares. After this controversy, several judges recused themselves from various cases on the grounds of conflict of interest. Justice S.H. Kapadia pulled out of a case concerning ITC Limited as he and his wife owned considerable shares in the company.[278] This recusal was important, as the parties to the case did not object to his being on the bench, but senior advocate Fali S. Nariman, who was incidentally present there though not connected with the case, registered his objection. It opened another Pandora's Box allowing a lawyer unconnected with the case to raise an objection. The case was listed for the seventh time before the bench, but the disclosure did not come earlier. Before this, he also pulled out of another case pertaining to the acquisition of

---

[276] See Arundhati Roy, 'Mr. Chidambaram's War', Cover Story Essay, *Outlook*, 9 November 2009, p. 44.

[277] 'Fresh Row: Dinakaran Ruled to Favour Friend', *Hindustan Times*, 30 November 2009.

[278] 'Justice Kapadia Recuses Himself from ITC Case', *Times of India*, 17 November 2009.

shares by London-based Vedanta Resources in Sesa Goa, an iron ore export-ing company, on the grounds that he owned shares in Sterlite Industries, a sister concern of Vedanta. Curiously, before his recusal, the Supreme Court issued a notice to advocate Prashant Bhushan to initiate contempt proceed-ings for his allegation that Justice Kapadia was guilty of misconduct by decid-ing a case involving Sterlite in which he had shares.[279] Justices Raveendran and Markandeya Katju also recused from different cases.[280] In 2014, Justice J.S. Khehar recused himself from Sahara group case as discussed earlier in this chapter. There are also examples when judges have decided cases despite clear conflict of interest. Justice K.L. Manjunath, then judge of the Karnataka High Court sat in judgement on a dispute involving his daughter's property but he was subsequently cleared by the Supreme Court inquiry. In his farewell speech after his retirement, he lambasted a judge of the Supreme Court and a former colleague of the same High Court for damaging his prospect of climbing higher through allegations of impropriety.[281]

Earlier Instances: This Issue Is Not New

The issue of conflict of interest is not a new one. When the Supreme Court was hearing the *Bank Nationalisation* case,[282] Justice Shah announced in the court at the outset that he and some other judges owned shares in private banks. But since the counsel of the union government did not object to their presence, they did not pull out of the case. Two days later, advocate R.K. Garg filed an intervention petition supporting the ordinance by which 14 banks were nationalized. The judges expressed amazement as to how such a petition could be entertained as a law was valid till set aside by the court. That was when Garg questioned the legitimacy of their being on the bench when they held shares of some of these banks. The Court took him to task stating that they had made the disclosure. However, the Court struck down the ordinance. Indira Gandhi was so convinced about Justice Shah's preju-dice, that later, during the Janata regime, she refused to appear before the Commission headed by him alleging bias. However, Justice M.H. Kania set

---

[279] 'Justice Kapadia Pulls out of Case', *Times of India*, 7 November 2009.

[280] 'Two SC judges Pull out of Different Cases', *Times of India*, New Delhi, 5 November 2009; 'Citing His Daughter, SC Judge Exits Ambani Case', *Indian Express*, 5 November 2009.

[281] 'Judge Accuses Colleagues of Ruining His Career', *Indian Express*, 21 April 2015.

[282] *R.C. Cooper v. Union of India*, AIR (1970) SC 564.

a good precedent in 1988 when he recused himself from the Bhopal gas leak case after disclosing that he had shares in Union Carbide. He did not consult lawyers either.

In 2008, Karnataka Congress MP N.Y. Hanumanthappa wrote to the Union Home Ministry pleading that the ministry should waive the export commitment of an arms and ammunition manufacturing firm, Dwarka Arms Stores and Ammunition Manufacturers. According to the factory's license, it has to export 40 per cent of its production of gun cartridges. Interestingly, the MP, who lobbied for the firm, had in his earlier avatar as a high court judge acquitted G. Lakshman, the firm's proprietor, of charges registered against him by the CBI for violating licensing conditions, illegally manufacturing arms, and possessing secret documents of the Ministry of Home Affairs. The arms manufacturer lives in a town near his Chitradurga parliamentary constituency.

Principle of Automatic Recusal

The principle of automatic recusal in a case of conflict of interest is well settled. The first case in the world of judicial review[283] has its genesis in this very conflict. In Britain, the regulation prescribed that no doctor would practice unless registered with the College of Physicians which was also empowered to prosecute and punish the violators of the rule. Dr Bonham was prosecuted and a fine of 10 pounds was imposed, of which half went to the State and the rest remained with the College. Bonham challenged this on the grounds of bias, stating that the College of Physicians had a pecuniary interest in the case, and so it could not be the judge. Allowing his petition, the court invalidated the regulation. Again, in *Dimes* v. *Proprietors of Grand Jn. Canal* (1852),[284] the orders of the Lord Chancellor were set aside as he had shareholdings in the company which was a party in the case decided by him, and he had not disclosed his financial interest. The House of Lords held that the dictum that no man could be a judge in his own cause and was 'not to be confined to a cause in which he is a party, but applies to a cause in which he has an interest'.

The Supreme Court of India upheld the Dimes principle.[285] In fact, in *Rupa Ashok Hurra* v. *Ashok Hurra*,[286] the Supreme Court allowed a person

[283] *Dr Bonham's case* (1608) 8 Co Rep 113.
[284] 3 HLC 759, 785.
[285] *A.K. Kraipak* v. *Union of India*, AIR (1970) SC 150; *Ashok Kumar Yadav* v. *Union of India*, AIR (1987) SC 454.
[286] (2002) 4 SCC 388.

aggrieved by a judgement of the court to file a curative petition, after the dismissal of his review petition, on two grounds. One of these was that the judge who decided the case had not disclosed his connection with the subject matter or the parties, giving scope for an apprehension of bias. Thus, the Supreme Court introduced the concept of curative petition when all other avenues of appeal and remedy are exhausted. It was taken from a judgement of the House of Lords in *Pinochet II*.[287] In this case, on 25 November 1998, the House of Lords by a majority of 3:2 restored the warrant of arrest of Senator Pinochet who was the Head of the State of Chile and was to face trial in Spain for some alleged offences. Later, it was revealed that one of the Law Lords (Lord Hoffmann), who heard the case, and his wife had links with Amnesty International (AI) which had become a party to the case. Hoffman had not disclosed this while hearing the case. On discovering this fact, Pinochet Ugarte sought the reconsideration of the judgement of the House of Lords on the grounds of an appearance of bias, though not actual bias. The House of Lords held:

> The principle that a Judge was automatically disqualified from hearing a matter in his own cause was not restricted to cases in which he had a pecuniary interest in the outcome, but also applied to cases where the Judge's decision would lead to the promotion of a cause in which the Judge was involved together with one of the parties. That did not mean that Judges could not sit on cases concerning charities in whose work they were involved, and Judges would normally be concerned to recuse themselves or disclose the position to the parties only where they had an active role as trustee or director of a charity which was closely allied to and acting with a party to the litigation. In the instant case, the facts were exceptional in that AI was a party to the appeal, it has been joined in order to argue for a particular result and the Law Lord was a director of a charity closely allied to AI and sharing its objects. Accordingly, he was automatically disqualified from hearing the appeal. The petition would therefore be granted and the matter referred to another committee of the House for rehearing.[288]

The case invoked the rule enunciated in *R* v. *Sussex Justices, Ex parte McCarthy*[289] that justice should not only be done, but it must also be seen to be done.

---

[287] *R* v. *Bow Street Metropolitan Stipendary Magistrate and Others ex p Pinochet Ugarte (No. 2)* (1999) 1 R England Reports 577.

[288] *R* v. *Bow Street Metropolitan Stipendary Magistrate and Others ex p Pinochet Ugarte.*

[289] (1924) 1 KB 256.

Dilution of the Dimes Principle

It appears from above decisions that the principle enunciated in the *Dimes* case has been diluted and judges may not be required to withdraw after making disclosures of their interests. An Australian court observed:

> The Dimes principle is not attracted simply by showing that a judge (or juror) owns a parcel of shares in a company whose pecuniary interests are in issue. If, as in the present case, the litigation could not possibly affect the value of shares, then it cannot be said that the judge has a direct pecuniary interest in the outcome of the litigation.[290]

In England, Judge Field held that a magistrate who subscribed to the Royal Society for the Prevention of Cruelty to Animals was not required to recuse from trying a charge brought by that body, of cruelty to a horse, observing that a mere general interest in the general object to be pursued would not be a reason for disqualification. There must be some direct connection with the litigation.[291] Jerome Frank, a judge, pointed out, 'if "bias" and "partiality" be defined to mean the total absence of preconceptions in the mind of the judge, then no one has ever had a fair trial, and no one ever will. The human mind, even at infancy, is no blank piece of paper'.[292]

It is true that everyone has an ideology or bias, but it must not be so pronounced as to affect reasoning and discretion. It appears that the thrust is on disclosure and the quantum of interest. Once a judge discloses the interest and the parties to the case do not object, they can continue on the bench. But this assumption of waiver of conflict after getting approval from the counsel of the parties concerned is erroneous. The unpleasant fact is that lawyers are tongue-tied in court and they would never like to antagonize judges by questioning their impartiality. It is, and should be, presumed that judges are truly impartial and no one would take exception if their credentials are impeccable. When a case involving Tata Iron and Steel Company (TISCO) came up before Chief Justice M.C. Chagla in the Bombay High Court, he disclosed his shareholding in TISCO. As no

---

[290] See Soli J. Sorabjee, 'Conflicts of Disinterest', *Indian Express*, 19 November 2009.

[291] See J.A.C. Griffith and H. Street, *Principles of Administrative Law* (Fourth Edition) (London: Sir Isaac Pitman & Sons, 1967), p. 156.

[292] Quoted by the Supreme Court in *Dr G. Sarma* v. *University of Lucknow and Ors.* (1976) 3 SCC 585, para 6. Also see P.P. Rao, 'Accusations of Bias against Judges', *The Tribune*, 10 November 2009.

parties objected, Chagla heard the case which was ultimately decided against TISCO.[293]

Apart from disclosure, the quantum of interest is important. Having a meagre share in a company is not likely to cloud the wisdom of a judge. But if it is substantial, the judge must recuse even if the parties have no objections. The UN-sponsored 'Bangalore Principles of Judicial Conduct' adopted in 2002 by judges from across the world, including India, the host country, is unequivocal that judges must recuse themselves if there is any conflict of interest. Clause 2.5 of the Bangalore Principles stipulates, 'A judge shall disqualify himself from participating in any proceedings in which ... the judge or a member of the judge's family has an economic interest in the outcome of the matter in controversy.'[294] However, in India, the 1997 'Restatement of Values of Judicial Life' allows a judge to continue on the bench after a disclosure, 'A Judge shall not hear and decide a matter in a company in which he holds shares ... unless he has disclosed his interest and no objection to his hearing and deciding the matter is raised.'[295]

Principle Followed in the US

In the US, judges have recused themselves *sua sponte* (on their own motion) under the 'extrajudicial source rule' recognized as a general presumption, although not an invariable one, by the US Supreme Court in *Litkey* v. *United Startes*.[296] In it, the district judge refused to accede to the defence motion that he recuse himself under Section 455 of Judiciary and judicial Procedure, which mandates that any justice, judge, or magistrate judge shall disqualify himself in any proceeding in which his impartiality might be questioned. The first motion was based on rulings and statements that the same judge made which allegedly betrayed impatience, disregard, and animosity towards the defence, during and after petitioner Bourgeois' 1983 bench trial on similar charges. The second motion was based on the judge's admonishment of Bourgeois' counsel and co-defendants in front of the jury at the 1991 trial. The Supreme Court held that 28 U. S. C. 455(a) which provides for a judge's recusal is subject to the limitation of the extrajudicial source doctrine. It laid

[293] *Jayantilal* v. *TISCO*, AIR (1958) Bom. 155.

[294] See, 'Judges Skirt Global Norms on Conflict of Interest', *Times of India*, 22 October 2009.

[295] Clause 11 of the Resolution adopted by the full bench of the Supreme Court on 7 May 1997.

[296] 510 U.S. 540 (1994).

down that the absence of the word 'personal' does not preclude the doctrine's application. The Court held that this doctrine is not a per se rule and, thus, is neither a necessary nor a sufficient condition for recusal. But it added that the source of bias is one factor a judge should consider in recusal.

There are also examples when judges have refused to recuse themselves, as did Justice Antonin Scalia in *Cheney* v. *United States District*,[297] involving his duck hunting partner, Vice President Dick Cheney.

Removal of Judges

The cumbersome procedure of impeachment for the removal of judges was laid down to ensure the independence of the judiciary. At one time in England, the king's judges could be dismissed by him. The result was that judges worked under the constant shadow of the fear dismissal if their verdict was distasteful to the king. Later, to ensure the independence of the judiciary, the tenure of the judge was fixed and the king was divested of the power to dismiss judges. Similarly, it was also decided that a judge's salary, fixed at the time of his appointment, could neither be increased nor diminished during his tenure. The reason is simple: no allurement should be offered to a judge by the executive.

But the Ramaswami episode demonstrated how our Parliament failed to perform its quasi-judicial function by refraining from voting on a momentous issue. There are instances when high court judges were removed when this power was in the hands of the government during the pre-independence days. Justice P.R. Das of the Patna High Court was forced by Chief Justice, Courtney Terell to resign. Terell threatened Das, stating that he had collected evidence of his (Das's) corruption and would be sending those papers to the Queen if he did not resign. Chief Justice Barnes of the Madras High Court was charged with firing. Though he was acquitted by the Presidency Magistrate, he put in his paper and returned home. In 1949, Justice Shiv Prasad Sinha of the Allahabad High Court was removed on the recommendations of the Federal Court after it found him guilty of favouring his friend, a lawyer, in a couple of cases. Then chief justice of the high court, K. K. Verma, wrote against him, and the Fazli Ali Commission found him guilty. But it was alleged by many legal luminaries that Sinha was victimized because he was considered anti-Congress and Verma acquiesced in the government design as he wanted to keep the government in good humour to

---

[297] 541 U.S. 913 (2004).

get his advocate son elevated as a judge of the high court and he ultimately succeeded in it. Justice Sinha happens to be the only judge of the higher judiciary to be removed in independent India, though prior to the enforcement of the Constitution.

The word 'misbehaviour', in the context of judges of the high courts in India, was first introduced in proviso (b) to Section 200(2) of the Government of India Act, 1935. Under the 1935 Act, it was initially the Privy Council and later, Federal Court of India that had to report to India's governor-general when charges were made of 'misbehaviour' against a judge of a high court. On 20 July 1948, a reference was made by the governor-general of India under Section 220 (2) (b) of the GOI Act, 1935, as adapted by the Indian (Provisional Constitution) Order, 1947, and the Indian (Provisional Constitution) Amendment Order, 1948, by forwarding a petition of the government of the United Provinces which levelled several allegations against Justice Shiv Prasad Sinha, who was appointed a permanent judge of the Allahabad High Court in October 1944. The governor-general filed affidavits and there was proper trial. He was held guilty in several cases. In Padrauna case, he gave relief to the petitioner without jurisdiction who had engaged his brother Shambhu Prasad Sinha. Further, he granted and rejected bails arbitrarily. He had his favourites in the Bar who could get desired orders. The Federal Court, in its report, said that 'Justice Sinha has been guilty of improper exercise of judicial functions, the cumulative effect of which was to lower the dignity of his office and undermine the confidence of the public in the administration of justice.'[298] It reported that four of the five charges brought against him had been established. Justice K.N. Singh, ex-CJI, told me that it was a common talk in the Allahabad HC Bar at that time that Prime Minister Jawaharlal Nehru had advised Justice Sinha to put in his papers so that he did not have to face the trial and the institution was not denigrated. But Sinha refused to relent.[299]

There is an instance of a judge of the Privy Council not allowed to continue on the charge of corruption. Justice M.R. Jayakar, former judge of the Federal Court of India, sat in the Judicial Committee of the Privy Council only during the Easter term of 1946, but he was never seen again as the Lord chancellor did not call him back. He allegedly influenced lawyers to engage his son.[300]

[298] http://indiancorruptjudges.com/Plot4Plot/008_07.htm (last accessed on 10 August 2013).

[299] In a personal interview to the author on 25 August 2013 on phone.

[300] Sen, Six Decade of Law, Politics & Diplomacy, p. 19.

It was to ward off any victimization and criticism that the Constitution conferred absolute protection to the judges. But this protection is proving counterproductive. The apex court itself should come out with a solution, since the Parliament has failed. The judiciary has interfered with government work precisely on this very ground that the executive has failed to discharge its duty. Earlier, judicial review was admissible only on the grounds that the issue in question was *ultra vires*. But now it is entertained on several other grounds of proportionality, unreasonableness, abuse of discretion, and so on. So, judges themselves should create some mechanism to contain corruption in the judiciary.

In-House Mechanism to Discipline Judges

In *C. Ravichandran Iyer* v. *Justice A.M. Bhattacharjee*,[301] a two-judge bench of the Supreme Court ruled that an in-house procedure would provide some forum to examine the allegations made against a high court or a Supreme Court Judge. Doubts were expressed even then about its effectiveness as it would depend solely on the CJI as to how he reacts. And secondly, it does not provide any solution if the CJI himself is accused of misconduct. Both these doubts have proved true. The CJI refused to act in Justice Punchhi's case or of the Judges of the Punjab and Haryana High Court, and several serious allegations were levelled against sitting CJIs in the recent past but no action was taken.

Further, the collegium of the Supreme Court even recommended those names for chief justiceships of high courts and elevation from district courts to high courts of those who were considered downright depraved. Ashok Kumar, formerly a session's judge in Tamil Nadu, was elevated to the Chennai High Court despite serious charges of corruption against him. The Intelligence Bureau, after investigation, gave a more damning and shocking report. He was still elevated and given a permanent position because of his proximity to the DMK government of the state which threatened to withdraw support from the UPA government. So, at the union law minister's insistence, the CJI gave him extensions and then made him a permanent judge.[302] Similarly, S.L. Bhayana, additional district judge in Delhi, was elevated to the Delhi High Court and then made a permanent judge in 2007, though

[301] (1995) 5 SCC 457.

[302] Shanti Bhushan's lecture on Judicial Accountability and Judicial Reforms, 10 March 2007, Indian Social Institute, New Delhi.

the Delhi High Court passed a severe stricture against him for acquitting the accused in the much publicized Jessica Lal murder case. The High Court went to the extent of recording that the judge was in a hurry to reach a particular conclusion. In yet another case, the Supreme Court collegium recommended the name of Justice Jagdish Bhalla of the Allahabad High Court as the chief justice of the Kerala High Court, despite official reports and documentary evidence that his wife bought a plot of 7200 sq. feet in Noida, UP, then worth Rs 7 crores for Rs 5 lakhs only. The president returned Bhayana and Bhalla's recommendations, but the collegium reiterated the recommendation for Justice Bhayana. Justice Bhalla was transferred to the Chhattisgarh High Court and made acting chief justice after some time. Justice Virendra Jain of the Delhi High Court was promoted as chief justice of the Punjab and Haryana High Court in 2006, though there were grave charges against him. He decided a case in the favour of Hari Ram, whom he knew so intimately that his (Ram's) granddaughter's marriage took place from Justice Jain's official residence. However, the CJI overlooked it saying that the Supreme Court did not have any disciplinary power over judges. When it was pointed out to him that under the Restatement of Judicial Values adopted at the Chief Justices' Conference, 1999, charges against a judge could be probed by an in-house committee of judges, the CJI said that he had looked into the charges and did not find any merit in it. It is flabbergasting that without holding an in-house inquiry, he was convinced about the innocence of the judge.

These instances clearly demonstrate that an in-house mechanism is totally incapable of chastening erring judges. If the Supreme Court's collegium does not withhold the promotion or elevation of corrupt judges, which is within its power, how can the CJI take any disciplinary action against them? Instead, the Supreme Court further fortified the position of judges by ruling that no investigation would be made against any judge without the prior approval of the CJI.[303] Obviously, no one would dare to register an FIR against any judge, much less one in the higher judiciary. Corruption is a crime under the IPC as well as the Prevention of Corruption Act, but judges enjoy immunity, as not even the president can sanction prosecution in a case of corruption against a judge of the higher judiciary without the recommendation of the CJI.

No judge was subjected to criminal investigation in the years after the condition was imposed by the Supreme Court till 2008–10 in the

[303] *K. Veeraswami* v. *Union of India* (1991) 3 SCC 650.

Ghaziabad provident fund scam, where the chief justice allowed the CBI to send written interrogatories to the judges involved. If an FIR cannot be registered against a judge, how can their crimes be investigated or proved? Article 14 of the Constitution has encrypted the sublime principle of equality before the law. The Supreme Court has itself held that the definition of 'the State' given in Article 12 includes the judiciary for the purpose of constitutional limitations on power.[304] Judges are public servants under Section 21 of the IPC, and in the Veeraswami case even the Supreme Court admits it. Further, Section 166 of the IPC provides for the punishment of public servants guilty of misconduct. The Judicial Officers' Protection Act, 1850 and Judges Protection Act, 1985, read with Section 166 of the IPC, do not give any immunity for crime. Unfortunately, no recourse has been made to this section to discipline or chastise judges. We find examples in other countries where judges are punished. A judge of the Supreme Court of Tokyo was punished for violating the law by a jurisdictional judge. In China too, a jurisdictional court punished a superior judge on similar grounds.

T. Devidas and Hem Lall Bhandari have rightly written:

> Judicial accountability is within the mandate of article 14. Its non-enforcement is part of the general malaise attending the judicial non-enforcement of any fundamental right, principal among which is article 14, which happens to be a catch-all and a cure-all. For judicial accountability to get started, all that would seem necessary would be for the judiciary to respect faithfully the mandate of article 14 and the denial of any time gap in the approximation of 'is' to the 'ought'. In this aspect, the pronouncement of the Supreme Court [*Bhaurao Dagdu Paralkar* v. *State of Maharashtra* (2005) 7 SCC 605] to the effect that any collusion or fraud on the court to procure a miscarriage of justice would be seriously noticed by the court is indeed salutary. Although it was so held in the context of property rights, the principle would have to be automatically applicable to every right. It can perhaps be hoped that this could provide a proper start for a new approach to revitalize article 14. But alongside, punishability of the erring judge who fails to give the protection of the applicable substantive law from the time of violation of rights would have to be predictable and automatic.[305]

---

[304] *Budhan Choudhary* v. *State of Bihar* (1995) 1 SCR 1045, 1049; *A.R. Antulay* v. *R.S. Nayak* (1988) 2 SCC 602.

[305] 'Judicial Accountability', *Journal of Indian Law Institute*, vol. 48, no. 1, 2006.

Code of Conduct for Judges

After several skeletons tumbled out of the judiciary's cupboard, the annual conference of chief justices in December 1999 adopted a Code of Conduct for themselves,

1. Justice must not merely be done, it also must be seen to be done. The behaviour and conduct of the members of the highest judiciary must reaffirm the people's faith in the impartiality of the judiciary. Accordingly, any act of a judge of the Supreme Court or a high court, whether in official and personal capacity which erodes the credibility of this perception, has to be avoided.
2. A judge should not contest the election to any office of a club, society, or other association; further he should not hold any such elective office, except in a society or association connected with the law.
3. Close association of a judge with individual members of the bar, particularly those who practice in the same court, must be eschewed.
4. A judge should not permit any member of his immediate family such as spouse, son, daughter, son-in-law, daughter-in-law, or any other close relative, if he or she is a member of the bar, to appear before him or even be associated in any manner with a cause to be dealt by him.
5. A member of a judge's family, if he or she is a member of the bar, should not be permitted to use the residence in which the judge actually resides or other facilities for professional work.
6. A judge should practice a degree of aloofness consistent with the dignity of his office.
7. A judge should not hear or decide a matter in which a member of his family, a close relation or a friend is concerned.
8. A judge shall not enter into a public debate or express his views in public on political matters or on matters that are pending or are likely to arise for judicial examination.
9. A judge is expected to let his judgments speak for themselves. He shall not give interviews to the media.
10. A judge shall not accept gift or hospitality except from his family, close relations, and friends.
11. A judge shall not hear and decide a matter in which a company in which he holds share is concerned unless he has disclosed his interest and no objection to his hearing and deciding the matter is raised.
12. A judge shall not speculate in shares, stocks, or the like.
13. A judge shall not engage directly or indirectly in trade or business, either by himself or in association with any other person (publication of a legal

treatise or any activity in the nature of a hobby will not be construed as trade or business).

14. A judge should not ask for, accept contributions, or otherwise actively associate himself with the raising of any fund for any purpose.
15. A judge should not seek any financial benefit in the form of a perquisite or privilege attached to his office unless it is clearly available.
16. Every judge must at all times be conscious that he is under public gaze and there should be no act or omission by him which is unbecoming of his office.[306]

Though these codes have no legal basis and are to be observed voluntarily, it is observed more in breach than in compliance.

Law Essential to Make Judges Accountable

The government brought the Judges Standards and Accountability Bill, 2011 to make judges of the higher judiciary accountable. Lok Sabha passed the Bill on 29 March 2012. The bill lapsed with the dissolution of the Lok Sabha. However, it sought to (a) lay down judicial standards, (b) provide for the accountability of judges, and (c) establish mechanisms for investigating individual complaints for misbehaviour or incapacity of a judge of the Supreme Court or high courts, and (d) it also provides for the removal of judges. It provided for establishing the National Judicial Oversight Committee (NJOC), the Complaints Security Panel, and an Investigation Committee. Salient features of the Bill are: Any person can file a complaint against a judge to the NJOC on grounds of 'misbehaviour', a motion for removal of a judge on grounds of misbehaviour can also be moved in the Parliament, such a motion will be referred for further inquiry to the NJOC, complaints and inquiries against judges will be confidential and frivolous complaints will be penalised, and the NJOC may issue advisories or warnings to erring judges and also recommend their removal to the president.

The Bill required judges to practice universally accepted values of judicial life. It explicitly prohibited (a) close association with individual members of the Bar who practice in the same court as the judge, (b) allowing family members who are lawyers practising in the same court to use the judge's residence for professional work, (c) hearing or deciding matters in which a member of the judge's family or relative or friend is concerned, (d) entering into public

---

[306] *The Indian Advocate*, vol. 29, 1999–2000, pp. 76–7. Godbole, *The Judiciary and Governance in India*, pp. 553–4.

debate on political matters or matters which the judge is likely to decide, and (e) engaging in trade and speculation in securities. Judges will be required to declare their assets and liabilities, and also that of their spouse and children, and it will be displayed on the website of the court to which s/he belongs. The Judicial Standards and Accountability Bill, 2010, which was introduced in December 2010, was brought to the Lower House with fresh amendments in December 2011, which included a controversial provision that seeks to restrain judges from making 'unwarranted comments' against any consti-tutional authority. Thus, any judge making verbal comments against other constitutional authorities and individuals would render himself/herself liable for 'judicial misconduct'. The then Law minister, Salman Khurshid, said that it was aimed at striking a 'balance' between maximizing judicial indepen-dence and laying down accountability at the same time for members of the higher judiciary.[307]

A Security Panel was proposed to be constituted in the Supreme Court and every high court, consisting of a former chief justice and two sitting judges of that court. The Oversight Committee was to consist of a retired CJI as the chairperson, a judge of the Supreme Court nominated by the sitting CJI, a CJ of the High Court, the attorney-general for India, and an eminent person appointed by the president. It provided that if the Security Panel recommended investigation into a complaint against a judge, the NJOC would constitute an investigation committee to investigate into the complaint. If the committee came to the conclusion that the charges warrant the removal of the judge, it would (a) request the judge to resign volun-tarily, and if s/he failed to do so, (b) advise the president to proceed with the removal of the judge. In such an eventuality, the president would refer the matter to the Parliament.

The Bill did not evoke positive reaction from the judiciary. Then CJI S.H. Kapadia, warned the Union Government against bringing the bill in a haste, saying it must not tinker with the constitutional philosophy of judicial inde-pendence. Justice Kapadia said that judges were not afraid of accountability law, but the move should not harm the constitutional principles and leave a ground for the country to regret later on.[308] Concerns were raised by some other quarters also about danger to the independence of the judiciary. The Union Ministry of Law and Justice issued a Press Release on 17 August 2012 clarifying misgivings about the Bill:

---

[307] 'Lok Sabha Passes Judicial Accountability Bill', *The Hindu*, 31 March 2012.
[308] *Times of India*, 16 August 2012.

Several national dailies have carried a news item on 16.08.2012 conveying that Judicial Standards and Accountability Bill will impair the independence of judiciary. The Ministry of Law & Justice, Department of Justice, would like to state that this is not true. In fact, it seems that the statement made by Hon'ble Chief Justice of India has been twisted and not seen and interpreted in full context. At the same time, the attempt to link the Bill with independence of judiciary, is not based on facts. The Judicial Standards and Accountability Bill has been prepared after holding wideranging consultations and after holding discussions with legal experts, eminent Jurists, Non-government Organizations (NGO) etc. The Bill has three parts. It lays down Judicial Standards which are derived from the Restatement of Values in Judicial Life, 1997 and have the acceptance and approval of the Full Court of Supreme Court. It makes it mandatory for the judges to declare their assets and liabilities. It makes provisions for filing of complaints by the citizens and the mechanism for their scrutiny and subsequent action for investigation or otherwise. For this, there are provisions for constituting Complaints Scrutiny Panel (CSP) which will scrutinize the complaints. They will be referred to National Judicial Oversight Committee (NJOC) for enquiry and action, only if there is a substance in them. All the bodies namely, CSP & NJOC comprise of persons who will be from judiciary and who are expected to exercise due care and circumspection while handling the complaints against Judges and before recommending action against them.

The Ministry of Law & Justice, Department of Justice, would like to clarify that by enforcing standards of behaviour, by declaration of assets by them and by providing a mechanism for making complaints against erring Judges and for their investigation, the Bill will establish the confidence and faith of the people in the judicial system without exposing them to unnecessary risk.

The provisions of the Bill do not in any way infringe on the independence of the judiciary which is hallmark of Indian democracy and which is guaranteed under constitution. The accountability and independence can co-exist in a reinforcing mode and without affecting the working of the judiciary. The apprehensions expressed are then devoid of the understanding of the Scheme of the Bill and without understanding of the fact that it meets the aspirations of the people in a functioning democracy like India having a functioning judiciary.[309]

The Bill was criticized on several counts, the definition of 'misbehavior' under Section 2(j) was such that a minor, inadvertent breach of judicial

---

[309] 'The Provisions of the Judicial Standards and Accountability Bill do not in any way Infringe on the Independence of the Judiciary', Press Release, 17 August 2012, issued by the Ministry of Law and Justice.

standards could constitute misconduct, while bigger acts if indiscretion and corruption may go unpunished. Secondly, the Oversight Committee was sought to be reduced to a post office referring each complaint to the Security Panel. This may lead to multiplicity of complaints and waste of time. Further, the Security Panel was to consist of three members, two of whom would be judges sitting in the same court as the judge against whom a complaint was filed. It would be extremely difficult for the judges to be totally dispassionate in inquiring against a brother judge while sitting with them day in and day out. Besides, the composition and tenure of the Investigation Committee had not been defined and even a lay person, without any knowledge and standing could become a member of the inquiry panel.

Thus, it allowed individuals who are not sitting judges to deal with complaints against them. It was being done to eliminate the in-house inquiry system in which judges receive and deal with complaints against fellow judges. And sought to repeal the Judges (Inquiry) Act, 1968, which deals with the manner of investigation, proof of misbehaviour, and incapacity of judges for their impeachment. It had several provisions from the Judges Inquiry Bill, 2006, which could not be enacted.

The Bill had some laudable provisions such as initiating investigations into charges against any judge on the complaint of any ordinary citizen and providing a statutory status to the Restatement of Judicial Values. But other provisions weaken the Council. The NJC comprises only peers with no outsider. Under the present 1968 Act, the Speaker forms a committee of three members out of whom one is a jurist who is not a serving judge. The Campaign on Judicial Accountability has rightly objected that the proposed Council is an in-house Council of sitting judges which is similar to the Judicial Council proposed when the Restatement of Judicial Values was adopted. This in-house body of sitting judges hardly ever inquired into allegations against judges, forget about recommending any action against them. However, there will be one difference: the NJC will have a statutory status and judges will not be able to say that they are not subject to any supervision as some of them reacted when the Supreme Court asked them to disclose their assets. But as discussed above, the manner in which the Supreme Court's collegium recommends the names of the judges under cloud, can it be expected that this committee of peers will investigate the conduct of their brother judges with whom they sit in the court every day? It is in the interest of the judiciary itself to include non-judges in the Council to inspire credibility.

If, instead of a committee of peers, a broad-based committee consisting of judges and eminent people from other walks of life probes the allegation, its findings will carry conviction. For example, the judges of the Karnataka High

Court, who were found with women lawyers, were reportedly absolved by a committee of judges but surprisingly, the report was not made public and so, people took it as a cover up. If something is hidden, people will genuinely be suspicious. Had there been an outsider in the committee, it would have been more credible and acceptable. India is a country bedevilled not only by casteism and communalism, but also by cadreism and it is not unnatural to presume that peers will stand by peers.

Section 33 of the Bill militated against the spirit of accountability which debarred the disclosure of any information relating to the complaint to any person. Thus, the complainant could not bring to the public notice the incriminating material against the judge once he complains to the NJC. In other investigations against non-judges such as ministers, bureaucrats, and so on, there is a general complaint of media trial but the facts are revealed to the people. What is more, though the truth has been made a defence by amending the Contempt of Courts Act, there is no guarantee that the Supreme Court and the high courts will honour it because as courts of records their power of contempt is not dependent on the this act. Moreover, very often (as in Arundhati Roy's contempt case) the judge against whom an allegation is made sits in judgement over his own contempt. So the alleged contemnor must convince the judge that his charge against the judge is true.

The government is toying with the idea of bringing another legislation to constitute a NJOC. The Union law minister is proposed to be one of the three members of the Committee which will deal with complaints against judges. The other two members would be CJI and an eminent person.[310]

Independence and Accountability Not Antagonistic

It must be understood that the independence and accountability of the judiciary are not antagonistic but complementary, because only an accountable institution can be independent of extraneous considerations. Justice J.S. Verma is forthright, 'Independence of Judiciary does not mean merely independence from outside influences but also from those within. To my mind, dangers from within have much larger and greater potential for harm than dangers from outside'.[311] Chief Justice S.R. Das of the Supreme Court also pontificated on it, 'If there is one principle of cardinal importance in the

---

[310] 'After NJAC, Govt Seeks Oversight Panel for Judges', *Times of India*, 8 February 2016.

[311] J.S. Verma, 'Constitutional Obligation of the Judiciary', in *New Dimensions of Justice* (Delhi: Universal Law Publishing Co. Pvt. Ltd., 2004), p. 18.

administration of justice, it is this: the proper freedom and independence of Judges and Magistrates must be maintained and they must be allowed to perform their functions freely and fearlessly and without any interference by any body, even by this court'.[312]

The Supreme Court has itself recognized that integrity and humility are non-negotiable for judges. In *State of Rajasthan* v. *Prakash Chandra*,[313] it exhorted that judges must be circumspect and self-disciplined in the discharge of their judicial functions. It added that the virtue of humility in the judges and a constant awareness that investment of power in them is meant for use in public interest, and all actions of judges must be judicious in character as erosion of credibility of the judiciary, in public mind, for whatever reasons, is the greatest threat to the independence of the judiciary. Justice D.A. Desai also cautioned about the loss of credibility:

> The people in rural and backward areas unfortunately illiterate have different kind of susceptibilities. A slight suspicion that the Judge is predisposed or approaches the case with a closed mind or has no judicial disposition would immediately affect their susceptibilities and they would lose confidence in the administration of justice. There is no greater harm than infusing or instilling in the minds of such people a lack of confidence in the character and integrity of Judge.[314]

Justice P.N. Bhagwati has written how some judges try to keep the government in good humour:

> It must be remembered that though, by and large, our judges (and their number, I am sure, is quite large) are made of sterner stuff and no threat of injury, however, grave or serious, would deflect them from doing their duty, without 'fear or favour', some judges may, on account of threat of transfer, be induced, albeit not consciously or deliberately, to do that which pleases the executive to avert such injury, and if they are competent and skilled in judicial craftsmanship, it will not be difficult for them to find arguments to justify their action in falling inline with the wishes of the executive, because reason is ready enough advocate for the decision, one, consciously or unconsciously, desire to reach. This would not only have a demoralising effect on the High Court judiciary, but would also shake the confidence of the people in the administration of justice in cases where the Government is a party.[315]

---

[312] AIR (1964) SC 707.
[313] AIR (1998) SC 1344.
[314] *Rama Dayal Markarha* v. *State of M. P.* (1978) 2 SCC 630, para 14.
[315] *Union of India* v. *Sankalchand Himatlal Sheth* (1977) 4 SCC 193, para 57.

Justice Bhagwati is very right and ironically and, maybe, unconsciously, he himself fell a prey to it and could hardly take a firm stand against the government, and its most glaring example is habeas corpus case. Similarly, he gave eloquent directions in *Bandhua Mukti Morcha* v. *Union of India*,[316] but did not take any cognisance when contempt petition was filed as none of the directions was complied with. As Indira Gandhi returned to power in 1980, Justice Bhagwati sent a congratulatory letter to her:

May I offer you my heartiest congratulations on your resounding victory in the elections and your triumphant return as the Prime Minister of India.... I am sure that with your iron will and firm determination, uncanny insight and dynamic vision, great administrative capacity and vast experience, overwhelming love and affection of the people and above all, a heart which is identified with the misery of the poor and the weak, you will be able to steer the ship of the nation safely to its cherished goal.[317]

Though he had written a confidential letter, it was somehow leaked to the press allegedly by the Prime Minister's Office. Justice V.D. Tulzapurkar reacted bitterly, 'If judges start sending bouquets or congratulatory letters to a political leader on his political victory, eulogizing him on assumption of a high office in adulatory terms, the people's confidence in the judiciary will be shaken.'[318] His behaviour was all the more shocking as he was a Supreme Court judge with no threat of transfer but he wanted to ensure his elevation as the CJI.

Prime Minister Narendra Modi also advocated self-regulation for judges when he asked the judiciary to evolve a mechanism of self-criticism, saying judges, unlike politicians were not subject to public scrutiny. Addressing a conference of chief justices and chief ministers, he said that even a slight erosion of faith in the judiciary would hurt the nation, 'If the politicians or the government make a mistake ... the judiciary can correct it, but if you make a mistake, it is the end'.[319]

However, despite all pontification and concern expressed by the apex court for the need to keep the credibility of the institution intact, there is a

[316] AIR (1997) SC 802, (1984) 3 SCC 161.

[317] Bhagwan D. Dua, 'A Study in Executive-Judicial Conflict: The Indian Case', *Asian Survey*, vol. XXIII, no. 4 (April 1983) https://ipc498a.files.wordpress.com/2007/04/evisceratingthejudiciary.pdf (last accessed on 4 March 2017).

[318] Dua, 'A Study in Executive-Judicial Conflict'.

[319] 'Modi Tells India's Top Judges to Introspect, Self-Regulate', *Hindustan Times*, 6 April 2015.

perception that the threat to the independence of the judiciary is more from within than from without. It is an irony that the Supreme Court has continued protecting judges on the grounds that a person dispensing justice must not be under any shadow of fear but has done nothing to ensure that these dispensers of justice do not fall from the lofty heights where they are located. Extraordinary punishments were given to police officials in Gujarat—even the SP of the concerned district was suspended when a judge of the subordinate court was handcuffed. Is it not essential that judges must also be awarded extraordinary punishments if they indulge in deeds unbecoming of them? After all, in the Mahabharata, we have the example of the Brahmin receiving the maximum punishment, and the Shudra the minimum, for the same offence because Brahmins are supposed to be enlightened people and enjoy an exalted position in society. Winston Churchill echoed the same feeling when he told the House of Commons that judges are 'required to conform to standards of life and conduct far more severe and restricted than that of ordinary people'.[320]

Stop Post-Retirement Assignments

One of the surest methods of rooting out judicial corruption is to make a provision, if possible a constitutional one by amending Articles 124 and 217 that judges of the high court and the Supreme Court shall not be given any assignment post-retirement. It is a bitter fact that pre-retirement judgments are influenced by prospects of post-retirement jobs. George H. Gadbois, JR, after doing an extensive research on the judges of the Indian Supreme Court from 1950 to 1989, wrote:

> India is a land of commissions—a 'commission culture' was the term used by one Chief Justice of India. Commissions are a highly institutionalized tradition, a deeply ingrained feature of the political culture. The British made occasional use of judge-staffed commissions, but after Independence they have exploded in number. At any time dozens are functioning, providing many job opportunities for retired Supreme Court of India and high court judges.... Not all commissions are established for noble purposes. Retired judges have acknowledged that some they headed were politically motivated, witch-hunts aimed at harassing political rivals.[321]

[320] V.R. Krishna Iyer, *Off the Bench* (Delhi: Universal Law Publishing Law Pvt. Ltd., 2001), p. 72.

[321] George H. Gadbois, JR, *Judges of the Supreme Court of India: 1950–9189* (New Delhi: Oxford University Press, 2011), p. 371.

It is not difficult to establish the quid pro quo between the government and the judge getting post-retirement jobs. Some judges never retire and move from one commission to another, and sometimes head more than one at a time. P.B. Gajendragadhkar headed six different official bodies while J.L. Kapur headed five. Judges who antagonize the government by their bold judgments hardly get any such offers. Gadbois has pointed out that none of the seven judges who ruled in favour of the basic structure doctrine in *Kesavananda Bharati* was asked to head any commission or tribunal nor was K. Subba Rao or M. Hidayatullah during Indira Gandhi's first tenure. However, the Janata Party's government offered jobs of one kind or another to all the seven judges.

It is true that some acts provide that only former judges can head the official tribunal or commission or regulatory body. It is argued that if a ban is imposed on post-retirement jobs of judges, these acts would become unworkable. This problem can be solved by making a minor amendment in the act which says that it will be headed by one who has been a judge of the Supreme Court/high court. Instead of 'who has been', it can be provided 'who is' so that only a serving judge becomes head or member of a commission or tribunal. The scope can be further enlarged by providing for eminent jurist or academic. To what extent can judges be hands in gloves with the powers has been depicted by M.V. Kamath. He has referred to an interesting episode during the hearing of the *Kesavananda Bharati* case:

> Another insight that Justice [P. Jaganmohan] Reddy provides of the goings-on behind the scene shows to what length the Indira Gandhi government was willing to go to change the Constitution to further its own interests. Writes Reddy: 'There was one occasion when J. Dwivedi made a startling proposal to Palkhivala. He said that if Palkhivala agreed to property rights being taken away, he (Dwivedi) would get Parliament to declare that other fundamental rights would not be taken away.' Palkhivala replied: 'Have I referred so far at any time to property rights? I was dealing with the implied limitations and natural rights etc.' How a judge could give such an assurance as Dwivedi offered and what authority he had to do so passed everyone's comprehension. Dwivedi rang me at about 9:30 p.m. and said that he had been indiscreet and ought not to have made that remark.[322]

The way the Misra Commission, headed by the then judge of the Supreme Court, Justice R.N. Misra, constituted to inquire into the massacres of Sikhs

---

[322] M.V. Kamath, *Nani A. Palkhivala: A Life* (New Delhi: Hay House India, 2007), p. 184.

after the assassination of the then Prime Minister Indira Gandhi, exonerated the Union Government and the Congress leaders of their complicity which was writ large on the face, made a mockery of the judicial commission. First of all, Justice Misra departed from the well-established tradition of conducting proceedings in the open and decided to do it in camera arguing that the victims would be able to depose fearlessly as their identities would remain secret. All this turned out to be humbug as he allowed a battery of lawyers who were anti-victims and were there to bolster up the proposition that it was not a pogrom but a spontaneous reaction to the murder of Indira Gandhi and earlier killings of Hindus in Punjab. According to H.S. Phoolka:

> Since they (lawyers) were permitted to participate in the inquiry, the lawyers representing those anti-victim groups received advance information from the commission about when each victim was due to depose. It became clear before long that those groups were actually proxies for culprits, as they were using that information to try and intimidate the victims just before their deposition. At times, victims received the commission's summons and the culprits' threats simultaneously. A number of witnesses complained about the threats to the commission, but to no avail ... The irony was that, while the rioters and police were being allowed to victimize the Sikhs all over again, the media and other public-spirited citizens interested in the inquiry, were shut out, as the proceedings were purportedly held in camera. This enabled Misra to distort the evidence in his report, and give a clean chit to the Congress Party as well as its leaders, and the government. Thus, the recourse to in camera hearings turned out to be a ploy to prevent the world from coming to know any evidence that might have emerged during the inquiry against the organizers of the carnage.[323]

The Citizens Justice Committee, headed by former CJI, Justice S.M. Sikri, made a blistering attack on the commission that the 'unusual procedure adopted by the commission subserves the purpose of those who are interested in shielding the culprits and suppressing the truth'.[324] Misra was suitably rewarded for brazening it out. He went on to become the CJI, and after retirement, he adorned the post of the first chairman of the National Human Rights Commission (NHRC). What a grotesque irony that a man who shielded the biggest violators of human rights became the first chairman of

---

[323] Manoj Mitta and H.S. Phookla, *When a Tree Shook Delhi* (New Delhi: Lotus Roli, 2014), pp. 125–6.
[324] Mitta and Phookla, *When a Tree Shook Delhi*, p. 135.

the NHRC! Later, shedding all pretentions of impartiality, he went to become a member of Rajya Sabha as a Congress candidate.

These retired judges generally give reports favouring the government which appoints them. The Gujarat government headed by Narendra Modi appointed the G.T. Nanavati Commission to inquire into the burning of the train bogies on the Sabarmati Express at Godhra on 27 February 2002 in which 58 people died. Six years later, the Commission in its report said that the attack on the 'kar sevaks' on the train from Ayodhya was pre-planned, and exonerated Chief Minister Narendra Modi for the consequent riots.[325] However, the U.C. Banerjee Commission set up by Railways Minister Lalu Prasad in 2004, brought out a different version: that the fire in the coaches was an accident and not pre-planned as claimed by Narendra Modi and the RSS.[326] Thus, the two judges gave diametrically opposite views which suited the political masters who appointed them. There is no dearth of such ignoble instances.

Most of the judges of the Supreme Court get some job or the other after superannuation. Justice Markandeya Katju was appointed chairman of the Press Council of India within days of his retirement. Actually, Justice V.S. Sirpurkar's name had almost been finalized for the post, but Katju got it at the last moment. Justice Mukundkam Sharma was nominated to head the central government appointed Vansadhara Water Dispute Tribunal at least four months prior to his retirement on 18 September 2011. People hardly know about this river. Justice H.K. Sema was appointed the chairman of the UP Human Rights Commission by the then UP chief minister Mayawati, immediately after his retirement from the Supreme Court and the state government issued a special order that his office would be located in Noida and not in Lucknow, with houses at both places. Curiously, earlier Justice Sema, while in the Supreme Court, reversed most of the adverse findings against Mayawati by the Allahabad High Court. Similarly, Justice Swatanter Kumar was nominated to head the National Green Tribunal in December 2012 while still being on the bench of the apex court. Such instances abound.

BJP leader Arun Jaitley said it umpteen times that there is a need to regulate the conduct of judges as pre-retirement judgments are influenced

[325] http://www.firstpost.com/politics/nanavati-reports-clean-chit-to-pm-modi-gujarat-riots-are-a-dead-issue-now-1810731.html (last accessed on 13 November 2016).

[326] 'Godhra Train Fire Accidental: Report', rediff.com, http://www.rediff.com/news/2005/jan/17godhra.htm (last accessed on 3 May 2015).

by post-retirement jobs. He repeated it while participating in a debate in Rajya Sabha as the leader of the Opposition on the Judicial Appointments Commission Bill on 5 September 2013.[327] Jaitley raised a pertinent issue, but it is difficult to forget that the NDA government gave lollypops to many retired judges. Two judges—one from the Allahabad and another from the Jabalpur high court—were transferred to the Rajasthan High Court as there were grave allegations against them. But they were made governors after retirement as reportedly they helped the son-in-law of Bharon Singh Shekhawat in different court cases. Justice Rama Jois was made governor and then was brought to the Rajya Sabha by the BJP. Rama Jois was arrested during the Emergency as he was the advocate of Lal Krishna Advani. So, he was rewarded with judgeship later on, and after retirement with these posts.

In September 2014, the appointment of former CJI, P. Sathasivam, as the governor of Kerala, touched off storm with opposition parties accusing the former CJI of quid pro quo and a reward for the relief he gave to Amit Shah in a fake encounter case on 8 April 2013.[328] Even many former judges, including former CJI, and leading members of the Bar, took exception to his gubernatorial assignment who feel that Sathasivam let down the judiciary by accepting the offer. It was not for the first time that a former judge was appointed governor, but it was for the first time that a former CJI occupied this post. Justice Sathasivam was on the Supreme Court bench that had quashed the second FIR against Shah in a fake encounter case on the ground that it was linked to the Sohrabuddin Sheikh encounter case that did not need to be separate. Denying the allegation he said that it is not legal to file a second FIR. However, it is true that when Justice Sathasivam gave the judgement, the BJP was not at the helms at the Centre.

So far as judges are concerned, there is a need to impose a total ban on any post-retirement jobs for them. The proposal was mooted in the Constituent Assembly on 7 June 1949 by Professor K.T. Shah who wanted to introduce a new article 193-A that read:

No one who has been a judge of the Supreme Court, or of the Federal Court, or of any High Court shall be appointed to any executive office under the Government of India or the Government of any State in the Union including the office of an Ambassador, Minister, Plenipotentiary, High Commissioner,

---

[327] Telecast on RS TV and DD NEWS, 5 September 2013.
[328] *Amitbhai Anilchandra Shah* v. *The Central Bureau of Investigation* (2013) 6 SCC 348.

Trade Commissioner, Consul as well as of a Minister in the Government of India or under the Government of any State in the Union.[329]

He elaborated, 'One way by which the executive has tried in the past to tempt the highest judicial officers is by holding out the prospect of more dazzling places on the executive side which would be offered to those who were more convenient or amenable to their suggestions.'[330]

However, the proposal was defeated.

The first Law Commission, headed by the then attorney-general, M.C. Setalvad, which submitted its report on 16 September 1958, recommended that judges of the higher judiciary should not accept any government job after retirement. Then chief justice of the Bombay high court, Justice M.C. Chagla, was a signatory to it as a member of the Commission. However, soon after it, in 1959, he resigned from his post only to be appointed India's ambassador to the US. He did not escape Setalvad's acerbic pen who commented in his autobiography later that the Commission had unanimously recommended that a constitutional bar should be imposed on judges accepting office under the Union or State governments as it would affect the independence of the judiciary:

> Chagla, who was the Chief Justice of Bombay High Court and a member of the Commission, had concurred in this recommendation. He had, however, always yearned to be in politics and, and had while Chief Justice expressed political opinions which a Judge ought not to. He was so keen to get into politics that after the Report was signed by him ('even before the ink of his signature on the report was dry'—as observed in a letter to the Press) he resigned his office to become India's Ambassador to the United States. His action was characteristic of the self-seeking attitude of many of our leading men.[331]

Chagla complained to him for his comment to which Setalvad replied that he thought it was too mild. Justice Chagla is an icon for judges who remained honest and impervious to any influence to a fault, but even he could not resist the temptation of accepting a government job. Later, he became a Union minister also.

However, some of them do not prefer any jobs and opt for the hugely lucrative field of arbitration. Such judges earn in tonnes and fix hearings at

[329] Constituent Assembly Debates, vol. VIII, no. 1, p. 676.
[330] Constituent Assembly Debates, vol. VIII, no. 1, p. 676.
[331] Motilal C. Setalvad, *My Life: Law and Other Things*, with an introduction by Fali S. Nariman (Delhi: Universal Publishing Co. Pvt. Ltd., 1999), p. 260.

exotic locations. Some former judges give their opinions which petitioners annex with the petition. There have been occasions when the Supreme Court has frowned upon such practices. On 20 January 2012, a bench of Chief Justice Kapadia and Justices A.K. Patnaik and Swanter Kumar flew into a rage and rebuked petitioner Grenadiers Association for citing opinions of four former CJIs. The bench was so upset that it passed a judicial order directing the Supreme Court Registry not to accept petitions where opinions of retired judges are annexed.[332]

However, there have been a few conscientious judges like late V.R. Krishna Iyer, M.N. Venkatachaliah, late J.S. Verma, Ruma Paul, et al., who refused to earn fortunes and did/are doing some social work. It does not behove the retired chief justices and judges of the Supreme Court to take up arbitration whose awards are challenged even in the civil court. The question of law and that of fact cannot be challenged, but on three limited grounds the award can be challenged—misconduct of the arbitrator, jurisdiction of the tribunal which the arbitrator has to decide, and if it is against public policy.

Don't Turn Courts into Fortresses

In the name of security, the Supreme Court and most of the high courts have been turned into fortresses making it well-nigh impossible for the common man to enter the premises. After a bomb blast near the Delhi High Court, security was tightened so much that courts also gave the look of elite institutions where access was restricted to privileged few. It is extremely difficult for even the in-person petitioners to enter without the help of some lawyer. A bomb was thrown into the chief justice's court at Patna on 5 October 1936. Chief Justice Courtney Terrell wrote a letter to Viceroy Lord Linlithgo pleading for a fresh outlook on young terrorists on the ground that they were mixed up than criminal. Linlithgo's son Glendevon has written, 'He (Chief Justice Terrell) was surprised to receive an immediate, personal and sympathetic reply. Research has not discovered whether there was any significant follow-up of this initiative but is certain that my father must have looked into the problem'.[333] Whatever was the follow-up, the High Court did not become inaccessible for the common man. No security was enhanced, and nothing untoward happened subsequently for decades. Around 48 years

---

[332] *Times of India*, 21 July 2012.

[333] Glevendon, 'Introduction', in Richard Terrell, *The Chief Justice: A Portraint from the Raj* (Salisbury: Michael Russell (Publishing) Ltd., 1979), p. 11.

later, in 1984, bid was made on the life of Justice P.S. Sahay in the open court. He was fired at, but it did not hit him. The assailant was grabbed by his orderly. Later it turned out that the assailant wanted to kill Justice P.S. Mishra and entered Justice Sahay's court because of the similarity in the two names. Ironically, he was acquitted many years later by the trial court as the witness turned hostile. Justice A.N. Grover was attacked in his court, the Supreme Court and he was injured and taken to the hospital by the then CJI M. Hidayatullah. But the Supreme Court was not converted into a fortress. Justice O. Chinappa Reddy has observed, '... the administration of justice is a vital concern for the public more than any private party. The public has the right to be present in court and watch the proceeding and its conduct except in the very rare cases where the very cause of advancement of justice requires that the proceeding be held in camera.'[334]

In fact, the right of reporting court proceedings also emanates from the concept that whatever transpires in court is public. In *Naresh Sridhar Mirajkar and Others* v. *State of Maharashtra*,[335] the Supreme Court clearly said that what takes place in court is public, and the publication of the proceedings merely enlarges the area of the court and gives to the trial that added publicity which is favoured by the rule that the trial should be open and public. In my view, it should apply not only to subordinate courts, but also to higher courts.

If the Common man is not allowed, it smacks of some design or conspiracy. In the Lahore Conspiracy case in which Bhagat Singh, Shivram Rajguru, and Sukh Dev were sentenced to death on 7 October 1930, the trial took place in a closed court which had been converted into a high security fortress. Armed guards kept vigil on roads leading to the trial. The district magistrate, the Legal remembrancer, the deputy inspector-general of Police, the senior superintendent of Police, Khan Bahadur Abdul Aziz, and other senior officers were present in large numbers. The general public was not allowed to enter the court-room in the Central Jail. Permits for admission were given to relations of the accused after arduous efforts. Defence counsel were stopped at the door and allowed to enter only after a lapse of some time. Bhagat Singh's legal advisor Lala Duni Chand, took exception to the trial being held in prison and in the ambience which gave it the appearance of 'a small gaol'.[336] He asserted that admission must not be restricted arbitrarily by permits. The court

---

[334] *Samarias Trading C. (P) Ltd. S. Samuel* (1984) 4 SCC 666, para 7.

[335] (1966) SCR (3) 744.

[336] A.G. Noorani, *The Trial of Bhagat Singh* (New Delhi: Oxford University Press, 1996), p. 55.

quipped, 'Should the whole city come here?' He replied, 'Everybody who wants to come should be admitted provided there is room.'[337]

* * *

Every democratic country needs a truly strong and independent judiciary to keep the government in check. Alexander Hamilton pointed out, 'Limitations on government can be preserved in practice no other way than through the medium of courts of justice…. Without this, all the reservations of particular rights or privileges would amount to nothing.'[338]

So, the judiciary enjoys tremendous power to discharge its function of protecting legal rights of all and chastening the government if it goes wayward. But power is accompanied by duty and accountability. The old English case of *Julius* v. *Bishop of Oxford*,[339] laid down a cardinal doctrine that whenever power was conferred on a public authority, it was coupled with a duty. Accountability is the mechanism to ensure that the duty is discharged judiciously without fear and favour. Power and accountability go hand in hand. Accountability and equality are cardinal principles of democracy, and the judiciary, being one of its estates, cannot have different standards for itself. Accountability and transparency heighten the credibility of an institution, and the judiciary, without the power of either the purse or the sword, subsists on its moral authority which far outweighs legal authority. Independence without accountability gets impaired. Accountability does not only mean total absence of consideration while deciding a case, but also entails the question of jurisdiction. If it directs the executive to do something which is beyond its domain and which has huge political and financial implications, it is negation of democracy. But courts pass such orders as they do not have any accountability. The judiciary cannot have finger in every pie.

To ward off accountability in the name of independence is appalling. Judges' plea that they are vulnerable and once they are made accountable, they will be harassed by disgruntled litigants, is frivolous. There is no reason to assume that every loser in each case will launch a smear campaign against the judge who decides the case. We must have faith in the common man's integrity and wisdom. Moreover, every criticism should not be dismissed as the ranting and raving of a disgruntled loser. Litigants know the merits of

---

[337] Noorani, *The Trial of Bhagat Singh*.

[338] Alexander Hamilton, *The Federalist*, no. 78, Clinton Rossiter ed., 1961, at pp. 465, 466.

[339] (1880) 5 AC 214.

their cases and can weigh the judgement accordingly. Several times there is real miscarriage of justice. Judges must not forget that by inflicting injustice in one case, they antagonize not just the loser, but all those who can evaluate impartially, thereby denting their own credibility. No one can blackmail an honest and impartial judge. Let us remember the words of William Jennings Brayan, 'The humblest citizen of all the land, when clad in the armour of a righteous cause, is stranger than all the hosts of error.'[340]

---

[340] Speech at the Democratic National Convention, 1896.

3

Binary Application of Laws

Society Is Barbarous without Justice

> What are kingdoms but great robberies? For what are
> robberies themselves, but little kingdoms?

> —St. Augustine in *The City of God.*

Justice is the beginning and end of any government and civil society. Craving
for justice is fundamental to human beings. That is why in Hindu scriptures,
justice has been equated with dharma and courts of justice have been described
as *dharmadhikaran*. An inalienable feature of justice is that it is blindfolded;
it does not discriminate and the law is applied uniformly. Fa-Hien recorded
(400 CE) how Emperor Asoka subjected himself to the majesty of the law.
After becoming a universal monarch, while passing through Jambudwipa
in the administration of justice, he came across a place of torture, situated
between two mountains and surrounded by an iron wall, where punishment
was inflicted on the wicked and crooked. On inquiring about it, he was told
that this was the place where Jemma, the infernal king, punished wicked men
for their crimes. Asoka thought that he too should have a place for punishments. Since only an extremely wicked man could create a hell and exercise
authority therein for the punishment of the dregs of the society, he dispatched
his ministers in all directions to find such a man. In the words of Fa-Hien:

> In the course of their search they saw, by the side of a running stream, a lusty
> great fellow of black colour, with red hair and light eyes, with feet like talons,
> and a mouth like that of a fish. When he whistled to the birds and beasts they

came to him, and when they approached he mercilessly shot them through, so that none escaped. Having caught this man, he was brought before the king. The king then gave him these secret orders, 'You must enclose a square space with high walls, and with this enclosure plant every kind of flower and fruit (tree), and make beautiful lakes and alcoves, and arrange everything with such taste as to cause men to be anxious to look within the enclosure. Then, having made a wide gate, the moment a man enters within the precincts, seize him at once, and subject him to every kind of infernal torture. And whatever you do, let no one (who has once entered) ever go out again. And I strictly enjoin you that if I even should enter that enclosure, that you torture me also and spare not....'[1]

It so happened that a Buddhist monk, while begging, entered the gate. The infernal keeper seized him and prepared to put him to torture. The monk was quite frightened and implored him to let him have his midday meal. Exactly, at this moment, another man entered the hell. The keeper pounced on him and, and putting him in a stone mortar, began to pulverise his body to atoms till a red froth oozed out from him. The monk, realizing the ephemeral nature of the body, arrived at the condition of a *Rahat*.[2] He was thrown into a cauldron of boiling water. Then a miracle took place. The heart of the monk bubbled with joy and his face was luminous. The fire was extinguished, the water became cold and in the middle of it sprang up a lotus, on the top of which the monk was seated. The dumbfounded keeper immediately rushed to the king and requested him to come and see this. According to Fa-Hein:

> The king said, 'I dare not come, in consideration of my former agreement with you'. The keeper replied, 'This matter is of great moment: it is only right you should come; let us consider your former agreement changed'. The king then followed him and entered the prison, on which, the Bikshu, for his sake, delivered a religious discourse, so that the king believed and was converted (obtained deliverance).[3]

Indian scriptures are replete with admonitions to kings. Sir William Jones, one of the first judges of the Supreme Court of Judicature of Bengal, did an authoritative translation of the *Manusmriti* from Sanskrit to English which

---

[1] *Travellers' India*, Second impression, chosen and edited by H.K. Kaul (Delhi: Oxford University Press, 1998), pp. 472–3.

[2] Rahat was a system of irrigation in ancient India to get water from well using oxen or water wheel.

[3] *Travellers' India*, p. 473.

was published in 1894. In the preface to the book, he makes this adulatory remark, 'The style of it [of the *Manusmriti*] has a certain austere majesty that sounds like the language of legislation and exhorts a respectful awe; the sentiments of independence on all beings but God, and the harsh admonitions even to kings are truly noble....'[4]

There can be a rule of law only when laws are applied uniformly, and it is rooted firmly in the interrelated notions of neutrality, uniformity, and predictability. It has nothing to do with the content of legal norms.[5] Judges are under an obligation to enforce laws without any discrimination. Lord Denning described it in a judgement: 'To every subject in this land, no matter how powerful, I would use Thomas Fuller's words: "Be you ever so high, the law is above you".'[6] According to A.V. Dicey:

> In England the idea of legal equality, or of the universal subjection of all classes to one law administered by the ordinary courts, has been pushed to its utmost limit. With us every official, from the Prime Minister down to a constable or a collector of taxes, is under the same responsibility for every act done without legal justification as any other citizen.[7]

Indian scriptures also mention in unambiguous words that members of a court must not connive with the king if he deviates from the path of justice. Rather, they must bring him to the right path by coaxing and persuasion. They would be parties to the sin if they agreed with the king in his unjust decisions and would fall head downwards into hell along with the king.

Laws Different for Different People

Show Me the Person and I shall Show You the Law

However, these lofty ideals are hardly put into practice in the modern age. Poor people rarely get the protection of the law; rather they are mostly discriminated against. Solon lamented, 'Laws are like spiders' webs: If some

---

[4] Quoted by Fali S. Nariman, *India's Legal System: Can It Be Saved?* (New Delhi: Penguin Books, 2006), p. 4.

[5] Roberto Mongabeira Unger, *Law in Modern Society: Towards a Criticism of Social Theory* (New York: The Free Press, 1976).

[6] *Gouriet* v. *Union of Post Office Workers* (1977), 1 QB 729, pp. 761–2.

[7] A.V. Dicey, 'The Rule of law: Its Nature and General Application', in *An Introduction to the Study of the Law of the Constitution with an introduction by E. C. S. Wade*, first published in 1885 (New Delhi: Universal Law Publishing Co., 2012), p. 193.

poor weak creature comes up against them, it is caught; but a big one can break through and get away'.[8] Oliver Goldsmith was equally forceful, 'Laws grind the poor, and rich men rule the law'.[9]

Voltaire was sent behind bars without trial when he took on the young French nobleman Chevalier de Rohan. In 1726, he responded to an insult from Rohan whose servants beat him a few days later. As Voltaire was seeking compensation and was even willing to fight in a duel, the Rohan family obtained a royal *lettre de cachet*, a decree signed by the French King, Louis XV which was invariably used to dispose of troublemakers of different ilks like drunkards, violent people, unequal marriages, and so on. The warrant led to Voltaire's incarceration in the Bastille without a trial and without an opportunity to defend himself. Fearing an indefinite jail term, he requested for being exiled to England which was accepted. The incident inspired him to make attempts to reform the French judicial system. After approximately three years in exile, Voltaire returned to Paris. At a dinner, mathematician Charles Mary de La Condamine proposed to buy the lottery that was organized by the French government to pay off its debt. Voltaire joined the consortium, earning perhaps a million livres. He invested the money wisely and on this basis could successfully convince the court that he bore a good moral conduct and so was able to receive an inheritance from his father that had been refused. He was then awfully rich.[10]

Torture was an accepted method in medieval Britain in treason trials. Queen Elizabeth, within four months of her accession to the throne, wrote to the Lieutenant of the Tower on 15 March 1559, asking him to examine two prisoners accused of robbery. She directed that if they denied guilt, they were 'to be brought to the rack, and feel the smart thereof as the examiners by their discretion shall think good for the better *boulting* out the truth of the matter'.[11] However, Coke claimed that torture was not applied to people of noble blood. In the Countess of Shrewsbury's Case, judges, Coke being one of them, declared that it was a 'privilege which the law gives for the honour and reverence of the nobility, that their bodies are not subject to torture'.[12]

---

[8] Quoted in Diogenes Laeritius, *Lives of the Eminent Philosophers*, translated into English by Robert Drew Hicks, Loeb Classical Library, Harvard University Press.

[9] See Arthur Morgan, *Handbook of Quotations*, Special Indian Edition (New Delhi: GOYL Saab, 1999), p. 174.

[10] Ian Davidson, *Voltaire: A Life* (London: Profile Books, 2010), p. 76.

[11] John Hostettler, *Sir Edward Coke: A Force for Freedom* (Delhi: Universal Law Publishing Co. Pvt. Ltd., 2006), p. 21.

[12] Hostettler, *Sir Edward Coke*, pp. 21–2.

There are instances galore which testify to the discriminatory application of laws. Judge Cadena referred to the case of a Houston policeman who was awarded two years' probation for pleading guilty to possessing 76 pounds of marijuana, though a San Antonio youth was sentenced to 25 years in jail for possession of 16 marijuana cigarettes.[13] Similarly, Indians were treated shabbily at the hands of the British in the garb of the law. An Indian was sentenced to three weeks of hard labour because he defended himself when some dogs, owned by an Englishman, attacked him. Poet Toru Dutt fulminated against it, 'The papers are speaking against the crying scandalous shame; the magistrate and the Sessions Judge ought to be dismissed for so monstrous a perversion of law. Imagine the row that would have been made in England at a Magistrate sending a boy to a treadmill under such circumstances.'[14]

Jawaharlal Nehru has written:

It was a notorious fact that whenever an Englishman killed an Indian he was acquitted by a jury of his own countrymen. In railway trains compartments were reserved for Europeans and however crowded the trains might be—and they used to be terribly crowded—no Indian was allowed to travel in them, even though they were empty. Even an unreserved compartment would be taken possession of by an Englishman and he would not allow any Indian to enter it.[15]

Penderel Moon, a distinguished British ICS officer, was so perturbed by the victimization of freedom fighters that he resigned from the service. He lambasted the British administration, especially its judicial system, and wrote that large numbers of innocent persons were convicted or hanged and officials who knew that they were innocent could do nothing about it.[16]

'Show me the man and I'll show you the law' is a Scottish proverb. Lloyd Duhaime Permalink has written:

One of the most significant disadvantages of the judge-based system of dispute resolution is that much rides on the person who sits as judge.

Often, though it is not supposed to, the personal feelings and biases of the judge enters into the equation.

[13] V.R. Krishna Iyer, *Law Versus Justice* (New Delhi: Deep and Deep Publications, 1983), p. 20.

[14] Amiya Rao, 'Toru Dutt', in *Women Pioneers In India's Renaissance*, edited by Sushila Nayar and Kamla Mankekar (New Delhi: National Book Trust, India, 2002), p. 7.

[15] Jawaharlal Nehru, *An Autobiography* (New Delhi: Penguin Books, 2004), p. 7.

[16] Penderel Moon, *Strangers in India* (London, Faber and Faber Ltd., 2011).

For example, almost all judges are former lawyers and so necessarily highly educated. Because education usually requires a significant investment, a very low proportion of judges are eventually drawn from the lower classes of society. Litigants and lawyers often suspect that a judge's ruling results from a lack of exposure to some of the hardships of a working class life.

Thus the expression 'show me the man and I'll show you the law' refers to the reality of judges that they are often persuaded not by the evidence before them but by personal consideration.[17]

Allegations of Double Standards against the International Criminal Court

The International Criminal Court (ICC) is struggling for credibility as South Africa, Burundi, and The Gambia decided to withdraw from it raising serious questions on its raison d'être. African leaders openly accused it of racial bias at the week-long deliberations of the ICC that kicked off in New York on 8 December 2014. Many of them, without mincing words, rued that they have lost faith in the court because only Africans were being tried, and some blamed a 'cabal' of wicked Western powers.[18]

It may be recalled that anguished by the Rwandan genocide in 1994 and the unpunished crimes of apartheid, it was African leaders who pushed for it. Thirty-four African countries are among the 139 countries that signed the Rome Statute. South Africa, a founding member, quit because it could not reconcile sharp conflict between its obligations to the African Union to grant immunity to serving heads of states and to the ICC which had issued a warrant against Sudanese President Omar al-Bashir, who participated in the African Union (AU) Summit hosted by South Africa in June 2015. On the one hand, it was obligatory for South Africa to arrest al-Bashir and hand him over to The Hague for his trial, on the other hand, it had to provide diplomatic immunity to him. However, Burundi was more forthright as it officially branded the ICC as a 'Western tool to target African governments'.[19] The fact that nine

---

[17] http://www.duhaime.org/LawMuseum/LawArticle-421/Show-Me-The-Man. aspx (last accessed on 20 June 2015).

[18] 'Nice Idea, Now Make It Work: The International Criminal Court Is Struggling to Justify Itself amid Accusations of Bias against Africa', *The Economist Newspaper Limited*, 2014, reproduced in *Indian Express*, 11 December 2014.

[19] Abraham Joseph, 'Why Did South Africa, Burundi and Gambia Decide to Leave the International Criminal Court', 1 November 2016, https://thewire.in/ 76869/why-did-south-africa-burundi-and-gambia-decide-to-leave-the-international-criminal-court/ (last accessed on 1 April 2017).

out of 10 situations being investigated then by the office of the prosecutor were in Africa (Mali, Cote D' Ivoire, Central African Republic, Libya, Kenya, Sudan, Uganda, and Democratic Republic of Congo) lent credence to the allegation. Georgia is the only country facing investigation that is not in Africa. The ICC's impartiality is also questioned because of its inability to try heads of state or other leaders of any of the permanent members of the Security Council (P5 countries) or even launch preliminary investigations against them for acts of impunity. But it is also true that Burundi's President, Pierre Nkrunziza was likely to be tried for widespread violence against political opponents as ICC chief prosecutor Fatou Bensouda had announced in April 2016 of the ICC's plan of opening a preliminary investigation into killings, imprisonment, torture, rape, and other acts of sexual violence in Burundi.

The Gambia accused the court of 'persecution and humiliation of people of colour, especially Africans'.[20] Curiously, Bensouda is a Gambian national. President of The Gambia, Yahya Jammeh, may have a poor human rights track record and liable to be prosecuted, but he rightly pointed out the non-prosecution of Tony Blair for his role in the Iraq war as a glaring example of how partial the court is. Of P5 countries, three—USA, Russia, and China—did not sign the Rome Statute, but Britain is a signatory, and so it has to accept the ICC's jurisdiction. But no prosecution was launched. George Bush was guilty of waging war against Iraq on concocted charges, but since the USA did not sign it, he would not accept its jurisdiction. Out of total 41 indictments made so far by the ICC, all except one are Africans.

Cardinal Principles Enshrined in the Constitution but with Discriminatory Application

After suffering so much of humiliation and injustice, the founding fathers of our Constitution gave place of pride to justice. Some of the essential prerequisites to ensure justice to all are: equality before the law; the independence of the judiciary; and the absence of arbitrary powers. Therefore, equality before the law and equal protection by the law to all citizens are the most fundamental rights enshrined in the Constitution. Granville Austin has written:

> During the British period, despite the presence of Indian in government, Indians had not been responsible for the laws that governed them. Indians had

[20] Joseph, 'Why Did South Africa, Burundi and Gambia Decide to Leave the International Criminal Court'.

neither law nor courts of their own, and both the courts and the law had been designed to meet the needs of the colonial power. Under the Constitution, all this would be changed. The courts were, therefore, widely considered one of the most tangible evidences of independence. And to the lawyers with which the Congress—and the Assembly—abounded, the opportunity to draft the judicial system under which they would function must have seemed the chance to write their own scriptures.[21]

Many laws enacted by the Parliament and state legislatures have been struck down by several courts on the grounds that they violate this basic principle of equality before the law. However, the courts generally stood by the propertied class, but in some cases, the Supreme Court did try to protect the rights of the underprivileged. In *Basheshar Nath* v. *Commissioner, Income Tax*,[22] the question arose whether a citizen could voluntarily waive his fundamental rights. Bhagwati and Subba Rao, JJ held with S.K. Das, J. dissenting, that one could not do so and laid down the principle that 'A large majority of our people are economically poor, educationally backward and politically not yet conscious of their rights. Individually or even collectively, they cannot be pitted against the state organizations and institutions, nor can they meet them on equal terms. In such circumstances, it is the duty of this court to protect their rights against themselves.'[23]

However, the Supreme Court itself appears to have forgotten these cardinal principles as is evident from some of its decisions that gave extraordinary relief to accused VIPs. In 1985, Justice E.S. Venkatramiah of the Supreme Court granted bail to Lalit Mohan Thapar, a major industrialist, in a criminal case at night at his residence. It was challenged in *Bihar Legal Support Society* v. *Chief Justice of India*,[24] in which the petitioner contended that the Supreme Court gives priority to important people at the cost of poor people. The Supreme Court disposed of the petition saying that it shares society's concern about the poor but it does not discriminate between the rich and the poor. Can this display of concern for the depressed and the clarification convince anyone? Laws, more often than not, are applied in such a way as to favour the 'privilegentsia', a word coined by Robin Crook who

[21] Granville Austin, 'The Judiciary and the Social Revolution', in *The Indian Constitution: Cornerstone of a Nation* (New Delhi: Oxford University Press, 2016), p. 204.

[22] AIR (1959) SC 149.

[23] AIR (1959) SC 149, 183.

[24] (1986) 4 SCC 767.

has commented, 'Discretion runs from top to bottom. In Bombay one hears of the well-connected businessmen who, in Indira Gandhi's time, had a shipload of prohibited chemicals waiting outside the docks; the ban was lifted for 24 hours.'[25] Dhirubhai Ambani was one such individual who could tweak the system as per his requirement, get the law changed, or get a favourable interpretation of the law. Hamish McDonald has written:

> Dhirubhai was not a law-breaker but had a creative attitude towards regulation. As one former colleague recalled: 'He would say: "You should not do anything illegal. First of all, the law should be changed."' 'He would not go into anything which was unlawful', agreed Kothary of the Silk and Arts Silk Mills Research Association (Sasmira). 'Everything he did was permitted to do by any other man. But his reading of the system! You have a law, the interpretation which you make—he would take advantage of a particular system in a way which others could not see. By the time other people started anything the government was also waking up and the system would be changed.[26]

Noted lawyer Fali S. Nariman has narrated an incident about how the same bench of the apex court gave conflicting orders in similar case. In 1975, before the proclamation of the Emergency, he had appeared (as the law officer of the Union) in a group of matters in the Delhi High Court on behalf of the government, where preventive detention orders on persons, later acknowledged to be smugglers, were challenged in writ petitions under Article 226 of the Constitution. The High Court, after reserving the judgement, delivered it on a Friday and quashed the detention orders saying the grounds of detention were inadequate. The same day he rushed to the Supreme Court and interrupted a part-heard matter before a Constitution Bench presided over by Chief justice A.N. Ray, and requested to stay the order of the High Court—undertaking that the special leave petition would be filed by next Monday. Declining the prayer, the chief justice pompously said, 'This is a matter of personal liberty and we have neither the judgement nor any written application from government and we cannot on mere oral application grant a stay.'[27] Later, in the first week of July the same year, after the emergency had been imposed, the then solicitor general, Lal Narayan Sinha presented a case concerning municipal councillors of Bombay who had been detained

---

[25]   Robin Crook, 'Rule of Law or Black Money', *Hindustan Times*, 12 May 1991.

[26]   Hamish McDonald, 'A First Class Journey', in *Ambani and Sons* (New Delhi: The Lotus Collection, 2010), p. 156.

[27]   Fali S. Nariman, 'Lest We Crawl', *Indian Express*, 25 March 2017.

under Maintenance of Internal Security Act (MISA). Mayoral election was going to be held and the Congress party had nominated its candidate. If the councillors detained under the preventive detention law were allowed to vote, the Congress would have lost the mayoral election. In a writ petition filed on behalf of those detenues in the Bombay High court, it was contended that they had not lost their right to vote and that they should be allowed to vote either at the detaining centre or be brought under guard to the voting centre. The High Court granted the prayer as it seemed quite reasonable. The following morning the solicitor general appeared in the Supreme Court without any paper or even the judgement of the High Court and orally asked the judges for a stay which was immediately granted. Nariman writes, 'the same Supreme Court, the same chief justice, and to the best of my recollection, the same set of judges, orally granted a stay of the decision of the high court—which resulted ultimately in the Congress nominee for the mayor being elected. So much (I then said to myself) for the court's abiding concerns for personal liberty!'[28]

In some other cases too, concerning VIPs, the court has given orders which defy all logic and reason. In 1996, in a cheating case against former Prime Minister P.V. Narasimha Rao, the Supreme Court directed that he would not be arrested even if his bail petition was rejected by the lower court.[29] This virtually amounted to nullifying the provisions of the Criminal Procedure Code. It must be understood that the Supreme Court has no power to create a law. Even the application of the 'complete justice' clause provided in Article 142 is limited and it cannot substitute a substantive law.

Legal experts as well as the common people were astounded when in 2001 it directly entertained the appeal filed by Lalu Prasad, former chief minister of Bihar, against the rejection of his bail petition in a fodder scam case by a special CBI court and granted him bail. Though Article 136 confers wide powers on the Supreme Court and a Special Leave Petition (SLP) can be filed against any order of any court, the convention is that an SLP is entertained only against the orders of high courts. Moreover, the Supreme Court rules mention only the orders of a high court, and not subordinate courts, against which SLPs are to be filed. There are a few precedents when the Supreme Court entertained SLPs directly against the orders of the subordinate courts but those were rare cases with extraordinary circumstances. What irreparable damage would have been done to the justice delivery system had Lalu Prasad

[28] Nariman, 'Lest We Crawl'.
[29] *Chandra Swami* v. *Central Bureau of Investigation* (1996) 6 SCC 751.

challenged the Special Court's order in the high court which is the proper forum for appeal? The Supreme Court ruled:

> In the above peculiar circumstance and the interconnections of the case with the facts in RC 64 A of 1997 in which bail was granted to these petitioners (Lalu Prasad and Jagannath Mishra) by this court we are not disposed to reject the Special Leave Petition purely for the purpose of directing them to go to the High Court first before approaching this court.[30]

It may be recalled that the Supreme Court has been dismissing petitions under Article 32 for the enforcement of fundamental rights, directing petitioners to first move the high court, though every citizen has a fundamental right to move the apex court directly in cases of fundamental rights violations. The reasoning is that the Court is overburdened. The magnanimity shown in Lalu's case is all the more intriguing when hundreds of thousands of undertrials are languishing in different jails for years and even decades for want of hearing, and it takes several weeks, even months for an ordinary bail petition to be listed for hearing. But in Lalu's case, not one but even two benches of the Supreme Court were available to hear his case.

In August 1998, the Supreme Court granted a stay on Lalu's arrest in RC 64-A/96 (the fodder scam case pertaining to fraudulent withdrawal of Rs 96 lakh from Deoghar treasury). It issued notices and directed the CBI to bring on record the charge sheets of RC 20-A/96 (fraudulent withdrawal of Rs 3.7 crore from Chaibasa treasury) and 64-A/96 since it was argued that Lalu was granted bail in RC 20, though the charges were similar. It was listed again on 21 September 1998 before a bench of M.M. Punchhi, CJ, and Srinivasan and Rajendra Babu, JJ. When the case was taken up, the other two judges pointed out in the open court that similar matters were pending before another bench, comprising M.K. Mukherjee, Sudhakar Panditrao Kurdukar, and K.T. Thomas, JJ, especially constituted to hear the fodder scam cases. Then Punchhi, CJI, ordered that the case may be put up before that bench, but directed that the stay on the arrest would continue.

Cases of Salman Khan and Jayalalithaa

The granting of bail to Salman Khan by the Bombay High Court on 6 May 2015, barely three hours after he was sentenced to five years of rigorous imprisonment by the district court for culpable homicide in a hit and run case, and

---

[30] Sudhanshu Ranjan, 'Binary Application of Laws', *Indian Express*, 14 January 2002.

that too on an oral prayer as the copy of the judgment was not available, is an eloquent commentary on the might of the haves. In fact, the prayer was made after the normal working hour of the high court. After two days, his appeal was admitted and sentence stayed. His lawyers and fans asked shamelessly: must a celebrity suffer just because hundreds of thousands of undertrials are behind the bars whose guilt is yet to be proved? They argued that even the unprivileged should get expeditious justice, but it is no ground to deny justice to those who have the resources to invoke their rights and move courts quickly.[31] M.K. Gandhi had a piece of advice for such influential people:

> [I]t will be asked, what when we are dragged, as we often are, to the courts? I would say 'do not defend'. If you are in the wrong, you will deserve the sentence whatever it may be. If you are wrongly brought to the court and yet penalized, let your innocence soothe you in your unmerited suffering. Undefended, you will in every case suffer the least and what is more you will have the satisfaction of sharing the fate of the majority of your fellow-beings who cannot get themselves defended.[32]

M.K. Gandhi also made another pithy, but apposite, comment, 'Justice in British courts is an expensive luxury. It is often "the longest purse that wins"'.[33] There was no change in the system after independence and moneybags are able to twist and tweak the judicial process with impunity which is often borne out when some celebrity or influential person is in the dock.

On 10 December 2015, the Bombay High Court finally acquitted Salman Khan of all charges. The Sessions Court had convicted him under Section 304(II) and Section 338 of the IPC, for charges relating to culpable homicide not amounting to murder and causing grievous hurt. Justice A.R. Joshi, in his judgement, expressed doubts over the statement of eyewitness Ravindra Patil, former police bodyguard of the actor, recorded by a magistrate, in which he had told that Salman was on the driving seat, and that he was drunk. The judge noted that the prosecution had failed to establish beyond reasonable doubt that Salman was driving and was under the influence of alcohol, and added that it was not clear whether the accident occurred due to bursting of the tyre prior to the incident or tyre burst after the incident. The trial court had accepted Patil's version and he was duly cross-examined.

---

[31] Sudhanshu Ranjan, 'Justice Served, with Partiality', *The Asian Age/The Deccan Chronicle*, 13 May 2015.

[32] *Young India* (23 July 1919), see M.K. Gandhi, *The Law and the Lawyers*, compiled and edited by S.B. Kher (Ahmedabad: Navjiavan Publishing House, 1999), p. 259.

[33] Gandhi, *The Law and the Lawyers*.

The High Court rejected it on the ground that the cross-examination was done when the actor was charged with the less serious offence of causing death by a rash and negligent driving, and that he was not cross-examined specifically after the charge was upgraded to culpable homicide not amounting to murder. This logic may not stand scrutiny on the touchstone of criminal jurisprudence. An FIR is admissible as evidence in criminal cases on the basic principle that what is stated immediately after the crime is committed, would be true. However, Patil was not the only witness. An employee of JW Mariott hotel testified that he saw Salman sitting on the driving seat. Another witness said he saw Salman getting out of the car from the right side. The High Court did not find these statements reliable because these were not corroborated by other witnesses. The question is why should these witnesses perjure and who would corroborate if there were no other witnesses present.

Surprisingly, the High Court also found the deposition of one Ashok Singh as per the rules. He popped in at the last moment, after 13 years, to claim before the Sessions Court that he was driving the car. Anybody could surmise that it was a last-ditch attempt to rescue the besieged actor. Otherwise, where was he for such a long time? He also turned out to be the family driver of Salman's father Salim Khan. The Court did not want any corroboration in this unusual claim! He also claimed that the tyre burst after the accident though Patil had reported that it happened due to the accident. Again Patil's version was not accepted in the absence of corroboration. Salman was also absolved of being under the influence of alcohol though the waiter and manager at the Rain Bar and restaurant at Vile Parle, where Salman had allegedly gone on a binge that evening, testified that Bacardi white rum had been served. Since his glass had a 'clear liquid', the defence was quick to claim that it was water. It is a common knowledge that Bacardi is a colourless liquid, and yet it was taken to be water in the absence of any further proof. Anil Dharker castigated the judgement in these words:

> TAKE YOUR PICK. Choice one: No one was driving the car. Choice Two: Salman Khan has the world's first Google self-driving car. Choice Three: The car was drunk. The facetiousness hides one stark fact: The high court judgment absolving Salman of all charges is a travesty of justice. If you look at the judgment, the court did deliver a 'guilty' verdict. Only, it was not against the Bollywood superstar. The court pronounced 'guilty' for the police and the prosecution team of lawyers. The police, according to the court, did a shoddy job of investigation, while the prosecuting lawyers did a poor job of presenting their case.[34]

[34] Anil Dharker, 'And Justice Lost', *Indian Express*, 21 December 2015.

Salman's case has another hideous facet as to how the prime witness against him, police constable Patil, lost everything, including his life, for speaking out the truth. Patil was Salman's unarmed bodyguard who was with the actor when he (Salman), while driving in an inebriated condition at a high speed, lost control and drove right on to the footpath on 28 September 2002, killing one and injuring four people. Patil had cautioned him not to drive and even asked him to slow down but he did not listen. After giving the statement that Salman was under the influence of alcohol and was at the driving seat, it was claimed that Patil received a lot of pressure to retract, but he stood firm. Later, he was sent to jail on the ground that he failed to appear in the court on five consecutive dates. He lost his job and was kept in the jail with inveterate criminals and was allegedly tortured inside the jail. The story of his misfortune does not end here. According to tehelca.com, after five years in 2007, he was found begging on the streets of Mumbai, and was suffering from TB for over two years. During his worst times, everybody abandoned him—police, media, as well as family. He passed away on 4 October 2007 of TB. Shockingly, his family had already cut him out of their life and they did not even claim or collect his body. It was around his death that Salman started his 'Being Human' initiative.[35] What a cruel irony that Being Human set up on 28 July 2007, could not be human to Patil!

Immediately after Salman Khan got reprieve from the High Court, the Karnataka High Court set aside the conviction of J. Jayalalithaa, ex-chief minister of Tamil Nadu, in a DA case by a subordinate court only to be upturned by the Supreme Court which restored the trial court's judgement in totality.[36] She was accused of amassing assets worth Rs 66,65,20,395 between 1 July 1991 and 30 April 1996 by hatching a criminal conspiracy with three others for her nefarious purpose. During this period, she was the chief minister drawing a token monthly salary of one rupee. The Supreme Court transferred the case to Karnataka in 2002. The trial court found her guilty and put her DA at Rs 53.6 crore and sentenced her to 4 years of imprisonment and imposed a fine of Rs 100 crore under Section 13(1)(e) of the Prevention of Corruption Act, 1988, following which she was disqualified from the Legislative Assembly. But the Karnataka High Court, relying on a pre-1988 judgement when the present Prevention of Corruption Act was

[35] 'How Salman Khan Hit and Run Case Ruined Bodyguard Ravindra's Patil's Life', http://www.tehelka.com/how-salman-khan-ruined-101-bodyguard-ravindra-patil/ (last accessed on 27 June 2015).

[36] *State of Karnataka* v. *Selvi J. Jayalalithaa*, 2017 (6) SCC 263: Cr. Appeal Nos. 300-303 of 2007, decided on 14 February 2017.

not in force, ruled that DA up to 10 per cent could be condoned. Through some arithmetic jugglery, Justice C.R. Kumaraswamy found that Jayalalithaa's unaccounted assets were only to the tune of 2.82 crore, which was just 8.12 per cent of her wealth, that is, below 10 per cent. The judge made errors in simple addition while calculating nine bank loans which cumulatively came to Rs 24,17,31,274 but according to his calculation, it was only Rs 10,67,31274. If the difference of Rs 13,50,00,00 is accounted, her DA would go up to 75.76 per cent. The judgement suffered from many other infirmities as Karnataka was not made a party during the entire appeal proceedings which was an essential legal prerequisite. Principle of natural justice was thrown to the wind as the defence counsel argued for two months in the absence of the public prosecutor who was not appointed. A prosecutor was appointed only after the argument of the defence was over and the prosecution was allowed 24 hours to make a written submission within 50 pages. The court also admitted foreign remittance of Rs 77 lakh and Rs 1.5 crore received as gifts on the occasion of her 44th birthday as her income.

Justice Kumaraswamy acquitted her of all charges. It is not surprising that the judge was himself accused of acquiring DA in the form of precious immovable properties in Bengaluru and Mysuru through Bangalore Development Authority, Karantaka Housing Board, Karnataka State Judicial employees Housing Society. He allegedly violated in the site allotment rules and housing building society bye-laws. The allegations were levelled by a group of RTI activists and advocates under the banner of Karnataka Bhrastachara Nirmoolan Vedike.[37] Finally, the High Court's judgement was set aside by the apex court.

Anti-Sikh Riot Cases, 1984

In 1984, in the anti-Sikh riots case, Sajjan Kumar, a prominent Congress leader, was granted anticipatory bail by the Delhi High Court on oral prayer, and that too after he was arrested, and the registrar made a phone call to the CBI not to arrest him as he had been granted bail. He was arrested on 11 September 1990 at 6:45 am by the CBI at his house in West Delhi. After the arrest, the CBI team started conducting the search of his house. While the search was on, a large crowd of his supporters assembled outside his house and raised provocative slogans against the CBI. They also installed a loudspeaker

---

[37] 'Judge in the Jayalalithaa Case in Soup over Sites', *Deccan Chronicle*, 25 August 2015, http://www.deccanchronicle.com/150825/nation-current-affairs/article/judge-jayalalitha-case-under-scrutiny (last accessed on 1 April 2017).

and repeatedly threatened the CBI officials of dire consequences if they had the audacity to take Kumar away with them. Their vehicles were damaged, and the CBI officials, instead of taking him away, were themselves detained. According to Manoj Mitta and H.S. Phoolka:

> The high drama in Sajjan Kumar's neighbourhood was actually a ploy to gain time and obtain anticipatory bail from the Delhi High Court, which was still being administered by Chief Justice RN Pyne, who had been ... especially transferred to the capital during Rajiv Gandhi's reign, to shield Sajjan Kumar. A lawyer mentioned the matter before Justice Pyne, who then directed Justice MK Chawla to hear Sajjan Kumar's anticipatory bail. There was no question of anticipatory bail at that stage because he had already been arrested early in the morning. But the vital piece of legal information was conveniently held back from the court. On his part, Justice Chawla, too, made no effort to find out Sajjan Kumar's status at that moment, even after he had been told that the CBI team was already there at the Congress leader's house. The only use that the judge made of that detail was that he got the court registrar to call up Sajjan Kumar's house and direct the CBI team to release him immediately.[38]

Some Laws Are Not Enforced

While laws are violated to give the privileged what is barred under the law, its opposite is equally true that certain laws are violated, or rather, not enforced to deny to the poor and deprived classes, that which is due to them under the law. CPI leader D. Raja has brought to light how Dalits are not allowed to become Panchayat presidents:

> The letter and spirit of the constitutional mandate for Dalit reservation in Panchayats is being openly flouted in several villages of Tamil Nadu without the authorities, in either Chennai or New Delhi, doing anything about it.
>
> In Pappapatti, a village in Madurai district where the post of sarpanch is reserved for Dalits, vested interest groups have repeatedly subverted the election process. Of 19 attempts made between 1996 and 2004 to elect a sarpanch, only thrice was the process allowed to be completed. Even on these three occasions, however, a candidate supported by the local dominant caste won, only to resign a few minutes later.[39]

[38] Manoj Mitta and H.S. Phoolka, *When a Tree Shook Delhi: The 1984 Carnage and Its Aftermath* (New Delhi: Lotus Collection Roli Books, 2007), pp. 158–9.

[39] D. Raja, 'Where Caste Oppression Mocks the Constitution', *The Hindu*, 24 June 2005.

Some Laws Are Also Discriminatory

Though the Constitution guarantees equality before the law, changes were not effected in some laws enacted during the colonial era and were clearly class-biased. It is not only a question of the law being applied differently; it is a question of some laws being inherently discriminatory. The IPC is one such example which clearly discriminates against the underprivileged. K.D. Gaur has pointed out some gaping holes in law:

> A careful study of the provisions of the (Indian Penal) code would reveal that it is undoubtedly a manifestation of the will of the dominant class determined by economic and political motives. It makes a broad classification of crimes against property, person and the state. Out of a total of 511 sections ... in the code, 85 sections have been devoted to offences against property and 33 sections to the offences relating to the documents and property-marks respectively to protect and safeguard the interest of the elite. But not even a single section is enacted to take care of the poor and the weak ... the rich man who refuses a mouthful of rice to save a fellow creature from death is a far worse man and criminal than the starving man (wretch) who snatches and devours the rice, but the law punishes the latter for theft and not the former for hard heartedness and killing the starving man.[40]

Two cases, *Re Sreerangyee*[41] and *Re Maragatham*[42] illustrate how heartless and apathetical our criminal justice administration is towards the poor. In *Sreerangyee*, the life of the accused woman is a saga of misfortune, dogged by hardship whose misery knew no bounds. Deserted by her husband, she made every effort to earn a living to support her five minor children and herself. Her penurious condition worsened further when her youngest child became seriously ill, and she failed to raise the money for her treatment despite her best efforts. Her brother-in-law (husband's younger brother) offered to give her a meagre amount on the condition that she slept with him. She bluntly repulsed his lascivious advances. With no ray of hope, she killed all her five children by throwing them into the well and then she herself jumped into it. But misfortune did not leave her here either. She was rescued, only to be prosecuted and finally convicted under Section 302 of the IPC for murdering her children. The High Court refused to accept poverty as an excuse for

---

[40] K.D. Gaur, *Poor Victim of Uses and Abuses of Criminal Law and Process in India*, *JILI*, vol. 35 (October–December 1993): 184–5.

[41] (1973) 1 M. L. J. 205.

[42] AIR (1961) Mad. 498.

murdering her children and attempting suicide. It is astounding that though the High Court lauded her moral tenacity, it refused to count it as a mitigating factor and convicted her.

Similarly, in *Re Margatham*, the accused husband and wife, having failed to get either work or alms, starved for almost 10 days, and then decided to end their lives along with their one-and-a-half-month old female child. The two tied themselves with a rope along with the infant and jumped into a well, Here again ill luck pursued them; the child slipped while jumping and the two accused were saved by a passer-by. They were also convicted by the district court for attempt to murder their child under Section 307 read with Section 34 of the IPC and under Section 309 for attempt to commit suicide. However, the High Court reversed it, ruling that the fact of the child slipping out and hitting his head had broken the chain of causation. Thus, the High Court ingeniously found out a way to acquit them that it did not happen the way they had planned.

One wonders whether it is a criminal justice administration or a criminal administration of justice. The state does not protect such peoples' fundamental right to life, fails to give them employment, and yet punishes them for attempting to end their lives along with their children's. The state just wanted to prolong their date of death, as they would have died without food in any case, after a few days. So, starvation deaths do not shock the conscience of the state, but cutting the painful journey to death short is severely punished.

In *Dr Subramanian Swamy* v. *Director, CBI*,[43] a five-judge Constitution Bench of the Supreme Court set aside Section 6-A of the Delhi Special Police Establishment Act, 1946 which requires the prior sanction of the Central government to conduct any inquiry or investigation into any offence alleged to have been committed under the Prevention of Corruption Act, 1988 if the allegation relates to the employees of the Central government of the level of joint secretary or above. The idea of equality is an anathema to the privileged class which ingeniously innovates justifications for creating privileges for itself. Section 6-A of the Delhi Special Police Establishment (DSPE) Act has its genesis in the 'Single Directive' (SD) which was introduced in the 1980s when P. Chidambaram was the minister of state for personnel. The justification adduced was that officials of the joint secretary level and above take policy decisions and exercise discretion. Hence, they needed to be protected from vexatious and frivolous litigation. When the British government enacted the

---

[43] (2014) 8 SCC 519.

Cr. P.C., government servants were given protection as Section 197 provides that prosecution against them cannot be launched without prior sanction of the government. The British had come to rule; so they wanted to protect their officers. They did not have such a provision in their own country. After independence, the Government of India, following in the footsteps of the colonial rulers, not only refrained from tinkering with these laws, but also provided for similar protections while legislating other laws. Thus, Section 19 of the P.C. Act also enjoins the investigating agency to take prior sanction from the government for prosecution. So, senior bureaucrats had double protection—both from investigation as well as prosecution. The Supreme Court, in *Vineet Narain and Ors.* v. *Union of India*,[44] set aside the SD on the ground that once the jurisdiction is conferred on the CBI to investigate an offence by virtue of notification under Section 3 of the DSPE Act, the powers of investigation are governed by statutory provision which cannot be curtailed by an executive instruction. The Court was quite forthright that the law does not classify offenders differently for treatment there under, including investigation of offences and prosecution for offences according to their status in life; every person accused of committing the same offence is to be dealt with in the same manner in accordance with the law, which is equal in its application to everyone.

However, the Court itself provided the escape route by reasoning that such an important provision cannot be by way of executive order; it must have a statutory basis. Finding the way out, the executive within no time, through the Central Vigilance Commission (CVC) Ordinance, 1998, restored the provision of obtaining prior approval of the CVC before investigation of the officers of the level of joint secretary and above. It was again set aside by the Supreme Court. The government finally incorporated it in the CVC Bill as the Court had directed in the same judgment to give statutory basis to the CVC. When the bill was referred to the standing committee of Parliament, all parties scrambled to have provision to protect senior civil servants. Kuldip Nayar was the only dissenting voice in the committee and he was flabbergasted to see the solidarity of political parties on the issue. Finally, through amendment, Section 6-A was inserted and came into force on 12 September 2003, which was challenged in this case. However, the government could not adduce a single instance of harassment when the SD was not in force between 18 December 1997 (the date of Vineet Narain judgment striking down the SD) and 11 September 2003 (when the CVC Act came into force), except

---

[44] (1998) 1 SCC 226.

the period between 25 August 1998 and 27 October 1998 when the CVC Ordinance, 1998 was in force. Moreover, there is no corresponding provision for officials of state government. Besides, local police of the state government are not required to take any prior approval for investigation. So the argument of frivolous litigation is hocus-pocus, rightly debunked by the Court.

The Supreme Court raised a valid question, namely, 'How can two public servants against whom there are allegations of corruption or graft or bribe taking or criminal misconduct under the P.C. Act, 1988 be made to be treated differently because one happens to be a junior officer and the other, a senior decision maker.'[45] This question should have been raised in Vineet Narain itself, instead of asking for its statutory base. However, better late than never, striking it down, Justice Lodha wrote:

> Criminal Justice System mandates that any investigation into the crime should be fair, in accordance with law and should not be tainted. It is equally important that interested or influential persons are not able to misdirect or hijack the investigation so as to throttle a fair investigation resulting in the offender escaping the punitive course of law. These are important facets of rule of law. Breach of rule of law, in our opinion, amounts to negation of equality under Article 14.[46]

In *State* v. *Indian Hotel and Restaurant Association*,[47] the Supreme Court struck down another arbitrary provision that discriminated between dance in bars and restaurants and that in five star hotels. Sections 33A and 33B of the Bombay Police Act allowed dance in five star hotels but prohibited it in bars and restaurants. The differential treatment was struck down as invidious and blatantly discriminatory and violation of Article 14.

Discrimination in Favour of Affluent Countries and Discrimination Inside India Also

Besides such unjust laws, the victims of which are the marginalized people, the applications of laws in general are discriminatory. The concept of equality breathes life into democracy, but exceptions in favour of the 'haves' stare into one's face. The Universal Declaration of Human Rights elucidates the concept of the rule of law which is based on three cardinal principles:

---

[45] *Dr Subramanian Swamy* v. *Director, CBI* (2014) 8 SCC 519, p. 730.
[46] *Dr Subramanian Swamy* v. *Director, CBI*, p. 736.
[47] (2013) 8 SCC 519.

no one is above the law;[48] all persons are entitled to equal protection of law;[49] everyone has the right to an effective remedy for acts violating the fundamental rights granted by the Constitution or by the law.[50] These are high-sounding principles only to be violated in practice. The American War of Independence and the French Revolution ushered in the first written Constitutions guaranteeing the right to equality. The American Declaration of Independence of 1776 reads:

> ... that all men are created equal; that they are endowed by their Creator with certain inalienable rights ... that to secure these rights, governments are instituted among men, drawing their just powers from the governed; that whenever any form of government becomes destructive of these ends, it is the right of the people to alter or abolish it....
>
> The French Declaration of the Rights of Man and of the Citizen says that 'Men are born free and equal in rights'.

The Bhopal Gas Tragedy: Victims of the World's Worst Industrial Disaster Are Also Victims of the Worst Injustice

Despite these high-sounding declarations of equality, there is considerable discrimination against poor countries in favour of the developed ones. One most glaring example is the Bhopal gas tragedy, the world's worst industrial catastrophe. The accident took place on the intervening night of 2/3 December 1984, when 40 tonnes of toxic methyl isocyanate gas leaked from the Bhopal-based Union Carbide India Limited (UCIL) pesticide plant. At the time, the company was the Indian subsidiary of the US company, Union Carbide Corporation (UCC) which subsequently became a subsidiary of Dow Chemicals Company. Over 3,000 people died instantaneously, 15,000 died within a week and around 5.74 lakh were maimed. According to unofficial figures, the number of casualties is around 25,000. The Indian government filed a claim of $3.3 billion in the US court against UCC, but Judge Keenan directed the transfer of the litigation to India; and the Government of India, in 1989, settled for a paltry compensation of $470 million.

The contrast with an accident involving Americans is simply appalling. When 11 American workers were killed in an oil rig blow-up in the Gulf of Mexico on 20 April 2010, Washington demanded $1.5 billion from

---

[48] Article 7, The Universal Declaration of Human Rights.
[49] Article 7, The Universal Declaration of Human Rights.
[50] The Universal Declaration of Human Rights, Article 8.

BP (British multinational oil and gas company based in London).[51] Further, the then US President, Barack Obama also threatened to penalize BP to the extent of several billions of dollars. When Exxon was fined $5 billion for the Alaska oil spill, about $40,000 was spent on the rehabilitation of every affected otter. The victims of Bhopal are, so far, entitled to $200 each.[52] The US refused to extradite Warren Anderson, then chairman of UCC, though he was the accused no. 1 and had been declared a proclaimed offender, and the case was transferred to India on the orders of the American court. The arrogance of the superpower refused to bow down before the rule of law! Anderson passed away at age 92 on 29 September 2014 at Vero Beach, Florida, though the news was broken after a month. With his death, the struggle to get him extradited hit a dead end. Survivors of the Bhopal gas tragedy assembled outside the defunct Union Carbide factory and spat at his photograph one by one.[53]

Anderson's behaviour was despicable beyond words. Indira Jaising has rightly commented:

> At a time like that, the UCC was expected to stand by the victims, and at the very least, provide the information required to treat those who had survived. Instead, it chose to cover up the poisonous nature of the gas, saying, 'it is nothing, just like tear gas'. Repeated efforts to get it to name an anti-dote to the poison fell on deaf ears. No advisory was issued, guiding people on what they could do to minimise the effects of exposure to the poison.[54]

Damage claims were filed in first, the New York District Court but Judge John Keenan declined to admit on the ground of forum non convenience. The decisions of the Indian courts did not redound to the glory of the legal system. The incident occurred on 2 December 1984 and the Station House Officer (SHO) of the local police station filed an FIR under Section 304-A of the IPC (causing death by negligence). Since it is a bailable offence, the police gave bail to Warren Anderson immediately. He was arrested along with Keshub Mahindra, chairman of UC India and senior official V.P. Gokhale and they were kept in the guest house of the factory for around six hours. He was released on the personal surety of Rs 25,000 and was taken out by

---

[51] *Deepwater Horizon*, a floating semi-submersible drilling unit, sank due to the explosion and the subsequent fire.

[52] M.J. Akbar, '"Justice" for Bhopal Is Just Political Farce', *Sunday Times of India*, 13 June 2010.

[53] *The Hindu*, 1 November 2014, New Delhi.

[54] Indira Jaising, 'Disaster in Progress', *Indian Express*, 3 December 2014.

the back door which was often shut under strict security, and was provided a special state plane to go to Delhi from where he flew to the US.

Since there was no law to deal with such a disaster, the Bhopal gas Leak Disaster (Processing of Claims) Act, 1985, was enacted after the accident, nay industrial genocide. Ushan Ramanathan has written:

> Three months after the disaster, the government gave to itself the 'exclusive right to represent, and act in place of ... every person who has made, or is entitled to make, a claim....' The problem was that this kindly assumption of the 'right to represent' was edging out the right of the affected people to be heard. And it was being taken over by a government that was itself being pilloried for being a wrong-doer, alongside the corporation. Why, because it was the government that had given the Union Carbide Corporation the license to operate, and had, even on the face of it, failed to ensure safety during the licensing process.[55]

The government did not take any cognizance of leakages earlier which caused death and injury of workers. Thus, the government's performance as a regulator was abysmal. Besides, the Factories Act mandates regular inspection, but no such inspection was done even in the face of lurking disaster which was writ large on the face. And on the top of it, the government had allowed the UCC to set up its plant in an area of dense human habitation defying common sense. The government, after assuming the right to represent victims, was accountable to them as a joint tortfeasor. The reason adduced to assume the right to represent was that individual litigants would not be able to fight a long-drawn legal battle against an MNC. However, the government itself cringed before it in 1989 for a settlement, even before it had assessed the extent of harm, for one-seventh of the claim to be adjudicated by the district court, and while the victims' challenge to the Claims Act, 1985, was pending in the apex court.

The CBI filed a charge sheet on 1 December 1987, the court took cognizance on 6 July 1988, and Anderson was declared an absconder. In the meanwhile, on 14 February 1989, the Supreme Court quashed all proceedings, past, present, and future, relating to and arising out of the Bhopal gas disaster.[56] In such a landmark case, the Court did not deem it essential to give

[55] Usha Ramanathan, 'Legislation of a Complicit State', *The Statesman*, 12 December 2014.

[56] *Union Carbide Corporation* v. *Union of India* (1989) Scale 1 380, JT (1989) 1 296.

even a reasoned judgment; it was satisfied to pass just a mere order. J.K. Jain has rightly commented:

> Two lawyers, the Attorney General of India and the counsel for Union Carbide, were allowed to reach a settlement, endorsed by the Supreme Court that effectively placed in suspension, the entire legal system of India. In a kind of judicial emergency that can find no basis in the Constitution, they suspended the power of every agency, including the criminal courts, to intercede in a matter that can be decided only on the basis of a settlement between the two parties in a conflict involving lakhs of victims. Fascinatingly, this decision, along with other aspects of the settlement, was communicated in a summary order barely 350 words in length, no logic, no jurisprudential reasoning, no concern for precedents.[57]

In all, 5,66,786 claims were filed. According to a rough estimate, approximately 95 per cent got only $500 each which was the minimum amount of compensation, about 4 per cent got somewhere between $700 and $1,250, and only 1 per cent got an amount between $2,000 and $4,000. Out of 22,149 claims of death, only 15,000 were admitted for compensation as this was the official figure.[58] However, the Court reviewed its order on a petition filed by the CBI and the case was committed for trial to the Sessions Court, Bhopal on 3 April 1992. The court framed charges against all the nine accused except the absconder, Anderson under Section 304-II of the IPC (culpable homicide not amounting to murder) under which the maximum punishment is 10 years of imprisonment, besides Sections 324, 326, and 429 with or without the aid of Section 35. The chief judicial magistrate (CJM) issued non-bailable warrants of arrest. The CBI moved an extradition request to the US on 8 September 1993 for the arrest and extradition of Anderson. The US government never acceded to this request. However, it is also true that the Government of India did not pursue it vigorously either.

The accused challenged the framing of charges in the Madhya Pradesh High Court which dismissed the appeal. They then filed an SLP in the Supreme Court. Allowing the appeal, a division bench, comprising Chief Justice A.M. Ahmadi and Justice S.B. Majumdar, in its order dated 13 September 1996,

---

[57] J.K. Jain, 'The Judiciary: Courts in Crisis', in *Constitution of India: In Precept and Practice*, edited by C.K. Jain (New Delhi: CBS Publishers), pp. 135–6. Taken from Madhav Godbole, *The Judiciary and Governance in India* (New Delhi: Rupa and Co., 2009), p. 83.

[58] Rajkumar Keswani, 'Bhopal Gas Trasdi', *Naya Jnanodaya*, December 2014, p. 13.

amended the charges to Sections 304A, under which the maximum punishment is two years of jail, Sections 336, 337, and 338 of the IPC with or without Section 35 of the IPC.[59] The prosecution placed before the Court the report of the Vardharajan Committee which established that apart from proximate reasons, there were a number of design defects and other criminally negligent operational practices which resulted in the leakage of the methyl isocyanate gas, and the management was fully in the know of all this, but they deliberately ignored these for commercial reasons. According to Section 32 of the IPC, an act also covers an illegal omission. Obviously, an omission which leads to an accident of this magnitude cannot be considered as a case of mere negligence. The Supreme Court propounded the principle of absolute liability and that of enterprise liability in the oleum gas leak from Shriram plant in Delhi.[60] In this case, the Court had given detailed instructions for ensuring the safety of the plant and also who would be responsible in case of any accident. However, the Court forgot to apply these eloquent principles in the Bhopal disaster.

The first conviction in the Bhopal case was pronounced after over 25 years on 7 June 2010 when the CJM handed down a punishment of two years each to the seven accused under Section 304A of the IPC, and they were immediately granted bail.[61] There were three foreign accused—Warren Anderson, CEO, UCC, USA; UCC, USA; and UCC, Eastern Hong Kong. The three have/had been absconding since 1992; one of them, Anderson, is dead. The verdict raised a storm at the international level and the blame game began. The opposition accused the Congress government of providing safe passage to Anderson, some leaders of the Congress pointed fingers at the then chief minister of Madhya Pradesh Arjun Singh, but finally the Union Finance Minister, Pranab Mukherjee, considered the number two person in the Union Government then, made a statement saying that Anderson was allowed to go because a law and order problem was anticipated.[62] But it came to light after the verdict of 7 June 2010, that Anderson, the prime accused on bail was given VVIP treatment. He was not only provided a special aircraft, but the then Superintendent of Police, Bhopal, Swaraj Puri, himself drove him to the Bhopal airport. Puri was removed as a member of

[59] *Keshub Mahindra* v. *State of M. P.* (1996) 6 SCC 129 (1996) 6 Suppl. SCR 285 (1996) (6) SCALE 522.

[60] *M. C. Mehta* v. *Union of India*, AIR (1987) SC 976 (1986) SCR (1) 312.

[61] *The Hindu*, 8 June 2010.

[62] 'Pranab Comes to Arjun's Aid on Anderson', *Time of India*, 14 June 2010.

the Grievances Redressal Authority, a post that he received after retirement, after a video surfaced showing him driving Anderson in an Ambassador car to the airport.[63]

The then Union Law Minister, M. Veerappa Moily, questioned the role of the judiciary in diluting the charges against the accused.[64] However, the fact remains that the victims of the disaster and their kin received a pittance even after decades, and the accused have got away with light punishments which are subject to several layers of appeal. After the public uproar, the Government of India filed a criminal curative petition in the Supreme Court on 1 August 2010, challenging the change of section under the IPC from 304(II) to 304A, but a Constitution Bench of five judges headed by Justice S.H. Kapadia, the chief justice, the Court dismissed it on 11 May 2011.[65] The Union filed another civil curative petition in the Supreme Court on 3 December 2010, demanding enhancement of the compensation settled at $470 million, is still pending. The government contended that the amount settled between the Government of India and the UCC at the behest of the Supreme Court on 15 February 1989 was inadequate. Besides the three foreign accused absconding, the Dow Chemicals has not shown up till date though the UCC merged with it in August 2000, and the victims have been demanding to call it. It audaciously proclaims that it has inherited the assets, but none of its liabilities. In 2005, it was issued the show cause notice by the CJM but the Jabalpur High Court stayed it. However, the High Court vacated the stay on 19 December 2012.

It is height of injustice and insensitivity that corporates have their exclusive claims over profit, but disasters are socialized and that too when it is man-made. Victims of Bhopal have been treated as subhuman.

Uphaar Theatre Fire Case

Victims of accidents in India caused by criminal negligence have always been treated contemptuously. The judgment handed down by the Supreme Court in the Uphaar theatre fire case, reducing the compensation by almost half confirms this and came as a bolt from the blue for the victims' families

---

[63] 'SP Who Drove Anderson to Airport Loses MP Job', *Indian Express*, 16 June 2010.

[64] 'Judiciary Is to Blame', *Times of India*, 13 June 2010.

[65] *CBI and Ors.* v. *Keshub Mahindra etc.* (2011) 6 SCC 216: Curative Petition (Crl) Nos. 39–42 of 2010 in Criminal Appeal Nos. 1672–1675.

waiting for justice for over 14 years.[66] The law of tort and tortious liability in India is not codified and is based on the English law and practice. In the absence of any statutory provision, the court decides a case on the touchstone of 'justice, equity and good conscience'. However, in matters of compensation to the kin of victims of such accidents, the courts have been extremely conservative. So, the judgement once again brought into focus the need to have a comprehensive law about the compensation policy. A division bench of the apex court, comprising Justices R.V. Raveendran and K.S. Radhakrishnan hoped that the legislature would bring in appropriate legislation to deal with claims in Public Law for violation of fundamental rights, guaranteed to the citizens at the hands of the state and its officials. It said that the absence of any such law was leading to arbitrary fixing of compensation to be paid by the government and its instrumentalities, and stressed that such a law was essential to slap compensation liability on the government and its officers under tortious liability in cases where disasters like Uphaar fire tragedy take place due to the inaction or non-performance of the official agencies.

To narrate the facts briefly, 59 people died of asphyxiation and 103 were badly injured in the Uphaar fire tragedy in New Delhi on 13 June 1997 during the screening of Hindi blockbuster 'Border'. When smoke billowed from the air-conditioning ducts, they remained stranded in the balcony, as they could not escape since the gangway and the exit were closed. The reason for slashing the compensation heavily—from Rs 18 lakh to 10 lakh for those above 20 and from Rs 15 lakh to 7.5 lakh for those below 20—is that the Supreme Court felt that the Delhi High Court erred in calculating the damage on the basis of an income of Rs 15,000 per month of each adult on the ground that they belonged to the higher income group as they had bought the balcony ticket. Damage is calculated in the common law on the basis of the capacity to earn and the period for which one would have earned. It is an elitist approach and the socialist ideologues have condemned it on the ground that class stratification is pronounced even in death. It is really abhorrent that though death is the greatest leveller which does not distinguish between prince and pauper, victims of the same tragedy should be compensated as per their status. However, the Supreme Court felt that someone cannot be clubbed in the Higher Income Group (HIG)

---

[66] *Municipal Corporation of Delhi* v. *Association of victims of Uphaar Tragedy and Ors.* (2011) 14 SCC 481, Civil Appeal Nos. 7114–15 of 2003, judgment delivered on 13 October 2011.

simply on the basis that they bought the balcony ticket, as there are fans of Hindi movies who do not mind parting with any amount of money for watching films.

As discussed in the Bhopal gas case, compare it also with the compensation given to the victims of the oil spill of the Gulf of Mexico. Oil giant BP, paid $20bn (£13.5bn) compensation for those affected by the Gulf of Mexico oil spill. Consequently, it did not make any payments to its shareholders in 2010. The company said that it was 'right and prudent' to take a conservative financial approach at present and that the value of the fund did not represent a cap on liabilities for the disaster. The agreement was hammered out after a meeting of BP executives with then US President, Barack Obama. In India, the cost of everything is skyrocketing except that of human life. It is inscrutable why the Supreme Court takes such a conservative estimate of compensation. Technically, the kin of the victims can approach the high court for higher compensation as the amount fixed by the apex court is only the base amount. But then how much time will it take? True, the Supreme Court has said that it would be summary proceeding, but the experience shows that it takes years even though there are directions for day-to-day hearing in criminal cases. In developed countries, the compensation slapped is so high that the accused accompanies go insolvent, and that is the only way to chasten them.

Earlier, victims felt cheated when the Delhi High Court, in the criminal liability, reduced the sentence of the convicts from two years to one year and acquitted four. Four had already died, which is quite natural when it takes decades to decide a case. The ground for reducing the sentence was that the convicts were educated, and had no criminal antecedents and were from good backgrounds; as if the victims were not educated or without criminal backgrounds. On 19 August 2015, the Supreme Court passed the order that Sushil Ansal and Gopal Ansal would stand sentenced to undergo rigorous imprisonment for two years but added that having regard to advanced age of the accused and other peculiar facts and circumstances, if they pay Rs 30 crores each, that is, Rs 60 crores, then the sentence would stand reduced to the period already undergone. The Court said that if they fail to pay the amount within a period of three months, they would undergo the sentence of two years each, excluding the term which they have already undergone.[67] Rs 60 crore is a pittance so far as Ansals are concerned. In all, Ansal companies'

---

[67] *Sushil Ansal* v. *State Through CBI*, Cr. Appeal No. 598 of 2010, decided on 19 August 2015.

revenue four years back, that is, 2014, was Rs 1,234 crore.[68] Neelam and Shekhar Krishnamoorthy have written:

> These two lines from the judge completely shattered our faith in the judiciary....
> I stood outside the Supreme Court of India, distraught and bereft of hope, tears streaming down my face as I spoke to the media. The Ansals walked past me with victorious smiles on their faces. I had just been robbed of my only hope of finding justice for the deaths of my children.
>
> The judgment has ensured the message is heard loud and clear: only the rich and powerful are human, the rest of us are mere commodities with a price tag.[69]

In the review petition filed against it, the Supreme Court, in a majority judgement of 2:1, decided to send Gopal Ansal back to jail for negligence, but spared his elder brother Sushil Ansal serving further sentence due to his advanced age.[70] Neelam Krishnamoorthy reiterated that she had lost faith in the judiciary:

> The Supreme Court has deeply disappointed the kith and kin of victims of Uphaar tragedy. The verdict has murdered justice. It would have been better if I had picked up a gun 20 years ago to seek justice for my children. I would have served 14 years and now would have been out of jail and would have been in peace.[71]

The lenience shown to Ansals, flies in the face of Supreme Court's order in Zaibunnisa Kazi's and Putti's cases, whose prayers for sparing jail terms on humanitarian ground were flatly rejected. Ninety-two-year-old Putti was convicted in a case of honour killing and sentenced to life imprisonment. The Court turned down his prayer that he be spared keeping in view his old age.[72] Similarly, Zaibunnisa, a convict in the 1993 Mumbai blasts case, made a similar prayer on the ground that she was suffering from cancer. She was convicted

---

[68] Anil Dharker, 'A Clockwise Justice', *Asian Age*, 24 August 2015.

[69] Neelam Krishnamoorthy and Shekhar Krishnamoorthy, *Trial By Fire* (Gurgaon: Penguin Books, 2016), p. 179.

[70] *Association of Victims of Uphaar Tragedy* v. *Sushil Ansal*, decided on 9 February 2017.

[71] 'Lost Faith in the Judiciary, Says Uphaar Victims' Mom', *Times of India*, 10 February 2017.

[72] '92-Year-Old Man to Undergo Life Imprisonment', 17 June 2016, http://timesofindia.indiatimes.com/city/delhi/92-year-old-man-to-undergo-life-imprisonment/articleshow/52800076.cms (last accessed on 2 April 2017).

on the basis of the retracted statement of a fellow accused. Many legal luminaries felt that her conviction was wrong, but the Court did not accede to her prayer. Justice (Retd.) Markandeya Katju issued an appeal for her release.[73]

The report of the magisterial probe, set up immediately after the accident, reveals everything, warts and all. It held the cinema management, Delhi Vidyut Board (DVB), city fire service, the Delhi police's licensing branch and the Municipal Corporation of Delhi (MCD) responsible for the tragedy. It said that all of them 'contributed to the mishap through their acts of omission and commission'. It further blamed the cinema management for losing precious time in alerting the fire services, and for not maintaining proper distance between the transformer room and the car park. It said, 'When the fire broke out at 1645 hours, the movie was not stopped nor any announcement made to evacuate the audience. Exit signs were not battery-operated and once the lights were out, panic struck people had to grope in the dark for exits, many of which were blocked by seats.'

This report speaks volumes about the omission and commission of various agencies. The transformer was installed there illegally. Surprisingly, the Supreme Court also exonerated the DVB and the MCD, though their omissions were too glaring to be glossed over. If the Court says that the absence of any law to fix the tortious liability of State and its agencies is creating problem, it had the option to invoke Article 142 for doing 'complete justice'. Further, like Vishakha, when the Supreme Court gave guidelines to be followed in cases of sexual harassment of women at work places, it could have laid down guidelines to be followed in cases of tortious liability till the Parliament makes a law in this regard. The court has missed a golden opportunity.

Cost of Defamation in Case of a Judge

In another case of binary application of law, Justice (Retired) P.B. Sawant, former chairman of the Press Council of India, was awarded Rs 100 crore as compensation for damage to his reputation by a Pune court.[74] The awarding of this huge amount, unprecedented so far, as compensation to Sawant for defamation raised serious questions not only about the freedom of the press, but also about the compensation policy in general. Sawant had sued

[73] 'Mumbai Blasts: After Supreme Court Rejects Zaibunnisa Kazi's Petition, Markandeya Katju Issues an Appeal', 24 February 2015, http://indiatoday.intoday.in/story/markandey-katju-zaibunnisa-kazi-mumbai-blast-shanti-bhushan/1/420728.html (last accessed on 2 April 2017).

[74] Special Civil Suit No. 1984 of 2008.

Times Global Broadcasting Company (TGBC), which owns TV channel TIMES NOW, for defamation and claimed a damage of Rs 100 crore. On 10 September 2008, the channel telecast a story about the Ghaziabad District Court Provident Fund Scam, wherein Justice P.K. Samantha, a serving judge of the Calcutta High Court, was alleged to have been involved. While airing the said story, the channel inadvertently showed the picture of P.B. Sawant. This happened only once for 15 seconds only. The channel telecast apology on its scroll, though belatedly, from 23 September for five days. However, this did not satisfy Sawant as the corrigendum was not issued immediately. The lower court allowed his claim. The Bombay High Court admitted the appeal against it but refused to grant stay on the execution of decree and asked TGBC to deposit Rs 20 crore in six weeks and bank guarantee of Rs 80 crore in 10 weeks. An SLP was filed against this order in the Supreme Court which refused to interfere with the direction of the High Court.

The question arises as to how the claim of such a gargantuan amount was allowed and that too in such a short time? Indian courts are not known for granting such a high compensation. A history of sort has been created that the court has allowed a claim of Rs 100 crore. Even in cases of death in police custody, the court grants a compensation of Rs 50 thousand or 1 lakh, though it is proved that the victim was tortured and killed. As mentioned earlier, the Supreme Court reduced the compensation, which was already meagre, in the Uphaar fire tragedy case. In the Bhopal Gas Tragedy case, the Supreme Court awarded a compensation of $470 million on 15 February 1989, when as per official estimate, the number the dead was 3,000. At the exchange rate of 1989, it amounted to Rs 58,166 per victim. Now compare it with Rs 100 crore awarded for defamation caused by the wrong display of photograph for 15 seconds, and for which apology was tendered. The life of a common man is worth much less compared to the dignity of a former judge when it is not even certain that the reputation was actually damaged.

Besides, the speed with which the case has been decided also speaks volumes about our legal process. Sawant filed the suit on 13 November 2008 and on 26 April 2011, the court delivered its judgment awarding Rs 100 crore to the plaintiff. Countless defamation cases are pending for decades, and the aggrieved parties get only next dates. S. Nambi Narayanan, then head at the Indian Space Research Organisation (ISRO), was falsely implicated in an espionage case. He was in-charge of the cryogenic project, and it was he who introduced the liquid fuel rocket technology in India in the early 1970s while A.P.J. Abdul Kalam's team worked on solid motors. He developed the Vikas engine used today by all ISRO rockets including the Polar Satellite Launch Vehicle (PSLV) that took Chandrayaan-1 to the moon on 22 October 2008.

In 1994, Narayanan was charged with selling ISRO secrets for millions to two alleged Maldivian intelligence officers, Marian Rasheeda and Fauzia Hassan. He, along with another scientist D. Sasikumaran, was alleged to have leaked secrets pertaining to the highly confidential 'flight test data' from experiments with rocket and satellite launches.

Narayanan was put behind bars and tortured. He suffered acute mental and physical agony and his wife lost her mental equilibrium. The CBI found the whole case against him false. He filed a suit of defamation claiming a compensation of Rs 1 crore in the Civil Court, Thiruvananthpuram in 1999, and the suit has been pending since then. However, on 14 September 2018, the Supreme Court absolved him of all charges and awarded a compensation of Rs. 50 lakh to him. A 3-judge bench headed by CJI Dipak Misra granted him compensation and allowed him to proceed with civil suit wherein he has claimed more compensation. (*S. Nambi Narayanan v. Siby Mathews & Others*, Civil Appeal Nos. 6637–6638 of 2018.) Nobody knows when it will be decided. If Sawant's suit can be decided in three-and-a-half years, why can't other cases? It proves that if the judiciary wants, cases can be disposed of expeditiously. But for that, one has to be a former judge of the apex court or a VIP. Huge compensation can also be allowed, but again for that one has to be a VIP.

Perception

On 5 April 2015, at a conference of judges of the Supreme court, chief justices of high courts and chief ministers, Prime Minister Narendra Modi made a caustic comment that the judiciary was being driven by star activists, 'The judiciary is not as fearless today as it used to be 10 years back. Are five star activists not driving the judiciary? Are they not attempting to do so? Judges fear what the reaction of five star activists would be when they render justice as per law and per Constitution.'[75] CJI H.L. Dattu later said, 'Judges today are as fearless as they ever were.'[76]

* * *

'Justice', Dante defined, 'is a certain straightness or rule, rejecting the oblique on either side.' But recent trends show that the status of the accused weighs

[75] 'Today's Judiciary Fears 5-Star Activists, Modi Tells Top Judges', *Times of India*, 6 April 2015.
[76] 'Today's Judiciary Fears 5-Star Activists, Modi Tells Top Judges'.

more heavily than the provisions of the law. In some cases, the laws themselves are discriminatory, while in others their applications are such. The net result is that the poor suffer. The high-flown principle of equality before the law and equal protection of law has failed to a great extent to animate our society. At least, Lord Thomas Babington Macaulay gave the IPC, which is universal with no distinction between two classes of people, but the application is not uniform.

During Oliver Cromwell's rule, a radical movement called the Levellers originated in the army. They advocated for the abolition of privilege, calling it the root of all evil, and demanded that all citizens should have political equality based on universal suffrage and a written Constitution. Harold Laski often said, 'Judge's mind is not a legal slot machine or a weighing machine that when a person puts a coin into that machine, a card comes out showing the weight. It passes through his mind, his philosophy of life, the inarticulate major premise gets reflected in his judgement. They are not at all independent.'

The Supreme Court has said:

> There can be no disagreement with the principle that that even the humblest citizen of the land, irrespective of his station in life, is entitled to present his case with dignity and is entitled to be heard with courtesy and sympathy. Courts are meant for, and are sustained by, the people and no litigant can be allowed to be looked upon as a supplicant or importuner.[77]

However, these magniloquent enunciations are seldom actuated into practice. Sheela Barse was herself taken out of this case, though she was the petitioner as she had protested against seemingly interminable adjournments and wanted to withdraw her petition.

---

[77] *Sheela Barse* v. *Union of India* (1988) 4 SCC 226, para 27.

4

Supreme Court's Power to Do Complete Justice

The word 'justice' figures in the Indian Constitution only 13 times—11 times in the main body and twice in the Schedules. First, it is in the Preamble when a pledge is taken to 'secure to all citizens: Justice, social, economic, and political'; which is reiterated in Article 38 which mandates that 'The State shall strive to promote the welfare of the people by securing and protecting as effectively as it may a social order in which justice social, economic and political, shall inform the institutions of the national life'. The term 'social justice' comes again in Articles 243-G and 243-W where state legislatures are given legislative authority to devolve powers on Panchayats and Municipalities for this purpose. The word comes twice in Article 39-A which enjoins the State to secure that the operation of legal system promotes justice. Article 139-A empowers the Supreme Court to transfer any case, appeal, or other proceedings pending before any high court to any other high court 'for the ends of justice'. Again we find the term 'administration of justice' in Article 225 which defines the jurisdiction of the high court. Before the 44th Amendment to the Constitution (1978), the word figured in Article 226 also, which bequeathed power to the high court to issue writs in the nature habeas corpus, mandamus, prohibition, quo warranto, and certiorari 'where such illegality had resulted in substantial failure of justice'. The amendment widened the power to issue writs for the enforcement of any of the rights conferred by Part III and for any other purpose. Articles 371A and 371G confer powers for the 'administration of civil and criminal justice' according to Naga and Mizo customary laws respectively in two states. Apart from all this, Article 142 which gives power to the Supreme Court for doing 'complete justice' in any matter or cause pending before it. Besides, the word 'injustice' figures in Article 46 which mandates the State to protect the weaker sections of the people 'from social injustice and all forms of exploitation'. At other places it is used in the context of designations like 'Chief Justice' or 'Chief Justice of India'.

While Articles 38, 39-A, and 46 form parts of the directive principles of state policy and so are not justiciable, the Preamble generally spells out the broad contours of the Constitution which its makers wanted to achieve, and therefore, it is not enforceable directly either. Article 139-A talks about the special power of the Supreme Court and Article 225 defines the jurisdiction of the high court. Thus, the word 'justice' that figures in Article 139-A and Article 142 is the only one which is substantive and justiciable while other provisions are definitional. Again, while Article 139-A gives a specific power to the apex court, Article 142 confers a wider power. However, its application is limited.

The power bequeathed under Article 142 is unique and has been given to the apex court as a matter of safety valve so that if need be, it can give extraordinary relief not even prayed for in some rare cases. The jurisdiction of the apex court under this special provision was not debated much in the Constituent Assembly, and for the first three decades, it was invoked in cases few and far between. However, subsequently, its liberal interpretation by the Supreme Court has spawned fierce controversy with respect to the power conferred by it. Article 142(1) reads, 'The Supreme court in the exercise of its jurisdiction may pass any decree or make such order as is necessary for doing complete justice in any cause or matter pending before it....' The words 'in the exercise of its jurisdiction' and 'any cause or matter pending before it' make it abundantly clear the power given under this article does not confer any extra jurisdiction and is to be invoked only in cases pending before the Court, precluding any scope of taking *suo motu* cognizance of any matter not pending before it.

This article was incorporated in the Constitution to do away with the handicap that the Federal Court faced in ensuring compliance of its orders. Under the Government of India Act, 1935, the Federal Court, while exercising its original jurisdiction, could do nothing more than pronouncing a declaratory judgment. Thus, it could lay down the law but could not enforce it. Similarly, if it allowed an appeal in exercise of its power under appellate jurisdiction, it remitted the case back to the court against whose order the appeal was filed with a declaration that the judgment, decree, or order would substitute the impugned judgment, decree, or order. Article 142 unshackles this barrier. The Federal Court only adjudicated constitutional matters, that is, the interpretation of the Government of India Act, 1935, or disputes between the Federation and the states or between states. Other cases went to the Privy Council which represented the Crown and could do 'complete justice' without any express provision as the Crown had all power.

Equity, Justice, and Good Conscience

The genesis of the concept of 'complete justice' is found in the concept of equity. Broadly speaking, equity connotes justice, that is, that which is fair and just. In developed legal systems, discretionary power has been vested so that justice does not elude. In England, during the medieval era, law courts enforced the king's laws. The king's judges, educated in law rather than theology, administered the realm's universal law. If any party was not happy with decisions given by them, he could appeal directly to the king. As sovereign, he was seen as the 'fount of justice' and responsible for the just treatment of his subjects. Subsequently, the king regularly delegated his power to the chancellor to dispose of such petitions. Thus, in England, it owes its origin to the exercise by the chancellor of the residual discretionary power of the king to do justice when a common law court was unable to do justice. Before the Judicature Act of 1873 came into force, the Court of Chancery had almost exclusive equity jurisdiction with common law courts kept out of the loop in this regard. If a defendant to a common law action had an equitable right, he had to move the Chancery with a prayer to grant injunction to stay the proceedings in the common law court and then start afresh in Chancery to prove his defence. This conflict of jurisdiction was resolved with the creation of the Supreme Court of Judicature by the Judicature Acts of 1873 and 1875. The chancellor, being the most important person after the king during the medieval period, discharged the important function of issuing royal writs which began an action at law. The litigant had to begin with it, but the common law court still enjoyed the power to adjudicate that the writ did not establish any claim recognized by the law. Jill E. Martin writes:

> A claimant could only sue at common law if his complaint came within the scope of an existing writ. In the thirteenth century the available writs covered very narrow ground. Even if the claim came within the scope of an existing writ, it may have been that for some reason, such as the power and influence of the defendant, his opponent could not get justice before a common law court. The King in his Council still retained wide discretionary power to do

justice among his subjects, and the claimant could petition to the King and the Council praying for his remedy.[1]

Litigant addressed petition to the chancellor complaining that he would not get justice under the ordinary mechanism. Subsequently, the equity jurisdiction was invoked in cases where the common law was not flexible enough to provide a remedy. So the chancellor tried to give relief in hard cases. He could do with ease as in the thirteenth and fourteenth centuries he was generally an ecclesiastic, learned in civil and canon law. He would give decisions according to his own sense of right and wrong in a given case. So his own understanding and idiosyncrasies played the decisive role. John Seldon wondered, 'Equity is roguish thing. For law we have a measure ... equity is according to the conscience of him that is Chancellor, and as that is longer or narrower, so is equity. 'Tis all one as if they should make the standard for the measure a Chancellor's foot'.[2]

Virtually, the Chancellor's jurisdiction was undefined and, therefore, sweeping. He could intervene because he felt that it was necessary on grounds of conscience.

It was at the fag end of the sixteenth century that quarrel over the sweeping power of the Chancery reached the flashpoint. The common law was virtually being made ineffectual and inoperative by the use of the injunction. The confrontation could have come earlier but for the statesmanship of men like Thomas More, and also because of the reluctance to challenge the powers of royal officers in Tudor times. Besides, Chief Justice Edward Coke was not the kind to take things lying down. He challenged the Lord Chancellor over the jurisdiction of the Court of Chancery which re-opened cases decided by common law courts. The Chancery could grant relief legitimately against any injustice where the common law had no remedy, but re-opening cases after judgements were delivered amounted to interference and complicated the system. However, Lord Chancellor Baron Ellesmere, encouraged recourse to Chancery after common law courts pronounced judgment. It opened a good avenue for litigants who could not succeed at common law courts. It led to a severe backlog of thousands of cases. Under him, Chancery issued injunctions to restrain suitors from suing at common law, or to prevent them from enforcing the judgment if it had been delivered. In a number of cases, Chief Justice Coke, decided that incarceration for disobedience to injunctions

---

[1] Jill E. Martin, *Hanbury and Martin: Modern Equity*, 16th Edition (London: Sweet and Maxwell Ltd, 2001), pp. 5–6.

[2] Martin, *Hanbury and Martin*, p. 7.

issued by Chancery was unlawful.[3] Coke ruled that where a decision had been given in a common law court, Chancery had no right to intervene, and that there could be no appeal from the king's bench, except to the High Court of Parliament.

Ellesmere, a diehard royalist, proclaimed that 'the monarch is the law' and equated him with a Roman emperor. He said, 'Our Constitution is to be obeyed and reverenced, not bandied by persons sitting in ordinaries drowned with drink, blown away with a whiff of tobacco'.[4] Coke was firm that such power of Chancery was contrary to the statute of Edward III's reign,[5] which provided that any person who sued in any court to defeat or impeach the judgment given in the king's court should be outlawed unless they withdrew. He then started issuing writ of habeas corpus to release prisoners committed by Ellesmere for contempt, though it was not always unreasonable, and encouraged them to prosecute the opposite parties for impeaching the judgments of the king's court. When the conflict became fierce, James I referred the matter to Francis Bacon, the attorney-general, and others learned in law. Bacon supported Ellesmere, referring to Chancery as 'the court of your Majesty's absolute power', and argued that the statute had referred only to appeals to Rome.[6] He even went to the extent of suggesting James that cases should often be withdrawn from the ordinary courts and sent for determination by the chancellor, who was 'ever a principla counselor ans instrument of monarchy, of immediate dependence upon the King: and therefore like to be a safe and tender guardian of the regal rights'.[7] Coke failed as James decided in favour of Chancery. However, pursuant to the Glorious Revolution, the power of Chancery was challenged again in 1690. A bill was introduced in the House of Commons to restrain Chancery from interfering in any suit for which the proper remedy was at common law. The bill could not be passed, and since then onward the jurisdiction of Chancery was not seriously challenged. According to Jill E. Martin, 'Thereafter, law and equity worked together, as parts of a consistent whole; and this enabled Maitland to say that Equity had come, not to

[3] *Heath* v. *Rydley* (1614) Cro.Jac. 335; *Bromage* v. *Genning* (1617) 1 Rolle 368; *Throckmorton* v. *Finch* (1598) Third Institute 124 at 25.

[4] John Hostteller, *Sir Edward Coke: A Force for Freedom* (New Delhi: Universal Law Publishing Co. Pvt. Ltd, First Indian Reprint, 2006), p. 85.

[5] 27 Edw. III. c. 1.

[6] 27 Edw. III. c. 1, p. 86.

[7] James Spedding, *Letters and Life of Francis Bacon*, vol. 236 (Longman, Green: Longman and Roberts, 1890). Hostteller, *Sir Edward Coke*, p. 86.

destroy the law, but to fulfil it.'[8] Between 1673, when Lord Nottingham took over as chancellor, and 1827 when Lord Eldon demitted office, equity got transformed into a system of established rules and principles. Thus, it no longer remained a nebulous area where the personal interference of the chancellor mattered. Lord Shaftesbury, who retired in 1672, was the last non-lawyer to hold the post of chancellor. Lord Nottingham is credited with harmonizing the whole system, who propounded the doctrine that there can be no 'clog on the equity of redemption'.[9] Lord Eldon was himself a great equity lawyer whose judgments were clear, erudite, thorough, and masterly. He worked hard to establish principles for equity, and his concern is reflected in his statement, 'Nothing would inflict on me greater pain in quitting this place than the recollection that I had done anything to justify the reproach that the equity of this court varies liked the chancellor's foot.'[10]

The Common Law Procedure Act, 1854, bequeathed certain powers to common law courts to give equitable remedies. Similarly, the Chancery Amendment Act, 1858, commonly called Lord Cairns' Act, empowered the Court of Chancery to award damages in addition to, or in place of, an injunction or an order for specific performance. However, the Judicature Acts of 1873 and 1875 effected historic change by abolishing the old separate Courts of Queen's Bench, Exchequer, Common Pleas, Chancery, Probate, the Divorce Court, and the Court of Admiralty. These were sub-stituted by the Supreme Court of Judicature with a high court divided into Divisions called the Queen's Bench Division, Chancery Division, and the Probate, Divorce, and Admiralty Division. There was further rechristening and reconfiguration of these courts subsequently. The high court created by the Judicature Act was conferred with the jurisdiction of both law and equity. It gave supremacy to equity in cases of conflict. Thus, the Act 'fused' the operation of law and equity.

The concept was imported to India when the East India Company set up courts here. Thus, the judges appointed in 1668 in Bombay (now Mumbai) were charged with behaving themselves 'according to good conscience'. Again, judges were obligated to act 'according to the rules of equity and good conscience' when courts were set up in Bombay under The Royal Charter of 9 August 1683. It was reiterated in the Royal Charter of 30 December 1687 while establishing Mayor's Court in Madras (now Chennai). However, the words 'justice, equity, and good conscience' were substituted by 'justice

---

[8] Martin, *Hanbury and Martin*, p. 12.

[9] *Howard* v. *Harris* (1681) 1 Vern. 33.

[10] Quoted by Martin, *Hanbury and Martin*, pp. 13–14.

and right' in the Royal Charters of 1726 and 1753 in regard to the Mayor's Court. It was codified in Section 60 of the Regulation 5 July 1781, 'That in all cases for which no specific directions are given, the respective judges do act according to justice, equity and good conscience'. Edward Otto Ives, the judge of the Murshidabad City Adalat since 1780, is credited with originating the formula.

Jurisdiction under Article 142

The article is couched in plain and unambiguous language. Late P.P. Rao, senior advocate, is right,

> the words 'in exercise of its jurisdiction' clearly shows that Art. 142 is not the source of any additional jurisdiction, but only of power. Jurisdiction means an authority to adjudicate a dispute. Power means the ability to alter the rights and liabilities of persons…. The Supreme Court derives its jurisdiction either from the Constitution or from a law made by Parliament.[11]

Still, its interpretation has been inconsistent and mercurial. As far back as in 1954, Justice Vivian Bose interpreted the constitutional provision in these eloquent words, 'We have upon us the whole armour of the Constitution and walk henceforth in its enlightened ways, wearing the breast plate of its protecting provisions and flashing the flaming sword of its inspiration.'[12]

Fali S. Nariman has written, 'I have always believed that the "breast-plate" and "flaming sword", about which Justice Vivian Bose had written, is located in Article 142(1)!'[13]

In *K.M. Nanavati* v. *State of Bombay*,[14] the Supreme Court held that Article 142 contains no words of limitation and it is unfettered. The Court was not asked to decide whether it could pass an order incongruous with a substantive provision of law in exercise of its power under Article 142. However, in *Prem Chand Garg* v. *Excise Commissioner*,[15] the Supreme Court made it abundantly clear that it cannot pass an order inconsistent with the express provision of

[11] P.P. Rao, 'Art. 142: Is the Power to do Complete Justice Subject to Rule of Law?', in *Reclaiming the Vision: Challenges of Indian Constitutional Law and Governance*, edited by Lokendra Malik (Gurgaon: Lexis Nexis, 2013), p. 185.

[12] *Virendra Singh* v. *State of UP*, 1954 AIRSC 447 at 454, para 34.

[13] Fali S. Nariman, 'Foreword', *Reclaiming the Vision*, p. viii.

[14] (1961) 1 SCR 497 at 527.

[15] (1963) Supp 1 ASCR 885 at 899–901.

any statute. A Constitution Bench, while deliberating on the scope of Article 142, struck down a rule made by the Supreme Court itself which required the petitioner to deposit security in proceedings under Article 32 for the enforcement of a fundamental right as it imposed a financial obligation on the petitioner, and the non-compliance with it would result in the dismissal of the petition. The Court refused to accept the plea of the solicitor-general that the language of Article 142 has a wide sweep and made its scope expansive, and that it should be interpreted liberally since it spells out the constitutional charter of the Court's powers. Dispelling any doubt, the Court held,

> The powers of the Court are no doubt very wide and they are intended to be and will always be exercised in the interest of justice. But that is not to say that an order can be made by this Court which is inconsistent with the fundamental rights guaranteed by Part III of the Constitution. An order which this Court can make in order to do complete justice between the parties, must not only be consistent with the fundamental rights guaranteed by the Constitution, but it cannot be even inconsistent with the substantive provision with the relevant statutory laws.[16]

However, this observation was taken to be *obiter dicta* as the question raised in the case did not pertain to an order made under Article 142 being repugnant with some substantive law. Nevertheless, subsequently, a larger bench of seven judges in *A.R. Antulay* v. *R.S. Nayak*,[17] endorsed the statement of law made in Prem Chand Garg's case making it a binding *ratio* that substantive law cannot be superseded. Proceeding on this principle, it set aside the directions given by the Court earlier on 16 February 1984 in *R.S. Nayak* v. *A.R. Antulay*,[18] transferring Special case No. 24 of 1982 and Special case No. 3 of 1983, pending against Antulay in the Court of Special Judge, Greater Bombay to the Bombay High Court with a request to the chief justice to assign the two cases to a sitting judge on the ground that since it was contrary to the relevant statutory provision, namely, section 7(2) of the Criminal Law Amendment Act, 1962, it violated Article 21 of the Constitution. Under Article 21, no person can be deprived of his life and personal liberty except according to procedure established by law. So, Article 21 comes into play only when there is a violation of the procedure established by law. Thus, Antulay's case reinforced the proposition that the Supreme Court does not have any

[16] (1963) Supp 1 SCR 885 at 899–901.
[17] (1988) Supp 1 SCR 56.
[18] (1984) 2 SCC 183, AIR (1984) SC 684.

power to pass an order under Article 142 which is incongruous with any other constitutional or statutory provision. However, In *Delhi Judicial Service* v. *State of Gujarat*,[19] the Supreme Court ruled that its powers are not fettered by provisions of statutory laws:

> This Court's power under Article 142(1) to do 'complete justice' is entirely of [a] different level and of a different quality. Any prohibition or restriction contained in ordinary laws cannot act as a limitation on the constitutional power of this Court. Once this Court has seisin of a cause or matter before it, it has power to issue any order or direction to do 'complete justice' in the matter. This constitutional power of the Apex Court cannot be limited or restricted by provisions contained in statutory law.[20]

In this case, the Supreme Court, in contempt proceedings against some police officials of Gujarat, for assaulting, handcuffing, and maliciously prosecuting a CJM, not only sentenced them to jail but also quashed criminal proceedings against the CJM under Article 142.

In *Union Carbide Corporation* v. *Union of India*,[21] the Supreme Court took recourse to this article for upholding the settlement between the Union of India and the UCC which, among others, terminated all civil and criminal proceedings pending before any court. It went to the extent of declaring that in order to do complete justice, it could even override the laws made by the Parliament as prohibitions or limitations or provisions contained in ordinary laws cannot curtail the powers of the apex court under Article 142. Nevertheless, the Court again realized its limitations that it cannot gloss over an express provision of law in *Supreme Court Bar Association* v. *Union of India*,[22] when it held that it could not suspend the license of a lawyer while punishing him for the contempt of court, as this power was specifically assigned to the Bar Council. It overruled its own decision in Vinay Chandra Mishra, in re,[23] wherein it had held that the jurisdiction and powers of this Court under Article 142, which are supplementary in nature, are independent of the jurisdiction, and the powers of this Court under Article 129, which cannot be trammelled in any way by any statutory provision including the provisions of the Advocates Act or the Contempt of Courts Act. The Court

---

[19] AIR (1991) SC 2176.
[20] (1991) 3 SCR 936 at 997 (1991) 4 SCC 406, AIR (1991) SC 2176.
[21] (1991) 4 SCC 584.
[22] (1998) 4 SCC 409.
[23] (1995) 2 SCC 584.

had suspended Vinay Chandra Mishra from practicing as an advocate for a period of three years and divested him of all nominated and elected offices held as an advocate, besides sentencing him to six weeks simple imprisonment which was kept in abeyance. Earlier, it had used this power in a contempt case against the Speaker of the Manipur Legislative Assembly for his production before the Court, 'Article 142 provides for enforcement of decrees and orders of Supreme Court and lays down that the Supreme Court shall have all and every power to make any order for the purpose of securing the attendance of any person, the discovery or production of any documents, or the investigation or punishment of any contempt of itself.'[24]

In *M.S. Ahlawat* v. *State of Haryana*,[25] reference was made to Supreme Court Bar Assn. Case,[26] wherein it was held that the order passed by the Supreme Court by issuing a show-cause notice and conviction summarily under Section 193 of the IPC for making false statement, was one without jurisdiction and that Article 142 could not be invoked for passing such an order. In *M.C. Mehta* v. *Kamal Nath*,[27] the Court clarified that power under this special jurisdiction cannot be exercised as it amounts to contravention of the specific provisions of a statute. A five-Judge Constitution Bench of the apex court reiterated this position in *E.S.P. Rajaram* v. *Union of India*.[28] Speaking for the bench, Justice D.P. Mahapatra observed that Article 142, even with the width of its amplitude, cannot be used to build a new edifice where none existed earlier, by ignoring express statutory provisions dealing with a subject and thereby achieve something indirectly which cannot be achieved directly. Again, in *Laxmidas Morarji (Dead) by LRS* v. *Behrose Darab Madan*,[29] the Supreme Court in a matter of eviction, made it clear that the constitutional power conferred upon it under Article 142 of the Constitution of India has to be used sparingly, though the same is not restricted by any of the statutory enactments. The case was pending for last 42 years. The Court clarified that acting under Article 142, it cannot pass an order or grant relief, which is totally inconsistent or goes against the substantive or statutory enactments pertaining to the case.

[24] *I. Manilala Singh* v. *H. Borobabu Singh* (1994) Supp (1) SCC 718, para 21, AIR (1994) SC 1033.
[25] (2000) 1 SCC 278.
[26] (1998) 4 SCC 409.
[27] (2000) 6 SCC 213.
[28] (2001) 2 SCC 186.
[29] Civil Appeal No. 5786 of 2002 with Civil Appeal No. 5787 of 2002, decided on 18 September 2009.

Passing Orders in Contravention of Substantive Laws

However, there seems to be total lack of unanimity so far as the exercise of power under Article 142 is concerned. Since the 1990s, the Supreme Court has been frequently passing orders in contravention of substantive laws. Even divorce has been granted by mutual consent and on the ground of irretrievable breakdown of marriage notwithstanding the fact that the Hindu Marriage Act, 1955, does not provide for it. In *Chandrakala Menon (Mrs) Anr.* v. *Vipin Menon (Capt.) & Anr.*,[30] the Supreme Court, in exercise of its powers under Article 142 of the Constitution, granted a decree of divorce by mutual consent under Section 13-B of the Act and dissolved the marriage between the parties in order to meet the ends of justice even though the consent given under Section 13-B of the Act was withdrawn within one week of the filing of the joint petition. In *Ashok Hurra* v. *Rupa Bipin Zaveri*,[31] the Supreme Court granted a decree of mutual divorce by taking recourse to its extraordinary powers under Article 142. Section 13-B(2) of the Hindu Marriage Act provides that on a motion by both parties, six months after the date of presentation of the petition under sub-section 1 of the Act, and not later than 18 months, the court shall, after inquiry, pass a decree of divorce by mutual consent. In this case, the wife withdrew the consent, but it was after 18 months of the filing of the joint petition. The Court should have laid down whether the consent withdrawn after 18 months was valid and whether the delay could be condoned under certain circumstances.

It was followed in *Anita Sabharwal* v. *Anil Sabharwal*,[32] in which case decree of mutual divorce was granted without waiting for the statutory period of six months. Again, the same view was echoed in *Kiran* v. *Sharad Dutt*.[33] After living separately for many years and after 11 years of litigation involving proceedings under Section 13 of the Hindu Marriage Act, 1955, the parties filed a joint application before the Supreme Court for amending the divorce petition. Treating the said divorce petition as one under Section 13-B of the Act, this Court, by invoking its powers under Article 142 of the Constitution, granted a decree of mutual divorce at the SLP stage. Using the same extraordinary powers in *Anjana Kishore* v. *Puneet Kishore*,[34] the Supreme

---

[30] (1993) 2 SCC 6.
[31] (1997) 4 SCC 226.
[32] (1997) 1 SCC 490.
[33] (2000) 10 SCC 243.
[34] (2002) 10 SCC 194.

Court directed the parties to file a joint petition before the family court at Bandra, Mumbai, under Section 13-B of the Hindu Marriage Act, 1955, for grant of a decree of divorce by mutual consent, along with a copy of the terms of compromise arrived at between the parties. It also directed that on such application being made, the family court could dispense with the need of waiting for six months as required by Sub-Section (2) of Section 13-B of the Act and pass final orders on the petition within such time as it deemed fit and directed the presiding judge to take appropriate steps looking to the facts and circumstances of the case emerging from the pleadings of the parties and to do complete justice in the case. The Court again used its special powers under Article 142 in *Swati Verma (Smt.)* v. *Rajan Verma & Ors.*,[35] and allowed the prayer for divorce by mutual consent to give a quietus to all litigations pending between the parties. The Court invoked this power in the similar way in many subsequent cases.[36]

In *Anil Kumar Jain* v. *Maya Jain*,[37] the Supreme Court was asked to adjudicate whether a decree can be passed on a petition for mutual divorce under Section 13-B of the Hindu Marriage Act, 1955, when one of the petitioners withdraws consent to such decree prior to the passing of such decree. The husband and wife filed a joint petition for divorce, but the wife withdrew her consent after six months, saying that she did not want the marriage dissolved, differences notwithstanding, even though she said that she would not live with her husband. The civil court dismissed the petition keeping in view the withdrawal of consent by the wife, and the Madhya Pradesh High Court also dismissed the appeal against it. The Supreme Court set aside the decision of the High Court and allowed divorce on the ground of irretrievable breakdown of marriage as the wife had refused to stay with the husband. What is astounding is that the Court did it not only without overruling the law laid down in *Smt. Sureshta Devi* v. *Om Prakash*,[38] but also reiterating that the law still holds good. In this case, the Court held that the consent given by the husband and wife to the filing of a petition for mutual divorce had to subsist till a decree was passed on the petition, and if either of the parties withdrew the consent before the passing of the final decree, the petition under Section 13-B of the Hindu Marriage

[35] (2004) 1 SCC 123.
[36] *Jimmy Sudarshan Purohit* v. *Sudarshan Sharad Purohit* [(2005) 13 SCC 410], *Sanghamitra Ghosh* v. *Kajal Kumar Ghosh* [(2007) 2 SCC 220]).
[37] (2009) 12 SCALE 115.
[38] (1991) 2 SCC 25.

Act would not survive and would have to be dismissed. Writing for the bench, Justice Altmas Kabir clarified,

> although irretrievable break-down of marriage is not one of the grounds indicated whether under Sections 13 or 13-B of the Hindu Marriage Act, 1955, for grant of divorce, the said doctrine can be applied to a proceeding under either of the said two provisions only where the proceedings are before the Supreme Court. In exercise of its extraordinary powers under Article 142 of the Constitution the Supreme Court can grant relief to the parties without even waiting for the statutory period of six months stipulated in Section 13-B of the aforesaid Act. This doctrine of irretrievable break-down of marriage is not available even to the High Courts which do not have powers similar to those exercised by the Supreme Court under Article 142 of the Constitution. Neither the civil courts nor even the High Courts can, therefore, pass orders before the periods prescribed under the relevant provisions of the Act or on grounds not provided for in Section 13 and 13-B of the Hindu Marriage Act, 1955 ... although the Supreme Court can, in exercise of its extraordinary powers under Article 142 of the Constitution, convert a proceeding under Section 13 of the Hindu Marriage Act, 1955, into one under Section 13-B and pass a decree for mutual divorce, without waiting for the statutory period of six months, none of the other Courts can exercise such powers. The other Courts are not competent to pass a decree for mutual divorce if one of the consenting parties withdraws his/her consent before the decree is passed. Under the existing laws, the consent given by the parties at the time of filing of the joint petition for divorce by mutual consent has to subsist till the second stage when the petition comes up for orders and a decree for divorce is finally passed and it is only the Supreme Court, which, in exercise of its extraordinary powers under Article 142 of the Constitution, can pass orders to do complete justice to the parties.[39]

The Court has itself admitted that in case of irretrievable breakdown of marriage, the Supreme Court alone can do justice, meaning thereby that those who cannot afford to move the apex court have to suffer in silence. Is it the way the Supreme Court dispenses justice and comes to the rescue of the affluent leaving the flotsams and jetsam high and dry? The Supreme Court is the mouthpiece of the Constitution, which is to interpret the law creatively and impartially to undo injustice and mitigate sufferings of the people. The Court could have made the irretrievable breakdown of marriage as a ground

---

[39] *Anil Kumar Jain* v. *Maya Jain* [(2009) 12 SCALE 115, paras 17 and 18].

for divorce by creatively interpreting Section 13(1-A) of the Hindu Marriage Act, 1955, which provides ample hint for it. It reads:

> Either party to a marriage, whether solemnized before or after the commencement of this Act, may also present a petition for the dissolution of the marriage by a decree of divorce on the ground–
>
> (i) that there has been no resumption of cohabitation as between the parties to the marriage for a period of one year or upwards after the passing of a decree for judicial separation in a proceeding to which they were parties; or
> (ii) that there has been no restitution of conjugal rights as between the parties to the marriage for a period of one year or upward after the passing of a decree of restitution of conjugal rights in a proceeding to which they were parties.

Making absence of cohabitation and non-restitution of conjugal rights grounds for divorce is nothing but irretrievable breakdown of marriage.

No Consistency

Surprisingly, the apex court did not take recourse to this extraordinary power in *Omprakash and Ors.* v. *Radhacharan and Ors.*,[40] and allowed the property acquired by a childless widow who died intestate (without leaving a will) to devolve on her husband's sister's sons. It is a touching story of one Narayani Devi who lost her husband within three months of her marriage. After that she was driven out of her matrimonial home, most probably taking her to be a bad omen. She stayed with her parents, was given education, and got a job. She amassed a fortune and also left huge amount in her provident fund account. After her death, her mother filed an application for grant of succession certificate in terms of Section 372 of the Hindu Succession Act, 1956. Ironically, her in-laws who had no qualms in driving her out, surfaced only after her death just to claim the fortune acquired by her. Section 15(1) of the Succession Act lays down that if a Hindu woman dies intestate (without leaving a will), her properties devolve in the following order: firstly, upon the sons and daughters (including the children of any pre-deceased son or daughter) and the husband; secondly, upon the heirs of the husband; thirdly, upon the mother and father; fourthly, upon the heirs of the father; and lastly, upon the heirs of the mother. Section 15(2) further says that notwithstanding anything contained in sub-section (1), any property inherited by a female Hindu from

[40] (2009) 15 SCC, p. 66.

her father or mother shall go, in the absence of any son or daughter of the deceased (including the children of any pre-deceased son or daughter), to the heirs of the father, and any property she inherited from her husband or father-in-law shall go to the husband's heirs. The Supreme Court observed that the law is silent on a Hindu woman's self-acquired property, and that such a property cannot be considered as property inherited from her parents. Going by Section 15(1), the Court allowed Narayani's husband's sister's sons' claims on her property. Justice S.B. Sinha admitted that it was a 'hard case', but nonetheless allowed the cruel in-laws to take away her property:

> This is a hard case. Narayani during her life time did not visit her in-laws' place. We will presume that the contentions … that she had not been lent any support from her husband's family is correct and all support had come from her parents but then only because a case appears to be hard would not lead us to invoke different interpretation of a statutory provision which is otherwise impermissible. It is now a well settled principle of law that sentiment or sympathy alone would not be a guiding factor in determining the rights of the parties which are otherwise clear and unambiguous.[41]

This does not seem to be a convincing reasoning based on equity and fair play. Justice A.M. Bhattacharjee, in his *Modern Hindu Law Under Constitution* has written, 'Under the provision of Section 15(1) read with sub-section (2) in the absence of children, the order of succession in the case of a female Hindu would vary according to the source of acquisition of property.' He raised the question why the source of acquisition should be a determinant in the case of a Hindu woman when it is not so in the case of a Hindu man, 'Unless we still want to perpetuate in a somewhat different form the old outmoded view that the ownership of the property cannot be full but must be somewhat limited'. Prabha Sridevan has commented:

> Ironically, some of the ancient texts have more pragmatic and equal approach in such cases. *Stridhan*, according to some texts, is categorized as technical and non-technical. Non-technical *stridahn* is that property which is acquired by a woman through her skill and mechanical arts (Vasishta). In the case of a woman who has no issues, the heirs to *stridhan* are her husband, mother, brother or father (*Devala*). *Aprajaayaaharedbhartaamatabhratapitaapiva*, says Devalasmriti (AD 600–900).
>
> In the 21st edition of *Principles of Hindu Law* (Mulla), it is observed that Section 15(2) 'seems to have been made on the ground that they prevent such

---

[41] *Omprakash and Ors.* v. *Radhacharan and Ors.* (2009) 15 SCC, p. 66, para 7.

property passing into the hands of persons to whom justice would require it should not pass and on the ground that the exceptions are in the interest of the intestate herself'. If the intention of this provision is to prevent property from devolving on persons to whom justice 'would require it should not pass', (sic) then the family that had refused to take care of Narayani should not have got anything.[42]

It is surprising why the Supreme Court did not invoke Article 142, which it has been doing at a frenetic pace, when it itself admitted that it is a hard case. When the Court says that its power is not limited by any provisions of any statutory law, then why it did not do 'complete justice' especially when the injustice was so glaring that it made it a hard case. In hard cases, intelligent judges, instead of distorting law, prefer to distort facts a little to meet the ends of justice. In this case, the Court could have taken the stand that had Narayani written her will, she would never have given her property to her in-laws. And this is a fact anyone could presume.

The technocratic decision of the Supreme Court may be contrasted with its decision in *Nandlal Wasudeo Badwaik* v. *Lata Nandlal Badwaik and Anr.*,[43] wherein it did disregard the express provision of Section 112 of the Indian Evidence Act that a child born during marriage is a conclusive proof of legitimacy. It is meant to prevent the bastardization of child. It reads:

> The fact that any person was born during the continuance of a valid marriage between his mother and any man, or within two hundred and eighty days after its dissolution, the mother remaining unmarried, shall be conclusive proof that he is the legitimate son of that man, unless it can be shown that the parties to the marriage had no access to each other at any time when he could have been begotten.

The wife claimed maintenance for herself and her daughter, but the husband claimed that the daughter was not his. She claimed that at the time of conception she was living with him, which he stoutly denied. DNA test proved that he was not the biological father of the child. Going by the report of the DNA test, the Court refused to allow her maintenance:

> We may remember that Section 112 of the Evidence Act was enacted at a time when the modern scientific advancement and DNA test were not

---

[42] 'A Law That Thwarts Justice', *The Hindu*, 27 June 2011.
[43] (2014) 2 SCC 576, decided on 6 January 2014, by C.K. Prasad and J.S. Khehar, JJ.

even in contemplation of the Legislature. The result of DNA test is said to be scientifically accurate. Although Section 112 raises a presumption of conclusive proof on satisfaction of the conditions enumerated therein but the same is rebuttable. The presumption may afford legitimate means of arriving at an affirmative legal conclusion. While the truth or fact is known, in our opinion, there is no need or room for any presumption. Where there is evidence to the contrary, the presumption is rebuttable and must yield to proof. Interest of justice is best served by ascertaining the truth and the court should be furnished with the best available science and may not be left to bank upon presumptions, unless science has no answer to the facts in issue. In our opinion, when there is a conflict between a conclusive proof envisaged under law and a proof based on scientific advancement accepted by the world community to be correct, the latter must prevail over the former. (pp. 16–17)

The Court glossed over Section 112 of the Indian Evidence Act without even taking recourse to Article 142. It could have adumbrated at the gaping hole in the law and left it to the legislature instead of grubbing about for the solution.

However, in *State of Gujarat* v. *Kishanbhai Etc.*,[44] decided only a day later, the Supreme Court acquitted the accused who had allegedly kidnapped a six-year-old girl, raped and brutally killed her. He had hit her head and other parts of the body with a brick and in order to steal the anklets she was wearing, he had chopped off her feet just above her ankles. All the circumstantial evidence pointed to the guilt of the accused, and the trial court awarded him death sentence. Howbeit, on appeal, the Gujarat High Court acquitted him, giving him the benefit of doubt. The accused was last seen with the deceased, her body was covered by the shirt that he was wearing, he pawned the anklets to a jeweller for Rs 1,000, he led the police to the field where the dead body was lying, and so on. Nonetheless, the High Court ruled that the prosecution was guilty of a grave lapse which did not produce the jeweller as a witness and said that the lapse could have easily been overcome by proving the identity of the person who had pledged the anklets, by identifying the thumb impression of the receipt. The prosecution could not establish why the accused had only Rs 940 in his possession when he had got Rs 1,000. The Supreme Court also upheld the High Court's verdict and lambasted the investigation and the prosecution

---

[44] (2014) 5 SCC 108, decided on 7 January 2014.

for the lapses and gave detailed directions to fix their accountability in cases of acquittals. The Court bemoans the failure to do justice:

> The investigating officials and the prosecutors involved in presenting this case, have miserably failed in discharging their duties. They have been instrumental in denying to serve the cause of justice. The misery of the family of the victim Gomi has remained unredressed. The perpetrators of a horrendous crime, involving extremely ruthless and savage treatment to the victim, have remained unpunished. A heartless and merciless criminal, who has committed an extremely heinous crime, has gone scot-free. He must be walking around in Ahmedabad, or some other city/town in India, with his head held high. A criminal on the move. Fearless and fearsome. Fearless now, because he could not be administered the punishment, he ought to have suffered. And fearsome, on account of his having remained unaffected by the brutal crime committed by him. His actions now, know of no barriers. He could be expected to act in an unfathomable savage manner, uncomprehendable (sic) to a sane mind.
>
> As we discharge our responsibility in deciding the instant criminal appeal, we proceed to apply principles of law, and draw inferences. For, that is our job. We are trained, not to be swayed by mercy or compassion. We are trained to adjudicate without taking sides, and without being mindful of the consequences. We are required to adjudicate on the basis of well drawn parameters. We have done all that. Despite thereof, we feel crestfallen, heartbroken and sorrowful. We could not serve the cause of justice, to an innocent child. We could not even serve the cause of justice, to her immediate family. The members of the family of Gomi must never have stopped cursing themselves, for not adequately protecting their child from a prowler, who had snatched an opportunity to brutalise her, during their lapse in attentiveness. And if the prosecution version about motive is correct, the crime was committed for a mere consideration of Rs. 1,000/-.[45]

It is inscrutable why the apex court did not invoke its power under Article 142 if it was so upset about justice being upended. Even the High Court had no difficulty as Section 482 of the Code of Criminal Procedure, 1973, unshackles it of all restraints:

> Saving of inherent powers of High Court: Nothing in this Code shall be deemed to limit or affect the inherent powers of the High Court to make such orders as may be necessary to give effect to any order under this Code,

---

[45] (2014) 5 SCC 108, decided on 7 January 2014, paras 15 and 16.

or to prevent abuse of the process of any court or otherwise to secure the ends of justice.

It has been reproduced from Section 561A of the Code of Criminal Procedure, 1898, about which the Supreme Court clarified in *Pampapathy* v. *State of Mysore*,[46] that the inherent powers cannot be invoked in respect of any matter covered by the specific provisions of the Code:

> It cannot also be invoked if its exercise would be inconsistent with any of the specific provisions of the Code. It is only if the matter in question is not covered by any specific provisions of the Code that Section 561A can come into operation. No legislative enactment dealing with procedure can provide for all cases that can possibly arise and it is an established principle that courts should have inherent powers apart from the express provisions of law, which are necessary to their existence and for the proper discharge of the duties imposed upon them by law.[47]

The High Court could have easily used its inherent powers as there was no clash with any specific provisions of the Code.

In *Academy of Nutrition Improvement* v. *Union of India*,[48] the Supreme Court held that Article 142 conferred unfettered independent jurisdiction to pass any order in public interest to do complete justice. In this case, the petitioner challenged the Prevention of Food Adulteration Act, 1954 and rules made there-under which seek to prevent adulteration of food stuffs. The rules were made by the Union Government in exercise of its power 'for the purposes of the Act'. In order to prevent iodine deficiency disorders (IDDs), the rules were amended in 2005, which provided that 'No person shall sell or offer or expose for sale or have in his premises for the purpose of sale, the common salt, for direct human consumption unless the same is iodised'. The Court was asked to adjudicate on the validity of this amended rule by those dealing in common salt. The challenge, among others, was on the grounds that the rule was arbitrary, made in violation of article 19(1)(g) of the Constitution and the same was *ultra vires* the parent legislation. Raveendran J, while conceding that the court had no power to review policy decisions of the government, clearly held that the impugned rule 44-I was

---

[46] AIR (1967) SC 286: (1966) Supp SCR 477.

[47] *Pampapathy* v. *State of Mysore*, AIR (1967) SC 286: [1966] Supp SCR 477, 482.

[48] (2011) 8 SCC 274.

ultra vires the parent legislation, as it was not a rule required to be made to carry out the provisions of the Act, having regard to the object and scheme, and it has nothing to do with curbing of food adulteration or to suppress any social or economic mischief. However, the Court did not lift the ban on the sale of non-iodized salt on the ground that it may not be in the interest of public health and allowed the impugned *ultra vires* rule to continue for a period of six months.

Unfettered jurisdiction makes the law unpredictable which attracts the basic principle of jurisprudence. Court has been vested with inherent powers. Section 151 of the Code of Civil Procedure reads, 'Nothing in this Code shall be deemed to limit or otherwise affect the inherent power of the court to make such orders as may be necessary for the ends of justice or to prevent the abuse of the process of the court'.

However, this power cannot be exercised in contravention of provisions of substantive law. In *Manohar Lal Chopra* v. *Raja Seth Hiralal,*[49] the Supreme Court ruled that these powers are not to be exercised if it may be in conflict with what had been expressly provided in the Code or against the intentions of the legislature. As quoted above, Section 482 of the Cr. P.C., 1973, confers similar inherent powers to the High Court.

These are procedural laws, and Article 142(1) is couched in similar language. So, the rationale behind making such a constitutional provision seems to be vesting the apex court with adequate powers to bypass procedural limitations in order to do complete justice and that it is not the source of any substantive power. Order XLVII, Rule 6 of the Supreme Court Rules, 1966 is also similarly worded. Article 142 corresponds to Article 118 of the Draft Constitution, which was incorporated without any discussion on the use of words 'complete justice'. This bolsters the view that it was only meant to cure procedural infirmities. In fact, Article 118 finds a place in the debate as a reference when Article 112 of the Draft Constitution was debated. Shri Alladi Krishnaswami Ayyar elucidated the concept of 'complete justice' in these words:

> ... If only we realize the plenitude of the jurisdiction under Article 112, if only, as I have no doubt, the Supreme Court is able to develop its own jurisprudence according to its own light, suited to the conditions of the country, there is nothing preventing the Supreme Court from developing its own jurisprudence in such a way that it could do complete justice in every kind of cause or matter.[50]

---

[49] (1966) 3 SCR 856: AIR (1966) SC 1899.
[50] Constituent Assembly Debates, Vol. VIII, p. 639.

Dr R. Prakash makes a valid point that the marginal note of Article 142 supports the view that the article does not confer any substantive power on the apex court:

The marginal note of Article 142 reads: '*Enforcement of decrees and orders of Supreme Court and orders as to discovery, etc.*'. The marginal note speaks of enforcement and discovery and not about complete justice. Had the makers of the Constitution wanted to confer the power to override statutory provision, its importance would have been spelt out in the marginal note. It is settled law that the marginal note is a part of the statute or the Constitution as the case may be and a permissible internal aid in construing a statute. Though the marginal note cannot cut down the scope of the enactment, it can be resorted to if there is an ambiguity in the enactment. The Supreme Court adverted to and relied on the marginal note of Article 368 in *Golak Nath* v. *State of Punjab*,[51] a decision by an eleven-Judge Constitution Bench. In *Bengal Immunity Co. Ltd.* v. *State of Bihar*,[52] a seven-Judge Constitution Bench of the Supreme Court construed the marginal note of Article 286 to find out the meaning of the phraseology employed in the article. Thus viewed, the marginal note of Article 142 suggests that the article concerns itself with procedural aspects.[53]

Article 142(2) reinforces this view as it confers three procedural powers on the Supreme Court in the arena of law of evidence: Securing the attendance of persons before it, discovery and production of documents, and investigation and punishment of contempt of itself. Further, Articles 129 and 142(2) of the Constitution deal with the contempt jurisdiction of the Supreme Court. While Article 129 bequeaths substantive power to the apex court to punish for contempt of itself, Article 142(2) supplements it by conferring the special power of investigation and punishment. It is well-known that the area of investigation falls within the ambit of the law of procedure.

The Supreme court accepted this premise in *Prem Chand Garg* v. *Excise Commr., U.P. Allahabad*,[54] as is evident from the following words of Gajendragadkar, J. (as he then was):

It may be pertinent to point out that the wide powers which are given to this Court for doing complete justice between the parties, can be used by this

---

[51] AIR (1967) SC 1643.
[52] AIR (1955) SC 661.
[53] 'Complete Justice Under Article 142', [(2001) 7 SCC (Jour) 14.], see http://www.ebc-india.com/lawyer/articles/2001v7a3.htm (last accessed on 19 January 2014).
[54] AIR (1963) SC 996.

Court, for instance, in adding parties to the proceedings pending before it, or in admitting additional evidence, or in remanding the case, or in allowing a new point to be taken for the first time. It is plain that in exercising these and similar other powers, this Court would not be bound by the relevant provisions of procedure if it is satisfied that a departure from the said procedure is necessary to do complete justice between the parties.[55]

A five-judge Constitution Bench of the Supreme Court, in *Union Carbide Corporation Etc.* v. *Union of India*,[56] also accepted the intention of the Founding Fathers of the Constitution that the article bequeathed procedural power as the Court dwelt upon its inherent jurisdiction under Articles 136 and 142 to withdraw or transfer and finally dispose of the main suits and pending criminal proceedings in the course of hearing of appeals, arising out of interlocutory orders in suits. In *Maniyeri Madhavan* v. *Sub-Inspector of Police*,[57] a division bench of the Supreme Court made it clear that while exercising its jurisdiction under Article 142, it need not follow the procedure prescribed under Section 6 of the Delhi Special Police Establishment Act, 1946.

In *B.C. Chaturvedi* v. *Union of India*,[58] Justice B.L. Hansaria, in his separate concurring judgment, opined:

It deserves to be pointed out that the mere fact that there is no provision parallel to Article 142 relating to the High Court, can be no ground to think that they have not to do complete justice, and if moulding of relief would do complete justice between parties, the same cannot be ordered. Absence of provision like Article 142 is not material; according to me I would say that power to do complete justice also inheres in every court, not to speak of a court of plenary jurisdiction like a High Court. Of course, this power is not as wide as which this Court has Under Article 142. That, however, is a different matter.[59]

Even the smaller bench of the Supreme Court has invoked this jurisdiction to overrule larger bench. The Court constituted a five-judge bench in *Islamic Academy of Education* v. *State of Karnataka*,[60] to explore the true import of

[55] AIR (1963) SC 996, 1003, para 13 (emphasis supplied).
[56] (1992) AIR 248: (1991) SCR Supl. (1) 251: (1991) 4 SCC 584: JT (1991) (6) 8.
[57] (1994) 1 SCC 536.
[58] (1995) 6 SCC 749: AIR (1996) SC 484.
[59] (1995) 6 SCC 749: AIR (1996) SC 484, para 23.
[60] AIR (2003) SC 3724.

the 11-judge bench's verdict in the T.M.A. Pai Foundation case regarding quota in unaided professional colleges and regulation of fee structure. It is flabbergasting that the five-judge bench overruled the 11-judge bench in the name of interpretation and imposed the old regulations which had been removed, and created government quotas even in unaided minority institutions. Perhaps the judges knew that it was out and out an unconstitutional act, and so, they legitimated it by invoking Article 142. It defies all rationale that the extraordinary jurisdiction was invoked to find out the ratio of the judgement given by a larger bench.

Exercising Extra-Constitutional Jurisdiction

The apex court has not only ignored statutory provisions while invoking powers under Article 142, but, on occasions, has also done nothing short of altering the Constitution. Its most glaring example is *Jagdambika Pal* v. *Union of India & Ors.*,[61] in which it ordered composite floor test to ascertain which of the two chief ministers of UP—Kalayan Singh and Jagdambika Pal—enjoyed the confidence of the House. The state government headed by Singh was dismissed on 21 February 1998 by Governor Romesh Bhandari and he appointed Pal as the chief minister. Singh moved the Allahabad High Court which reinstated his government on 23 February, holding the dismissal of the state government unconstitutional. Pal challenged the High Court's decision in the Supreme Court. On 24 February, a bench headed by Chief Justice M.M. Punchhi, directed to hold a composite floor test on 26 February. Both Singh and Pal sat as chief ministers on the designated day and floor test was conducted in which Singh emerged victorious. It was a unique incident in which the apex court recognized two chief ministers of a state at a time. The Court should have upheld or set aside the decision of the High Court. But it preferred to keep mum on the main issue and ordered for the floor test which is not provided for anywhere in the Constitution. In a sense, it followed the principle laid down in *S.R. Bommai* v. *Unoin of India*,[62] that the House is the only place to test the strength of the government. But there is no provision for the composite floor test which would make the office of the governor redundant. Obviously, it was done under Article 142. Perhaps the Court presumed that Singh would secure the majority, which he did only to fall the next day. Making a pun of Chief Justice Punchhi's name, the order of the apex court was ridiculed as 'Punchhaiti Raj' sounding like 'Panchayati Raj' which was

[61] (1999) 9 SCC 95.
[62] AIR (1994) SC 1918: (1994) 3 SCC 1.

not bound by the written law. In the Jharkhand case,[63] the Supreme Court gave a detailed direction as to how the floor test in the Jharkhand Legislative Assembly would be conducted, though it has no such jurisdiction.

Though any order or decision delivered under Article 142 of the Constitution does not have any precedential value, the Supreme Court, in *Union of India* v. *Harish Chandra Singh Rawat*,[64] in its order on 9 May 2016, referred to its directions in Jagdambika Pal and Jharkhand cases, and ordered for floor test debarring the Speaker from presiding over it:

> This Court, being the sentinel on the qui vive of the Constitution is under the obligation to see that the democracy prevails and not gets hollowed by individuals. The directions which have been given on the last occasion, was singularly for the purpose of strengthening the democratic values and the constitutional norms. The collective trust in the legislature is founded on the bedrock of the constitutional trust. This is a case where one side even in the floor test does not trust the other and the other claims that there is no reason not to have the trust. Hence, there is the need and there is the necessity to have a neutral perceptionist to see that absolute objectivity is maintained when the voting takes place. Solely for the aforesaid purpose, we intend to modify the order by directing that the Principal Secretary, Legislative and Parliamentary Affairs who belongs to the cadre of the District Judge shall remain present to conduct the affairs with perceptible objectivity and singularity of purpose of neutrality along with the Secretary Legislative Assembly.[65]

Law and Morality

Some judges think that whatever is right in their opinion can find a place in their judgement, irrespective of whether it is supported by any law. In Britain, Lord Patrick Devlin, in *Shaw* v. *Director of Public Prosecution*,[66] held that punishment would be awarded in case of offence against public morality. Till then, there was no act defined as offence against public morality. Shaw had published a directory of 600 socialite women with details of their sexual preferences. Lord Devlin held it to be an offence against public morality. Renowned law scholar Professor H.L.A. Hart, criticized the decision that

---

[63] *Anil Kumar Jha* v. *Union of India* (2005) SCC 150.

[64] Petition(s) for Special Leave to Appeal (C) No(s). 11567/2016.

[65] Petition(s) for Special Leave to Appeal (C) No(s). 11567/2016, second last para.

[66] (1962) AC 220.

punishment cannot be handed down in the absence of any law. It led to a fierce Hart-Delvin debate in the 1960s. Professor Hart endorsed J.S. Mill's opinion that it was not the law's business to regulate morality.[67]

Actually some extraordinary powers have been vested in courts of all levels so that they do not feel asphyxiated due to procedural bottlenecks and fail to deliver justice. It has its provenance in the concept of 'justice, equity, and good conscience'. Aristotle opined that *'justitia'* needs and presupposes *'acquitas'*. *Acquitas* has the arduous role to adjust the written statute to the particular circumstances of the case. This is done in two ways: (a) to correct, modify, and, if necessary, amend the statute law; and (b) to supplement and otherwise remove the difficulties of the written sources of law. There is also a third sense of *acquitas*—it is where the judge is to fall back upon his 'office' to give a decision *ex bono et acquo*, which means 'according to good conscience'. It was developed in England and made part of the legal system.[68] The preamble to the Act of Succession, 1536, contains the words 'equity, reason and good conscience'.

It is a well-established principle of interpretation of statute that legislations alter the pre-existing common law and principles of justice, equity, and good conscience only to the extent of repugnancy between the two. Judicial review of administrative action was in existence even in the pre-Constitution era. Courts invoked the principle of justice, equity, and good conscience and the relevant statutes to rectify illegalities in administrative action. Even the Constitution did not wipe out the pre-existing law if it did not attract any provision of the Constitution, as Article 372(1) itself clarifies. A nine-judge bench of the Supreme Court also reiterated it, 'it is well-known that the common law of England was applied as such in the original sides of the High Courts of Calcutta, Bombay and Madras, and that in the mofussil courts the principles embodied in the common law were invoked in appropriate cases on the ground of justice, equity and good conscience'.[69]

Sometimes, there may be genuine confusion. In the United Kingdom, in *R (JK)* v. *Registrar General*, the Queen's Bench Division (Administrative Court) for England and Wales[70] had to grapple with a unique situation.

---

[67] H.L.A. Hart, *Law, Liberty and Morality* (California: Stanford University Press, 1963).

[68] A.R. Biswas, 'Justice, Equity and Good Conscience', in *Encyclopedic Law Dictionary* (Calcutta: Eastern Law House, 1979), p. 465.

[69] (*Superintendent & Legal Remembrancer* v. *Corporation of Calcutta* (1967) 2 SCR 170 at 180).

[70] (2015) EWHC 990 (Admin).

A man, who was born as a male, married a woman in 2007 and in 2012 the couple had a biological child. In the birth certificate issued by the registrar general, the names of parents were mentioned as father and mother respectively. After the birth of the first child, the biological father developed a desire to live like a woman and he took drugs for it after which he was referred for gender reassignment surgery. In the meantime, the wife got pregnant from him a second time. Now the biological father wrote to the registrar general asking whether the birth of the first child could be re-registered and the birth of the next child registered with the claimant's female name showing her identity as parent, and not as father. The registrar general declined to accede to the request saying that as per the law, the claimant could be registered only as father. The claimant moved the court on the ground that the registrar's decision violated Articles 6, 8, and 14 of the European Convention of Human Rights (ECHR). Article 6 of the Human Rights Act mandates that a public authority must act in accordance with ECHR. Article 8 provides a right to respect for one's 'private and family life, his home and his correspondence' and Article 14 prohibits discrimination based on 'sex, race, colour, language, religion, political or other opinion, national or social origin, association with a national minority, property, birth or other status'. The court was between two horns of a dilemma as to which part of the right under Article 8 weighed heavier. The Births and Deaths Registration Act, 1953, in the UK had been amended drastically to accommodate parentage acquired through assisted reproduction, surrogacy, and adoption. So, the petitioner argued that as a transsexual parent, she was discriminated against, which violated Article 14. The Queen's Bench held that though her right to private life guaranteed under Article 8 was hit by requiring a transsexual to disclose her previous gender and not allowing her to get the original document changed for showing her chosen gender, failure to give correct gender of parents at the time of birth may interfere with the child's right. The court ruled that any change in the birth certificate subsequently would interfere with the child's rights to have its fundamental identity recognized. Judges may use their discretion in such cases.

Actually, Article 142 was incorporated into the Constitution to deal with those rare cases in which law may not be adequate, and complete justice cannot be done on its basis. But such cases are not many.

* * *

Many state statutes authorize judges to be guided, in the absence of any express law, by principles of 'justice, equity and good conscience' while deciding cases. Courts at all levels have been conferred inherent powers so that the stream of justice does not dry up in the dreary desert of wilderness. As discussed in the chapter, prior to the adoption of the judicature system, the principles of the common law and equity were administered in separate courts. Thus, common law did not recognize equitable obligations. Besides, a defendant in a common law court could not get his/her matter transferred to a court of equity. The only remedy available was to obtain a common injunction from the equity court to either prevent the plaintiff from setting up an inequitable plea at common law or to restrain such a plaintiff from pursuing and enforcing a judgment obtained at common law. The English Judicature Act of 1873 resolved the conflict between equity and common law. Section 25(11) of the Act stipulated that the equitable right would prevail in case of conflict, though this provision was rarely invoked subsequently. Debates on the subject in the English Parliament clearly suggest that it was being enacted to serve as an administrative reform. However, equitable rights were not to be enforced totally ignoring the principles of common law. This is how Lord Justice Cotton explained it:

> It has been argued before us that the difference between legal and equitable interests has been swept away by those statutes. But it was not intended by the legislature, and it has not been said, that legal and equitable rights should be treated as identical, but that the Courts should administer both legal and equitable principles. I think that the clause enacting that the rules of equity shall prevail ... shews that it was not intended to sweep away altogether the principles of the common law.[71]

As has been mentioned earlier, equity developed as a body of articulate rules and principles, and was no longer dependent on the whims and caprice of the chancellor. Similarly, Article 142 does not give a carte blanche to judges to do as per their personal proclivities and propensities. As the maxim 'Equity will not suffer a wrong to be without a remedy' means that equity will intervene to protect a right which is being denied because of some technicality, so is the case with the power to do 'complete justice'. But while doing so, another maxim about equity must not be forgotten that 'Equity follows the law'. Thus, equity does not gloss over statute law, except in exceptional circumstances. In England, the writ (now called a claim form in the Civil Procedure Rules, 1998) *ne exeat regno*, which applies to equitable debts, will not be granted unless the conditions of the Debtors Act 1869, allowing arrest in the case of a

---

[71] *Joseph* v. *Lyons*, (1884) 15 QBD 280 at 285–6.

legal debt, are satisfied.[72] Principle of justice and equity definitely takes over in case of legal vacuum as the court cannot sit with its fingers crossed witching the macabre dance of injustice. The story of African chieftain Somersett illustrates this. Captured by slave traders, he was being taken to the US, but the luck smiled on him and he escaped from the ship and landed in England. His captor chased him. Two Englishmen moved court for the writ of habeas corpus to secure his release. He argued unabashedly that he was not doing anything illegal by slave-trading, as no law of England prevented it. Lord Mansfield rejected the argument observing that the air of England was too pure for a slave to breathe. On being inquired where the law was prohibiting slavery, Lord Mansfield quipped that the law was in the 'air' of England, that is, it was in the legal and political climate of England, in which the institution of slavery could not survive even for a moment.[73]

So, Article 142 has to be used to avoid miscarriage of justice in the absence of any express legal provision. Frequent invocation of Article 142 is creating uncertainty, though certainty in law is a prerequisite for justice. It does not mean that there should be no evolution. But without consistency, it is not evolution but caprice. Something meant to obviate injustice should not be used to obfuscate clearly defined law.

[72]   *Felton* v. *Callis* (1969) 1 Q.B. 200.

[73]   V.S. Deshpande, 'Nature of the Indian Legal System', revised by Thomas Paul in *Indian Legal System*, 2nd edition (Revised) (New Delhi: The Indian Law Institute, 2006), pp. 2–3.

5

Judicial Delays

Matter Is in the Court, Incompetence Is the Main Reason

Soapy, the protagonist of O. Henry's famous short story 'The Cop and the Anthem' is a homeless destitute who is in the dire need to find some sort of shelter for the winter. He knows of Blackwell's Island, the local jail, as the *de facto* homeless winter shelter. He wants to get arrested and for this, he resorts to criminal acts one after another, but he is not arrested. Desperate and dejected, he lingers by a small Christian church ruing his misery. There he listens to an anthem being played and experiences a spiritual epiphany. It gives him an impetus to discard the life of a vagrant and regain his self-respect. He resolves to do something and remembers that a big businessman had offered him a job. He decides to find out the man the very next day and apply for a job. As Soapy makes his plan standing on the street, a cop taps him on his shoulder and asks him what he is doing. As he answers 'Nothing', he is taken into custody.

Mohammed Saleem, a physically challenged person, was arrested on 3 June 2005 in New Delhi for allegedly attempting to attack a judge with a knife at the Patiala House Court complex in New Delhi. The reason he said was that he was 'frustrated over the delay' in the grant of compensation to him in a motor accident claim case. 'I know I will go to jail. In fact, that is exactly what I want. It is better than living in penury or begging',[1] he exclaimed.

[1] *Hindustan Times*, Patna, 4 June 2005.

The difference between the character of Saleem and O' Henry's Soapy is that while Saleem was instantly arrested for his act of violence, the fictional character was not. Saleem's plight is a poignant commentary on the problem of judicial delays. After the brouhaha created over the acquittal of accused in the infamous Jessica Lall murder case by the trial court in Delhi in February 2006, we witnessed a spate of judicial decisions over the next two to four weeks thereafter. For instance, in the case of rape of a German girl in Alwar, the accused, Biti Hotra Mohanty, a 23-year-old computer engineer who happened to be the son of a top Odisha police officer, was convicted within nine working days. The rape was committed on the night of 20 March 2006 and the verdict was delivered on 12 April 2006.[2]

We also have some precedents wherein the trial concluded within a few days—though the same were frowned upon—raises the question whether justice hurried is justice buried. The famous *Nagarwala* trial is one such example. On 21 May 1971, Ved Prakash Malhotra, chief cashier at the State Bank of India, Sansad Marg, New Delhi, received a phone call from someone who identified herself as Prime Minister Indira Gandhi. She instructed him to withdraw 6 million rupees in 100 rupee notes and make over to *Bangladesh ka Babu* (a gentleman from Bangladesh) at a particular place in Delhi. Malhotra met the man and delivered the money in cash to him. The man turned out to be Rustom Sohrab Nagarwala, a former army captain. After this, Malhotra rushed to the prime minister's office to inform P.N. Haksar, her principal secretary that he had carried out the PM's instructions and acted accordingly. Haksar was taken aback and asked him to register an FIR with the police as the prime minister had not given any such instructions. Nagarwala was arrested immediately. He confessed to impersonating Indira Gandhi on the phone. In perhaps the fastest ever investigation and trial, he was convicted and sent to jail, all in a matter of only three days.[3]

The scandal rocked the Parliament with the Opposition alleging that it was Indira Gandhi who authorized this transaction and then got Nagarwala silenced. In jail, Nagarwala retracted from his confession and pleaded that the trial be carried out afresh, but ultimately he died while in prison. The investigating officer, D.K. Kashyap, also died in a car accident. All this deepened the mystery and raised serious questions on the hurried trial as well.

[2] 'Express Justice: Alwar Rapist Gets 7 Years in Jail', *Times of India*, New Delhi, 13 April, 2006.

[3] Katherine Frank, *Indira: The Life of Indira Nehru Gandhi* (Noida: HarperCollins Publishers, 2010), pp. 332–3.

In another instance of an expeditious trial, on 15 May 2010, a Gaya court sentenced three youths to life imprisonment exactly 30 days after they gang raped a 25-year-old Japanese tourist on the night of 16 April.[4] It kindled a hope that if there is a will there is a way, and all alibis for the delay are nothing but a humbug. However, in one of the most publicized cases of rape and murder of a 23-year-old paramedic, committed in a moving bus in Delhi on the night of 16 December 2012, the judgment of a Delhi fast track court came on 10 September 2013.[5] So, even in such a case which spawned some unprecedented public protests and which led to the long-awaited amendment to the criminal law, it took over eight months for the trial court to pronounce its judgment in the matter. Of all the six accused, one died in the jail, while another one was a juvenile and so was tried accordingly. The remaining four adult accused were awarded death sentence. Since there were 85 prosecution witnesses and 17 defence witnesses, the trial did take some time. But the judgment was delivered in less than nine months, perhaps, on account of the fact that it not only shook the nation's conscience, but also, considering the public anger that the incident triggered, the trial court directed its focus only on this case. The Delhi High Court confirmed the trial court's judgment and on 5 May 2017, the Supreme Court dismissed the appeal filed against the decision of the High Court.[6] In general, the disposal of a criminal case takes many years, sometimes decades also. This highlights the need to urgently deal with the problem of judicial delays. No alibis justify delays.

Suits Running into Generations, Trials into Decades

Protracted litigations and trials are a common phenomenon in the Indian set up and the nation has also earned notoriety on account of these factors. It is a common belief that if you want to ruin someone permanently, get him implicated in litigation. A court case has a lifespan longer than that of a human being. Civil cases continue for several generations. India has the record of having witnessed a longest contested lawsuit according to the Guinness Book of World Records. In Pune, on 28 April 1966, Balasaheb Patloji Thorat received a favourable judgment in a suit filed by his ancestor

[4] '3 Get Life Terms a Month after Raping Japanese Tourist', *Times of India*, New Delhi, 16 May 2010.

[5] *Times of India, The Hindu, Hindustan Times, Dainik Hindustan, Dainik Jagran, Jansatta*, and other newspapers, 11 September 2013.

[6] *Mukesh and Anr.* v. *State for NCT and others* (2017) 6 SCC 1.

Maloji Thorat, 761 years earlier in 1205 CE. The points at issue were concerning the right to preside over public functions and precedence at religious festivals.[7]

A case filed in Kolkata in 1833 is yet to be decided. In the late eighteenth century, the Governor General of India, Robert Clive ruled that thousands of acres of land, historic buildings, and temples spread across Kolkata remain in the custody of Raja Naba Krishna Deb, a Royal of the Sovabazar court. The only condition for the Raja's continued rule was that he was to pay a tax of Re 1 per day—a duty that the state still collects. After the death of Deb and his son, the property was divided among family members who began to sell-off the buildings. In 1833, Kesto Sakha Ghosh, an executor of the Will of Raja's son, moved the court to stop the sale. After pondering over the case for 22 years, the judges appointed Hamingston, a British lawyer, to oversee the property, effectively making him a ward of the court as the case dragged on.

In 1862, control was passed over to a 'temple committee' comprising the members of Sovabazar family, British officials, and respected citizens. The committee lodged Rs 10,000 with the court and the interest it earned was used to maintain the buildings and temples. The compromise was continuously challenged by one or the other of the 2,000 family members since the case was lodged. Now the money has got depleted, and a petition by Alok Krishna Deb, a sixth generation scion of Raja Naba Krishna Deb, in 2006, sent court clerks scurrying for documents that were gathering dust. According to Deb, 'We are still kings in letter and spirit.... The court took the decision after a family member went to the court with a dispute over the property. Since then, no decision has been taken to return the property to the inheritors. Now the city high court possesses the property. And the case hangs fire.'[8]

Ramjanmabhoomi-Babri Masjid Dispute

An analysis of the litigation pertaining to disputed structure at Ayodhya, pertaining to the question as to whether it was the Rama Mandir or the Babri Masjid that existed anterior in time at that place, conclusively demonstrates and is a text book illustration of the fact that some suits do remain inconclusive, perhaps forever. In 1949, some primitive images of Hindu Gods and

---

[7] T.V.R. Shenoy, 'A Record We Can Do Without', http://in.rediff.com/news/2002/mar/08flip.htm (last accessed on 22 March 2015).

[8] *Realestatetimes*: News for use, 2 January 2007.

Goddesses mysteriously appeared in one section of the unused mosque. It triggered a huge controversy leading to communal frenzy. The issue went to the district court for the first time on 13 January 1950 when Gopal Singh Visharad filed a suit in the Faizabad court.[9] In 1955, the Allahabad High Court lamented that a decision was still awaited even after passage of four years.[10] The second suit was filed by the Nirmohi Akhada in 1959,[11] the third in 1961 by the Sunni Central Board,[12] and the fourth one was filed in 1989 on behalf of Ramlala by Justice (Retd) Deoki Nandan Agrawal.[13] All suits were clubbed together and called before the Lucknow Bench of the Allahabad High Court in the representative capacity. The litigation kept hanging fire and after many political convulsions that it touched off, the disputed structure called Babri Masjid, said to have been erected at Ramjanmabhoomi, was pulled down allegedly by some obscurantist Hindu activists on 6 December 1992 during a political rally which triggered large-scale communal riots and made a huge impact on the politics of the country as well. Ultimately, after a long wait, a three-judge bench of the High Court pronounced its verdict on 30 September 2010.[14] It ruled that the 2.77 acres (1.12 hectares) of the land be divided into three parts, with 1/3rd going to the Ramlala (infant Lord Rama) represented by the Hindu Mahasabha for the construction of the Rama temple, 1/3rd going to the Islamic Sunni Waqf Board, and remaining 1/3rd going to the Hindu religious denomination, Nirmohi Akhara. While the Bench was sharply divided over the issue whether the disputed structure was erected after demolishing a temple, it was unanimous as to the finding that a temple or a temple structure predated the mosque at the same site. The court heavily relied upon the reports of the Archaeological Survey of India (ASI), which carried out excavations, that the predating structure was a massive Hindu religious building. Ironically, the decision came seven long years after the ASI excavated the site in 2003 on the direction of the Lucknow Bench of the Allahabad High Court.

Excavations were carried out earlier also, but surprisingly, the court could not take any advantage out of it. The Banaras Hindu University was

---

[9] Suit no. 2 of 1950.

[10] Swapan Dasgupta, 'A Truth Nobody Will Ever Admit', *Sunday Times of India*, 5 July 2009.

[11] Suit no. 26 of 1959.

[12] Suit no. 12 of 1961.

[13] Suit no. 236 of 1989.

[14] *Gopal Singh Visharad* v. *Jahoor Ahmad; Ramlala Virajman* v. *Sunni Central Waqf Board* (2011) 86 ALR 646, OOS No. 5 of 1989.

the first to excavate the site in 1967. The second such exercise was undertaken in 1975–6 by the ASI, but its findings were not published then. Again, between 1975 and 1985, excavation activity was carried out in Ayodhya to examine some site related to the Ramayana story. 14 sites were examined including the Babri Masjid site. The ASI team (led by B.B. Lal), claimed to have found the pillar bases which may have been of a temple and which appeared to be belonging to a larger building than the Babri Mosque. In his submissions before the High Court in 2003, Lal averred that after he submitted his seven-page preliminary report to the ASI mentioning the discovery of pillar bases, adjoining south of the Babri Mosque structure, all technical facilities were withdrawn, and despite repeated requests, the project was not revived for 10–12 years. In July 1992, eight noted archaeologists, including former ASI directors, Y.D. Sharma and K.M. Srivastava, went to Ramkot hill to evaluate and examine the findings. These findings included religious sculptures and a statue of Lord Vishnu. They added that the inner boundary of the disputed structure rests, at least on one side, on an earlier existing structure, which 'may have belonged to an earlier temple'.[15]

The issue was referred to the Supreme Court for its advice under Article 143 of the Constitution of India. The apex court took undertakings from the Union as well as the state government that they would comply with the advice notwithstanding the fact that the advice given under Article 143 is not binding, and in a belated development, it returned the reference unanswered in 1994.[16] In the majority opinion of three judges, the reference could not be taken as an 'alternate dispute settlement mechanism', and thus, it could not substitute the pending suits and legal proceedings. In the opinion of the Court, the reference had become 'superfluous and unnecessary'. It further said that the reference should not be answered because it favoured some religious community over another, and also because the Union Government was not interested in settling the issue according to the Court's opinion, but wanted to use it as a springboard for negotiations. It added that the principal protagonists of the two sides had not appeared before the court to lead evidence or for cross-examination.

However, the appeal against the Allahabad High Court's judgment is pending before the Supreme Court. On 21 March 2017, the Court urged

---

[15] *Indian Express*, 4 July 1992.

[16] *Dr. M. Ismail Farooqi* v. *Union of India* (Special reference No. 1 of 1993) (1994) 6 SCC 360.

the opposing parties to settle the issue through negotiation. CJI, J.S. Khehar advocated an approach of give and take and offered himself as a mediator.[17] Though compromise in civil case is always welcome, the suggestion by the CJI in this case is puzzling as all the reasons adduced by the Court for returning the reference remain unchanged. If it was averse to be used as a springboard for negotiations, how is it so keen to mediate now? Further, if the principal adversaries did not show up in the Court to lead evidence and for cross-examination, how can it be sanguine about ensuring their appearance in the out of court settlement? The Court virtually put the case in the cold storage by refusing to advance the hearing.

Other Cases Running into Decades

On 20 September 2007, a division bench of the Supreme Court, comprising A.K. Mathur and Markandeya Katju, JJ, disposed of a 60-year-old case with a terse warning:

> (B)ecause of delay in disposal of cases people in this country are fast losing faith in the judiciary. We saw in the media news of lynching of suspected thieves in Bihar's Vaishali District, the gunning down of an undertrial prisoner outside Patna City Civil Court, and other incidents where people have taken the law into their own hands. This is obviously because many people have started thinking that justice will not be done in the Courts due to the delays in Court proceedings. This is indeed an alarming state of affairs, and we once again request the concerned authorities to do the needful in the matter urgently.[18]

The instant appeals by Moses Wilson and others arose out of a suit filed way back in 1947 at Kanyakumari and the subsequent proceedings. Since the facts involved were very complicated and also stretched over a long period of 60 years, the Court, with the consent of counsel of the parties, directed that the entire property be divided equally between the appellants and the respondents. Sometime later, the then president of India, Pratibha Patil, expressed her concern while inaugurating a seminar on judicial reforms in New Delhi

---

[17] http://timesofindia.indiatimes.com/india/sc-calls-for-talks-to-resolve-ayodhya-dispute-cji-khehar-offers-to-mediate/articleshow/57761624.cms (last accessed on 4 April 2017).

[18] *Moses Wilson and Others* v. *Kasturiba and Others*, AIR (2008) SC 379 (2007) 14 SCC 452.

that the judiciary could not escape blame for delayed justice that was fraught with the risk of promoting the lynch mob phenomenon.[19] Then CJI, K.G. Balakrishnan, sharing the dais with the president, countered the charge that the judiciary was the main culprit for the snail-paced justice and said that the root of the malaise lay in governance deficit.

The incidents of mob lynching are on a rise these days. In one of the most macabre incidents, Syed Sarifuddin Khan, a 35-year-old man from Assam, accused of rape, was dragged and beaten to death in Dimapur, Nagaland, by a mob of thousands. He was accused of rape by a Naga woman, the cousin of his wife. He was arrested and sent to jail for 10 days when a strong mob of several thousand people, including a large number of young women, on 5 March 2015, stormed Dimapur Central Jail. Barbarism was on its full display as he was dragged out, beaten and pelted with stones, stripped naked, tied to a motorcycle and dragged wounded and bleeding for about 7 km when he succumbed to the injuries. Not satisfied, the mob strung his body up on a fence for the perverted onlookers to see and jeer. The allegation of rape could never be established. Khan was initially misrepresented to be a Bangladeshi which made the barbarism justifiable. His father and brothers served in the Indian Army, and he was living in Dimapur with his Naga wife and daughter. Ananya Vajpeyi writes:

> What was at stake in Dimapur then was not Khan's true nationality as a Bangladeshi or an Indian, but the underlying fact in Nagaland it is possible to see both these identities as equally foreign, and equally likely to be placed at the receiving end of xenophobic violence. For the unfortunate Syed Sarifuddin Khan, the suspicion of a rape that he may or may not have committed was enough to set alight a tinderbox of regional discontent with the political dispensation, the permanent state of emergency, conflicting identities, thwarted aspirations and vexed histories, into a conflagration that incinerated him. His bewildered relatives were left saying—'But he was Indian', 'But we are a fauji family'—because in their view these qualifications ought to have protected him from the extraordinary and ultimately deadly ferocity with which he was wrenched out of the legal process and simply torn to pieces in the town square.[20]

However, apart from the regional discontent, the failure of our justice delivery system in punishing the guilty expeditiously was the main cause for such

[19] 'Delayed Justice Leading to Lynch Mobs: Pratibha', *Times of India*, New Delhi, 24 February 2008.

[20] Ananya Vajpeyi, 'The Prison House of Identity', *The Hindu*, 14 March 2015.

mass frenzy. Sampat Pal Devi, from Bundelkhand, Uttar Pradesh, openly espouses vigilante justice. She founded the Gulabi Gang with a group of lathi-wielding women (who wear pink sari) to fight gender and other forms of social injustice. She heads the largest vigilante group in the world and emphatically asserts that it is no use asking for help from men who rule the country, and that women must fight themselves. US academic Hillel Gray justifies vigilantism, 'Certainly, yes. In the absence of a legal order, or when legal authorities are blatantly unjust, it can be ethically appropriate to act without authorisation of law'.[21]

In another shocking case of an unjust delay, it took a woman over 25 years to get a sum of Rs 84/- only as part of her bonus from her employer. Padmawati worked as a packer on piece-rate basis for her employer, M/s Superbazar Cooperative Store. She was promised, along with other labourers, that a bonus of Rs 84 would be given to her. In 1984, she was informed that the bonus would not be paid. She and her other colleagues moved the labour court in Tis Hazari, New Delhi, where the hearing began in 1984 and continued for 15 years. Eventually, the court decided the case in December 1999 in their favour and directed the store to pay them within three months. The respondent challenged the order in the Delhi High Court which granted a stay of the order. Finally, in May 2010, the petitioners got relief when the cooperative store agreed before the High Court to pay them their due on a pro-rata basis and a sum amounting to over Rs 2,000/- (including interest) for each labourer was given. But the pertinent question here is whether it is worth fighting over for a quarter of a century?[22]

One can find innumerable such instances and with time the situation has only worsened. In fact, delay is the rule and expeditious disposal is an exception to it. All this reminds me of the comment made by Shrilal Shukla, a noted Hindi satirist, that the doctrine of re-birth was born in civil courts so that the plaintiff and the defendant may not die with this repentance that the litigation remained inconclusive. They can die in peace that there is still a next life to hear the decision of the case.[23]

A curious example of how lethargic and unaccountable our courts can be is a case filed by a government employee challenging his retirement, on

[21] Quoted by Baijayant Jay Panda, 'Fifth Shades of Grey', *Times of India*, 4 August 2016.

[22] 'She Fought 25 Years for Rs. 84', *Times of India*, New Delhi, 24 May 2010.

[23] Shrilal Shukla, *Rag Darbari* (New Delhi: Rajkamal Paperbacks, 1991), Chapter 5, p. 31.

attaining the age of 58, in the Allahabad High Court, on the basis that according to the rules governing his service, his age of superannuation was 60. At the preliminary hearing, the court passed an *ex-parte* interim order directing the government to ensure that he continues in service during the pendency of the writ petition. The case could not be heard for several years, and when it ultimately came-up for final hearing, it was found that his age of retirement was indeed 58, and so, his petition was dismissed. But by then he was already 67, and had remained in service till then, that is, nine years more than his age of superannuation.[24]

It is not only the civil cases that drag on for decades, even the criminal cases are not decided expeditiously. Machal Lalung of Assam remained in custody for 54 years without any case against him or any record of the crime that he allegedly committed. His case was taken up by the Supreme Court on the basis of a report in a newspaper, depicting the plight of the man who was behind the bars since 1951.[25] He was freed on a personal bond of a rupee after the NHRC, during its routine visit to the prison, detected the facts of the case. The Supreme Court ordered for formation of a committee, comprising the Guwahati High Court registrar general or a judicial officer to be nominated by the chief justice of the High Court and a secretary-level officer of the state government, to carry out a probe into the matter in order to fix responsibility on officials liable for this gross miscarriage of justice. The reports submitted before the apex court revealed that there was no record traceable in the court. Ultimately, the Supreme Court, on 9 January 2006, dismissed the case and ordered for grant of Rs 3 lakhs and a monthly pension of Rs 1,000 to the concerned person.[26]

Similarly, Sarla remained behind bars for 43 years before the NHRC took up her case. She was accused of murder and was acquitted. As the court said that she was not mentally stable, she was sent to a mental asylum where she remained from 1963 to 2006. According to the documents available with Naini prison, where she was lodged in 1961–3, Sarla came to Allahabad on a train as a nurse in 1961. Deserted by her husband a few years after her marriage, the ill-fated woman from Andhau village, Ghazipur district, had

[24] Justice S.S. Sodhi, 'Writ Run Wild', in his book *The Other Side of Justice* (Australia, Canada, Hong Kong, South Africa, UK, US: Hay House India, 2007), p. 110.

[25] News Item, '38 Years in Jail without Trial', published in *Hindustan Times*, in Re (2007) 15 SCC 18.

[26] 'After 54 Years in Jail, Some Relief for Laung', *Indian Express*, New Delhi, 10 January 2006.

nothing to fall back on when the police nabbed her for the murder of her batchmate Bela. The trial court acquitted her after two years, and recorded that her mental health was precarious. The state government however, challenged the orders of her acquittal pleading that she be brought to trial when she is in a fit state of mind and health. Sarla was rearrested and sent to the Varanasi asylum. The Allahabad High Court ordered the medical superintendent to submit a report on her health within a week. This week stretched to 43 years.[27] Ultimately, the NHRC had to intervene.

In a curious judgment delivered on 7 April 2010, the apex court refused to show any leniency to a serial killer 'Ripper' Chacko, sentenced to three life terms in jail. A division bench, headed by Justice H. S. Bedi, while deciding a five-year-old petition filed by Chacko[28] from his cell at Kannur Central Jail in Kerala, directed him to serve his full life term unless the state government remitted it. Surprisingly, the Court was oblivious of the fact that Chacko had already died by hanging himself in the prison cell on 24 November 2005. Chacko had filed the petition in February 2005 praying for mercy, 'Now I apologise for the offences committed. That part of my life, was full of unpredictable behaviour, and has ended'.[29]

On 1 September 2009, the Bombay High Court directed the Maharashtra government to pay Rs 1 lakh as compensation to Bapu Pandu Mali, a 40-year-old man, who languished in prison for over 10 years for a crime he never committed. He was in jail for five years as an under trial prisoner battling against rape and murder charges. Even after being acquitted by the trial court, the poor Mali remained incarcerated for five years longer as he was not able to pay the bail amount when his case went into appeal. A division bench of Bilal Nazki and A.R. Joshi, JJ, lamented, 'This is a sorry state of affairs in which not only the prosecuting agency but also the Courts are involved. This is a reflection on our own system, which needs to be corrected.'[30] Delay in getting justice, forced a retired septuagenarian engineer of the Madhya Pradesh State Electricity Board to commit suicide. The officer, V.K. Brahmankar, shot himself dead with his licensed revolver on 7 December 2009. A suicide note left behind said that he was ending his life

---

[27] 'After 43 Years Locked Away, This Woman Gets a Second Shot at Justice', *Indian Express*, New Delhi, 19 September 2006.

[28] Convict No. 8735.

[29] '5 Years after Killer's Suicide, SC Rejects His Plea', *Indian Express*, New Delhi, 12 April 2010.

[30] *State of Maharashtra* v. *Bapu Pandu Mali*, Criminal Appeal No. 17 of 2003, para 3.

since he was tired of responding to court summons in an anti-corruption case filed against him in 1998.[31]

Nisar-ud-din Ahmad walked out free from Jaipur jail after remaining behind bars for 23 years after the Supreme Court acquitted him of all charges.[32] He was arrested on a charge of carrying out blasts in trains on the first anniversary of the Babri Masjid demolition and was tried under Terrorist and Disruptive Activities (Prevention) Act (TADA). His gut-wrenching story demonstrates as to how the police can implicate anyone either with malice or without exercising due diligence. The Court held that there was no material other than his confession in the police custody, and so the conviction was not sustainable. He walked out like a living corpse as he told *Indian Express*:

> I have clocked 8150 days of the prime of my life inside the jail. For me, life is over. What you are seeing is a living corpse. I was yet to be 20 years old when they threw me in jail. I am 43 today. My younger sister was 12 when I saw her last. Her daughter is 12 now.... My cousin was two years younger than me, she is now a grandmother. A generation has completely slipped from my life.[33]

H.D. Sikand had to wait for 26 long years to get justice for his son who was killed by a parcel bomb on 2 October 1982.[34] At the ripe old age of 98, his last wish in life was fulfilled when the additional sessions judge, on 28 April 2008, convicted Lieutenant Colonel (Retd), S.J. Chaudhary for the murder of 40-year-old Kishan Sikand. The convict had been out on bail during the trial. The trial in this case began on 31 May 1984 and dragged on for years. It was only after the old father moved the High Court on 23 February 2007 praying for a speedy trial that the court directed the lower court to complete the trial even if the judge was neck deep in work. Besides, the Supreme Court also directed that the court should conclude the case by carrying out hearing in the case on a day-to-day basis.[35] Thus, the verdict of the trial court

[31] 'Retired Engineer Kills Self over Graft Case', *Asian Age*, New Delhi, 8 December 2009.

[32] *Mohd. Jalees Ansari and Others* v. *Central Bureau of Investigation*, AIR (2016) SC 2461: (2016) (5) SCALE 326 (Criminal Appeal No. 546 of 2004).

[33] *Indian Express*, New Delhi, 30 May 2016.

[34] 'Court Convicts Retired Army Officer in 1982 Sikand Murder Case', *The Hindu*, New Delhi, 29 April 2008; '26 Years On, Justice for 98-Year-Old Sikand', *Times of India*, 29 April 2008.

[35] Lt. Col. *S. J. Chaudhary* v. *State (Delhi Administration)* (1984) 1 SCC 722, AIR (1984) SC 618.

came after 26 long years, and that too only after the directions from the high court. However, the Delhi High Court set aside his conviction on 15 May 2009.[36] H.D. Sikand passed away before the High Court pronounced its verdict. The Supreme Court upheld the decision of the High Court acquitting Chaudhary.[37] The FIR was registered on 2 October 1982 and the case was finally decided by the Supreme Court on 15 December 2016. Thus, the legal process consumed over 34 years. Similarly, an 80-year-old Buddha Singh had to fight a legal battle against the police for over 15 years for taking them to court for killing his physically-challenged son Raj Narain in a fake encounter. On 12 September 2007, an Etawah court awarded life sentences to 15 policemen.[38]

However, it was a bolt from the blue for the victims of Hashimpura, Meerut, who, having waited for nearly 28 years since 22 May 1987, when 42 Muslims were shot dead allegedly by Provincial Armed Constabulary (PAC) *jawans* (soldiers), were in for a huge shock when 16 accused cops walked scot free after being acquitted by the court on the strength of getting benefit of doubt. The additional sessions judge at the Tis Hazari Court in Delhi, in *State v. Surendrapal Singh*, on 21 March 2015, said that the court was giving the 'benefit of doubt for want of sufficient evidence regarding their identity'.[39] Three other PAC personnel, who made up the initial 19 accused, died during the course of trial. They had all been charged with murder, criminal conspiracy, and tampering of evidence. It all happened three days after one Dr Prabhat Singh was killed by a 'Muslim' mob when he was going to attend to a Muslim patient. The PAC arrested all the able-bodied men of Hashimpura, totalling 324 according to official records and packed them into police trucks. Around 50 of them were allegedly taken to a lonely place, dragged out, shot, and thrown into a ditch (Gangnahar) in Ghaziabad. However, six survived and one of them, Zulfiqar somehow fled to Delhi, met Syed Shahabuddin, and both broke the story of the massacre at a press conference. Many bodies were found floating in the canal. The state government was not ready to admit that so many people were killed in a cold blooded murder, and so, no death certificates were issued. People's Union for Democratic Rights (PUDR) moved the Supreme Court, which was initially reluctant to admit the case.

[36] *S. J. Chaudhary* v. *CBI*, 159 (2009) DLT 673, MANU/DE/0584/2009.
[37] *H.D. Sikand (D) Though Lrs.* v. *C.B.I. & Anr*, AIR (2017) SC 164 (2017) 2 SCC 166.
[38] 'Disabled Son Shot in "Encounter", Father Took Cops to Court: 15 Years Later, Life in Jail for 15', *Indian Express*, 19 September 2007.
[39] *Sunday Express*, New Delhi, *Sunday Times*, New Delhi, 22 March 2015.

The Vacation judge, Justice Ranganath Misra, asked the petitioner to go to the Allahabad High Court first. However, the case was admitted, and the kin of the victims got a major relief that they got death certificates issued.

After big brouhaha, the state government directed the Crime Branch of Central Investigation Department (CBCID) to investigate the case. But its report, submitted in 1994, was never made public. The kin of those killed, and the survivors moved the Supreme Court in 1995 for a direction to make the report public and initiate action against those indicted in it. The Court however did not accede to the prayer and instead directed the petitioners to approach the high court. The case is still pending there. The state government in 1996 had filed charge sheets (under section 173(2), CrPC) against 19 PAC personnel. No senior police officer was however charge sheeted. None of the charge sheeted jawans was arrested despite 23 non-bailable arrest warrants issued against them by the court between January 1997 and April 2000. They remained in active service, though the state government pleaded that they were absconding throughout. Thus, they were in a position to influence the investigation, tamper with the evidence, and intimidate witnesses. It is a sad commentary on the collusion existing between the state and the accused. Policemen did not inform their uniformed brethren and misled the court that they were not traceable. But the court cannot go unscathed as it could have directed the Director General, Police, Uttar Pradesh, to produce them in the court, failing which it could request the High Court to initiate contempt proceedings against him.

Later, some activists and relatives of the victims moved the Supreme Court seeking transfer of the case from the state of Uttar Pradesh to Delhi and the Court acceded to the prayer in September 2002. However, still the case continued to be adjourned on some technical grounds. Ultimately, charges were framed in May 2006, that is, 19 years after the incident took place. However, a silver lining in our civil society, not the judicial system, is that Dr Harpal Singh, the father of Dr Prabhat Singh, who fell to communal violence, kept fighting along with the relatives of the victims to bring those policemen to justice.[40] On 24 May 2007, two survivors and members of 36 victim families filed 615 applications at the office of the Director General of Police, UP, under the RTI Act, 2005, seeking information about the case. The reply made some startling disclosures that all accused remained in service, and none had any mention of the incident in their Annual Confidential Reports (ACRs). At

---

[40] 'Until Justice Is Done, These Two Old Men Refuse to Take a Break', *Indian Express*, New Delhi, 24 September 2007.

the end of May and early June 2000, 16 of them surrendered and were also granted bail. The trial court fixed dates in September and October 2000 for framing of charges for which the government counsel was not prepared. On 13 December, the CBCID submitted that it needed some time for appointing a special public prosecutor.[41] The fact that 28 years after the brutal massacre of Muslims, the guilty in police fatigue were let off on grounds of lack of identification though they were on duty at Hashimpura on the fateful day, speaks volumes about the shoddy investigation and corruption in police force. Delay derails the trial as evidences disappear, witnesses leave this world or are not traceable. How delay pays dividends is evident in this case as three investigating officers passed away, three accused died, and the surviving guilty were let off to roam free. It is a mockery of justice that not a single person was found guilty though it is indisputable that many were killed.[42] However, on 31 October 2018, the Delhi High Court upturned the trial court's decision and sentenced all the accused to life imprisonment.

In December 2009, the verdict of the trial court, Chandigarh, in the Ruchika Girhotra case, shocked the conscience of the whole nation when former Director General of Police of Haryana, S.P.S. Rathore, got away with a light punishment of six months rigorous imprisonment and that too after 19 long years of trial. He came out of the court with a smirk which created a national furore. Ruchika Girhotra, a promising tennis player of 14, was molested by Rathore on 12 August 1990. He threatened, intimidated, and tortured her using all the influence and resources at his command. Her brother was implicated in several cases of theft and subjected to torture that is beyond description. A hapless Ruchika ultimately decided to end her life three years later, but nothing moved.

It was her first signed complaint, which was submitted as a memorandum on 16 August 1990 before the then Governor of Haryana, which acted as the foundation on which the case was registered and later contested for 19 long years. On the basis of this memorandum, which was also handed over to the Financial Commissioner, Home Secretary, and even the Haryana government, an FIR was registered on 29 December 1999 under Section 354, IPC (outraging the modesty of a woman). The memorandum narrated

[41] Iqbal A. Ansari, 'Is Their Any Hope of Justice?', http://www.pucl.org/reports/UttarPradesh/2001/hashimpura.htm (last accessed on 23 March 2015).

[42] Sudhanshu Ranjan, 'The Injustice of Justice', *Asian Age*, 31 March 2015; Sudhanshu Ranjan, 'Nyayaik Deri ka Shikar Hashimpura', *Dainik Hindustan*, 26 March 2015; Sudhanshu Ranjan, 'Phir kathghare mein kanoon', *Dainik Jagran*, 27 March 2015.

Ruchika's story in her own words. The document claimed that a few young girls use to play at the tennis court situated in Panchkula's Sector 6. Rathore was the president of the Haryana Lawn Tennis Association. On 11 August 1990, Rathore visited Ruchika's house and met her father S.C. Girhotra. He told him that he should not send Ruchika abroad as she was a very promising player and that he would arrange special coaching for her. The senior cop also told Girhotra to send Ruchika to his office on 12 August 1990 at 12 noon in connection with this issue. On 12 August 1990, Ruchika along with her friend Aradhana went to play at the lawn tennis court and met Rathore. On seeing both of them, Rathore told Aradhana to call the tennis coach to his room. But she returned halfway.

> *Is beech Ruchika ko akeli paa kar Rathore sahib aisi ghinoni harquat pe uttar aye jo manavta ke liye kalank se bhi badtar hai. Apni beti ki umar se bhi choti Ruchika se unhone chedchad ki* (in the meanwhile, finding Ruchika alone Rathore performed a shameful act which is a blot on humanity. He molested Ruchika, who was younger than his daughter),

the document claimed.[43]

The then CJI, K.G. Balakrishnan, just months before demitting office, made a candid admission of trials being delayed by the rich and powerful, while commenting on the Ruchika Girhotra case, 'What they do is challenge the summons issued to them, appeal against framing of charges and also every interim order of the trial court up to the Supreme Court. If they get an interim stay from either the High Court or the Supreme Court, the trial gets stayed and delayed'.[44] However, after an uproar created by the media and the civil society in the whole country, the CBI appealed for enhancement of Rathore's punishment and the Sessions Court at Chandigarh, on 25 May 2010, enhanced his punishment to one and a half years of imprisonment, and he was thus immediately taken into custody.[45] The Supreme Court finally upheld his conviction on 23 September 2016.[46] However, the Court reduced his sentence from 18 months to the period

[43] 'Ruchika Girhotra Case: Molestation of Minor, Abuse of Power', *Times of India*, New Delhi, 23 December 2009.

[44] '19 Years on, First Arrest in Ruchika Case: Classic Example of the Powerful Exploiting Legal Loopholes, Says CJI', *Times of India*, 11 January 2010.

[45] 'Justice, Finally: Molester Cop Sent to Jail for 18 Months', *Times of India*, New Delhi, 26 May 2010; 'Sentence Enhanced, Rathore Goes to Jail', *Indian Express*, New Delhi, 26 May 2010.

[46] *S.P.S. Rathore* v. *C.B.I. & Anr.*, AIR (2016) SC 4486, MANU/SC/1096/2016.

already undergone, that is, six months, in view of his advanced age. So, he did not have to go to jail again.

The Supreme Court recorded its concern that if the problem of delays is not addressed, people would take to extra-legal means, in the following words:

> The time is running out for doing something to solve the problem which has already grown into monstrous form. If a citizen is told that once you resort to legal procedure for realisation of your urgent need you have to wait and wait for 23–30 years, what else it is if not to inevitably encourage and force him to resort to extra-legal measures for realising the required reliefs.[47]

Bhopal Gas Tragedy Case

Justice continues to evade for decades even in some of the most publicized cases. Victims of the Bhopal gas tragedy, the world's biggest ever industrial disaster, had to wait for over 25 long years for the first criminal conviction to be pronounced when the court of the CJM of Bhopal handed down light punishments to seven accused who were awarded two years jail and fined about Rs 1 lakh each on 7 June 2010.[48] The tragedy struck Bhopal on the intervening night of 2/3 December 1984, when 40 tonnes of a lethal and highly reactive chemical called methyl isocyanate (MIC), which was stored in liquid form at the pesticide factory owned by UCC, got contaminated with water and other impurities and escaped from the factory in gaseous form due to the resulting exothermic reactions. The victims kept fighting and imploring for justice, which was consistently denied. The CJM held former chairperson of the Union Carbide India Limited (UCIL) , UCC's Indian subsidiary, Keshub Mahindra and six others guilty under Section 304-A of the IPC (causing death by negligence) and Sections 336, 337, and 338 of the IPC, which are bailable offences and immediately granted them bail. The FIR was lodged on 3 December 1984 and the CBI filed the charge sheet on 1 December 1987. In fact, the Sessions Judge had framed charges under Section 304-II (culpable homicide not amounting to murder) besides Sections 324, 326, and 429 of the IPC. Subsequently, the High Court of Madhya Pradesh at Jabalpur vide order dated 1 August 1995, upheld the said order of the CJM. However, on 13 September 1996, the Supreme Court quashed the charges and directed the court to frame charge under

[47] *Gaya Prasad* v. *Pradeep Srivastava* (2001) 2 SCC 604, para 9.

[48] 'Justice Delayed, Denied', *Times of India*, New Delhi, 8 June 2010.

Sections 304-A and 336, 337, and 338 of the IPC.[49] Thus, the CJM had apparently limited options.

However, the light punishment awarded after an inordinate delay ignited such a storm worldwide that the Union Government reconstituted a Group of Ministers headed by the then Home Minister, P. Chidambaram, which was earlier headed by Arjun Singh, to examine all issues including remedial measures and make appropriate recommendations relating to the relief and rehabilitation of the victims and their families.[50] The then Union Law Minister, M. Veerappa Moily admitted that the long delay in giving justice to the victims and their kin brought the case into the category where justice delayed is justice denied.[51] Under public pressure, the CBI filed a curative petition in the Supreme Court on 1 August 2010 seeking orders for recalling its judgment and order dated 13 September 1996 in *Keshub Mahindra* v. *State of M.P.*,[52] when the Court quashed the charges framed against the accused under sections 304 (Part II), 324, 326, and 429 of IPC and directed the trial court to frame charges under section 304A, under which the punishment is imprisonment for maximum two years, and Sections 336, 337, and 338 of the IPC. A Constitution Bench of the Supreme Court dismissed it on 11 May 2011 as it did not find any justification behind the delay of about 14 years in filing the petition.[53] Nevertheless, Court, in para 4 of the same order had noted as follows:

> If according to the curative petitioner, the learned Magistrate failed to appreciate the correct legal position and misread the decision dated 13.9.96 as tying his hands from exercising the power under Section 323 or under Section 216 of the Code, it can certainly be corrected by appellate/revisional court. In fact, the revision petitions though belatedly filed by the State of M.P. and the CBI (which are still pending) have asserted this position in the grounds of revision.

[49] *Keshub Mahindra* v. *State of MP* (1996) 6 SCC 129: (1996) 6 Suppl SCR 285: (1996) 6 SCALE 522: MANU/SC/1236/1996.

[50] 'Congress Joins Chorus on Bhopal Verdict, GoM Reconstituted', *Indian Express*, New Delhi, 10 June 2010.

[51] 'Not Satisfied, Need to Change Law, Says Moily', *Indian Express*, New Delhi, 8 June 2010.

[52] *Keshub Mahindra* v. *State of M.P.* (1996) 6 SCC 129: (1996) 6 Suppl SCR 285: (1996) 6 SCALE 522: MANU/SC/1236/1996.

[53] *CBI and Others* v. *Keshub Mahindra etc.*, AIR (2011) SC 2037 (2011) 2 SCC (Cri) 863.

In other words, in the opinion of the Supreme Court, the Sessions Court had ample power and opportunities to rectify the mistakes committed by the CJM.

Earlier, on the eve of the 25th anniversary of the tragedy, the Madhya Pradesh High Court struck another blow to the victims' quest for justice. The victims were so far given just one-fifth of the compensation promised to them under the 1989 agreement, since the compensation meant for 105,000 gas-victims as per terms of the settlement was effectively disbursed among 573,588 gas-victims as determined by the Claims Courts. The government agreed for a final settlement with the UCC for a meagre sum of 470 million US dollars which amounted to Rs 700 crore at the then exchange rate of around 1:15. On 13 September 2004, the Bhopal Gas Peedith Sangharsh Sahayog Samiti (BGPSSS) and the Bhopal Gas Peedith Mahila Udyog Sanghathan (BGPMUS) filed an application before the Supreme Court seeking enhancement of compensation by a factor of five, that is, in terms of the magnitude of the disaster as acknowledged by the Supreme Court in its order dated 19 July 2004.[54] The Court admitted the petition to reopen the compensation issue. But on 4 May 2007, it rejected the plea of the petitioners on the grounds that it was the task of the Welfare Commissioner, Bhopal to determine the facts. Initially, the settlement was hammered out on the basis that the number of victims was 1,05,000 (3000 dead and 1,02,000 injured). But 40 claims courts set up under the welfare commissioner determined, after processing the claims, that the actual number was 573,588 which included 5295 deaths (total death claims = 22,150, awarded death cases = 5295; in 10,047 death claim cases while Claim Courts acknowledged that the victims were dead, compensation was awarded only for injury). The number of deceased has crossed 25,000, but the registration of claims was closed in April 1997, though the injured are still dying.

On 28 August 2008, nine victims (members of BGPMUS and BGPSSS) filed a joint petition (unregistered) before the welfare commissioner with a prayer to order grant of compensation at least at the value of the rupee vis-a-vis US dollar prevailing on the date of settlement. The welfare commissioner rejected the petition *vide* its order dated 31 January 2009. On 28 October 2009, the crestfallen victims challenged this order in the Madhya Pradesh High Court which rejected the petition on 30 November 2009.[55] Again, on 3 April 2010, the same members of BGPMUS and BGPSSS filed

---

[54] I. A. No. 46–7 on C. A. Nos. 3187–8 of 1988.
[55] Writ Petition No. 11276 of 2009.

an SLP against the order of the High Court in the Supreme Court.[56] The Court admitted the SLP and issued notices to the concerned parties. On 3 December 2010, the Government of India also filed a civil curative petition in the apex court seeking enhancement of the compensation.[57] In its petition, the government submitted that the number of the deceased and that of injured had increased. At the time of settlement, the number of the dead was approximately 3,000 and that of injured 1,02,000, and the settlement was reached without processing the claims. As the processing and disbursement went up to 2004, the amount of 700 crore also went up to 3,000 crore as the rate of dollar increased vis-a-vis rupee, since the bulk of the settlement amount was retained in a dollar account. In its curative petition, the government averred that the number of deceased was 5,295 and that of injured was 568,293, and prayed for enhancement of compensation accordingly. A Constitution Bench of five judges has to decide it, but no such bench has been constituted. The petition is still pending after only preliminary hearing.

On 9 August 2012, the Supreme Court, in a PIL filed by the BGPMUS, Bhopal Group for Information and Action, and BGPSSS, on 14 January 1998, gave various directions including computerization of health records of gas-victims by and issuance of health booklets to each gas-victim with their complete medical records.[58] It asked the Monitoring Committee to ensure that 'health booklets' and smart cards are provided to each gas victim irrespective of where such victim is being treated, and clarified that this direction would apply to all hospitals being run by the government or otherwise. The Court also directed the state government to provide assistance in all respects to the Empowered Monitoring Committee and take appropriate action against the erring officials in the event of default and complete computerization of the medical information in the government as well as non-government hospital/ clinics within a period of three months from the date of judgment. However, it is yet to be done and the case is pending before the Madhya Pradesh High Court, Jabalpur, since the same had been assigned to it by the Supreme Court to oversee its implementation.[59]

Thus, since 1984, the victims of the Bhopal gas tragedy continue to suffer while the ping-pong game continues. The appeal against the CJM's order in criminal cases is pending in the court of District Judge, Bhopal. The main

[56] Special Leave petition (CC No. 5631) of 2010.
[57] Curative Petition (Civil) Nos. 345–7 of 2010.
[58] *Bhopal Gas Peedith Mahila Udyog Sangathan & Ors.* v. *Union of India & Ors.*, AIR (2012) SC 3081 (2012) 8 SCC 326.
[59] WP (Civil) No. 156–8 of 2012.

accused, then CEO of Union Carbide, Warren Anderson, died in the US in September 2014 at the age of 92. Andersen was arrested but was let-off within a few hours and Swaraj Puri, then superintendent of police, Bhopal, himself accompanied him to the airport ensuring his free passage. On 19 December 2016, the CJM, Bhopal ordered the CBI to interrogate Puri and also the then district magistrate Moti Singh who also helped him escape.[60] Abdul Jabbar had filed the case in 2010, and the court asked him to explain the delay in filing the case. He said that he could file only after obtaining the evidence. He cited Moti Singh's book, *Unfolding the Betrayal of Bhopal Gas Tragedy*[61] in which the author, who was the district magistrate of Bhopal at that time, has admitted how Anderson's escape was facilitated by orders from above. Though the court objected to delay in filing the case, it took over six years to pass the order. However, Puri and Singh got stay order by the Sessions Court against the order of the CJM. Keshub Mahindra and a few others were arrested after the accident and they remained in jail for 10 days. After this, nobody has gone to jail so far and the interminable judicial process goes on and on.

Cases Related to Anti-Sikh Riots of 1984

Similarly, culprits of the 1984 massacre of the Sikhs are yet to be brought to justice. The CBI filed charge sheets against Sajjan Kumar, a former Congress MP from outer Delhi, in two separate cases relating to anti-Sikh riots on 13 January 2010. He was charged under sections 302 (murder) and 153-A (promoting enmity between communities) in two cases of rioting at Sultanpuri and Delhi Cantonment police stations on 1 November 1984.[62] One of the reasons for the delay is that the government, in order to deflect public attention, constituted an inquiry commission. These take years and even decades to submit reports. In the meanwhile, the police sit with their fingers crossed and wait for the outcome on the basis of which charge sheets are filed.

Abuse of Judicial Process with Impunity

The court is supposed to come to the rescue of those whose rights are violated. It does so by adjudicating disputes between two parties or pronouncing a

---

[60] *Abdul Jabbar v. Swaraj Puri and Moti Singh* of 2010.

[61] Moti Singh, *Unfolding the Betrayal of Bhopal Gas Tragedy* (New Delhi: B.R. Publishing Corporation, 2008).

[62] '84 Riots: CBI Charge Sheets Sajjan', *Hindustan Times*, 14 January 2010.

person guilty or innocent of an offence, and punishing or acquitting them accordingly. It ensures rule of law and good governance. But these cardinal values evaporate into thin air once a person suffering injury has to wait on and on for decades, not sure whether justice will be done during their lifetime. The horrendous delay in adjudication is a huge incentive for wrong doers and criminals to continue with their illegalities and criminal activities milking the labyrinthine judicial process. In most of the criminal cases, the accused ultimately go scot free as the evidence vanishes. Delay gives them an opportunity to destroy evidences and intimidate witnesses into submission. Similarly, its converse is equally frightening if an innocent person is falsely implicated. They remain behind bars for years or even decades and face the ordeal of a tortuous legal process till they are finally acquitted. During the excruciating long period, they feel like taking to arms and settling it once and for all.

Suits for recovery of money are delayed inordinately and the interest granted to the affected party is a pittance. Similar is the case with specific performance. Apart from affecting the quality of justice, delays encourage falsehood and perjury. Arun Mohan, in his voluminous and monumental work on the problem of delays, has rightly pointed out:

> As it is, today, there is little 'fear' which would dissuade a party from making false averment in the pleadings or filing a false/fabricated/forged document or denying a genuine document, but with court delays being what they are, the parties often look to (or are advised to) doing so. Sometimes they even deny their own signature. The object is that by doing so, issues will arise, voluminous evidence will have to be led and the case will remain pending for years to come, which would then force the other party to settle by either giving up a part of the entitlement or paying something on the side. In the remote event the other party does not, and also continues to stand, the delays—till the case is adjudicated and prosecution for falsehood ordered—will take it beyond the lifetime of the person resorting to falsehood as aforesaid … although there may be a million instances of falsehood, perjury, forgery, etc., there would hardly be a person who has actually gone through a prison sentence for having done so.[63]

Inquiry Commissions and Committees

Inquiry commissions, generally headed by former high court or Supreme Court judges, seldom submit their reports within the stipulated time frame

[63] Arun Mohan, 'Effect of Court Delays', in *Justice, Courts and Delays*, Vol. 1 (Delhi: Universal Law Publishing Co., 2009), p. 13.

and generally provide reports that the people in power want. An inquiry commission, headed by Ved Marwah, then additional commissioner of Police, Delhi, was appointed in November 1984. It was assigned the job of inquiring into the role of the police during the anti-Sikh carnage of November 1984. As Ved Marwah completed his inquiry towards the middle of 1985, he was abruptly directed by the Union Home Ministry not to proceed further. This was because the Akali leader Sant Harchand Singh Longowal, listed a set of preconditions when Rajiv Gandhi, in 1985, desperate for a breakthrough in Punjab, mollycoddled him into agreeing to sign a peace accord with him. Setting up a judicial commission to inquire into the massacre was one of the preconditions.

Thus was born the Ranganath Misra Commission of Inquiry in May 1985. He submitted his report in August 1986 and the report was tabled in the Parliament six months thereafter in February 1987. In his report, Justice Misra stated that it was not part of his terms of reference to identify any person and recommended the formation of three committees. The People's Union for Civil Liberties criticized the Misra Commission for keeping information on the accused secret while revealing the names and addresses of the victims of violence.[64] Human Rights Watch lambasted the report as biased:

> It recommended no criminal prosecution of any individual, and it cleared all high-level officials of directing the riots. In its findings, the commission did acknowledge that many of the victims testifying before it had received threats from local police. While the commission noted that there had been 'widespread lapses' on the part of the police, it concluded that 'the allegations before the commission about the conduct of the police are more of indifference and negligence during the riots than of any wrongful overt act'.[65]

Subsequently, nine commissions and committees (Kapur Mittal Committee, Jain Banerjee Committee, Potti Rosha Committee, Jain Aggarwal Committee, Ahuja Committee, Narula Committee, and so on, and finally the Nanavati Commission) were set up to get to the truth. However, they were either disbanded midway or not allowed access to documents and evidence. Ultimately, the G.T. Nanavati Commission, set up in May 2000, identified several VIPs for their role in the riot, in its report submitted in February 2005.

[64] *Justice Denied*, People's Union for Civil Liberties and People's Union for Democratic Right, 1987.

[65] Patricia Gossman (1991), *Punjab in Crisis*, Human Rights Watch.

The M.S. Liberhan Commission, set up to inquire into the demolition of the disputed structure at Ayodhya on 6 December 1992, submitted its report after nearly 17 years on 30 June 2009. When the Commission was appointed, the notification, dated 16 December 1992, issued by the Union Home Secretary, Madhav Godbole, clearly stated that the Commission should submit its report to the Union government 'as soon as possible but not later than three months'.[66] However, it received 48 extensions, and did not submit any interim report either. It reflects on the extraordinarily languorous ways of the Indian judicial system. Moreover, the Commission could not determine anything new that was not known earlier. In fact, the live footage of the episode, taken by some government agency that Sharad Pawar showed to a group of friends and colleagues just a week later, on 13 December established everything.[67] The inconvenient fact is that the people in power wanted it delayed and the former justice conveniently acquiesced and received his pay and perks from the taxpayers' money. M.J. Akbar observed:

> Every government between 1992 and 2004 had a vested interest in delay. The minority governments of Deve Gowda and Inder Gujral could not have survived a day without support from the Rao-Sitaram Kesri Congress. (Mrs. Sonia Gandhi was not the party president then).... The BJP-led coalition that ruled for six years had the guilty on its first row. Only Uma Bharti has been candid enough to say that she was delighted when the mosque fell.[68]

V. Balakrishna Eradi headed the commission, set up in 1986, on the sharing of the Ravi-Beas river water between Punjab and Haryana till his death on 30 December 2010.

However, there have been some commissions which submitted reports even ahead of time. The commission headed by Justice S.R. Pandian to inquire into the Chhattisinghpora massacre of 36 Sikhs in March 2000, during US President Bill Clinton's visit to India, was given six months to submit its report, but it was submitted a month in advance. Besides, Justice Pandian spent his salary on distributing gifts to villagers and did not take a single farthing from Kashmir to Kanyakumari, his home. Justice G.N. Ray headed the Gaisal train accident (1998) and completed his work ahead of time. He

---

[66] '17 Years, 48 Extensions: That's What the Liberhan Commission Took to Complete its Probe', *Indian Express*, New Delhi, 1 July 2009.

[67] M.J. Akbar, 'Does Justice Matter after 17 Years?', *Sunday Times of India*, 5 July 2009.

[68] Akbar, 'Does Justice Matter after 17 Years?'.

did not accept any emoluments either. Justice J.S. Verma Committee, constituted in the wake of gang rape of Nirbhaya (Jyoti Singh) on the night of 16 December 2012 in a moving bus, to recommend amendments to the criminal law so as to provide for quicker trial and enhanced punishment for criminals accused of committing sexual assault against women, submitted its report on 23 January 2013, ahead of schedule. The Committee in its letter to the prime minister said, 'it is the Committee's hope that the promptitude with which the Committee was constituted within a few days of the brutal gang rape in Delhi on December 16, 2012, will continue to accomplish the task by speedy implementation of its Recommendations to retain public confidence in good governance'.[69]

Right to a Speedy Trial and the Huge Backlog of Cases

It is now well-established that the right to life under Article 21 includes the right to a speedy trial.[70] Article 21 confers a fundamental right on every person not to be deprived of his life or liberty, except according to the procedure established by law. Such a procedure must be 'reasonable, fair, and just'. From here flows the right to a speedy trial. Earlier, the Supreme Court adopted a bureaucratic approach to the interpretation of this right and held that the expression 'procedure established by law' meant any procedure with no kind of judicial evaluation about its nature. In *A.K. Gopalan* v. *State of Madras*,[71] the Court clearly held that only such a speedy trial was available as the Cr. P.C. provided. Again in *State of West Bengal* v. *Anwar Ali Sarkar*,[72] the Court ruled that 'the necessity of a speedy trial is too vague and uncertain to form a basis of valid and reasonable classification'.

But after 27 years, the apex court felt that this was too textual an interpretation and influenced by the abuse of power approach. In *Maneka Gandhi* v. *Union*,[73] the Court overturned this position and ruled that the procedure prescribed by the law must be reasonable, fair, and just and held that speedy trial, which means a reasonably expeditious trial, is an integral and essential part of the fundamental right to life and liberty enshrined in Article 21. Again, in

---

[69] http://www.firstpost.com/india/full-text-recommendations-of-the-justice-js-verma-committee-report-599874.html (last accessed on 13 November 2016).

[70] *Hussainara Khatoon* v. *Home Secretary, Bihar* (1980) 1 SCC 81: AIR (1979) SC 1360; *A.R. Antulay* v. *R.S. Nayak* (1992) 1 SCC 225: 1992 Cri. L. J. 2717.

[71] AIR (1950) SC 27: (1950) SCR 88: (1950) 2 MLJ 42.

[72] AIR (1952) SC 75: (1952) SCR 284: (1952) Cr. LJ 510.

[73] AIR (1978) SC 597: (1978) 1 SCC 248.

Aladankundu Puthiyapurayil Abdulla v. *Food Inspector*,[74] the Supreme Court ruled that in the spirit of Article 21, trial courts should ensure that food and adulteration cases, which involve imprisonment, are tried expeditiously so that neither the prosecution nor the accused is prejudiced by unusual judicial procrastination. It further directed that the high court concerned would issue peremptory directions to trial judges demanding expeditious disposal of such cases. Going further, in *Kadra Pahadia* v. *State of Bihar*,[75] the Court laid down that if a person is denied speedy trial, which is a fundamental right under Article 21, then s/he is entitled to move the Supreme Court for the enforcement of such a right, and the Court, in the discharge if its constitutional obligation, has the power to give necessary direction to the state government and other appropriate authorities to secure this right to the accused. The Court gave such a direction in several other cases later.[76]

However, the Court diluted this position when it held in *State of Maharashtra* v. *Champalal Punjaji Shah*,[77] that though a speedy trial is an implied ingredient of a fair trial guaranteed by Article 21, the converse is not necessarily true. It clarified that a delayed trial is not necessarily an unfair trial. But again in *T.V. Vatheeswaran* v. *State of T.N.*,[78] the Court emphasized the significance of the right to speedy trial. Extending it to the post-conviction stage as well, it ruled that undue delay in carrying out the death sentence entitles the accused to ask for a lesser sentence of life imprisonment. But a few months later, in *Sher Singh* v. *State of Punjab*,[79] another division bench of the Supreme Court held that no such time limit could be fixed for the commutation of death sentence as it would depend on the facts of each case. Finally, a Constitution Bench of the Supreme Court in *Triveniben* v. *State of Gujarat*,[80] overruling Vatheeswaran, laid down that it may consider the question of inordinate delay in the light of all circumstances of the case to decide whether the execution of death sentence should be carried out or it should

---

[74] (1979) SCC (Cri) 948: (1979) 4 SCC 187.

[75] (1981) 3 SCC 671: (1981) SCC (Cri) 791: AIR (1981) SC 939: (1981) Cri LJ 481.

[76] *R.D. Upadhyay* v. *State of U.P.* (1996) 3 SCC 422; *Common Cause, A Registered Society* v. *Union of India (Arrears Case I)*, (1996) 4 SCC 33; *Common Cause, A Registered Society* v. *Union of India (Arrears Case II)* (1996) 6 SCC 775.

[77] (1981) 3 SCC 610: (1981) SCC (Cri) 762: (1981) Cri LJ 105.

[78] (1983) 2 SCC 68: (1983) Cr LJ 481: (1983) 2 MLJ 39: (1983) 2 SCR 348: AIR (1983) SC 361 (2).

[79] (1983) 2 SCC 344: AIR (1983) SC 465.

[80] (1988) 4 SCC 574.

be commuted to life imprisonment. In *Shatrughan Chauhan & Anr.* v. *Union of India & Ors.*,[81] this Court held that undue, inordinate, and unreasonable delay in the execution of death sentence does certainly attribute to torture which is indeed a violation of Article 21 and is a valid ground for commuting it into life term. It clarified that it would be within its right to exercise its power under Article 32 of the Constitution to commute the sentence on this ground alone, however, after satisfying itself that the delay was not caused at the instance of the convict. However, it refused to give any exhaustive guidelines in this regard saying that it would depend on the facts of individual cases whether the delay is unreasonable. It commuted the death sentence of 15 convicts into life imprisonment. Again, within a month, the Supreme Court commuted the death sentence of three convicts in the Rajiv Gandhi assassination case.[82] Expressing its deep concern over the delay in the disposal of mercy petitions, the Court held:

> We are confident that the mercy petitions filed under Article 72/161 can be disposed of at a much faster pace than what is adopted now, if the due procedure prescribed by law is followed in verbatim. The fact that no time limit is prescribed to the President/Governor for disposal of the mercy petition should compel the government to work in a more systematized manner to repose the confidence of the people in the institution of democracy. Besides, it is definitely not a pleasure for this Court to interfere in the constitutional power vested under Article 72/161 of the Constitution and, therefore, we implore upon the government to render its advice to the President within a reasonable time so that the President is in a position to arrive at a decision at the earliest.[83]

The concern of the apex court over the delay by the executive is laudable. However, it is inscrutable why the Supreme Court does not look inward to set its own house in order and reduce the unreasonable delay caused by courts. Cases can also be disposed of at a much faster pace, provided there is an intention to do justice.

In *Sheela Barse* v. *State of Maharashta*,[84] it reiterated that the right to a speedy trial is a fundamental right, the violation of which would lead to questioning of the prosecution. In *Rakesh Saxena* v. *State*,[85] the Court

---

[81] (2014) 3 SCC 1.

[82] *V. Sriharan @ Murugan* v. *Union of India* (2014) 2 SCC 282.

[83] *V. Sriharan @ Murugan* v. *Union of India*, para 29.

[84] (1986) 2 SCC 96: AIR (1986) SC 1773.

[85] AIR (1987) SC 740: (1986) Supp SCC 505: (1987) SCC (Cri) 156.

quashed the proceedings on the grounds of delay and held that any further continuance of the prosecution after a delay of more than six years was uncalled for.

The Allahabad High Court held that the delay of 18 years in prosecution was an instance of gross abuse of the process of law.[86] In *A.R. Antulay* v. *R.S. Nayak*,[87] the Supreme Court categorically stated that it was in the interest of all concerned that the guilt or the innocence of the accused is established as early as possible, but added that every single delay did not necessarily prejudice the accused. In *Kartar Singh* v. *State of Punjab*,[88] affirming that a speedy trial is one of the facets of the fundamental right to life and personal liberty, it said that its constitutional guarantee is reflected in Section 309 of the Cr. P.C.

In *Common Cause, A Registered Society* v. *Union of India (Arrears Case I)*,[89] the Court gave categorical guidelines on bail. If the offences for which the accused is charged, are punishable with imprisonment up to three years with or without a fine, and if the trial is pending for one year or more, and the accused is in jail for six months or more, the criminal court concerned shall release the accused on bail or on a personal bond. Similarly, for offences punishable by incarceration extending up to five and seven years respectively, if the trials are pending for two years and the accused are in jail for six months and one year respectively, they will be granted bail. If the offence is non-cognizable and bailable, and the case is pending for over two years and the trial is yet to commence, then the criminal court shall discharge or acquit the accused. Later, the Court clarified that the direction for discharge or acquittal will apply to cases wherein the accused themselves are not responsible for the protraction of the trial.[90] In *Anil Rai* v. *State of Bihar*,[91] the Court laid down that the inordinate delay in pronouncing judgement by the High Court negates the right of appeal conferred on the convict under the provisions of the Cr. P. C. Justice R.P. Sethi wrote: 'Any procedure or course of action which does not ensure a reasonable quick adjudication has been termed to be unjust. Such a course is stated to be contrary to the

---

[86] *Shahabuddin Kureshi* v. *State of UP*, (1998) All Cr Law 303.

[87] (1992) 1 SCC 225: (1992) Cr LJ 2717: (1992) SCC (Cri) 93.

[88] (1994) 3 SCC 569: (1994) (Cri) 899.

[89] (1996) 4 SCC 33.

[90] *Common Cause, A Registered Society* v. *Union of India (Arrears Case II)* (1996) 6 SCC 775.

[91] (2001) 7 SCC 318: (2001) SCC (Cri) 1009: Air (2001) SC 3173.

maxim *actus curiae neminem gravabit*, that an act of the court shall prejudice none'.[92]

However, a seven-judge Constitution Bench in *P. Ramachandra Rao* v. *State of Karnataka*,[93] affirmed the right to speedy trial under Article 21 but dissipating the need to observe a time limit, it held that the guidelines laid down in A.R. Antulay case were not exhaustive but illustrative, and the time required to decide a case varied from case to case. So the Court ruled that it was neither advisable, nor feasible, nor judicially permissible to prescribe an outer time limit to conclude all criminal proceedings. It must be left to the judicious discretion of the court to find out from the totality of circumstances of a given case if the quantum of time consumed up to a given stage amounted to violation of Article 21, and if so, to terminate the particular proceedings, and if not, then to proceed.

Again in *PUCL* v. *Union of India*,[94] the Court declared the speedy trial to be the essence of Article 21. In *Pramod Kumar Saxena* v. *Union*,[95] the Court gave relief to the petitioner even in corruption cases on the grounds that the petitioner was in jail for over 10 years. In *Vakil Prasad Singh* v. *State of Bihar*,[96] the Supreme Court quashed criminal proceedings on the grounds of delay even though the allegations were serious. It held that the court can quash the charges or the conviction, as the case may be, if it finds that the right to the speedy trial of an accused has been infringed:

> Inordinately long delays may be taken as presumptive proof of prejudice. In this context, the fact of incarceration of the accused will also be a relevant fact. The prosecution should not become persecution. But when does the prosecution become persecution, again depends upon the facts of a given case.
>
> The right to speedy trial is applicable to not only to the actual proceedings in court but also includes within its sweep the preceding police investigations as well. The right to speedy trial extends equally to all criminal proceedings and is not confined to any particular category of cases.[97]

The Supreme Court upheld the monitoring by the High Court where the progress of investigation was tardy and slow.[98]

---

92 (2001) 7 SCC 318: (2001) SCC (Cri) 1009: Air (2001) SC 3173, p. 328.
93 (2002) 4 SCC 578: AIR (2002) SC 1856.
94 (2004) 9 SCC 580: AIR (2004) SC 456.
95 (2008) 9 SCC 685.
96 (2009) 3 SCC 355.
97 (2009) 3 SCC 355, para 24.
98 *Babubhai Jamnadas Patel* v. *State of Gujarat and Others* (2009) 9 SCC 610.

Constitutional Mandate for Expeditious and Cheap Justice

The Preamble of the Constitution mandates the state to secure justice, social, economic, and political, to all its citizens. The Directive Principles of State Policy of the Constitution declare that the state shall strive to promote the welfare of the people by securing and protecting, as effectively as it may, a social order in which justice shall inform all the institutions of national life.[99] Article 39-A further enjoins: 'The State shall secure that the operation of the legal system promotes justice ...; to ensure that opportunities for securing justice are not denied to any citizen by reason of economic or other disabilities'. Interpreting this provision, the Supreme Court has emphasized the need of dispensing quick and cheap justice:

> The Indian people are very patient, but despite their infinite patience, they cannot afford to wait for twenty-five years to get justice. There is a limit of tolerance beyond which it would be disastrous to push our people. This case and many others like it strongly emphasise the urgency of the need for legal and judicial reform. A little tinkering here and there in the procedural laws will not help. What is needed is a drastic change, a new outlook, a fresh approach which takes into account the socio-economic realities and seeks to provide a cheap, expeditious and effective instrument for realization of justice by all sections of the people, irrespective of their social or economic position or their financial resources.[100]

The Constitution enjoins the state to dispense speedy justice, and resource crunch is not a valid ground for denial of right to justice emanating from Articles 14, 19, and 21 and also the Preamble of the Constitution as well as the Directive Principles of State Policy. The solicitude of the Supreme Court in this regard is manifest from its decision in *Brij Mohan Lal* v. *Union of India*,[101] where the Court directed that the exercise for the appointment to the Fast Track Courts should be complete within two months, that is, by 31 March 2004. It further ordered that in case premises for the courtrooms were not available, they would either be constructed or taken on lease for which the requisite charges by way of rent, and so on, would be borne by the state concerned.

Credibility of the System at a Premium

The 85th Report of the Parliament's Standing Committee on Home Affairs (Law's delays: Arrears in courts) in 2002 gave bewildering statistics which

---

[99] Article 38 (1).
[100] *L. Babu Rao* v. *Raghunathji Maharaj*, AIR (1976) SC 1734, 1735.
[101] (2004) 11 SCC 344.

reveal the magnitude of the problem. These numbers have gone up since then. In 2002, the Government of India set up a Committee on Reforms of the Criminal Justice System headed by Justice V.S. Malimath, which submitted its report in March 2003. It was asked to make recommendations to make the police, the prosecution, and the judiciary more effective. Prison was left out as the facts and figures of jails would have shocked the world in general and human rights bodies in particular. Justice Malimath described the pendency and arrears of civil and criminal cases in different courts in these words:

> It is common knowledge that two major problems besieging the criminal justice system are huge pendency of criminal cases and the inordinate delay in disposal of criminal cases on the one hand and the very low rate of conviction in cases involving serious crimes on the other. This has encouraged crime. Violent and organized crimes have become the order of the day. As chances of conviction are remote, crime has become a profitable business. Life has become unsafe and people live in constant fear.[102]

The Committee recommended dividing the IPC into four different codes—Social Offences Code, Correctional Offences Code, Economic Offences Code, and Indian Penal Code. The first code should comprise offences which are actually of civil nature and can be settled by the administrative processes without the involvement of the police and should not be penal in nature. The second should consist of offences punishable up to three years of imprisonment with provisions for parole, probation, and conditional sentences in lieu of jail terms which can be dealt with under the summary/summons procedure with ample scope for plea bargaining and is free from the taint of conviction. The third code would look after property offences which destabilize the financial viability of the country and can be tackled by criminal and administrative strategies including plea bargaining. The last code should deal with major crimes with 10 years' imprisonment or more.

To carry out this mandate, both the judiciary and the executive must come forward to mitigate the agonies of litigants. Addressing a conference of chief ministers and chief justices on 16 August 2009, Prime Minister Manmohan Singh, spoke of a joint effort, 'I can assure ... that my government will not be found wanting at any level in this joint effort.... We promise to match each step of the judiciary with two of our own'.[103] It is essential for quick disposal.

---

[102] The Committee on Reforms of Criminal Justice System, Ministry of Home Affairs, Government of India, March 2003, pp. 4–5.

[103] 'Reduce Pendency of Cases: Manmohan', *The Hindu*, 17 August 2009.

It is seen that warrants issued by the court keep gathering dust at police offices. If summons are issued, the efficiency of the postal department lies in their quick delivery. Besides, the government must implement the orders/judgements of courts immediately and must not file unnecessary appeals.

Victims are losing faith in the judicial system. N.R. Madhava Menon has emphasized making the criminal justice system victim-centric:

> What does 'victim-centric' mean in the criminal justice system? It means restoring the confidence of victims in the system and achieving the goal of justice in whichever sense the idea is conceived.... Today, a victim-centric approach in criminal justice can also mean healing the wounds through reconciliation and restorative means or justice rather than letting it get prolonged in the system, leading to frustration and more wrongs. Restorative justice is more akin to indigenous system of quick, simple systems of resolution of wrongs which enjoy community support, victim satisfaction and offender acknowledgement of obligations.[104]

As far back as in 1924, Rankin Committee lamented:

> Unless the court can start with a reasonably clean slate, improvements of methods is likely to tantalize only. The existence of a mass of arrears takes the heart out of a presiding officer. He can hardly be expected to take a strong interest in the preliminaries when he knows that the hearing of the evidence and the decision will not be by him but by his successor after his transfer. So long as such arrears exist, there is a temptation to which many presiding officers succumb, to hold back the heavier contested suits and devote attention to the lighter ones. The turn-out of decisions in contested suits is thus maintained somewhere near the figure of institutions, while the really difficult work is pushed further into the background.[105]

The Allahabad High Court recorded that people are losing faith in the judiciary because of delay.

> There was, no doubt, a time when Judiciary was highly respected by the people who had faith in the quality of justice, dispensed with promptly by the Judges. Now the people have started losing faith in the entire judicial system because of every day increasing arrears. Remarks have come to be

---

[104] N.R. Madhava Menon, 'Towards Restorative Criminal Justice', *The Hindu*, 5 April 2016.

[105] Quoted by Bibek Debroy, 'The Problem at the Top', *Financial Express*, 19 November 2016.

made expressing the lamentation in various forms. The whole nation, it was said, is in a Juridical abyss. Many today are dissatisfied over the courts' conduct. All through the years men have protested at the laws' delay and counted it as a grievous wrong, hard to bear. It is linked amongst the whips and scorns of the time. Some talk of it. how it exhausts patience, courage and hope. In substance, it is a Judicial anathema, for all who are concerned with the litigation process. Even the aggrieved persons have, at times, been found remorseful and repentant for filing the case. It is a usual phenomenon to hear the conversation between suitors that they are not likely to reap the fruits of litigation during their life time. Eminent Jurists have gone even to the extent of observing that our Justice Delivery System is cracking under the oppressive weight of delay and arrears. It has been repeated ad nauseam that to delay Justice is to deny justice. An eminent person not less than the former Chief Justice of India, J. C. Shah made the following remarks, which amply exhibits the present situation:

'..... The accumulation has reached such a proportion that there is danger of Judicial administration breaking down in future years, if the cases before the courts increase at the rate at which they are mounting today. One shudders to think what the position of Judicial administration will be in a decade or two, if the present worst disparity between in flow and disposal of cases continues. Unless this problem is tackled the litigants might be gripped with a sense of frustration and loss of confidence in courts and Tribunals.[106]

Judge-Population Ratio

Who is to blame for this chaos? Not surprisingly, judges, instead of show-ing some magnanimity to own up even a share of blame, apportion it to the executive stating that it does not appoint an adequate number of judges and nor does it fill existing vacancies. In *P. Ramachandra Rao* v. *State of Karnataka*,[107] the apex court diagnosed the root cause of delay as the appallingly low judge-population ratio, which, according to it, is 10 times lower than the corresponding ratio in the US and five times in the UK. Successive CJIs have lamented that the existing judge-population ratio in India is around 14 per million, which is one of the lowest in the world. The corresponding ratios in the US and the UK are 107 and 50.9 and is 25 to 30 in India's neighbourhood. For decades, judges have been blaming the

[106] *Siddhartha Kumar and others* v. *Upper Civil Judge, Senior* (1998) 1 AWC 593 (1998) 1 UPLBEC 587.

[107] (2002) 4 SCC 578: AIR (2002) SC 1856.

poor population-judge ratio for the excruciatingly slow pace of the wheels of justice. The then CJI S.C. Bharucha, in his Law Day address delivered in the Supreme Court on 26 November 2001, put the responsibility of arrears on the utterly inadequate number of judges. He entirely agreed with the suggestions made by the Law Commission in its 127th Report in 1988 that the state should improve the judge-population ratio, which at that time was 10.5 judges per million population, to at least 50 judges within the next five years. The Commission had further recommended that by 2000, India should command at least 107 judges per million population. Justice Bharucha said the current ratio was 12 or 13 judges per million, whereas 12 years ago it was about 41 in Australia, 75 in Canada, 51 in the UK, and 107 in the US. Justice Bharucha rightly diagnosed the cause why India could not better its judge-population ratio:

> The States are, quite simply, not interested in doing anything about it. They have no money to spend on the judiciary. That it is the obligation of the state to secure justice for its citizens does not bother the States: litigants are not a vote bank they need to cater to. That the obligation of the state to secure justice to its citizens is honoured in the breach every day is evident from the fact that the jails in the country are chock-a-block and a very large proportion of those who are within are not convicted criminals but accused awaiting trial.[108]

The Law Commission, in its 120th report (1987) on Manpower Planning in Judiciary, also highlighted this problem. To increase the number of judges in order to lessen the mismatch between demand and supply, the Supreme Court directed 'the increase in the judge strength to 50 judges per million people to be effected and implemented with the filling up of posts in a phased manner ... within a period of five years'.[109] It is also argued that in a country like Britain, judges are highly paid and they never retire, but in India even the tenure of judges is not extended. In 2009, after examining figures for both civil and criminal cases over seven years, the Supreme Court, for the first time assessed that the judiciary needs, '1,547 High Court judges and 23,207 subordinate court judges, only to clear the backlog in one year'.[110]

---

[108] V. Venkatesan, 'The Law and Delays', *Frontline*, vol. 19, no. 05 (2–15 March 2002).

[109] *All India Judges' Association and Others* v. *Union of India and Others* (2002) 4 SCC 247.

[110] 'To Clear Backlog, SC Calculates: 1500 Judges in HCs, 23,000 in Lower Courts', *Indian Express*, New Delhi, 12 August 2009.

In 2016, it was a running feud between Justice T.S. Thakur, the CJI, and the Union Government over the lack of the number of judges, with the former not sparing any opportunity to slam the government. On 24 April 2016, CJI T.S. Thakur, like his predecessors, again blamed the executive for not making adequate appointments of judges to tide over the crisis. He almost broke down in the presence of the prime minister in the conference of chief ministers and chief justices as he lamented that the judiciary was being condemned unnecessarily for the mounting arrears. He gave a hackneyed example that if five labourers are required to construct a road in 10 days, 50 labourers would be required to construct the same in one day.[111] The comparison is simplistic; he did not realize that judges are not labourers and that each case does not call for equal time and energy. A few days later, he repeated it at Cuttack asserting that the country needed 70 thousand judges.[112] He raised eyebrows by expressing disappointment while reacting to Prime Minister Narendra Modi's Independence Day speech on 15 August 2016. After hoisting the tricolour in the Supreme Court, he said:

> You (government) frame schemes, take steps to remove poverty and to keep the country united. But you should also think about providing justice to citizens.
>
> Today we heard the country's very popular and loving Prime Minister for one-and-a-half hours and we also heard the law minister's speech (in SC premises). I was hoping that they will talk about speedy justice and appointment of judges.[113]

On 11 September, he told a conference of judicial officers at Bilaspur that 'we may keep on inviting foreign direct investment and raising slogans about progress' but it is essential that the judicial system should also improve to deal with disputes arising from this progress.[114] On 23 October, Justice Thakur again lambasted the government addressing the global conference on arbitration organized by National Institution for Transforming India (NITI) Ayog while sharing dais with Prime Minister Narendra Modi that delay in justice delivery keeps investors away: 'We have over 3000 foreign companies with

---

[111] *Times of India*. New Delhi; *Indian Express*, New Delhi, *Hindustan Times*, New Delhi, 25 April 2016.

[112] *Times of India*, New Delhi, 9 May 2016.

[113] 'PM's I-Day Speech Disappoints CJI', *Times of India*, New Delhi, 16 August 2016.

[114] *Indian Express*, New Delhi, 12 September 2016.

operations in India. In 2015–16, there has been a 29 percent increase in foreign direct investments. We wish to overtake China and the United States by 2050. Yet we are ranked 130 among a total 189 countries in the ease of doing business'.[115]

Shortly afterwards, on 29 October, Justice Thakur slammed the government in the open court for delay in the appointment of judges, 'Today we have a situation where court rooms are locked because there are no judges.... You are scuttling the working of the institution'.[116]

Justice Thakur's concerns may be genuine but the judiciary cannot go unscathed as by harping on the number of judges, it cannot see the wood for the trees. Moreover, if we talk about the judge-population ratio, we also must take into account the number of litigations in India. Marc Galanter has exploded the popular myth that Indians are highly prone to litigation.

> Since British times, it has been widely believed that the Indian population is extremely litigious. This piece of received wisdom is however far from the mark. Indeed, the rate of utilization or invocation of these courts by the citizens of India is very low. Reliable data are scarce and the state of record-keeping makes collecting them a daunting task, but there are sufficient bits to suggest that India is among the lowest in the world per capita use of courts. Before his untimely death, the late Professor Christian Wollschlager, the trailblazer of comparative judicial statistics, presented a comparison of the per capita filing of civil cases in some 35 jurisdictions for the ten-year period 1987–96. Rates of filing in courts of first instance per 1000 persons ranged from 123 in Germany and 111 in Sweden at the high end to 2.6 in Nepal and 1.7 in Ethiopia at the bottom. Since no national figures are available for India, Professor Wollschlager included in his comparison figures on Maharashtra, which ranked thirty-second of the thirty-five jurisdictions with an annual per capita rate of 3.5 filings per 1000 persons. There is no reason to believe that Maharashtra has less litigation than India as a whole, since no data point to a general correlation of court use with economic development.... The suspicions aroused by the Wollschlager study gain some confirmation from an earlier study by Robert Moog, who examined litigation rates in Uttar Pradesh from 1951 to 1976; a stopping point dictated by the fact that the state stopped issuing these statistics then. He found that per capita civil filings in all district level courts in UP had fallen dramatically from the early days of Independence,

[115] *The Hindu*, New Delhi, 25 October 2016.

[116] http://www.hindustantimes.com/india-news/sc-slams-centre-over-delay-in-appointment-of-high-court-judges/story-EvddfTj2hfaWHIsOVDgMYJ.htm (last accessed on 26 January 2017).

when there were 1.63 per thousand persons in 1951 to 1976 when there were only 0.88 per thousand.[117]

Shailesh Gandhi has also challenged the popular notion that there has been an explosion of litigation.

I have studied the data from the Supreme Court's website, and if one understands it rationally, it can be eye-opening. Analysing the data leads one to the conclusion that a simple and doable solution stares us in the face. First, it destroys the myth that the backlog is growing at a rapid pace. The total number of pending cases each year on January 1, 2009–14 were 303, 214, 315, 316, and 322 lakhs. This shows that the backlog is not growing at a galloping pace as is commonly believed. To appreciate these figures, we must also understand that each year, about 200 lakh cases are instituted and around the same number of cases is being disposed. The increase in backlog over this six-year period is just about 19 lakh, or about 3 lakh per year. This would represent just about a 1.5 per cent increase per year.[118]

Some statistics are misleading. Sometimes numerous petitions are filed by similarly situated people, for example government school teachers for some benefits denied to them. The high court, instead of adjudicating the issue, would direct the petitioner in each case to file representation before the concerned authority with a direction that it would be disposed of judiciously. Thus, the high court would decide several hundred cases in one day or in a few minutes. Again, the same petitioners would file contempt petitions that they did not get any response, though they had filed representations or that their demands were rejected. So, again the same number of petitions would be filed. Thus, the court encourages litigation, as it could have heard the state and decided the case in one go, saving the time of the court, and the petitioners would have been spared of avoidable harassment, delays, and expenses.

The problem of pendency has been discussed for a very long time. The Civil Judge Committee, popularly known as the Rankin Committee, was set up in 1924 under the chairmanship of Justice George Claus Rankin of the Calcutta High Court to examine the problem of delay in disposal of civil cases both

[117] Marc Galanter, 'Fifty Years On', in *Supreme but Not Infallible: Essays in Honour of the Supreme Court of India*, edited by B.N. Kirpal, Ashok H. Deasi, Gopal Subramanium, Rajeev Dhavan, and Raju Ramchandran (New Delhi: Oxford University Press, 2010), p. 58.

[118] Shailesh Gandhi, 'Buck Stops at Bench', *Indian Express*, 27 April 2016.

in high courts and subordinate courts as civil cases were not being disposed of in six months. Imagine, a period of over six months was a matter of worry. Justice Rankin, in his report, attributed it to adjournments and delay in serving summons which is still the order of the day. The High Courts Arrear Committee, was appointed in 1949, headed by Justice S.R. Das, to examine the possibility of curtailing the right of appeal and revision. Subsequently, the matter was raised in the Parliament that cases were not being disposed of expeditiously. Prime Minister Jawaharlal Nehru, conceded it and the Law Commission was set up by an executive order, and the then Attorney General M.C. Setalvad was appointed the first chairman of the Commission.

The Commission traversed the whole country, and then in its 14th Report, it suggested measures so that cases are disposed of within six months. It made many recommendations such as increasing the number of judges, speedy filling up of judicial vacancies, making judicial posts more attractive to legal talents, appointment of additional judges to clear up backlogs, re-fixation at a higher figure of the pecuniary jurisdiction of high courts to entertain First Appeals, fixation of the working days of the high court at 200 days per annum, better supervision and control of the subordinate judiciary, and so on. A committee was appointed in 1969 under Justice M. Hidayatullah to suggest ways and means to reduce arrears in high courts. These, and several other committees have expressed concern over the inadequate number of judges.[119] Again, the Law Commission, headed by Justice H.R. Khanna, in its 79th Report 'Delay and Arrears in High Courts and Other Appellate Courts', suggested ways to secure elimination of delays and speedy clearance of arrears.

It is ironical, if not amazing, that judges, while accusing the police of a slow pace of investigation or failing to control crime or bureaucrats for various omissions, never bother to make any such comparisons of their strengths for a population of 1 million vis-à-vis other countries. It is true that the judiciary is not responsible for vacancies in government services; nonetheless handicaps of the administration ought to be taken into consideration. This does not mean that the administration is doing its job efficiently and honestly. In fact, systemic atrophy at various levels of governance, leading to deliberate denial of justice to the people, has led to the unprecedented explosion, which is the biggest challenge before the Indian judiciary. However, the judiciary has not been able to mitigate the miseries of the victims of injustice either. Rather, it aggravates their miseries by delaying, and virtually denying justice.

---

[119] Law Commission of India headed by Justice H.R. Khanna, '79th Report on Delay and Arrears in High Courts and other Appellate Courts'.

As far as vacancies in the superior judiciary are concerned, the judiciary itself is to blame for this. The Supreme Court rejects panel after panel sent by high courts for the appointment of judges. There was hardly any unanimity in the collegium on any name as there are extraneous considerations. The collegium system was sought to be replaced by the National Judicial Appointments Commission (NJAC) by the 99th constitutional amendment, but a Constitution Bench of the Supreme Court with 4:1 majority struck it down as unconstitutional.[120] Justice J. Chelameshwar dissented and upheld the NJAC and quoted from this author's book *Justice, Judocracy and Democracy in India: Boundaries and Breaches*.

After 1993, the Supreme Court had full authority over the appointment and transfer of high court judges. However, the government and the judiciary have been engaged in a blame game in owning up responsibility for the delays in filling up vacancies of judges. While the government holds the judiciary responsible for not recommending the names, the judiciary blames the Union Government for not clearing the names recommended by the Supreme Court collegium and also state governments for not providing them with the requisite infrastructure to expedite the decision-making process for the appointment of judges. The blame game continues, while the people suffer. Justice V.R. Krishna Iyer's comment on the role of the collegium in this regard is apposite:

> It is unpleasant to investigate the performance of the collegium in India and the inordinate delay inflicted on the country in failing to fill in time vacancies in the High Courts and the Supreme Court. Rajinder Sachar recently wrote of course, the negative aspect of arrears and long delays and even 150 unfilled vacancies of High Court judges (due to non-recommendation by the judiciary collegium) have cast a shadow on the effectiveness of the present legal system (*Hindu* dated 9 October 2003) while the patronage of the political bosses has largely vanished, the patronage of the 'robed' bosses has not improved the quality of the judges selected.[121]

The judge-population ratio is a flawed and stereotyped alibi handed out by the judiciary to hide its own weaknesses. The malaise is deep and referring to the

---

[120] *Supreme Court-Advocates-on-Record Association* v. *Union of India* (2016) 5 SCC 1, MANU/SC/1183/2015.

[121] V.R. Krishna Iyer, 'A National Judicial Commission—A Command for Reforms', *Random Reflections*, Universal Law Publishing Co. Pvt. Ltd., New Delhi, 2004, pp. 133–4.

low judge-population ratio ad nauseam is simplistic. The Law Commission's 120th Report (1987), which recommended increasing the number of judges, itself admitted that this 'judge-population ratio' reasoning was based on 'a very poor substitute for sound scientific analysis'. It also lamented that even after four decades of independence, we did not have even the minimal of vital statistics which could be the basis for concrete proposal on judicial manpower planning. Governments at the Centre and in the states have differed with the Supreme Court with respect to the creation of additional courts, which according to them, should be based on the case-load of existing courts in a particular region. Against this backdrop, the Supreme Court asked the Law Commission to examine it afresh and recommend measures for the creation of additional courts. The Commission felt as handicapped because of the absence of vital data, as it felt in 1987. The data given by high courts were not only inadequate, but in some cases patently wrong as the Commission recorded:

> Besides gaining access to appropriate data from all High Courts, a major challenge was determining its accuracy. Potential errors could be seen upon close scrutiny of the data. For example, data received from the Delhi High Court indicates that in 2010, 40054 Negotiable Instrument Act, matters were instituted in the Delhi Subordinate Courts and 111517 were disposed of. Since a negative number of institutions is patently impossible, this number appears to have been inserted to balance the backlog tally and make up for a previous mistake in the number of pending negotiable instrument act matters. It is not known how many other errors like this have not occurred. Also, such adjusting of the statistics to get a correct backlog tally then misrepresents the number of institutions in a given year, distorting the overall institution rate.[122]

However, the Law Commission examined six different probable methodologies including the judge-population ratio basis. Finding that filings of cases per capita varied across states and are associated with economic and social conditions, it observed that the justice needs of different societies thus vary, and no universal standard can be prescribed in this regard. Thus, it came to the conclusion that 'while population might be the appropriate metric to measure the availability of essential services like healthcare and nutrition,

---

[122] Law Commission of India, Report No. 245, 'Arrears and Backlog: Creating Additional Judicial (Wo)Manpower', July 2014, p. 11. http://lawcommissionofindia. nic.in/reports/Report_No.245.pdf (last accessed on 3 July 2016).

it was not the appropriate standard for measuring the requirement of judicial services'.[123]

The author has been stressing this point for long that increasing the number of judges is no solution. Judges are not labourers and handling of cases is different from constructing roads. It is the quality of the judges that matters, not the quantity.[124] Further, each case does not require equal time. There are cases which have larger legal and constitutional implications and call for cool cogitation, while many are just run-of-the-mill type which can be disposed of in minutes. The Union Government also took the stand in the Parliament that the rate of disposal and number of 'judicial hours' needed to finish a case are key criteria for reducing pendency. In its first official rebuttal to CJI T.S. Thakur's stand linking inadequate number of judges to backlog, the Law Ministry reportedly relied on the example to Delhi which had the highest 'judge-to-population ratio' in India. According to the government, the capital has 47 judges per million population, almost touching the UK at 51, and yet suffers from a huge backlog. The then Law Minister Sadanand Gowda's reply quoted a 2014 report prepared by former chief justice of the Delhi High Court A.P. Shah titled, 'Arrears and Backlog: Creating Additional Judicial (Wo)Manpower'.[125] A study by the Union Law Ministry also punches holes into the judge-population ratio theory that the less number of judges is responsible for the pendency. The study, based on data between 2005 and 2015, listed several states with higher judge-population ratio—such as Delhi (47), judges per million persons and Gujarat (32 judges)—which are still struggling to dispose of cases, while states like Tamil Nadu (14 judges per million population) and Punjab (24 judges) have a much better record with lowest pendency rate.[126]

On the issue of judge-population ratio, it will be pertinent to recall what US President Nixon said on 11 March 1971, expressing his concern on the administration of the criminal justice system:

> But if we limit ourselves for more judges, more police, more lawyers operating in the same system, we will produce more backlog, more delays, more litigation, more jails and more criminals.

---

[123] Law Commission of India, Report No. 245, 'Arrears and Backlog', p. 20.

[124] Sudhanshu Ranjan, 'Small can be Beautiful', *Asian Age*, OP-ED, 29 April 2016, Sudhanshu Ranjan, 'Jujon ki sankhya badhana hi samadhan nahin hai', *Amar Ujala*, 29 April 2016.

[125] *Times of India*, New Delhi, 14 May 2015.

[126] *Times of India*, New Delhi, 20 June 2016.

More of the same is not the answer, what is needed now is genuine reform—the kind of change that requires imagination and daring and demands a focus on ultimate goals.[127]

Justice V.R. Krishna Iyer echoes a similar sentiment:

The truth is: more courts, more arrears, more lazy judges, more examples of Parkinson's Law and Peter Principle. The real cause of the escalating arrears is the absence of accountability and transparency.... For more disposals and inexpensive justice, the purposeful therapy is not the arithmetical illusion of judicial numbers but intelligent selection of robed brethren, of result-oriented technology, and summary procedure.[128]

The then Speaker of Lok Sabha and noted lawyer, Somnath Chatterjee made a similar comment on the decision to increase the number of Supreme Court judges, 'My humble experience is more the number of judges, more would be the arrears. I would prefer quality and determination, not showmanship. Much greater scrutiny is required at the time of admission of cases'.[129] He was forthright that increasing the number would be counterproductive, as has been seen in the high courts and lower courts. One has just to compare the disposal of a competent court with a not-so-competent court, and one can easily surmise that the crux of the problem is competence, not number, but the judiciary is unnecessarily dotty about increasing the number of judges without caring for the quality of judges and judging.

Competence and Dedication of Judges

Judges should take inspiration from Thomas More (1478–1535), who, as chancellor, made himself notable for the speed at which he dispatched his cases. He was efficient in his work and even encouraged litigants to lay their claims before him at his own home. The speed of his disposal and

---

[127] Speech of US President Richard Nixon delivered at the National Conference of the Judiciary, Williamsburg, Virginia, 11 March 1971, as quoted by Katz, Litwin, Lawrence B. Litwin, and Richard H. Bamberger, in *Justice is Crime* 35 (Cleveland: The Press of Case Western Reserve University, 1972). Nixon's speech is also available on net: http://www.presidency.ucsb.edu/ws/index.php?pid=3344 (last accessed on 14 October 2018).

[128] V.R. Krishna Iyer, 'Everything for Justice', *The Hindu*, 3 August 2009.

[129] 'More Judges, More the Delay', *Times of India*, New Delhi, 25 February 2008.

efficiency had a tremendous impact on the people, which is reflected in a popular rhyme:

> When More some time had Chancellor been,
> No more suits did remain;
> The like will never more be seen,
> Till More be there again.

A stereotype has been successfully created that judges are overworked and that the judicial system is crumbling under the load of work. A visit to subordinate and superior courts is sufficient to explode this myth. Judges seldom come to the court before noon and get up by 1 pm or latest 1:30 for lunch. In the second half, they sit for the same duration. Thus, they hardly sit for three hours a day. In consumer courts or other such tribunals, it is difficult to find any judges after noon even though they come after 10 am. The Supreme Court sits for only 193 days a year while the high courts have 210 working days and trial courts have 245 days. The British practice of the olden days when judges availed of long vacations and went to England still continues. On 30 July 2016, the then CJI R.M. Lodha told a private news channel that the courts should work 365 days every year without break.[130] However, he did not get any support either from judges or lawyers who go abroad during summer or winter vacation. Lawyers argue that they also need breaks. True, but like government employees and even those working with private companies who get their weekly offs besides casual, earned, and medical leaves, lawyers and judges can also avail of these leaves and weekly offs. Malimath Committee had recommended curtailing long vacations and increasing the number of working days of the apex court and the high courts to 206 and 231 days respectively.

Focus should be more on the competence of judges than their number. In some states, the high court is monitoring the performance of each and every judge. In Jharkhand, for example, in 2015, Ambuj Nath, the district judge of Dhanbad, was adjudged the best judge with the disposal rate of 78 per month, while the average rate of disposal was 21; the second highest rate was 24. The average disposal rate would have still been lower, but for the high rate of 78 by one judge. In 2016 also, he maintained the disposal rate of 78. All judges get the same facilities and salaries as per their rank and seniority, but the competent ones are quick at disposal and the quality of disposal is such that leaves little scope for going in appeal.

---

[130] *Indian Express*, New Delhi, 31 July 2016.

Lack of confidence is the prime reason that judges do not decide cases, particularly the high-profile and the high-stakes ones. Since they are not sure of the rightness of the judgements to be delivered, they prefer to keep them hanging fire, lest they are under fire. Many judges of the lower court stop working once they get their transfer orders, even though they may not be relieved immediately. It is to avoid the common perception that once the transfer order comes, a judge decides cases with pecuniary self-interest not caring a fig for their reputation as they have to leave the place. The question arises after all, why such a perception has been built up. Justice is a sovereign function, but for most judges it is a routine job which may or may not be discharged. Their concern for justice is underwhelming, the concern for career, controversy free tenure, and extraneous things is overwhelming. Judges are supposed to be persons with exemplary sang-froid, but they are afraid or apathetical to the extent of being incapacitated.

Dispensation of justice should be the only concern of judges and they should learn from Justice Lord Alfred Denning, one of the greatest jurists. In 1944, he became a Judge of a high court, was promoted to the Court of Appeal in 1948, and was finally elevated to the House of Lords in 1957. But he astounded the whole world and created a history of sorts when he voluntarily reverted to the Court of Appeal, when Lord Evershed resigned as Master of the Rolls and Denning was appointed to succeed him on 10 April 1962. Although he himself described it as 'a step down', he opted for it. The reason for his voluntary demotion was that the annual output of the Appeal Court was about 800 cases while that of House of Lords was about 50–60 cases, and he preferred a place where he could be more essentially preoccupied with dispensation of justice. Another reason was that the Court of Appeal judges sit in threes while the Lords sat in fives or more. So, he could have his way in the Court of Appeal by persuading just one judge, whereas in the House of Lords it was at least two.[131]

There are judges who come late and rise early; there were those who would say they were not in a good mood and so did not feel like working. One lady Supreme Court judge was notorious for coming late, perhaps seldom before noon. She had the same reputation as a high court judge and still she was promoted as chief justice, high court. The promotion brought no improvement in her punctuality and yet she was elevated to the apex court. In every period of history, we find that even kings were very meticulous as judges and never absented themselves from court. Megasthenes, in his book *Indica*,

---

[131] http://en.wikipedia.org/wiki/Alfred_Denning,_Baron_Denning (last accessed on 21 May 2015).

writes that Emperor Chandragupta Maurya sat for a few hours every day to decide cases. The Mughal kings attended to ordinary cases in *darbar* (court) every day, while for important cases they had a fixed day in the week. Akbar had reserved Thursdays, Jehangir, Tuesdays, and Shah Jahan, Wednesdays. This routine was never disturbed, come what may, even though the king went on military expeditions, pleasure trips, or was touring the provinces. Distinguished lawyers and eminent people from other disciplines may be appointed as additional judges for short periods for the disposal of backlogs. There is no dearth of such people who would do yeoman service without charging anything.

Judges with conscience and intention to do justice walk extra miles to settle disputes and do not give alibis of lack of strength or that of infrastructure. Justice Courtney Terrell, who served as the chief justice of the Patna High Court between 1928 and 1936, went to a village in Araria (Bihar) to settle disputes between landlords and tenants. In a letter to his wife, he has described the case:

The landlords are Brahmins and the tenants Nonias. For years there have been fierce quarrels and litigation because the Brahmins said the Nonias were only 'tenants at will' and could be turned out at any time. The Nonias said they were 'occupancy tenants' with permanent rights. This culminated in a pitched battle. The police behaved badly and sided with the landlords and the Nonias were driven back. One of their men was killed, many injured and the Nonia village burned to the ground. Both sides were arrested and tried by the sessions judge who sent the Brahmins to jail for three years and Nonias to jail for one year. Both appealed to the High Court, and it seemed to me that there was a chance of putting an end to the entire trouble. So I let the whole lot out of jail *on bail* and told them they were to enter into an agreement by which the Brahmins gave a proper written lease to the Nonias as permanent tenants and settling all disputes outstanding forever. I said I would myself go to the village and if this had not been done when I arrived I would send the whole lot back to jail again! It was an enormous success. I went to the place and both sides met me with cheers. I went with them through their village, a Brahman on one side and a Nonia on the other and talked to them. Then I made them all sit down together and photographed them. I said that, when I sent them a copy, they were to hang it up in their temple forever. They cheered loudly and then all came and touched my feet. Then we walked to the waiting car and they fetched a cow and milked her to give me a drink, and I drove off amid cheers.[132]

---

[132] Richard Terrell, *The Chief Justice: A Portrait from the Raj*, with an Introduction by Lord Glendevon (Salisbury: Michael Russell (Publishing) Ltd, 1979), p. 50.

He mentioned in the letter about another case in which two Rajput families have had a terrible fight which cost one life. One man was sentenced to death and three to transportation for life. He wrote: 'I am going to do the same thing again. The result will be that, instead of ruining the families for ever and perpetuating the strife, I shall enable them to settle down in peace for some years, at any rate. The Government is quite pleased at this experiment'.[133] Bihar witnessed the worst kind of bloody internecine caste wars during the 1980s and 1990s, though earlier also there were caste killings but not so frequently, which took a huge toll on life. Did it ever occur to the chief justice or the judges of the Patna High Court that they could proactively use their vast power to bring about peace in the battered regions?

Keeping Judgements Reserved

Judges should cogitate on how to improve the system instead of exculpating themselves and excoriating the government. One glaring example of their omission is the new trend of keeping judgements reserved for a long time. The Supreme Court itself expressed annoyance over it in *Anil Rai* v. *State of Bihar*,[134] and lambasted this practice:

> The inordinate, unexplained and negligent delay in pronouncing the judgement is alleged to have actually negatived the right of appeal conferred upon the convicts under the provisions of the Criminal Procedure Code. It is submitted that such a delay is not only against the provisions of law but in fact infringes the right of personal liberty guaranteed by Article 21 of the Constitution of India. Any procedure or course of action which does not ensure a reasonable quick adjudication has been termed to be unjust. Such a course is stated to be contrary to maxim *actus curiae neminem gravabit*, that an act of the court shall prejudice none.... Delay in disposal of an appeal on account of inadequate number of judges, insufficiency of infrastructure, strike of lawyers and circumstances attributable to the State is understandable but once the entire process of participation of the justice delivery system is over and the only thing to be done is the pronouncement of judgement, no excuse can be found to further delay for adjudication of the rights of the parties.[135]

The Court laid down certain guidelines for high courts for quick pronouncement of judgements till the Parliament makes a suitable enactment to

---

[133] Terrell, *The Chief Justice*, pp. 50–1.
[134] (2001) 7 SCC 318.
[135] (2001) 7 SCC 318, pp. 328–9.

deal with the problem. The Supreme Court even suggested drawing inspiration from section 353(1) of the Cr. P.C. to pronounce judgement 'immediately' after the termination of the trial. No act of courts should harm a litigant and it is the bounden duty of the courts to ensure that if a person is harmed by a mistake of the court, he should be restored to the position he would have occupied but for the mistake. The Court expressed dismay that two judges of the Patna High Court took two years to pronounce judgement after the conclusion of the argument, though in 1961 a judge of the same court passed a stricture against a magistrate who took nine months to deliver his judgement, stating that such a magistrate ought not to do any judicial work.

The Supreme Court in its guidelines ruled that if the judgement is not delivered within two months from the date of reserving the judgement, the chief justice of the high court would draw the attention of the bench to it; if it is not delivered within three months, any of the parties may file an application for early judgement, and such a petition would be listed before the concerned bench within two days, excluding intervening holidays; if it is not pronounced in six months then either party can move an application for the transfer of the case to another bench. Earlier, reminding a judge about a judgement was considered contemptuous, but now delays are so common that litigants are forced to remind judges frequently about it. Unfortunately, even these directions were never followed. It simply means that high court judges kept committing contempt of the Supreme Court.

Order XX, Rule 1 of the Civil Procedure Code also mandates that the court shall pronounce judgement in open court either at once or soon thereafter, but it shall not ordinarily be beyond 30 days on which the hearing was concluded. However, at least in one-third of cases, judgements are delayed. In some cases, after the case is posted for judgement, one party will file petition for arguing on law points and that time may be granted. The court may allow or reject rehearing, but a date is given. It is funny that the law allows for arguing on law points after the conclusion of hearing as if earlier it was argued on extra-legal points. It is alleged that many a time, such petitions are filed at the instance of the court as the judge is not able to deliver judgement within the specified period.

It is clear that inordinate delay in the pronouncement of a judgement after the conclusion of the hearing speaks of incompetence and irresponsible behaviour of judges. Earlier, judges generally dictated judgements running into hundreds of pages in the open court immediately after the hearing was over or at least pronounced the operative part to be followed by a detailed judgement. Thus, the parties knew the outcome of their cases. Judgements were reserved only in murder cases as even the slightest of errors may result in ending a person's life. Today, there are judges who reserve judgements for months and even years, and conveniently retire. Such cases are released and reheard causing avoidable harassments to litigants. There have been a few high court judges who hardly wrote any judgement except 'I agree'. There are instances of judges who seldom wrote a judgement during their entire career as judges of high courts and were only known for reserving judgements never to be delivered are elevated to the apex court. Justice Cyriac Joseph is one such example who was warned by his then chief justice of the Kerala High Court, Justice Jawahar Lal Gupta, that no cases would be listed in his court till he delivered the judgements he had reserved for a long period. Earlier, he earned such a dubious distinction of not delivering judgments in the Delhi High Court also. However, he was promoted as the chief justice of the Uttarakhand High Court and also served the Karnataka High Court in the same capacity. But his style of functioning remained the same. Still, he was elevated to the Supreme Court, and during his tenure from 7 July 2008 to 27 January 2012, he authored exactly seven judgments, and was a signatory to as many as 309 judgments, and 135 orders, all authored by his colleagues on the bench.[136] Even these seven judgements were penned at the fag end of his tenure when the Court's corridors were abuzz with murmurs that a judge would retire without writing a single judgement. He was further rewarded post-retirement for being a lotus eater with the membership of the NHRC.

On the other hand, there are judges who write verbose and lengthy judgements only to exhibit their erudition and cause delays. Former CJI, Y.V. Chandrachud commented:

> Judges are after all human beings and the desire for immortality is a common human failing. We seek immortality through the pages of law reports and our judgements are frightfully long, almost so long as to discourage the most ardent followers of law from reading them. So much scholarship is often wasted on the desert air and full many a judgement is born to blush unread.[137]

There are judges who write that the law is well-settled in this regard, and yet go on writing reams of pages quoting long paragraphs from different judgements, sometimes lifting passages without even acknowledging the source.

---

[136] V. Venkatesan, 'Judges have to Watch Their Scoreboard', *The Hindu*, 27 May 2013.

[137] 'Social Watch India: Citizens Report on Governance and Development', 2004, p. 65.

Conflicting Judgements Creating Uncertainty

Law is not clear on many vital issues of general concern because the apex court has not been consistent on a particular stand. For instance, on the issue of registration of FIRs, there were conflicting judgments. Seven judgments say that it is mandatory for the police to register FIRs once a complaint has been made. But three judgments speak otherwise. On 27 February 2012, in *Lalita Kumari* v. *Govt. of UP*,[138] a division bench of three judges referred it to the Constitution Bench for an authoritative judgment as different judgments of the apex court were in conflict with one another. The Court recorded that it had become extremely important to have a clear enunciation of law for the benefit of all concerned.

Finally, the Constitution Bench ruled that registration of FIR is mandatory under section 154 of the Code of Criminal Procedure if the information discloses commission of a cognizable offence and that no preliminary inquiry is permissible.[139] However, if it does not reveal any cognizable offence but indicates the necessity for an inquiry, a preliminary inquiry is permissible only to ascertain whether a cognizable offence is made out, and if it ends in closing the complaint, a copy of the entry of such closure must be supplied to the first informant forthwith and not later than a week. The closure report must also disclose reasons in brief for closing the complaint. The Court added that action must be taken against erring officers who do not register the FIR on receiving information that discloses cognizable offence.

Such instances of divergent judgements are galore. The total erosion of judicial collectivism leads to complete uncertainty about the legal position on several issues. Naturally, high courts and lower courts too are baffled. Even on the issue of death sentence, there are conflicting judgments and even the Supreme Court itself lately admitted in 2009 in *Santosh Kumar Satishbhushan* v. *State of Maharashtra*[140] that some judgments are per incuriam (without basis of law) and that some convicts were executed wrongly. Justice S. B. Sinha wrote:

> [T]he judicial principles for imposition of death penalty are far from being uniform. Without going into the merits and demerits of such discretion and subjectivity, we must nevertheless reiterate the basic principle, stated repeatedly by this Court, that life imprisonment is the rule and death penalty an

---

[138]   AIR (2012) SC 1515: (2012) 4 SCC 1 (Cr. Appeal No 1410 of 2011).

[139]   *Lalita Kumari* v. *Govt. of UP*, AIR (2014) SC 187: (2014) 2 SCC 1.

[140]   (2009) 6 SCC 498: (2009) 9 SCR 90.

exception. Each case must therefore be analyzed and the appropriateness of punishment determined on a case-by- case basis with death sentence not to be awarded save in the 'rarest of rare' case where reform is not possible.[141]

The Supreme Court has given conflicting judgements even in cases pertaining to divorce, invoking its powers under Article 142 of the Constitution, though laws on the subject are crystal clear. In *Chandrakala Menon (Mrs.) & Anr.* v. *Vipin Menon (Capt.) & Anr.*,[142] the Court granted a decree of divorce by mutual consent under section 13-B of the Act and dissolved the marriage between the parties in order to meet the ends of justice, ignoring the fact that the consent given under section 13-B of the Act was withdrawn within one week of the filing of the joint petition. In *Ashok Hurra* v. *Rupa Bipin Zaveri*,[143] the Supreme Court granted a decree of mutual divorce by taking recourse to its extraordinary powers under Article 142. Again, in *Anita Sabharwal* v. *Anil Sabharwal*,[144] the Court granted decree of mutual divorce without waiting for the statutory period of six months. The same view was echoed in *Kiran* v. *Sharad Dutt*[145] (all this has been discussed in detail in the chapter Supreme Court's Power to Do Complete Justice). Such judgments, lacking statutory basis, encourage litigation as everyone thinks of taking a chance because the law appears to be labile. So, everything is uncertain and unpredictable.

On a vital issue of governance, the Supreme Court has given differing judgments on the precondition of sanction to prosecute a public servant under the Prevention of Corruption Act, 1988. Section 19 of the Act requires that without prior sanction, no court shall take cognizance of an offence alleged to have been committed by a public servant. However, it does not put any bar on an investigation either under the P.C. Act or the Criminal Procedure Code by registering an FIR or a court-monitored investigation under section 156(3) Cr. P.C. But a division bench of the Supreme Court, in *Anil Kumar* v. *M.K. Aiyappa*,[146] ruled that section 19 of the P.C. Act applies at the threshold level and an application under section 156(3) of Cr. P.C. is not maintainable without obtaining the sanction from the competent authority. This view was reiterated in *Narayan Swamy* v. *State of Karnataka*.[147] This is in sharp contrast

---

[141] (2009) 6 SCC 498: (2009) 9 SCR 90, second last para.
[142] (1993) 2 SCC 6: (1993) 1 SCALE 119.
[143] AIR (1997) SC 1266: (1997) 4 SCC 226.
[144] (1997) 1 SCC 490.
[145] (2000) 10 SCC 243: MANU/SC/1415/1999.
[146] (2013) 10 SCC 705.
[147] (2016) 9 SCC 598.

with established legal position that sanction is not required at the level of investigation. Investigation into the fodder scam was done by the CBI on the direction of the Patna High Court under its monitoring, though there was no prior sanction. The chief minister of Bihar, Lalu Prasad and several others were chargesheeted and sanction was obtained subsequently. In *R.R. Chari* v. *State of UP*,[148] a bench of three judges held that previous sanction was not needed to order an investigation under section 156(3) of Cr. P.C. The Court, in *State of Rajasthan* v. *Raj Kumar*,[149] took the same view that no sanction was required for filing a charge sheet under section 173 of Cr. P.C. Finally, a Constitution Bench of five judges of the Supreme Court, in *Subramanian Swamy* v. *Union of India*,[150] struck down section 6A of the DSPE Act as unconstitutional, as it required previous sanction for investigation into crimes by the employees of the Central government of the Level of Joint Secretary and above; and such officers as are appointed by the Central government in corporations established by or under any Central Act, government companies, societies, and local authorities owned or controlled by that government. The Court laid down:

> Insofar as investigation is concerned, an investigation into a crime may have some adverse impact but where there are allegations of an offence under the PC Act, 1988 against a public servant, whether high or low, whether decision-maker or not, an independent investigation into such allegations is of utmost importance and unearthing the truth is the goal. The aim and object of investigation is ultimately to search for truth and any law that impedes that object may not stand the test of Article 14.[151]

Notwithstanding the unanimous verdict of the Constitution Bench, these verdicts (*Aiyappa* and *Narayan Swamy*) are confounding the legal position. It is flabbergasting that the apex court delivered a conflicting judgment in *Narayan Swamy* even after the Constitution Bench's unequivocal judgment in *Subramanian Swamy* ignoring the principle of *stare decisis*. Actually, even without this judgement, there was never any bar on the court to direct for an investigation under section 156(3) of the Cr. P.C. In the Jain Hawala case,[152] the Supreme Court ordered the CBI to investigate alleged payments to several

---

[148]   (1951) 2 SCR 312.
[149]   [(1998) 6 SCC 551].
[150]   (2014) 8 SCC 682.
[151]   (2014) 8 SCC 682, para 90.
[152]   *Vineet Narain* v. *Union of India* (1996) 2 SCC 199.

politicians. In the Fodder Scam case,[153] the apex court not only upheld the decision of the Patna High Court directing the CBI to probe it, but also ruled that the investigation would be monitored by the High Court. So, there was never any doubt about the jurisdiction of the courts to order investigation under section 156(3) of the Cr. P.C. Unscrupulous elements in the higher echelon of power may invoke these two judgments to scuttle any direction for investigation. High courts are openly ignoring Aiyappa and Narayan Swamy. However, in a rare act of confession of having gone wrong, Justice Anand Byrareddy of the Karnataka High Court refused to follow the apex court which upheld his own judgment in *M.K. Aiyappa* v. *State of Karnataka*, delivered on 21 May 2013 that a special judge/magistrate cannot order for investigation on a complaint against a public servant without valid sanction from the government. A division bench of the Supreme Court comprising Justice K.S. Radhakrishnan and A.K. Sikri, upheld it in *Anil Kumar* v. *M.K. Aiyappa*.[154] The Kerala High Court in *Maneesh E.* v. *State of Kerala*,[155] has even observed that this judgment by the apex court is *per incuriam*.

Actually, sanction is required only at the stage of cognizance. Investigation is at the pre-cognizance level. The word 'cognizance' is not defined in the Cr. P.C., but it figures in so many sections. The Supreme Court grappled with this word for the first time in *R.R. Chari* v. *State of UP*.[156] A three-judge bench headed by Chief Justice H.J. Kania, quoted with approval the observation of the Calcutta High Court in *Superintendant and Remembrancer of Lagal Affairs, West Bengal* v. *Abani Kumar Banerjee*,[157] that before it can be said that any magistrate has taken cognizance under Section 190 (1) (a) of the Cr. P.C., he must not only have applied his mind to the contents of the petition, but must have done so for the purpose of proceeding in a particular way as indicated in subsequent provisions, but for taking action of some other kind, for example, for ordering investigation under Section 156(3), or ordering search warrant for the purposes of the investigation, he cannot be said to have taken cognizance.

The apex court is duty bound to lay down law. Therefore, Article 145(3) of the Constitution provides for the setting up of Constitution Bench comprising minimum five judges for deciding any case involving a substantial question of law as to the interpretation of this Constitution or for the purpose

---

[153] *Union of India* v. *Sushil Kumar Modi* (1997) 4 SCC 771.

[154] (2013) 10 SCC 705.

[155] (2016) 1 KLJ 169, MANU/KE/2529/2015.

[156] AIR (1951) SC 207.

[157] AIR (1950) Cal 437.

of hearing any reference from the president under Article 143. However, the number of cases decided by Constitution Benches is declining continuously. Nick Robinson has found that between 1950 and 1954, about 15 per cent of the total cases decided by the Supreme Court were decided by the Constitution Benches. In the 1970s, the percentage dropped to below 1, and between 2005 and 2009, this figure came down to a negligible 0.12 per cent.[158] It may be noted that the minimum number was fixed at 5 when the original Constitution of 1950 provided for a Supreme Court with a CJI and 7 puisne judges, leaving it to the Parliament to increase this number which was raised from 8 to 11 in 1956, 14 in 1960, 18 in 1968, 26 in 1986, and 30 in 2008. The Statement of Objects and Reason of the Supreme Court (Number of Judges) Amendment Act, 2008, reads:

> The pendency of cases in the Supreme Court of India has constantly been on the rise largely due to higher rate of institution of cases. As on the 31st day of March, 2007, 41,581 cases were pending in the Supreme Court. The Chief Justice of India has intimated that the Judges in the Supreme Court feel over-burdened and have been working under acute work pressure. It has also not been possible for the Chief Justice of India to constitute a five Judge Bench on a regular basis to hear cases involving interpretation of constitutional law as doing that would result in constitution of less number of Division Benches which in turn will result in delay in hearing of other civil and criminal matters.[159]

It is clear that the formation of Constitution Benches was a major objective of increasing the number of judges. But surprisingly, it is not happening and division benches of two or three judges are giving conflicting judgments because some brilliant idea strikes some judge who ignores the principle of *stare decisis*. It may also be remembered that five is the minimum number required for a Constitution Bench; the CJI may constitute larger benches. The largest bench so far was of 13 judges in *Kesavananda Bharati* v. *State of Kerala*,[160] when the Supreme Court had the strength of 14 judges. It may be mentioned that in the initial years, all judges of the apex court generally sat

[158] Nick Robinson et al., 'Interpreting the Constitution: Supreme Court Constitution Benches since Independence', *Economic and Political Weekly*, vol. 46, no. 9 (2011).

[159] http://www.prsindia.org/uploads/media/1209532839/1209532839_The_Supreme_Court__Number_of_Judges__Amendment_Bill__2008.pdf (last accessed on 15 October 2016).

[160] (1973) 4 SCC 225.

together to decide cases, but slowly, division benches started deciding cases except the few when Constitution Benches are set up. Because of the erosion of judicial collectivism, the high courts and the lower courts are flummoxed as the law is not certain. If different benches speak in different voices, which one would be binding, remains a conundrum. Because of this uncertainty, everybody feels like taking chance even though the statute goes categorically against them, as even certain laws have been made uncertain by inconsonant judgements of various benches.

False Cases

Filing false cases is a major cause of burgeoning litigation. How the police build up false cases and present doctored witnesses has been described elaborately by the Supreme Court in *Prem Chand (Paniwala)* v. *Union Of India (Uoi) And Ors.*[161] Petitioner Prem Chand, earned his living as a *paniwala* or a vendor of soft drinks near Delite Cinema in Delhi. He had a few mobile carts which he used for refrigerating water and parked them on the roadside due to the indulgence of the police. Thus, he came to be known as Prem Chand paniwala. Since he thrived due to his close association with police and their connivance and indulgence, he became a pawn in the hands of the police and he was persuaded and pressurized to be their personal stooge and stock witness. He averred that once he yielded to the pressure of the police to give false testimony disclosing a rubberized conscience and unveracious readiness to forswear himself, there was escalation of demands upon him and he became a regular peddler of perjury 'on police service'.[162] The counsel for the petitioner made sensational disclosure that his client was a stock witness because he had to keep the police in good humour and oblige them with tailored testimony in around 3,000 cases because the alternative was police wrath. When he refused to be their witness any further, the police avenged themselves by initiating externment with the intent of giving a body blow to his business and shattering him financially. Justice V.R. Krishna Iyer wrote:

> We were flabbergasted at this bizarre confession but to lend credence to his assertion counsel produced a few hundred summonses where the petitioner

---

[161] AIR (1981) SC 613 (1981) CriLJ 5 (1981) 1 SCC 639 (1981) 1 SCR 1262 (1981) 13 UJ 27 SC.

[162] AIR (1981) SC 613 (1981) CriLJ 5 (1981) 1 SCC 639 (1981) 1 SCR 1262 (1981) 13 UJ 27 SC, para 5.

was cited as a witness. Were he not omnipresent how could he testify in so many cases save by a versatile genius for loyal unveracity? For sure, the consternation of the community at this flood of perjury will shake its faith in the veracity of Police investigation and the validity of the judicial verdict. We have no doubt that the petitioner, who has given particulars of a large number of cases where he had been cited as witness, is speaking the truth even assuming that 3,000 cases may be an exaggeration. In Justice, Justices and Justicing and likewise in the Police and Policing, the Peril to the judicial process is best left to imagination if professional perjurers like the self-confessed Paniwala are kept captive by the Police, to be pressed into service for proving 'cases'. Courts, trusting the Police may act on apparently veracious testimony and sentence people into prison. The community, satisfied with such convictions, may well believe that all is well with law and order. We condemn, in the strongest terms, the systematic pollution of the judicial process and the consequent threat to human rights of innocent persons. We hope that the higher authorities in the Department who, apparently, are not aware of the nefarious goings-on at the lesser levels will immediately take measures to stamp out this unscrupulous menace.[163]

In *Pankaj Chaudhary & Others* v. *State (Govt of NCT of Delhi)*,[164] the Delhi High Court slammed the police for filing false cases against innocent persons. Justice S. Muralidhar, in the opening sentence of the judgment, says, '*This is an instance of how a false criminal case, instituted in connivance with obliging police officials, can virtually ruin the lives of innocent persons*'. Four appellants had been facing criminal proceedings for the offence of gang rape for over 12 years. The prosecutrix, a prostitute, was used to frame them. She was in the custody of police one hour before and after the time of alleged rape. While acquitting them, the court said that the state should consider suitably compensating them, monetarily and/or in any other appropriate manner, and directed the state to take a decision to this effect within a period of 12 weeks and file a compliance report. The court also clarified that these directions would not come in the way of the appellants seeking appropriate remedies available to them in law to seek redress for the violation of their fundamental and human rights to life and liberty. It added that the cost awarded by the court would be independent of any other amount awarded by the state.

However, the Supreme Court refused to entertain a joint petition by six persons acquitted by it in the 2002 Akshardham terror attack case seeking

---

[163] AIR (1981) SC 613 (1981) CriLJ 5 (1981) 1 SCC 639 (1981) 1 SCR 1262 (1981) 13 UJ 27 SC, para 5.

[164] MANU/DE/4327/2009: (2009) 3 RCR (Criminal) 750.

compensation for their wrongful arrest, prosecution, and incarceration almost for a decade.[165] A division bench comprising Justices Dipak Misra and R. Banumathi said that awarding compensation would set a dangerous precedent even though the Supreme Court, while acquitting them, had censured the Gujarat government for fabricating false evidence to implicate them. It is in conflict with what the Supreme Court ruled earlier in *Ankush Shivaji Gaikwad* v. *State of Maharashtra*[166] that though the award or refusal of compensation in a particular case may be within the court's discretion, there exists a mandatory duty on the court to apply its mind to the question in every criminal case. Justice T.S. Thakur wrote:

> The power to award compensation was intended to reassure the victim that he or she is not forgotten in the criminal justice system. The victim would remain forgotten in the criminal justice system if despite the legislature having gone so far as to enact specific provisions relating to victim compensation, courts choose to ignore the provisions altogether and do not even apply their mind to the question of compensation. It follows that unless Section 357 of the IPC is read to confer an obligation on the courts to apply their mind to the question of compensation, it would defeat the very object behind the introduction of the provision.[167]

Earlier, the Supreme Court awarded compensation in *Rudal Shah* v. *State of Bihar*.[168] Justifying it, Chief Justice Y.V. Chandrachud wrote:

> The right to compensation is some palliative for the unlawful acts of intrumentalities which act in the name of public interest and which present for their protection the powers of the State as a shield. If civilisation is not to perish in this country as it has perished in some others too well known to suffer mention, it is necessary to educate ourselves into accepting that, respect for the rights of individuals is the true bastion of democracy.[169]

The discharge of eight accused in the Malegaon blasts case by a Mumbai court on 26 April 2016, also reflects on the tendency of the police to implicate innocent people. A series of bomb blasts that took place on 8 September 2006 claimed 37 lives. Nine Muslim men were arrested and made accused. The

---

[165] *Times of India*, New Delhi, 6 July 2016.
[166] (2013) 6 SCC 770.
[167] (2013) 6 SCC 770, para 54.
[168] (1983) 4 SCC 141.
[169] (1983) 4 SCC 141, para 10.

sessions court directed that eight men be set at liberty—the ninth accused Shabbir Ahmed, died in an accident one year before—noting that there was not sufficient ground to proceed against them.[170]

Delay is another tempting factor that encourages falsehood and perjury. The court has to recognize it and act accordingly. In *Ramrameshwari Devi* v. *Nirmala Devi*,[171] the Supreme Court categorically ruled that in order to curb uncalled for and frivolous litigation, the courts have to ensure that there is no incentive or motive for such litigations. The Court again expressed its anxiety like this:

> Those who indulge in immoral acts like perjury, prevarication and motivated falsehoods have to be appropriately dealt with, without which it would not be possible for any court to administer justice in the true sense and to the satisfaction of those who approach it in the hope that truth would ultimately prevail. People would have faiths in courts when they would find that truth alone triumphs in the courts.[172]

Creation of Tribunals Not Helping Either

Many tribunals and boards were created to ease the pressure on high courts but they have become just like other courts with the speed of disposal remaining equally tardy. Central Administrative Tribunals (CATs) were created for expeditious disposal of service matter disputes. But cases keep pending for 5–10 years, and the method of disposal is so ludicrous in several cases that the respondents are directed to dispose petitioners' representations and that too after keeping the case pending for several years. According to the rule, the court has to decide a matter if it comes before it. And secondly, it is a matter of common sense to wonder why an employee should move the court if the respondents are so justice-loving. They do not even comply with high court directions to dispose a case within the stipulated period. The Supreme Court, in *L. Chandra Kumar* v. *Union of India*,[173] held that judicial review is a basic feature of the Constitution and thus declared clause 2(d) of Article 323-A and clause 3(d) of Article 323-B, to the extent they oust the writ jurisdictions of

---

[170] http://indianexpress.com/article/india/india-news-india/malegaon-blast-case-mumbai-court-discharges-all-eight-accused/ (last accessed on 6 August 2016).

[171] (2011) 8 SCC 249.

[172] *Maria Margarida Sequeira Fernandes* v. *Erasmo Jack de Sequeira* (2012) 5 SCC 370, para 45.

[173] (1997) 3 SCC 261: JT (1997) 3 SC 589.

the high courts under Articles 226 and 227, and that of the Supreme Court under Article 32, unconstitutional. Since then, an appeal against CAT's judgment goes to the high court, and not directly to the Supreme Court, as was the case earlier. Earlier, in *S.P. Sampath Kumar* v. *Union of India*,[174] the apex court did not find anything unconstitutional in excluding the jurisdiction of the high court, holding that as a substitute for the high court, the tribunals are so constituted as to generate the same faith and confidence in them as the high court. Now, after *L. Chandra Kumar* v. *UOI*,[175] there is no justification to have CAT as the Supreme Court has struck at its very *raison d'etre*. Now three tiers contribute to delays, but the government is not winding it up, despite a cabinet decision in this regard, under pressures from lawyers, and also from bureaucrats and judges who find sanctuaries post-retirement. So, protecting the vested interest gets preponderance over ensuring justice.

However, still there are many tribunals like Telecom Disputes Settlement and Appellate Tribunal (TDSAT), Securities Appellate Tribunal (SAT), Competition Appellate Tribunal Armed Forces Tribunal (CATAFT), National Green Tribunal (NGT), the orders of which are challenged only in the Supreme Court, not the high court. Though in case of each of these tribunals, the concerned act provides that the presiding officer would be a person who has been a judge of the Supreme Court or a chief justice of a high court, in the case of CAT, the Act provides that the presiding officer would be a former high court judge. However, the dilution or elevation of status of the presiding officer does not vanquish the logic that the writ jurisdiction of the high court is a basic feature of the Constitution.

Similarly, to reduce the load on high courts, the Customs Excise and Gold Control Appellate Tribunal (CEGAT) was established in 1981–2 to hear appeals under the Central Excise, Customs and Gold Control Act. It was rechristened as Customs, Excise and Service Tax Appellate Tribunal (CESTAT). Today, thousands of cases are pending in CESTAT, Mumbai, and come up for hearing after eight to nine years. Similar is the case with the Foreign Exchange Regulation Act (FERA) Board, which was constituted in 1973–4 to hear appeals under the Foreign Exchange Regulation Act—cases do not get listed for 10 to 15 years. Frequent transfers of the members of the tribunal and the board cause delays as partially heard matters have to be reheard on the transfers of members. Curiously, the Supreme Court itself does

[174] AIR (1987) SC 386: (1987) 1 SCC 124.
[175] AIR (1997) SC 1125: (1997) 3 SCC 261.

not observe the principle of delivering quick judgements. In 2003, the Centre of India Trade Unions, in an open letter to the CJI, sought his intervention in a case in which judgement was pending for over two years after the hearing was complete, on 1 May 2001. The case pertained to the Employees' Pension Scheme, a social security measure. Justice Ruma Paul, a former judge of the Supreme Court, has commented:

> [T]he 'tribunalisation' of justice has not worked in India. In 1997, the Supreme Court acknowledged, 'Tribunals have been functioning inefficiently.... The situation at present is that different tribunals constituted under different enactments are administered by different administrative departments of the Central and the State Governments. The problem is compounded by the fact that some tribunals have been created pursuant to the Central legislations and some others have been created by State legislations'. More than a decade later, if one is to go by the Report of the Chairperson of the Intellectual Property Appellate Board submitted to the Madras High Court recently, the situation has not improved.
>
> The litigant, in whose apparent interest tribunalisation has and is taking place, has been the worst sufferer. When most of the rights are claimed by citizens against the Government how can people have faith in a body if even one member is perceived as being part of the Government? The credibility of the judicial process comes from the office of the judge and his or her individual and institutional reputation for independence.
>
> Additionally, every decision of a tribunal is subject either to appeal before a high court or the Supreme Court and subject to judicial review. This has only meant further delay and expense for a litigant because of additional rounds of litigation. Some brave high court judges have tried with faultless reasoning to set right this constitutional anomaly in their decisions but have unfortunately failed to convince the Supreme Court up till now.[176]

Adjournments: The Major Irritant

Judges, Lawyers, and Influential Litigants are Responsible for the Avoidable Bane

Adjournment is the biggest bane of the Indian legal system. Lawyers seek repeated adjournments. What is more amazing is that the adjournments are

---

[176] Justice Ruma Paul, 'An Independent Judiciary', in *Choosing Hammurabi: Debates on Judicial Appointments*, edited by Satya Paul (Gurgaon: LexisNexis, 2013), pp. 23–4.

granted. This is because several judges do not come to the court prepared. If they do not go through the case files before they come to court, they are not aware of the pleadings of the parties, the issues they have to decide on, and the law applicable to the case. Thus, they are not capable of controlling the proceedings of the court and grant adjournments just on the asking or on the slightest pretext. The Supreme Court observed in the *Lt. Col. S.J. Chaudhary* v. *State (Delhi Administration)*[177] that not only should the trial proceed from day-to-day, but also that an advocate, who accepts a brief in a criminal case, is duty-bound to attend the trial daily, otherwise he will be guilty of breach of professional duty. Lawyers are notorious for delaying trials/suits when their cases are weak. They resort to strikes, the judgement of the Supreme Court stating that they have no right to strike notwithstanding.[178]

Because of such adjournments Sheila Barse, in 1988, described the Supreme Court as dysfunctional and wanted to withdraw her petition. She filed her petition on 9 September 1985 under Article 32 against the Union of India and 24 states, charging them with violating the Children's Act by illegally detaining 1,400 children below 16 years in jails. She appeared before the court in person. By 22 July 1988, 24 adjournments were granted. Of them only one was due to Barse's illness. She finally made a submission that 'an honest-to-goodness final hearing date should be set up or I should be allowed to withdraw the petition from the court'. She was snubbed by the court and taken out of the case.

When Professor D.C. Wadhwa filed a petition in the Supreme Court on 16 January 1984 against the ordinance rule in Bihar, it did not come up for hearing after its admission for over two years. Wadhwa published his book *Re-Promulgation of Ordinances: A Fraud on the Constitution of India* on 15 August 1983,[179] in which he presented detailed and comprehensive evidence about the extension of hundreds of ordinances in Bihar. The book created a sensation and there was a debate in the Parliament (Rajya Sabha) on 22 December 1983. Then Wadhwa filed a petition and annexed his book to it—the first Brandeis Brief ever filed in India. But even such a sensitive and well-publicized case did not come up for hearing and on every date its serial number in the list slid down further. Some commentators even wrote that the case was not being heard as Chief Justice Y.V. Chandrachud was

[177] (1984) 1 SCC 722: AIR (1984) SC 618.

[178] *Harish Uppal (Ex-Capt.)* v. *Union of India* (2003) 2 SCC 45.

[179] D.C. Wadhwa, *Re-Promulgation of Ordinances: A Fraud on the Constitution of India*, Gokhale Institute of Politics and Economics, Pune: Vedpal Law House, Indore, 1983.

scared of the government. In fact, it did not come up for hearing during his tenure. When Justice P.N. Bhagwati took over as the CJI, he passed an order that this case would be listed first when the Constitution Bench was constituted. But when it was constituted it did not figure as the first case. Wadhwa was so agitated that he told Justice Bhagwati in open court that he (Bhagwati J) had committed contempt of his own court by not complying with his own order and wanted to know where he should file the contempt petition. When asked whether he knew the consequences of what he was saying, Wadhwa replied that he knew and was prepared to go to jail, where he would read and write, which were his only hobbies. Then Justice Bhagwati pacified him.[180] Ultimately the case was heard and the judgement was delivered on 20 December 1986 which became a landmark.[181] It is said that both Justice Chandrachud and Justice Bhagwati had their eyes on the post of president or vice-president, and so they did not want to be on the wrong side of the government. The Supreme Court, in *Shiv Cotex* v. *Tirgun Auto Plast (P) Ltd,*[182] has itself likened adjournments to cancer which corrodes the entire body of the justice delivery system.

Judges control the courts and they can act tough by refusing adjournments. Granting adjournments reflects on the incompetence of the judge. However, lawyers are to blame more for delays, as they virtually act as the villain of the piece. One of the parties is invariably interested in prolonging the trial and lawyers adopt dilatory and other reprehensible tactics. It is only in some exceptional cases that both parties want an expeditious trial. Protracted litigation is an incentive to the advocate, for example, in Land Acquisition Act cases where high rates of interest are available for delayed payments. Though they are supposed to protect the interests of their clients, they must not forget that they are the officers of the court that is supposed to help it arrive at justice. So, a fine balance is to be struck. However, instead of striking a blow for justice they virtually behave like scofflaws.

Sometimes, it appears that the legal system could function more efficiently without lawyers. There are lawyers, including eminent ones, who feign illness or even give false medical certificates to get adjournments and are found present in other courts. The court should send them to jail for perjury. In such cases, senior counsel will sacrifice their juniors without compunction that the junior sought adjournment without his/her instruction. So, the court

[180] D.C. Wadhwa shared it with the author on 3 October 2004 at Pune in a personal interview.
[181] *D.C. Wadhwa* v. *State of Bihar* (1987) 1 SCC 378: AIR (1987) SC 579.
[182] (2011) 9 SCC 678.

should never grant adjournment without written request by the counsel. The tendency in some lawyers to instigate frivolous litigation is also responsible for delays in trials.

It is well-nigh impossible to get adjournment in developed countries. If an advocate has cases listed in two cities, s/he uses chartered flight to reach the other court in time as adjournment is not granted, while in India, it is granted at the drop of a hat. Even the express provision in this regard is not followed. The Civil Procedure Code provides that more than three adjournments are not to be granted, but it is being granted. Busy lawyers seldom refuse any briefs because of dearth of time. They seek adjournments on false and flimsy grounds because they are engaged in different courts and also to help their clients who want to prolong. Nevertheless, lawyers do not accept their role in causing delays and unconscionably blame judges who grant it. They argue that they only make prayers but it is judges who grant adjournments. It is like saying that if someone jumps red lights they are not to blame as it is for the traffic constables to catch and penalize them. Renowned lawyers get adjournment without much problem. Neelam and Sanjay Krishnamoorthy, who lost both their children in the Uphaar Cinema fire in Delhi on 13 June 1997 and have been fighting for justice since then have written:

> We have noticed that the wealthy and powerful with the means to engage high profile counsels (sic) do so not only to avail their legal skills and expertise, but also to take advantage of the many courtesies accorded to them by the courts. By now, we can say with a fair degree of certainty that if a high profile lawyer seeks adjournment citing even the most frivolous of reasons, he or she will be assured the adjournment will be granted without any fuss.
>
> There were instructions that the matter be taken up on day-to-day basis. It was listed thirty-seven times between January and September 2008, but was not heard for more than fifteen minutes on each occasion. During this period the Ansals (the main accused) were granted bail.[183]

They have also mentioned how a senior counsel got adjournment by lying to the apex court:

> Predictably, the counsels (sic) for the accused were not available to argue the matter once bail had been granted, and they continued to seek adjournments....

---

[183] Neelam Krishnamoorthy and Sanjay Krishnamoorthy, *Trial By Fire* (Gurgaon: Penguin Random House India, 2016), pp. 154–5.

The counsels' pattern became extremely clear to us—they were available for quick completion of arguments when their clients were behind bars, but they did the vanishing trick once they were granted bail. Eight adjournments were sought by the counsel for Sushil Ansal in span of two years between 2010 and 2012. In May 2011, an adjournment was sought on the grounds that the senior counsel appearing for Sushil Ansal, who was leading the matter, was unwell. However, as per media reports, he was arguing a high-profile case in the Patiala House Courts that day.[184]

This senior counsel was Ram Jethmalani who was arguing the case of Kanimozhi, an accused in the 2-G scam. He was guilty of perjury, but no action was taken against him. However, he is not the only one to do so. Many lawyers do it without any qualms. If they are prosecuted for perjury and sent to jail, it will mark the death knell for the abominable practice of seeking adjournments. However, it is true that lawyers do not seek adjournments in those courts which are strict and do not grant it. Judges allow prayer for adjournments because they have not taken the pains of going through the brief. Some judges do not bother to read briefs in advance as they anticipate that adjournment may be asked for. The scourge of adjournment on the ground of the non-availability of advocate can easily be resolved by having a system of two lawyers for every brief so that the other one steps in if the lead counsel is not available for whatever reason.

There are not many cases which are technical and ticklish, where some important principle is to be decided. The majority can be decided on the basis of common sense within a few days. In 2002, the chief justice of the Andhra Pradesh High Court, Justice S.B. Sinha, had an exhilarating experience. He had gone to a subdivision on the occasion of the 150th anniversary of the local court. There he discovered that around the time the court was set up, that is, around 150 years ago, the *pradhan* (Head) of a village in that particular subdivision, adjudicated the disputes of the villagers, and the practice continued even after the setting up of the court. In one case, an aggrieved party moved the court challenging his order. The court inquired into it and found that most of the judgements delivered by the pradhan were legally correct.[185]

The Supreme Court has bewailed time and again over the tendency to grant adjournments, as it is the bounden duty of the court to scuttle any

---

[184] Krishnamoorthy and Krishnamoorthy, *Trial By Fire*, p. 160.
[185] Justice Sinha narrated it at a seminar at Patna in 2003 and later gave details to the author on phone.

design to delay and derail, as unscrupulous lawyers do more often than not. In *Gurnaib Singh* v. *State of Punjab*,[186] it said:

> We are compelled to proceed to reiterate the law and express our anguish pertaining to the manner in which the trial was conducted as it depicts a very disturbing scenario. As is demonstrable from the record, the trial was conducted in an extremely haphazard and piecemeal manner. Adjournments were granted on a mere asking. The cross-examination of the witnesses was deferred without recording any special reason and dates were given after a long gap. The mandate of the law and the views expressed by this Court from time to time appears to have been totally kept at bay. The learned trial Judge, as is perceptible, seems to have ostracised from his memory that a criminal trial has its own gravity and sanctity. In this regard, we may refer with profit to the pronouncement in *Talab Haji Hussain* v. *Madhukar Purshottam Mondka*[187] wherein it has been stated that an accused person by his conduct cannot put a fair trial into jeopardy, for it is the primary and paramount duty of the criminal courts to ensure that the risk to fair trial is removed and trials are allowed to proceed smoothly without any interruption or obstruction.

Earlier, in *Swaran Singh* v. *State of Punjab*,[188] the Court was forthright and trenchant:

> It has become more or less a fashion to have a criminal case adjourned again and again till the witness tires and gives up. It is the game of unscrupulous lawyers to get adjournments for one excuse or the other till a witness is won over or is tired. Not only is a witness threatened, he is abducted, he is maimed, he is done away with, or even bribed. There is no protection for him. In adjourning the matter without any valid cause a court unwittingly becomes party to miscarriage of justice.[189]

The Court went on to comment that if the criminal justice system is to be put on a proper pedestal, the system cannot be left in the hands of unscrupulous lawyers and the sluggish state machinery, and stressed on the need to monitor all trials properly by linking all courts: district courts, and subordinate courts, to the high court with a computer to keep a proper check on the adjournments and recording of evidence.

---

[186] (2013) 7 SCC 108.
[187] AIR (1958) SC 376.
[188] (2000) 5 SCC 668.
[189] (2000) 5 SCC 668, para 37.

In *State of U.P.* v. *Shambu Nath Singh*,[190] the apex court excoriated the practice of court, adjourning a case in spite of the presence of the witnesses willing to be examined fully. The Court expressed its anguish without mincing words:

> Witnesses tremble on getting summons from courts ... not because they fear examination or cross-examination in courts but because they fear that they might not be examined at all for several days.... The witnesses, perforce, keep aside their avocation and go to the courts and wait and wait for hours to be told at the end of the day to come again and wait and wait like that. This is the infelicitous scenario in many of the courts in India so far as witnesses are concerned. It is high time that trial courts should regard witnesses as guests invited ... for helping such courts with their testimony for reaching judicial findings. But the malady is that the predicament of the witnesses is worse than the litigants themselves.[191]

The Court directed:

> We make it abundantly clear that if a witness is present in court he must be examined on that day. The court must know that most of the witnesses could attend the court only at heavy cost to them, after keeping aside their own avocation. Certainly they incur suffering and loss of income. The meagre amount of bhatta (allowance) which a witness may be paid by the court is generally a poor solace for the financial loss incurred by him. It is a sad plight in the trial courts that witnesses who are called through summons or other processes stand at the doorstep from morning till evening only to be told at the end of the day that the case is adjourned to another day. This primitive practice must be reformed by the presiding officers of the trial courts and it can be reformed by everyone provided the presiding officer concerned has a commitment towards duty.[192]

In *N.G. Dastane* v. *Shrikant S. Shind*,[193] the Supreme Court held that seeking adjournments for postponing the examination of witnesses who were present, without making other arrangements for examining such witnesses is a dereliction of the duty that an advocate owed to the Court which amounts to professional misconduct. The Court was pained to see

---

[190] (2001) 5 SCC 667.
[191] (2001) 5 SCC 667, para 1.
[192] (2001) 5 SCC 667, para 10.
[193] AIR (2001) SC 2028 (2001) 3 SCALE 619 (2001) 3 SCR 442.

how the two advocates sought repeated adjournments to derail the course of justice:

> We are much grieved, if not peeved, in noticing how two advocates succeeded in tormenting a witness by seeking numerous adjournments for cross-examining him in the Court of a judicial magistrate. On all those days the witness had to be present perforce and at considerable cost to him. It became a matter of deep concern to us when we noticed that the judicial magistrate had, on all such occasions, obliged the advocates by granting such adjournments on the mere asking to the incalculable inconvenience and sufferings of the witness.[194]

However, courts seem little bothered and the anguished observations of the apex court seems to have made little impact either on judges or on lawyers. In *Vinod Kumar* v. *State of Punjab*,[195] the Supreme Court bemoaned again that despite series of judgments of this Court, the practice of granting adjournments continues:

> If one is asked a question, what afflicts the legally requisite criminal trial in its conceptual eventuality in this country the two reasons that may earn the status of phenomenal signification are, first, procrastination of trial due to non-availability of witnesses when the trial is in progress and second, unwarranted adjournments sought by the counsel conducting the trial and the unfathomable reasons for acceptation of such prayers for adjournments by the trial courts, despite a statutory command under Section 309 of the Code of Criminal Procedure, 1973 … and series of pronouncements by this Court. What was a malady at one time, with the efflux of time, has metamorphosed into malignancy. What was a mere disturbance once has become a disorder, a diseased one, at present.[196]

Speaking for the bench, Justice Dipak Misra said:

> It is imperative if the examination-in-chief is over, the cross-examination should be completed on the same day. If the examination of a witness continues till late hours the trial can be adjourned to the next day for cross-examination. It is inconceivable in law that the cross-examination should be deferred for such a long time. It is anathema to the concept of proper and fair trial. The duty of the court is to see that not only the interest of the accused as per law is protected but also the societal and collective interest is safe-guarded. It is

---

[194] AIR (2001) SC 2028 (2001) 3 SCALE 619 (2001) 3 SCR 442, para 1.
[195] AIR (2015) SC 1206: (2015) 3 SCC 220 (decided on 21 January 2015).
[196] AIR (2015) SC 1206: (2015) 3 SCC 220, para 1.

distressing to note that despite series of judgments of this Court, the habit of granting adjournment, really an ailment, continues. How long shall we say, 'Awake! Arise!'. There is a constant discomfort. Therefore, we think it appropriate that the copies of the judgment be sent to the learned Chief Justices of all the High Courts for circulating the same among the learned trial Judges with a command to follow the principles relating to trial in a requisite manner and not to defer the cross-examination of a witness at their pleasure or at the leisure of the defence counsel, for it eventually makes the trial an apology for trial and compels the whole society to suffer chicanery. Let it be remembered that law cannot allowed to be lonely; a destitute.[197]

It speaks volumes about the desperation of the apex court that despite Article 141 of the Constitution which declares categorically that the law declared by the Supreme Court would be binding on all courts, the Court has to circulate it to trial judges with a command to follow the principles laid down. It raises many questions as to why no action was taken against any judge for not following the directions given earlier by the Court in different cases. Besides, ignorance of law is no excuse even for the common man. So, how can judges feign ignorance of any judgment by the apex court, more so when they are provided law journals of reported cases and even online subscriptions? Ironically, the Supreme Court and high courts are themselves liberal in granting adjournments, but who will chasten them?

Fix Timeframe

There is a flip side also of the court's attitude which apparently commiser-ates with litigants for not getting quick justice. This flip side is baffling and has frustrated even the noble initiatives of the Parliament. In 1999, many amendments of far reaching consequences were introduced to the Civil Procedure Code. One of it put a cap of maximum three adjournments that the courts could grant during the hearing of a suit. Another amendment fixed the timeframe for another important provision, disallowing the courts from enlarging the time granted by them for doing any 'act prescribed or allowed by the Code' beyond a maximum period of 30 days. However, the Supreme Court, in *Salem Bar Association-II* v. *Union of India*,[198] virtually nullified these amendments by interpreting this restriction as curtailing the court's power to allow more than three adjournments, and also ruled that the timeframe does not attenuate the court's inherent power to '*pass orders*

---

[197] AIR (2015) SC 1206: (2015) 3 SCC 220, para 41.
[198] (2005) 6 SCC 344.

as may be necessary for the ends of justice or to prevent abuse of process of the Court'. This interpretation is wrong and retrogressive as it derails the system. Such judgements are byproducts of the ego of the judges who think that their discretion must not be diluted. It debunks their concern for speedy justice, expressed eloquently in so many decisions quoted above. Maybe, the judge needs to be allowed some discretion in some exceptional circumstances. But such exceptions have become the rule. It is almost impossible to find even one case in the whole country in which more than three adjournments were not granted. Similarly, extending timeframe may be permissible in some rare circumstances, but the discretion is abused so much that the law becomes a dead letter and the discretion becomes the law. Further, recourse is taken to all technicalities to defeat the very purpose of any legislation. Many a time, the party, interested in prolonging the litigation, does not seek adjournment for the fourth time and produces witnesses or evidence, and thus, they stick to the rule. But having done it, they seek fresh adjournment on next dates and it is now counted afresh, though the law allows maximum three adjournments to both parties during the entire hearing.

Surprisingly, in the same judgement, the Supreme Court is also solicitous about the load of cases that increases with every new legislation. It asked the government to examine whether or not there should be a 'judicial impact assessment' whenever any bill is introduced in the Parliament or in the state legislature. The Court also suggested that the financial memorandum attached to each bill should also mention, among other things, how many courts would be required, how many judges and staff would be needed, and what would be the infrastructure necessary.

Section 35B of the Civil Procedure Code provides that if a party to the suit obtains adjournment, the court may, for reasons to be recorded, make an order requiring such party to pay to the other party such costs as would, in its opinion, be reasonably sufficient to reimburse the other party in respect of the expenses incurred by him in attending the court on that date, and payment of such costs, on the next date, shall be a condition precedent to the further prosecution of the suit by the plaintiff where he was ordered to pay, or the defence by the defendant where the defendant was ordered to pay. But this deterrent provision is almost a dead letter and the party interested in protracting the matter keeps seeking adjournments. In some cases, adjournments are granted even 20 or 30 times. Many times, even the court refuses to record evidence citing workload which is an automatic adjournment. According to the Limitation Act, the court hour is from 10 am to 4 pm with a lunch break of half-an-hour between 1:30 and 2 pm. If a party comes to file petition on the last day after 4 pm, it will not be entertained. In some states, the filing time is up to 2 pm, as decided by the respective high courts. But the court hardly sits for over three hours. Thus, not entertaining petition on the last day after the court hour, or refusal to record evidence on the ground of workload is ludicrous.

In another significant amendment, an outer time limit of 30 days for service of summons was fixed for prosecution of cases filed by litigants. The Supreme Court diluted this provision also by holding that 30 days' timeline designated only the outer timeframe within which steps must be initiated by the plaintiff to enable the court to issue the summons.[199] Thus, the time limit of serving summons within 30 days was extended indefinitely by the apex court. What is more shocking is that in this digital age, courts still follow antediluvian techniques of serving summons only through process servers, that is, delivery by hand through *baildar* (court staff), and not e-mails, couriers, or even government's speed post service as mandated in the 2002 Civil Procedure Code amendment. It was brought to the notice of the apex court during a workshop organized by its e-committee when judges of the subordinate judiciary complained that they were not able to use the modern mode of communication for lack of required amendments in the respective high court rules which still specify that summons be delivered only through process servers.[200] Justice Madan B. Lokur, then head of the Supreme Court's e-committee, had to direct registrars of the high courts to carry out the required update.

First, the effort to put a time cap by the Parliament was frustrated by the apex court, and then even the required rules were not framed by the high courts. The respondent easily manages the court server by greasing his palm. The court server reports that the respondent was not available, or if he was available, he refused to receive summons, or he received but refused to sign acknowledgement. If the court server reports that the respondent refused to receive or sign, he (court server) will be examined under Order V, Rule 19 of the Civil Procedure Code. However, there is a move to update litigants, lawyers, and other stakeholders through Short Message Service (SMS) and e-mail regarding the progress of the case and the next date of hearing or of delivery of judgement. It is also proposed to equip the court staff with a hand-held Global Positioning System (GPS) camera enabled palmtops or personal digital assistants (PDA) instruments. The PDA will track time and location of the delivery of summonses, and the recorded

---

[199] *Salem Advocate Bar Association* v. *Union of India-I*, AIR (2003) SC 189.
[200] *Times of India*, New Delhi, 18 August 2016.

data will be put online curtailing any scope of mischief that summonses were not delivered.

Another significant amendment introduced in 2002 required the filing of the written statement within 90 days from the date of the service of the summons. However, the Supreme Court again interpreted it as merely directory and not mandatory, thus taking the sting out of the law.[201] So, even the written statement is not filed within 90 days in many cases; sometimes, it is filed even after one year. However, it is true that due to this amendment, the delay is not so rampant now. The court has the discretion to impose the fine of up to 50 thousand rupees, but the court hardly uses this deterrent provision to teach a lesson to the party trying to delay.

The apex court dilutes reforms in procedures calling them handmaidens of justice. The irony is that by doing so, it blithely helps the party which tries to subvert justice by abusing the process of law and delaying the case indefinitely. Thus, the reasoning that procedures must not frustrate justice, ironically does the same as procedures are abused to frustrate justice.

The party in the wrong, uses all obstructionist shenanigans to prolong. Order VI, Rule 17 of the Civil Procedure Code provides that the court may at any stage of proceedings allow either party to alter or amend their pleadings in such manner or such terms as may be just, and all such amendments shall be made as may be necessary for the purpose of determining the real question in controversy. Thus, amendment petition is filed at the last stage, sometimes even after the case is posted for judgement, and later, even at the stage of second appeal. Similarly, under Order XLI, Rule 27, additional evidence can be filed at any stage. Further, Order VI, Rule 17 provides that no amendment shall be allowed after the trial has commenced unless the court comes to the conclusion that in spite of due diligence the party could not have raised the matter before the commencement of the trial. Substitution petitions are also filed at the last stage as the law allows it. The party interested in delay, misuses these provisions. Surprisingly, Order XX, Rule 4 provides that once the case is posted for judgement, it must be pronounced even if one of the parties dies, and though the judgement may not be binding on the judgement debtor (the loser in the case). It is incongruous with the provision of amendment which is allowed till the second appeal. So, it is the court's savoire-faire to see through whether there is a genuine disclosure of some new fact or it is just a ploy to derail.

There was no provision in the Civil Procedure Code for a final hearing or closing arguments. Sub-Rules (3A), (3C), and (3D) were inserted in Rule 2

---

[201] *Kailash* v. *Nankhu*, AIR (2005) SC 2441.

of Order XVIII which deal with the filing of written arguments and fixing of time limits for oral arguments. According to Arun Mohan, the placement of these Sub-Rules as part of Order XVIII is erroneous:

> The preceding Sub-rules refer to what are the opening statements before the recording of oral evidence and are altogether separate. While the ensuing Rules 3 to 17 & 19, all refer to recording of oral evidence. The final arguments are after, and not before, the recording of evidence has been concluded. Therefore—after the conclusion of the evidence per Order 18—a separate Order, pertaining only to the final hearing and written arguments, would have been more desirable.[202]

However, the advance filing of written arguments will benefit the legal process tremendously as the judge as well as the adversary will be prepared leaving little scope for seeking adjournments. If still adjournment is sought, it is only with the nefarious purpose to delay, which the court can always refuse. The court can also decide on the basis of written arguments, how much time to be awarded to each party for argument. Fixing equal time for each case may not be rational or practical as each case has different demands.

In civil cases, a large number of miscellaneous petitions are filed. Sometimes, it is filed by a third party even after the judgement is pronounced that they must be heard as their interest is also involved. Many a time, it is at the behest of the judgement debtor (the party which loses) so that the decree is not executed. For harassing the opposite party, the party in the wrong files first appeal if he loses, and then second appeal in the high court, and finally an SLP in the Supreme Court. If s/he finally loses from the apex court, s/he makes a third party move the court who also exhausts all appellate channels up to the Supreme Court. This makes the execution of decree extremely cumbersome.

Indian courts should learn from the system followed by the ICJ, The Hague, where everything is decided before pleadings are completed. It includes the time given for the argument to each party. Adjournment is not granted in any case. There is no division bench, but it is always the full court which sits. There are 15 judges but the quorum is 11. If any judge is absent due to inevitable reasons, s/he is supplied the copy of the written arguments. All the 15 judges write judgements and then a ratio is derived leaving little scope for any confusion.

---

[202] Arun Mohan, *Justice, Courts and Delays*, Vol. 2 (Delhi: Universal Law Publishing Co., 2009), pp. 1339–40.

Quality of Judgments

The quality of judgments is also responsible for appeals after appeals. The scope for filing appeals/revisions against a well-reasoned and legally sound judgment is not much. According to Section 2(9) of the Civil Procedure Code, a judgement is the statement given by the judge on the ground of a decree or order. A judgement is not a bland statement but a reasoned one encapsulating the details of the parties involved, their contentions, the issues, the evidence, and the principles of law considered, besides the rationale for drawing an inference and adjudicate on the dispute. The Supreme Court has said that after hearing the two sides, the judges cannot have the luxury to lean back and say, 'The suit is decreed' or 'The suit is dismissed'.[203] Reasons must be recorded for arriving at a particular conclusion. Describing the Statement of Reasons, the Supreme Court, in *Swarna Lata Ghosh* v. *H.K. Banerjee*,[204] commented that a mere order deciding the matter in dispute not supported by reasons is no judgement at all:

> In a judicial trial the Judge not only must reach a conclusion which he regards as just, but, unless otherwise permitted, by the practice of the court or by law, he must record the ultimate mental process leading from the dispute to its solution. A judicial determination of a disputed claim where substantial questions of law or fact arise is satisfactorily reached, only if it be supported by the most cogent reasons.... Recording of reasons in support of a decision of a disputed claim serves more purpose than one. It is intended to ensure that that the decision is not the result of whim or fancy, but of a judicial approach to the matter in contest: it is also intended to ensure adjudication of the matter according to law and the procedure established by law. A party to the dispute is ordinarily entitled to know the grounds on which the court has decided against him, and more so, when the judgment is subject to appeal. The appellate court will then have adequate material on which it may determine whether the facts are properly ascertained, the law has been correctly applied and the resultant decision is just.[205]

In *Union of India* v. *Madan Lal Capoor*,[206] the Supreme Court reiterated that reasons should reveal a rational nexus between the facts considered and the conclusions reached, as only in this way can opinions and decisions recorded

---

[203] *Balraj Taneja* v. *Sunil Madan* (1999) 8 SCC 396: AIR (1999) SC 381.
[204] (1969) 1 SCC 709: AIR (1969) SC 1167.
[205] (1969) 1 SCC 709: AIR (1969) SC 1167, p. 711, 1169.
[206] (1973) 2 SCC 836: AIR (1974) SC 87.

be shown to be manifestly just and reasonable. Again, in *Maharashtra State Board of Education* v. *K.S. Gandhi*,[207] the Court ruled:

> What is necessary is that the reasons are clear and explicit so as to indicate that the authority has given due consideration to the points in controversy. The need for recording reasons is greater in a case where the order is passed at the original stage. The appellate or the revisional authority, if it affirms such an order, need not give separate reasons. If the appellate or revisional authority disagrees, the reasons must be contained in the order under challenge.... It also excludes the chances to reach arbitrary, whimsical or capricious decision or conclusion.... The recording of reasons is also an assurance that the authority concerned consciously applied its mind to the facts on record.[208]

In *State of West Bengal* v. *Atul Krishna Shaw*,[209] it said that reasoned decision is not only for the purpose of showing that the citizen is receiving justice, but also a valid discipline on the Tribunal itself, and so, statement of reasons is one of the essentials of justice. In *Rupan Deol Bajaj* v. *Kanwar Pal Singh Gill*,[210] it held that reasons introduce clarity and minimize chances of arbitrariness. In *Hindustan Times Ltd.* v. *Union of India*,[211] the Supreme Court criticized the Delhi High Court for dismissing the petition *in limine* and observed that the reasons should have been recorded:

> Obligation to give reasons introduces clarity and excludes or at any rate minimises the chances of arbitrariness and the higher forum can test the correctness of those reasons. It becomes difficult for this Court in all such cases to remit the matters to the High Court inasmuch as by the time the cases reach this Court, several years would have passed.

In an article On Writing Judgments, Justice Michael Kirby of Australia[212] has approached the problem from the point of view of the litigant, the legal profession, the subordinate courts/tribunals, the brother Judges and Judges' own conscience. To the litigant, the duty of the Judge is to uphold his own integrity and let the losing party know why he lost the case. The legal profession is entitled to have it demonstrated that the Judge had the correct principles in mind, had properly applied them and is entitled to examine the body of the judgment for the learning and precedent that they provide and for the

---

207 (1991) 2 SCC 716: (1991) 1 SCR 772.
208 (1991) 2 SCC 716: (1991) 1 SCR 772, p. 38
209 1991 (Supp 1) SCC 414: AIR (1990) SC 2205.
210 (1995) 6 SCC 194: AIR (1996) SC 309.
211 (1998) 2 SCC 242: AIR (1998) SC 688.
212 (1990) Vol. 64 *Australian Law Journal*, p. 691.

reassurance of the quality of the judiciary which is still the centre-piece of our administration of justice. It does not take long for the profession to come to know, including through written pages of published judgments, the lazy Judge, the Judge prone to errors of fact, etc. The reputational considerations are important for the exercise of appellate rights, for the Judges' own self-discipline, for attempts at improvement and the maintenance of the integrity and quality of our judiciary. From the point of view of other Judges, the benefit that accrues to the lower hierarchy of Judges and tribunals is of utmost importance. Justice Asprey of Australia has even said in *Pettit* v. *Dankley*[213] that the failure of the Court to give reasons is an encroachment upon the right of appeal given to a litigant. In our view, the satisfaction which a reasoned judgment gives to the losing party or his lawyer is the test of a good judgment. Disposal of cases is no doubt important but quality of the judgment is equally, if not more, important.[214]

The Supreme Court of India has reiterated the need to record reasons in several other cases.[215] Lord Denning M.R., in *Breen* v. *Amalgamated Engineering Union*,[216] also observed that the giving of reasons is one of the fundamentals of good administration. Justice Kirby wrote:

The legal profession is entitled to have it demonstrated that the Judge had the correct principles in mind, had properly applied them and is entitled to examine the body of the judgment for the learning and precedent that they provide and for the reassurance for the quality of the judiciary which is still the centre-piece of our administration of justice. It does not take long for the profession to come to know, including through written pages of written judgments, the lazy Judge, the Judge prone to errors of facts, etc. The reputational considerations are important for the exercise of appellate rights, for the Judges' own self-discipline, for attempts at improvement and the maintenance of the integrity and quality of our judiciary. From the point of view of other Judges, the benefit that accrues to the lower hierarchy of Judges and tribunals is of utmost importance. Justice Asprey of Australia has even said in *Pettit* v. *Dankley*[217]

---

[213] (1971) 1 NSWLR 376 (CA).

[214] (1971) 1 NSWLR 376 (CA), pp. 247, 691.

[215] *Fauja Singh* v. *Jaspal Kapoor* (1996) 4 SCC 461: (1996) 4 SCALE 326; *State of Orissa* v. *Dhaniram Luhar* (2004) 5 SCC 568: AIR (2004) SC 1794; *State of Rajasthan* v. *Sohan Lal*, (2004) 5 SCC 573: JT (2004) 5 SC 388: (2004) 5 SCALE 86; *Union of India* v. *Essel Mining & Industries Ltd* (2005) 6 SCC 675: JT (2005) 7 SC 424.

[216] (1971) 1 ALL ER 1148.

[217] (1971) 1 NSWLR 376 (CA).

that the failure of a Court to give reasons is an encroachment upon the right of appeal given to a litigant.[218]

The bad quality of judgment is a major provocation for filing appeals. Incompetent judges dispose of cases in a perfunctory manner without recording reasons for reaching a conclusion. Such poor judgments can easily be inveighed legally. Poor quality of disposal and the high probability of dragging the case for years and decades in appeals are great incentives for moving higher courts in appeal. Ironically, the Indian Supreme Court which is so effusive in exhortations to give reasons for every judgment, hardly writes a single sentence while dismissing or granting leave to an SLP or sometimes even a statutory appeal.

Symptom of Laggard States

In the developed countries, cases are decided within a few months and the entire time for disposal is not more than two years even if a case is fought from the lowest to the apex court. Delay in disposal is symptomatic of underdeveloped countries. Countries notorious for judicial delays do not attract foreign investments. In August 2003, ex-CJI, B.N. Kirpal, appearing in a New York Court for a Japanese firm that had a dispute with ICICI Bank, preferred its trial in the US, not in India, on the grounds that in India the trial would take at least 20 years. Having presided over the system, Kirpal knew what it means to fight a case in an Indian court and to protect the interest of his client, he argued unabashedly to avoid litigation in Indian courts: 'It is anybody's guess when the case will be finally decided'. The New York Supreme Court accepted his plea but the Appellate Division reversed this decision granting ICICI Bank's plea, that the dispute could well be tried in Indian courts.[219]

Alas, general litigants in India have not been able to invent any mechanism to avoid litigation in Indian courts, nor are their lawyers so privileged to speak about this pungent truth in court, as it would invite criminal contempt of court. Of course, Kirpal could make such a statement even in India with impunity as the law of contempt is applied selectively.

---

[218] Justice Michael Kirby, 'On Writing Judgments', *Australian Law Journal*, vol. 64 (1990): 691, Arun Mohan, *Justice, Courts and Delays*, Vol. 2 (Delhi: Universal Law Publishing Co. Pvt. Ltd, 2009), p. 1400.

[219] *CJ v. CJ in New York*: 'US Court Rules Let Indian Courts Decide', *Indian Express*, New Delhi, 16 June 2004.

In 1995, the Third Circuit of the United States Court of Appeals held that the delay in the judicial system was so *'profound and extreme'* that a remedy before an Indian court was clearly inadequate.[220] It is said that if the legal system could be fixed, there would be an increment of 1 per cent in Gross domestic product (GDP).[221]

Social Watch India (Citizens Report on Governance and Development, 2004) identified the following major problems that have fettered the judicial system in India:

1. Extreme delays in the passing judgements
2. High pendency of cases
3. The labyrinth of antediluvian court procedures
4. Perennial adjournments
5. Miscarriage of justice in the form of a low rate of conviction (some estimates peg the rate of conviction at a mere 6 to 7 per cent)
6. Secrecy surrounding the procedures for assessing the competence or the efficiency of the judges
7. Lack of appropriate standard of remuneration of judges, especially those in the subordinate courts

It is true that court and investigation procedures are almost as outmoded as during the pre-independence days when Justice Sir Cecil Walsh of the Allahabad High Court was constrained to comment: 'Whereas the English detective begins with his available witnesses, and works his way up to the discovery of truth, the Indian sub-inspector begins with the accused, and from him works his way up to witnesses.'[222]

Trials in Lalit Narain Mishra and Chief Justice A.N. Ray's Cases

Investigation is generally shoddy and tardy, and sometimes even in the most sensational cases it does not move at all. How slow moves the wheels of justice is evident from two sensational bomb attack cases of 1975—one, successful against Lalit Narain Mishra, the then minister for Railways on 2 January, and another, unsuccessful one on the then CJI A.N. Ray, near the Supreme Court in New Delhi on 25 March when he was returning home. Anand Margis

---

[220] Abhinav Chandrachud, 'Not above the Law', *Times of India*, 7 April 2009.

[221] Bibek Debroy, '324 Years, 100 Days', *Indian Express*, 26 October 2009.

[222] Chandr Mohan Upadhyay, *Human Rights in Pre-trial Detention APH Publishing* (New Delhi: APH Publishing, 1999), p. 377.

were accused in both cases. The case pertaining to the assassination of Lalit Narayan Mishra epitomizes the syndrome of delay. Mishra was fatally injured in an explosion in a public meeting at Samastipur and succumbed to injuries the next day. On 9 December 2014, that is, almost 40 years after the assassination, the Karkardooma court of Delhi convicted four men—Santoshananda Avadhuta (75), Sudevananda Avadhuta (79), Gopalji (73), and Advocate Ranjan Dwivedi (66); the first three convicts being Anand Margis.[223] The trial in the case of Mishra's murder was transferred from Samastipur to a Delhi court in December 1979 on the orders of the Supreme Court. The pace of the trial was annoyingly slow; many important witnesses had to be dropped either because they remained untraced or because they did not come forward to depose.

The accused moved the Supreme Court for quashing the trial on the ground of delay. Dismissing the petitions on 12 August 2012, that is, over 37 years after the incident, the Court held that the length of the delay is not sufficient in itself to warrant a finding that the accused was deprived of the right to a speedy trial, as it is only one of the factors to be considered, and must be weighed against other factors. The Court ruled:

[A]mong factors to be considered in determining whether the right to speedy trial of the accused is violated, the length of delay is least conclusive. While there is authority that even very lengthy delays do not give rise to a per se conclusion of violation of constitutional rights, there is also authority that long enough delay could constitute per se violation of right to speedy trial. In our considered view, the delay tolerated varies with the complexity of the case, the manner of proof as well as gravity of the alleged crime. This, again, depends on case to case basis. There cannot be universal rule in this regard. It is a balancing process while determining as to whether the accused's right to speedy trial has been violated or not. The length of delay in and itself, is not a weighty factor.[224]

The Court recorded that more than 30 judges tried the case at one stage or the other and they did their best to see that the trial is completed at the earliest, and so they are not to blame. It gave directions for day to day hearing of the case even though such a direction was given earlier also:

We certainly say that our system has not failed, but, accused was successful in dragging on the proceedings to a stage where, if it is drawn further, it may

---

[223] *Times of India*, New Delhi, 10 December 2014.
[224] *Ranjan Dwivedi* v. *CBI Through Director General* (2012) 8 SCC 495, para 21.

snap the Justice Delivery System.... The system has done its best, but, has not achieved the expected result and certainly, will not fit into the category of cases where (late) N.A. Palkhiwala, one of the most outstanding Senior Advocates in the Country had said that '... the law may or may not be an ass, but in India it is certainly a snail and our cases proceed at a pace which would be regarded as unduly slow in a community of snails.... Therefore, in our view at this stage the one and the only direction that requires to be issued is to direct the learned trial judge to take up the case on day to day basis and conclude the proceedings as early as possible, without granting unnecessary and unwarranted adjournments.[225]

It is an eloquent commentary on the criminal justice administration that it took 40 years for the trial court to decide despite repeated directions for a day-to-day hearing and that too when the victim happened to be a powerful Union minister.

In Justice Ray's case, to his good luck, the bomb did not explode. The four accused—Santosanand Avadhoot, Sudevanand Avadhoot, Ranjan Dwivedi, and Vikram—were common to both cases. Vikram turned approver subsequently. The sessions court convicted the three accused in November 1976 on the testimony of the approver in the attack on Justice Ray, who himself was examined as a witness. The convicts immediately moved the Delhi High Court against their conviction where the appeal is pending since then.

Participating in a debate in 2002 in the Rajya Sabha, Jethmalani, MP, commented wryly, 'in 1975, L. N. Mishra was murdered. The case is still going on in the trial court. Who can have respect for this kind of system?'[226] Hemant Shahi, an MLA in Bihar, was murdered in 1991 and the police could never file the charge sheet.

Dilatory Tactics and Systemic Failures

Affluent and influential litigants use every provision of law to delay and derail the trial or the suit by challenging every order of every court in higher courts until the channel of appeal or revision is exhausted. In criminal trials, the accused will first challenge the cognisance taken by the magistrate in the high court. If it is rejected, he will move the high court for quashing once charges are framed. It takes a long time. Once revision petition is filed, the trial does

[225] *Ranjan Dwivedi* v. *CBI Through Director General*, para 25.
[226] CJI attacked in '75, Appeal Still Pending in HC', *Times of India*, New Delhi, 11 September 2006.

not proceed even though there may not be any stay. Generally, the high court takes years to dispose of revision petitions. Sometimes they move even the Supreme Court. They exploit all legal provisions to delay the trial so that the doctor and the investigative officer are transferred or they retire or die a natural death. Once they are transferred, it is difficult to trace them. These procedural latches must be plugged by amending the law. It must be seen that the rights given to accused are not abused to derail the process of law. The high court can use its inherent power to impose penalties on vexatious litigants, but this power is seldom used.

Time taken in framing charges after the charge sheet is filed is the failure of the whole system including the judiciary. Police papers are not supplied to the accused for months and years together. There is no official mechanism to do it expeditiously, and neither the government nor the high court or the Supreme Court has taken cognisance of the problem. If the judge is conscientious, s/he takes personal interest and gets them served. The problem can be solved just by providing one photocopy machine and stationery and assigning one clerk to oversee that it is done without delay. Another major reason behind delay in criminal trials is the non-production of witnesses. Firstly, summonses are not served to them in time. It is the duty of the investigating officer, that is, the police, to produce witnesses. Police in India is inefficient and corrupt enough to be managed easily. However, it cannot be denied that since investigation has not been separated from the law and order despite several recommendations of the police commission and also the direction of the Supreme Court,[227] policemen are generally too preoccupied with law and order problem and security of VIPs, finding little time for these things. Further, there is no judicial police in India as countries like France and Mexico have. Moreover, witnesses are treated like dregs of the society even though they come to assist the court. They are not even offered a glass of water. If the judge is conscientious, s/he takes initiative and police papers are served and witnesses are produced.

Civil suits crawl, not walk, much less run, and take decades to get resolved. The situation has come to such a pass that money suits are not being filed. Instead, criminal cases are filed by adding some criminal intent or offence. The party interested in delay would file an amendment petition on some ground, for example, that certain facts have been missed. Now, the opposite party would file rejoinder and then the hearing would follow. If it is not

---

[227] *Prakash Singh* v. *Union of India* (2006) 8 SCC 1 (2006) 9 SCALE 444, MANU/SC/8516/2006.

allowed, civil revision will be filed in the high court. It will take years. Section 35A of the Civil Procedure Code, 1908, lays down that if a court finds that the case dismissed by it was vexatious, it is empowered to award compensatory costs to the innocent party; however, such costs shall not exceed a grand sum of Rs 3,000. This amount was fixed in 1908, when it was a big amount that could have deterrent effect. The figure has not been revised, huge depreciation notwithstanding. In the U.K., courts award cost on the 'cost follow the event' formula, under which the losing party is directed to bear the entire cost incurred by the winning party. Since the cost is pretty high, it disincentivizes frivolous litigation.

The Supreme Court put its anxiety on record when the Sahara Group adopted the nastiest of shenanigans to prolong the litigation and escape punishment, and suggested to the legislature to make a law that the party which has won must be compensated by the party which lost, in order to discourage frivolous litigation:

> A lot of these hearings consumed this Court's full working day. Hearing of the main case, consumed one full part, of the entire summer vacation (of the Supreme Court) of the year 2012. For the various orders passed by us, including the order dated 31.8.2012 (running into 269 printed pages) and the present order (running into 205 printed pages), substantial Judge hours were consumed. In this country, judicial orders are prepared, beyond Court hours, or on non-working days. It is apparent, that not a hundred, but hundreds of Judge hours, came to be spent in the instant single Sahara Group litigation, just at the hands of the Supreme Court. This abuse of the judicial process, needs to be remedied. We are, therefore of the considered view, that the legislature needs to give a thought, to a very serious malady, which has made strong inroads into the Indian judicial system.
>
> The Indian judicial system is grossly afflicted, with frivolous litigation. Ways and means need to be evolved, to deter litigants from their compulsive obsession, towards senseless and ill-considered claims. One needs to keep in mind, that in the process of litigation, there is an innocent sufferer on the other side, of every irresponsible and senseless claim. He suffers long drawn anxious periods of nervousness and restlessness, whilst the litigation is pending, without any fault on his part. He pays for the litigation, from out of his savings (or out of his borrowings), worrying that the other side may trick him into defeat, for no fault of his.... The suggestion to the legislature is to formulate a mechanism, that anyone who initiates and continues a litigation senselessly, pays for the same. It is suggested that the legislature should consider the introduction of a 'Code of Compulsory Costs'.... What is sought to be redressed is a habituation, to press illegitimate claims. This practice and pattern is so rampant, that in most cases, disputes which ought

to have been settled in no time at all, before the first Court of incidence, are prolonged endlessly, for years and years, and from Court to Court, upto the highest Court.

This abuse of the judicial process is not limited to any particular class of litigants. The State and its agencies litigate endlessly upto the highest Court, just because of the lack of responsibility, to take decisions.... And there are some litigants who continue to pursue senseless and ill-considered claims, to somehow or the other, defeat the process of law. The present case is a classic illustration of what we wish to express. Herein the regulating authority has had to suffer litigation from Court to Court, incurring public expense in its defence, against frivolous litigation. Every order was consistently and systematically disobeyed. Every order passed by the SEBI was assailed before the next higher authority, and then before this Court. Even though High Courts have no jurisdiction, in respect of issues regulated by the SEBI Act, some matters were taken to the High Court of Judicature at Allahabad (before its Lucknow Bench). Every such endeavour resulted in failure, and was also sometimes, accompanied with strictures. Even after the matter had concluded, after the controversy had attained finality, the judicial process is still being abused, for close to two years. A conscious effort on the part of the legislature in this behalf, would serve several purposes. It would, besides everything else, reduce frivolous litigation.... At the end of the day, Court time lost is a direct loss to the nation.[228]

The Court has rightly suggested that the legislature should evolve ways and means to curtail this unmindful activity as in the present setting of the adjudicatory process, a litigant, no matter how irresponsible he is, suffers no consequences. However, it is inscrutable why the Court did not impose extraordinary fine on the Sahara Group for protracting the litigation with a mala fide intention. It is the same court which, in 1996, had imposed a hefty fine of Rs 50 lakh on Satish Sharma, the then Union minister of Petroleum[229] and Rs 60 lakh on Sheila Kaul, the then Union minister of Housing[230] for arbitrary allotments of petrol pumps and houses respectively. It was for the first time that the apex court evolved the principle of punishment for constitutional tort. Though the apex court's concern about frivolous litigation is laudable, in Sahara's case, it moved ahead though there was not even an FIR against Sahara.

[228] Writ Petition (Criminal) No. 57 of 2014 *Subrata Roy Sahara* v. *Union of India and others*, AIR (2014) SC 3241 (2014) 8 SCC 470 (2014) (6) SCALE 257 (paras 49–53), decided on 6 May 2014.

[229] *Common Cause* v. *Union of India* (1996) 6 SCC 530.

[230] *Shiv Sagar Tiwari* v. *Union of India* (1996) 6 SCC 599.

Use of Technology and Video Recording of Court Proceedings

Many irritants in quick disposal can be removed with the help of technology. There is a move towards digitization, and slowly courts are becoming e-courts which are supposed to be paperless. However, it will still take some time to be totally paperless. Some courts are now e-courts where filings of cases are done electronically and even summons and notices are being sent electronically. But under the Evidence Act, a document downloaded from any website is not admissible. Even the orders or judgements of the Supreme Court posted on its website cannot be downloaded and used in the court. The certified copy must be obtained for it to be used in any court. This hurdle may be over once electronic signatures of judges are also there on the orders/judgements. The downloaded documents will then be admissible in the court. However, cent per cent population is not literate, much less digiterate. So, a large number of people do not use internet. It will take time to have total coverage of the population, but digitization is going to benefit a lot. At the click of the mouse, all information pertaining to any case is available on the computer screen. The judge can know how many times adjournments were sought by which party and how much time was wasted in it and also what has been the past conduct of any party. The creation of National Judicial Data Grid is a welcome development which has the latest data of each and every case.

Analysis of some data pertaining to backlog may help diagnose the malaise. The number of cases pending in the apex court in 1950 was 771 which went up to 23,092 in 1978, crossed 100,000 in 1983, and further increased to 134,221 in 1991. But in 1998, we find a sharp fall in the number; it came down to 19,806. The precipitate fall in arrears was attributed to the use of IT and better case management and also statistical rejigging. However, the backlog again began rising and went up to 59,595 in 2016. About it, the Supreme Court's website itself says, 'out of 59,595 pending matters as on 31-03-2016, if connected matters are excluded, the pendency was only of 34,562 matters as on 31-03-2016'.

The judiciary should step one step further and breaking the conservative view should allow video recording of court proceedings. Now the technology is cheap and installing CCTV is neither cumbersome nor so expensive now a days. It has been allowed in many countries. In the US, video recording of court proceedings is common. In some countries, even television broadcasts of court proceedings are allowed. The proceedings of the UK Supreme Court are open to not only video recording, but also telecast since 1 October 2009. India is still cocooned in the conservative thought that photography or videography inside the courtroom is not desirable. Many judges fear that it will make the atmosphere very formal. There is nothing wrong if the atmosphere is formal as it will prevent lawyers from making false averments and committing perjury. They obtain adjournments and pass-overs on false grounds and then subsequently deny what they say. Video recordings will clinch the issue. No party can back out from the undertakings given in the court verbally. It will help the court a lot at the trial and also at the appellate level.

In deciding criminal cases, scientific tools can be of tremendous help. The Supreme Court also advocated it:

> In this age of science, we have to build legal foundations that are sound in science as well as in law. Practices and principles that served in the past, now people think, must give way to innovative and creative methods, if we want to save our criminal justice system. Emerging new types of crime and their level of sophistication, the traditional methods and tools have become outdated, hence the necessity to strengthen the forensic science for crime detection. Oral evidence depends on several facts, like power of observation, humiliation, external influence, forgetfulness etc. whereas forensic evidence is free from those infirmities. Judiciary should also be equipped to understand and deal with such scientific materials. Constant interaction of judges with scientists, engineers would promote and widen their knowledge to deal with such scientific evidence and to effectively deal with criminal cases based on scientific evidence.[231]

Judges' Salaries and the Financial Autonomy of the Judiciary

As far as remunerations are concerned, it is not correct to say that it is inadequate though earlier it was so. When the high courts were set up in 1861, a judge was given a salary of Rs 4,000 per month. It was at the suggestion of the viceroy who said that a *nawab*[232] could lead a luxurious life in Rs 500 per month, and a high court judge should be paid eight times that amount. So, judges got this salary till January 1950. When the Constitution was enforced, the salary of high court judge was reduced to Rs 3,500, but for the chief justice of the high court it was Rs 4,000 and the same was for the Supreme Court judge, and the CJI got Rs 4,500. But judicial salaries remained frozen

---

[231] *Dharam Deo Yadav* v. *State of UP* (2014) 5 SCC 509, para 30.

[232] An honorific title conferred by the Mughal emperor to semi-autonomous Muslim rulers of princely states.

for 37 years at the amount fixed on 26 January 1950. It had a debilitating impact on the quality of judicial functioning, as the best talents in the bar were reluctant to accept judgeships. However, the government belatedly realized this and raised the salaries of judges substantially by the Constitution (54th Amendment) Act, 1986. Further, the Parliament passed an Act which increased the perquisites and other benefits conferred on judges. Today, judges of the High Courts and the Supreme Court get perks and privileges, in the form of manpower (orderlies, peons, gardeners, chauffeurs, and so on), and bungalows which are unimaginable even in a developed country. Besides, they get Rs 12,000 per month as sumptuary allowance, reimbursement for 200 litres of petrol, and LTC (Leave Travel Concession) twice a year which never lapses. Even the salaries of the judges of the subordinate courts are quite attractive after the recommendations of the Shetty Commission were implemented.[233] Eight state governments submitted that their financial health did not allow to increase the salaries to such an extent, but the Supreme Court rejected the plea on the grounds that resource crunch was not a valid reason for not implementing its directive. Of all the government officials, they are the highest paid. Besides, they get fabulous perks. It was a clear-cut case of overstepping by the Supreme Court as pay and perks are decided by the government. Today, salaries of judges of the subordinate are much more than what a leading lawyer of the lower court can earn. If perks are added, an advocate's earning is nothing in comparison.

It is also said that the judiciary is handicapped as it does not have financial autonomy and it has to depend on the executive for every rupee. Before the 13th Finance Commission, the expenditure on the judiciary in India in terms of Gross National Product was extremely low, not more than 0.2 per cent. The comparative spending on this head in other developed countries is much higher—in Singapore it is 1.2 per cent, in the UK, 4.3 per cent and the US, 1.4 per cent. In fact, the administration of justice in India was a state subject, but it was made a concurrent subject in the 42nd Amendment. Moreover, expenditure on the judiciary does not figure in the plan but it appears in the non-plan expenses. In 2002, in the Five Year Plan, the expenditure on the judiciary was fixed at approximately Rs 700 crores. Of this, nearly Rs 500 crores came from the judiciary itself through the collection of fines, court fees, and stamp duty. Then what does the government do for it? Establishment of one court incurs an expenditure of about Rs 70 lakh. Why does the government

---

[233] *All India Judges Association* v. *Union of India & Ors.*, AIR (2002) SC 1752 (2002) 4 SCC 247.

not establish new courts? The Supreme Court suggested in July 2005 that the government should carve out a separate fund before promulgating any new law, as every law means extra litigation and burden on courts.

However, the 13th Finance Commission recommended an allocation of Rs 5,000 crores to improve the justice delivery system. It was for the five-year period 2010–15. Never before in India's judicial history has the government come forward to invest such a large sum to improve the judicial infrastructure and make justice more accessible. After Verappa Moily took over as the Union Law minister, problems relating to the judiciary at last received the proper attention. He avowed to implement his Vision Plan of reducing the lifespan of a case in the system to three years, a target to be achieved within a three-year period. Half the money was earmarked to increase the number of courts. According to N.R. Madhava Menon:

> There are six components to which the money is earmarked, all of which may not be equally relevant to all the States. Obviously the focus of the expenditure is on the trial courts where over 90 per cent of all arrears reside. However, the administrative and supervisory control exercised over them by the respective High Courts is so absolute that nothing much can happen without the Chief Justice and the portfolio judges in charge of the districts concerned allowing them the freedom to innovate and change. It is hoped that High Courts for once would welcome the initiatives from below and provide the leadership for the effective implementation of the plan even if they do not personally support the changes proposed. This may require amendment to the rules of the court: on an experimental basis this could be allowed in those districts where the plan is to be implemented. The causes of delay are not the same everywhere and a district-wise approach alone can be effective in the beginning. It is more so because the support of the Bar and court staff are critical for the success of the plan. This is easier to mobilise at the local level.[234]

However, reducing the life span of a case remained a wishful thinking. The number of cases can be brought down drastically if the legislature and the executive do their jobs properly. In India, almost every legislation or appointment means litigation. We have a penchant for enacting laws but it is done without proper cogitation or deliberation. One amendment in the Negotiable Instruments Act brought over 25 lakh cases of bounced cheques to the court. The Income Tax Act, 1961 has been amended over several thousand times and nobody knows how many more amendments will have to be effected. It

---

[234] N.R. Madhava Menon, 'Judicial Reforms to Get a Fillip', *The Hindu*, 11 March 2010.

provoked Nani A. Palkhivala to comment: 'The tragedy of India is the tragedy of national power, energy and manpower. Tens of millions of man-hours, crammed with the intelligence and knowledge of tax-gatherers, tax-payers and tax-advisers are squandered every year in grappling with a torrential spate of mindless amendments. The cardinal error of our times is to mistake amendment for improvement and change for progress.'[235]

Legislators must know that they have been elected to make laws for the welfare of the people. Parliamentary and Assembly sessions should be fully used for this function and a great amount of effort has to go into law-making to ensure that there are no lapses and loopholes that attract any provisions of the Constitution. If this is taken care of, a large amount of litigation with respect to the constitutionality, usurpation of power, and so on, can be reduced. Similarly, any appointment has to be made with utmost transparency ruling out any scope for foul play. The government should bring in an act à la the Administrative Procedures Act of the USA (1946). It is an attempt to bring in transparency, certainty, accountability, and public action in administration. It has laid down clear checks on the administrative action to avoid arbitrariness and to uphold the concept of the Rule of Law. It lays down that any rule or regulation of the administrative authority has to be published to bring it to public notice. This is to ensure that people are aware of all rules and regulations before they approach the authorities.

Alternative Disputes Resolution (ADR)

There is a growing consensus that ADR mechanisms have to be devised to ease the unnecessary burden on courts. The primary object of the ADR is to provide cheap, quick, and effective remedy. The Arbitration and Conciliation Act, 1996, laid down the minimum standards for an effective ADR mechanism. Now, arbitration has become a thriving business for lawyers and retired judges and the same problem of delay has defeated its purpose. First of all, there is a huge challenge of finding impartial arbitrators. Nowadays, it is seen that arbitrators behave like the advocates of the parties who nominate them. This is creating a crisis of credibility. The 1996 Act defined the procedures to be followed, but with the passage of time, it lost its charm as an effective ADR forum. It is also infected by the same court culture and adjournments are sought which are generally granted. In case, it is denied, the aggrieved party

---

[235] Quoted by Subhash Kothari, 'Courting Disaster: A Case for Judicial Reform', *Times of India*, 28 June 2000.

moves the high court which may direct to give a chance. Though the award can be challenged only on three limited grounds—misconduct of the arbitrator, award going beyond the jurisdiction of arbitration, and going against public policy—the loser goes to the high court which also treats it as the first appeal. Further, the party interested in prolonging the case moves the high court against any interim relief or denial of adjournment, and so on. Thus, it takes many years. Many arbitrators, who are generally the retired chief justices or judges of the apex court, complain that situation may improve if high courts change their attitude.

So, it was felt necessary to amend the Act to do away with theses irritants, and the amended Arbitration and Conciliation Act came into force on 28 October 2015. It mandates that the award must be made within 12 months from the date of initiation, extendable further by six months with the consent of the parties. It has also added cost consequences as both a penalty for delay and as bonus for early disposal. Newly introduced Section 29B provides for passing an award within six months if both parties in a case consent to conduct it in a fast track or summary manner where oral arguments are not allowed and adjudication is on the basis of written arguments only.

India has *ad hoc* arbitration in which even the works that are done by the registry in a regular court are done by arbitrators. So, they have to see that the notice pleadings are completed—claims, replies, rejoinders, and so on, are in place. In institutional arbitration, parties are not encumbered with the problem of finding independent arbitrators, and further the arbitration institutions have the infrastructure like building and well-equipped and efficient secretariat required for the smooth functioning of arbitration. Further, parties, lawyers, or arbitrators do not have to spend extra hours formulating rules and procedure in a case. Some private bodies have arbitration institutions such as the Indian Council of Arbitration run by Federation of Indian Chambers of Commerce and Industry (FICCI), Nani Palkhivala Arbitration Centre, International Centre for Alternative Disputes Resolution, and so on. Now some high courts also have arbitration institutions and their fee structure is also quite conservative. So, sometimes it is difficult to get arbitrators for them. Institutional arbitrations are also cost-effective and arbitrator's fees and other administrative expenditure are predetermined. So, the parties know in advance the expenses they are likely to incur. The Supreme Court has also expressed concern on the rising arbitration cost and commented with approbation on institutional arbitration:

> There is no doubt a prevalent opinion that the cost of arbitration becomes very high in many cases where retired Judges are Arbitrators. The large

number of sittings and charging of very high fees per sitting, with several add-ons, without any ceiling, have many a time resulted in the cost of arbitration approaching or even exceeding the amount involved in the dispute or the amount of the award. When an arbitrator is appointed by a court without indicating fees, either both parties or at least one party is at a disadvantage. Firstly, the parties feel constrained to agree to whatever fees is suggested by the Arbitrator, even if it is high or beyond their capacity. Secondly, if a high fee is claimed by the Arbitrator and one party agrees to pay such fee, the other party, who is unable to afford such fee or reluctant to pay such high fee, is put to an embarrassing position. He will not be in a position to express his reservation or objection to the high fee, owing to an apprehension that refusal by him to agree for the fee suggested by the arbitrator, may prejudice his case or create a bias in favour of the other party who readily agreed to pay the high fee. It is necessary to find an urgent solution for this problem to save arbitration from the arbitration cost. Institutional arbitration has provided a solution as the arbitrators' fees is not fixed by the arbitrators themselves on a case-to-case basis but is governed by a uniform rate prescribed by the institution under whose aegis the arbitration is held.[236]

The problem is that India does not have an arbitration culture and the weak party always resorts to dilatory tactics for which it is not punished. Adjournment should not be allowed even in courts, but seeking adjournment in arbitration is nothing short of blasphemy. In India, people abusing the process of law are not punished. In Singapore, any one seldom asks for adjournment as the penalty is very high. If it is asked for 12 weeks in advance, then the party asking for it has to pay 40 per cent of the cost (arbitrator's fees and other administrative expenses), it goes up to 60 per cent if it is done eight weeks before the date, and it is 100 per cent when the request is made four weeks before. Now, only time will tell how far the amendment is able to bring about the desired changes.

The Code of Civil Procedure, 1908, was amended with effect from 1 July 2002 to make ADR an integral part of the judicial process. The newly inserted Section 89 (1) provides for settlement of disputes outside courts through mediation, arbitration, conciliation, Lok Adalat. It was done to resolve disputes between parties quickly and minimize costs and reduce burden on courts. In many countries, especially the developed ones, over 90 per cent of cases are settled out of court; cases go to trial only if the mediation fails.

---

[236] *Union of India* v. *Singh Builders Syndicate*, para 10 (2009) 4 SCR 563 (2009) 4 SCC 523, MANU/SC/0490/2009.

However, lawyers felt threatened that it would punch holes into their pockets as disputes would be resolved. As minimizing litigation is not their concern, they challenged the constitutional validity of the amendment. The Supreme Court upheld the amendment in *Salem Advocate Bar Association, Tamil Nadu* v. *Union of India*,[237] but there were questions about its functionality. Modalities had to be formulated for the manner in which Section 89 and other provisions introduced by the amendment had to be made operational. So, in *Salem Advocate Bar Association, Tamil Nadu* v. *Union of India* II,[238] the Supreme Court directed the constitution of an expert committee headed by the then chairman of the Law Commission, Justice M. Jagannadh Rao, to formulate the manner in which Section 89 and other provisions introduced in the Code of Civil Procedure have to be made effective. It also directed the creation of the Model Case Flow Management Rules along with rules and regulations to be observed while taking recourse to ADR. The committee framed the model rules called Civil Procedure-Alternative Dispute Resolution and Mediation Rules, and high courts were given the liberty to frame their own rules in consonance with the model rules if they so desired. The case management policy can yield remarkable results in achieving more disposal of the cases. Its mandate is for the judge or an officer of the court to set a timetable and monitor a case from its initiation to its disposal. Model Case Flow Management Rules have been separately dealt with for trial courts and first appellate subordinate courts and for the high courts. These draft rules extensively deal with the various stages of the litigation.

In *Afcons Infrastructure* v. *Cherian Verkay Construction*,[239] the Supreme Court dwelt upon Section 89(1) and virtually rewrote it and laid down which cases are fit for mediation. It also pointed out drafting errors in Section 89 and suggested amendments which may be considered by the Law Commission. The first anomaly, it pointed out, is the mixing up of the definitions of 'mediation' and 'judicial settlement' under clause (c) and (d) of sub-section (2) of Section 89. Clause (c) mandates that for judicial settlement, the court shall refer the matter to a suitable institution or person who shall be deemed to be a Lok Adalat. However, according to Clause (d), where the reference is to mediation, the court shall effect a compromise between the parties by following such procedure as may be prescribed. The two are contradictory as it is ridiculous calling a compromise effected by the court, as mediation, as is

---

[237] (2003) 1 SCC 49.
[238] 2 August 2005.
[239] (2010) 8 SCC 24.

done in Clause (d). Similarly, it makes no sense to describe a reference made by a court to a suitable institution or person for hammering out a settlement as judicial settlement provided in Clause (c). Judicial settlement is prevalent in the US which means settlement of a civil case with the help of a judge who is not authorized to decide the dispute, while mediation refers to a method of non-binding dispute resolution with the help of a neutral third party. The words as ordinarily understood have interchanged meanings in their definition in Section 89 that causes confusion. So, the Court said that if the word 'mediation' in Clause (d) and the words 'judicial settlement' in Clause (c) are interchanged, the said clauses make perfect sense. The Law Commission, in its 238th Report in December 2013, proposed amendments to Section 89 Code of Civil Procedure, as well as Order X Rules 1-A to 1-C, and also to Section 16 of the Court Fee Act.

However, many a time the court prefers to send cases to the mediation centre as judge gets points against it which is one of the criteria to assess his performance. Due to this, sometimes even such cases are sent to Lok Adalat which are on the verge of disposal. However, the court is not bound to accept if compromise is thrashed at the mediation centre. The government is spending a lot on ADR, but there is no review on how far it is helping reduce pendency. There is an opinion that result is dismal compared to the money spent and better result could have been achieved by using the same resources to strengthen the infrastructure of the court and increase the number of judges. Though the impact of this amendment is yet to show results, parallel ADR fora have already arisen. Dawood Ibrahim is getting economic disputes settled in Dubai.

Parliament's Responsibility

It is time for the Parliament to make law for quick disposal of cases as suggested by the Supreme Court itself.

Abolish/Minimize Adjournment

Adjournment is the slow poison. It kills at a slow pace, and so, no one is guilty of murder. Code of Civil Procedure was amended to ensure that more than three adjournments are not granted, and summons is served within 30 days as discussed earlier. Unfortunately, the Supreme Court set aside and diluted all these amendments on the ground that procedure should not defeat justice. Ironically, this is happening as procedures defeat justice. The Parliament may conduct referendum over these amendments so that the higher courts are mindful of the fact that people have put their seal directly on these amendments and they abhor delays. In fact, adjournment should be abolished altogether. Otherwise, if it is minimized, again it will be misused and the court will exercise discretion. Abolition of adjournments will not lead to miscarriage of justice as the petition carries the facts and arguments of the petitioner and so does the reply. B. Sen, who practised in the Privy Council in the 1940s, has written about it, 'The established tradition in those days was just to say "If your Lordships have read the petition, I have nothing further to add" and sit down if there was no point of substance to urge'.[240] If the lawyer is not present for some unavoidable reasons, they may submit written argument subsequently. Alternatively, two-lawyer system may be introduced so that in case the lead counsel is not available, the next counsel will take over. It may be argued that it will put extra burden on litigants who would have to pay two advocates. But it can be worked out with the cooperation of lawyers who can charge less, as lawyers will get double cases as every case will have two lawyers.

Withhold Pension If Judge Retires without Writing Judgements, No Transfer without Delivering Judgements

The Parliament should also ensure by making appropriate law that the judges who do not discharge their duties and retire keeping judgements reserved forfeit their pension and other benefits. But, it also must be ensured that to save their pension, judges do not dispose of cases, burying justice. The transfer policy of judges should be rationalized and a judge after transfer should be asked how much time does s/he need to complete the cases s/he is hearing. In the lower court, judges stop doing any work once the transfer order comes. In the Uphaar Cinema Fire trial, the judge hearing the matter was transferred after 36 hearings and the matter was assigned to another judge causing colossal waste of judicial time and setback to the victims' families.[241] The Supreme Court should also do some introspection and bring about some mechanism to deal with the problem of delay. Its pontification to the Gujarat government, led by Narendra Modi, in the aftermath of 2002 communal riots, to observe Raj Dharma and quit if it cannot punish the rioters, sounds strange when it cannot perform its own duty. The basic work of the judiciary is to resolve disputes between two parties but instead of doing that, it is busy with PILs to remove encroachments from roads, protect the environment, and so on.

[240] B. Sen, *Six Decades of Law, Politics & Diplomacy: Some Reminiscences and Reflections* (New Delhi: Universal Law Publishing C. Pvt. Ltd, 2010), p. 14.
[241] Krishnamoorthy and Krishnamoorthy, *Trial By Fire*, p. 139.

Install CCTV in Courts

CCTV should be installed in all courts—from the lowest to the highest. It will ensure that lawyers do not mislead the court nor seek adjournments on false grounds. It happens that an advocate is arguing in a different court, but will seek adjournment in another court on health or some other grounds. CCTV footage will give a lie to their claims. It can be proved even without CCTV footage from the records of the court that a particular lawyer was arguing in one court and feigning illness in another court. But the CCTV footage will make it easier. Further, many lawyers give some assurance in the court and get adjournment on that basis but back out from making any such assurance on the next date. CCTV footage will expose them, warts and all, and they can be prosecuted for perjury.

The measures suggested are implementable. In the Babri Masjid demolition case,[242] the Supreme Court transferred proceedings from the court of Special Judicial Magistrate, Rai Bareilly, to the court of Additional Sessions Judge (Ayodhya Matters) at Lucknow, with a clear direction to conclude it within two years by conducting day to day hearing with no adjournment on any grounds except when the Sessions Court finds it impossible to conduct trial on a particular day for which reasons will have to be recorded, and also ordered that there would be no transfer of the judge during this period. It is not understandable that the Supreme Court dilutes the amendment when the Parliament tries to cut delays by reducing adjournments but it itself imposes a blanket ban on adjournment when it so desires.

In the US, the delay is never inordinate. Trial is held in the state court, then if some constitutional issues are raised, it goes to the Federal Court which decides the issue and directs the trial court to proceed with the case in the light of its finding. Let us not forget the age-old aphorism: *Lex dilationes semper exhorret.*[243]

* * *

Charles Dickens, in his novel *Bleak House*, describes a case, *Jarndyce* v. *Jarndyce* pertaining to a will. Jarndyce is in debt and continues taking loans in the hope that he will win the case and settle the debt. The case drags on and on,

---

[242] *State (Through Central Bureau of Investigation)* v. *Kalyan Singh and Others* (2017) 7 SCC 444.

[243] The law always abhors delays.

and though he finally wins, he remains in debt as the legal cost was high. No wonder, Voltaire commented that he was ruined twice in his life—once when he lost a lawsuit and again when he won a lawsuit. This is the international standard which gets further aggravated in India. A gypsy curse says, 'May you have a lawsuit in which you are in the right'. It is interesting to know that gypsies had their provenance in India. An American jurist once famously commented that once someone files a case, they should execute their nominee who would fight it after their death. Litigation ruins permanently as it drags on for generations. Lawyers are hardly interested in expeditious disposal as a prolonged trial or suit only fetches them more money. Adjournment should be granted only in the rarest of rare cases. In developed countries, getting an adjournment is well-nigh impossible, whereas in India, one invariably gets only the next date, not an order or justice. India should learn from the ICJ, The Hague, where everything is decided in advance. Pleadings are completed before the registrar within fixed timeframe and date and time of hearing/argument is fixed. Duration of argument is fixed which cannot be exceeded even by one minute. Adjournment is not granted in any case. In India also, it can be done by introducing two-lawyer system so that a lawyer cannot ask for it even on the ground of health.

Judgements should be pronounced as soon as the hearing concludes. The Bombay High Court had developed the practice of delivering judgment in the court immediately after the conclusion of argument. It has many advantages—the judge comes prepared, listens to parties carefully, and does not forget anything as the judgment is dictated then and there. If there is any confusion, the lawyer is available to clarify.

Besides, judgement must be couched in an unequivocal and lucid language which does not leave any space for equivocation. More important than disposal is the quality of disposal. There may be total disposal with no arrears and yet there may not be any justice. If the judgement is impeccable, it leaves little scope for appeal/revision/review. The court should also tear into the designs of those trying to protract the matter by some way or the other and challenging every order of every court till the appellate channel is exhausted. Further, if a counsel makes a submission in the court regarding some fact, the judge should record it, and it should not be be controverted later on; there is no need to ask the party to file an affidavit. Till the 1960s, it was rare for the court to ask for filing affidavit. If a statement made before a magistrate under Section 164 of the Cr. P.C. is admissible which cannot be recanted, why not the statement made before the court be taken as plain truth?

Further, judges should ensure that the courts' orders are complied with immediately. The executive is generally reluctant to implement the judgement that is not to its liking and tries to interpret the order according to its convenience. Such officers should be dealt with stringently. It is the power of civil contempt which should be exercised ruthlessly, though the jurisdiction of criminal contempt should be invoked sparingly. Once senior officers are sent to jail for non-compliance, the number of contempt petitions will come down drastically. If a party adopts devious shenanigans to buy time, s/he should be punished commensurately. Judges can also help by calling both parties to their chambers in person, not to be represented by lawyers and settle disputes. Many a time, injustice is writ large on the face and even a blind person can feel it. Justice may be blind but judges are not. There are many groups in government services who do not get any promotion in the entire career as there are no promotional avenues for them. But if the aggrieved employee moves the court, the case goes on and on. The government has unlimited money, manpower, and resources to prolong the case unconscionably and then challenge any order favourable to the employee up to apex court and then not implement it if it goes in favour of the employees. The employee gets tired, retired, and ruined. If the court fixes responsibility and punishes senior bureaucrats severely for it, there will be no occasion for knocking at the court's door.

So far as the number of judges is concerned, the judiciary is missing the wood for the tree by consistently harping on improving the judge-population ratio. If any improvement is required, it has to be qualitative first. There are judges who seldom write independent judgments, and some of them have even been elevated to the apex court. Besides, the courts should not go expanding their jurisdiction. The Supreme Court is deciding everything from cricket to *Jallikattu* (taming of bulls) in Tamil Nadu, to fixing the height of *Dahi-Handi* (earthen pot filled with butter) on the occasion of Janmashtami in Mumbai. These are not the jobs of the judiciary. Courts have time for such things, but not for the general resolution of disputes.

The government has to play a proactive role in reducing arrears as it is the largest litigant. Those officers who contribute to the growth of litigation by denying justice to aggrieved parties and file unnecessary appeals should be punished. Responsibility should be fixed on the officers because of whose omission or commission someone was forced to knock at the door of the court. The government should cooperate with the judiciary in carrying out its work. Unfortunately, the executive works like an impediment in the judicial process.

The police administration has to be thoroughly revamped and made accountable. If a policeman like Sir William Sleeman could rid India of 'thugee', even now several ills can be exterminated if we can give a free hand to upright police officials who are still not as rare as the dodo, but for that we need a minister like Sir Robert Peel, who put policemen on their feet in England. Judges should be made accountable for their judgements and be penalized for keeping the judgements reserved.

Unfortunately, judicial reform has not been on the agenda of the government or that of political parties which hardly discuss the issue in their manifestos. The 188-page document on the 10th Five Year Plan 2002–7, issued by the Planning Commission, made a passing reference to the issue in less than four lines: 'There is an urgent need to bring about judicial reforms with a view to speeding up the process of delivering justice. Alternatives to the regular delivery mechanism through a hierarchy of alternate courts like Family Courts, Lok Adalats [sic], Nyay Panchayats, etc., need to be resorted to more often.'[244]

[244] 10th Five Year Plan, Planning Commission, Government of India, 2002–7, vol. I, 2002, p. 187. Madhav Godbole, *The Judiciary and Governance in India* (New Delhi: Rupa and Co., 2009), p. 5.

6

Lawyer, Heal Thyself

'The first thing that we do, let's kill all the lawyers'.[1] Though it was intended as a comic relief and not something to be taken seriously, it, nonetheless, reflects on the image lawyers have. They have been reviled from the time immemorial. Socrates, in the *Theaetetus*, derided lawyers in these words:

> He is a servant, and is disputing about a fellow servant before his master, who is seated and has the cause in his hands.... The consequence has been, that he has become keen and shrewd; he has learned how to flatter his master in word and indulge him in deed; but his soul is small and unrighteous. His slavish condition has deprived him of growth and uprightness and independence ... he has been driven into crooked ways; from the first he has practised deception and retaliation, and has become stunted and warped ... and is now, as he thinks, a master in wisdom.

Jesus also spoke about lawyers' despicable conduct. In the New Testament, St. Luke says: 'Woe unto you also, ye lawyers! For you lade men with burdens grievous to be borne, and ye yourselves touch not the burdens with one of your fingers'. This quote is often cited to denounce lawyers but Overton challenged that Jesus did not mean lawyers. The word translated was Greek *nomikos*, which does mean lawyer, but is the Biblical equivalent to 'scribe' or 'Pharisee'. Moreover, Radin emphatically suggests that lawyers had a good reputation in early Christian times. One of Paul's followers, Zenas, was a lawyer who became a saint in the Greek Orthodox Church, and other lawyers

---

[1] William Shakespeare, *Henry VI*, Act IV, Scene 2.

have attained sainthood. Writing about the historic incident of the capture of London in late fourteenth century after the social rising of 1381, G.M. Trevelyan has hit out at lawyers, 'unpopular characters were murdered, including the mild Archbishop Sudbury, whose head was placed over London Bridge. Lawyers were specially obnoxious'.[2]

Anyway, lawyers are generally perceived as parasites on society, which is summed up in William Makepeace Thackeray's comment on the Court of Chancery, 'a sty for fattening lawyers in on the bones of honest men'.[3] Disraeli denounced lawyers in these words: 'The chief characteristics of the legal mind are expounding the obvious, illustrating the self-evident, and expatiating on the commonplace'.[4]

Evolution of Lawyers

In ancient Greece there were great orators called Sophists who were profes-sional teachers and educators. The advent of democracy made it possible for the common man to attain the highest position if he could win over the people by eloquent oratory. Thus, people wanted to hone their skills of oratory and demagoguery and hence the demand for such an education. According to W.T. Stace:

> It was this demand which the Sophists undertook to satisfy. They wandered about Greece from place to place, they gave lectures, they took pupils, they entered into disputations. For these services they extracted fees. They were the first in Greece to take fees for the teaching of wisdom. There was nothing disgraceful in this in itself, but it had never been customary. The wise men of Greece had never accepted any payment for their wisdom.[5]

In Athens during the second half of the fifth century BCE and first half of the fourth century BCE, there were orators, called *synegoros*, who occasionally spoke on behalf of litigants or defendants. After the principal uttered a few words, a *syndic* (friend) took over the case. The line between the *synegoros* and the *syndic* slowly got blurred. The orator did not merely adduce facts

---

[2] G.M. Trevelyan, *English Social History* (London: Longmans, 1944), p. 14.

[3] Quoted by Nani A. Palkhivala, 'The Law and Lawyers', in *We the People* (Bombay: Strand Book Stall, 1986), p. 340.

[4] Palkhivala, 'The Law and Lawyers', p. 341.

[5] W.T. Stace, 'The Sophists', in *A Critical History of Greek Philosophy* (London: Macmillan and Co. Ltd, 1954), p. 109.

and arguments in support of the brief but also vouched for the probity and rectitude of the litigant and justness of his cause.

Modern advocate is an evolution of the gladiator of yesteryears. William the Conqueror, after coming to England, introduced a system of trial called 'Ordeal by battle' in which the plaintiff and the defendant in a civil suit or the prosecutor and the accused in a criminal case were required to combat each other physically. It was thought that in such wrestling, the party in the right would win with the blessings of God. The loser was pronounced guilty and the winner was declared innocent and to have justice on his side. Only women and the Church were allowed to hire champions who fought for them. Thus, the champion was the precursor of the present day advocate. In due course, the freedom of employing an 'advocate' to appear for the litigant was extended from priests and women to other classes of litigants. William Graham, a gladiator, was the most famous advocate in the thirteenth century. Though this form of trial became antiquated, under the law it remained open to litigants in England until the nineteenth century. The practice was abolished in 1919 after a man convicted of murder in 1918 moved the appellate court in appeal and his counsel pleaded that his client be allowed to challenge the prosecutor in a physical combat. Chief Justice Lord Ellenborough, found that the right did exist. It was then that this method of trial was abolished.[6] The 'trial by ordeal' was quite brief compared to today's protracted trials which go on interminably.

Legal Profession in India

The modern legal system of India is a boon or bane gifted by the British. The contemporary Indian legal profession is the superimposition of the British legal system on the traditional institutions of caste, family, and village panchayat (an assembly of villagers). Though we find the significant role of judges in the literature of Hindu and Mughal India, there is no reference to lawyers. In ancient India, justice was dispensed in open assemblies known as *sabha* or *samiti*. Kautilya's *Arthashastra* gives a quaint description of 'King's court of justice'. There were different courts—court for the *sangraha* (for a group of ten villages), court for the *dronamukha* (for a group of hundred villages), court for the *sthaniya* (for a group of eight hundred villages), and at the top of all was the court presided over by the king's judges.

During the Mughal period, there did exist a multi-tiered judicial and revenue system; they did not tinker with the autonomy of the local traditional

---

[6] Nani A. Palkhivala, 'Obedience to the Unenforceable', in *We, the People*, p. 30.

judicial system. Lawyers as a class of legal experts, advocating the cause of litigants perhaps did not exist. Hindu pundits, Muslim muftis, and Portuguese lawyers served under the earlier regimes, but they did not have any say in the system of law and legal practice. The first British court was set up in 1672 in Bombay by Governor General Aungier after King Charles II, who was presented the island of Bombay by the king of Portugal at the time of his marriage with Infanta Catherine of Braganza in June 1661, transferred it to the East India Company by a royal charter dated 27 March 1669. George Wilcox was appointed attorney-general.

However, for about a century, the British East India Company was in a dilemma whether to introduce a legal profession and did not send out either a trained judge or an attorney or a law clerk. It prophetically apprehended that the members of the legal profession might lead the freedom movement against the British regime. In fact, lawyers were the leading lights during the freedom movement. Mayor's Courts were set up in the early eighteenth century in the presidency towns of Bombay, Calcutta, and Madras when King George I, on 24 September 1726, by a charter, granted courts of records to be established. Ironically, mayors or officers who presided over the court, utterly lacked legal knowledge and, so, were not in a position to question the submissions of the attorneys who practiced before them. The deficiency of the system was eventually recognized and it led to the establishment of a Supreme Court at Fort William in Calcutta (now Kolkata) through a Charter issued on 26 March 1774. However, only the English and Irish barristers and members of the Faculty of five Advocates in Scotland were entitled to practice as per Clause 11 of the Charter. The attorneys mentioned in the Charter were Irish attorneys and solicitors. Thus, the Supreme Court bar was shut for Indians as it was an exclusive preserve for members of the British legal profession.

Two years earlier, in 1772, civil and criminal courts were set up in all district headquarters with a *sudder adalat* (provincial court) at the top. Thus, two discrepant systems co-existed at the *mofussil* (rural area) and the city levels and there was hardly any interaction between the practitioners of mofussil courts and the barristers or solicitors of the courts in the presidency cities who were British. For the first two decades, in the sudder courts, it was free for all with no limitations on those who could draft pleadings or the fees they could charge. Bengal Regulation VII of 1793 introduced some order as the *sudder diwani adalat* (provincial civil court) was empowered to appoint *vakils* (pleaders) and regulate their conduct. Now vakils were required to be trained at Hindu and Muslim religious schools at Banaras and Calcutta. *Mukhtars* were attorneys who could appear in the criminal court in the mofussil.

It may be mentioned that former CJI, late Mehar Chand Mahajan began his career as a mukhtar.

In 1846, the segregation between the two systems was slightly bridged when barristers were allowed to practice in the sudder courts. However, a unified judicial system was introduced after the British government assumed the reins of the government, superseding the British East India Company in 1858. High courts were established in Calcutta, Bombay, and Madras in 1862, leading to a uniform system in the whole country. It also marked the beginning of the Indianization of the court system. Now, the vakils practicing before the sudder court could also appear before the high court. However, a distinction between barrister (called advocate then onwards) and solicitor (attorney) was maintained for those high court cases that would have been heard in the erstwhile Supreme Court, but not for appellate matters. Vakils became eligible for promotion as advocate. The pleaders, mukhtars, and Revenue Agents Act, 1865 and Legal practitioners Act, 1879 defined the different classes of legal practitioners more articulately as to how advocates, attorneys and vakils were different in the high court and pleaders, mukhtars, and revenue agents in the lower court. To remove any doubts about the eligibility of woman to be enrolled as an advocate, the Legal Practitioners (Women) Act, 1923, was enacted to provide that notwithstanding anything contained in previous legislations or other provisions in this regard, 'no woman shall, by reason only of her sex, be disqualified from being admitted or enrolled as a legal practitioner or from practicing such; and any such rule or order which is repugnant to the provisions of this Act shall, to the extent of repugnancy be void'.[7]

When the Federal Court was set up on 1 October 1937 in Delhi, every advocate could not appear before it. It was mandatory to practice for five years in the high court before one could appear before it, and three years' practice in the district court was essential for getting enrolled at the high court. The same applied to the Supreme Court after it replaced the Federal Court in January 1950. Since Delhi did not have any tradition of legal learning, leaders of provincial bars came over to appear in important cases and went back; they did not shift to Delhi as they had roaring practice back home. The Advocate General of India (now called attorney general, as every state has an advocate general), B.L. Mitter, appointed in 1937, was from the Calcutta High Court, who was succeeded by S.N. Bose from the same High Court. Then came N.P. Engineer from Bombay (now Mumbai). Delhi did not have its high court which came under the jurisdicature of the Lahore

---

[7] Section 3.

High Court. So, only district court practitioners were available in Delhi, making the Supreme Court bar very poor. The Advocates Act, 1961 introduced a unified bar obliterating difference between different classes of advocates, and any advocate could practice in any court including the Supreme Court from day one.

The Act was legislated as the bar was not satisfied with the Bar Councils Act, 1926, which did not did not set up a unified Indian bar. The 1926 Act was itself a result of seething resentment in the legal fraternity over the distinction that existed between barristers and vakils, and the special privileges enjoyed by the British barristers and solicitors. Recognizing the dissatisfaction, the Government of India constituted the Indian Bar Committee in November 1923 called the Chamber Committee to examine the possibility of constituting Indian bar, whether on all India or provincial basis, and the extent to which it might be possible to remove the distinction enforced by statute of practice between barristers and vakils. The Act introduced a major change by making a separate provision for advocates, while the Legal Practitioners Act of 1879 continued to be applicable to other legal practitioners. The Act failed to perk up the legal fraternity as it did not cover pleaders, mukhtars, and revenue agents practising in the mofussil courts and revenue offices. Several non-official members' bills were introduced to amend the law pertaining to the legal profession but had lapsed. After the enforcement of the Constitution on 26 January 1950 and the establishment of the Supreme Court of India, the Union Government set up the All India Bar Committee under the chairmanship of Justice S.R. Das of the Supreme Court. It recommended the creation of a unified all India bar as well as the establishment, composition, and functions of the State and All India Bar Councils. Subsequently, the Law Commission of India, headed by the then Attorney-General M.C. Setalvad, supported the recommendations of the All India Bar Committee, in 1955, in its 14th report.

Pursuant to it, the Legal Practitioners Bill, 1959, was introduced in Lok Sabha on 19 November 1959. It was changed into Advocates Act when the bill was to be passed. The bill, having been passed by both Houses of Parliament, received president's assent on 18 May 1961 and was enforced. However, section 30 of the Act giving freedom to an advocate to practice throughout the territories to which this Act extends came into force only in 2011. Earlier, even the Supreme Court was moved at least twice for the issuance of the writ of mandamus to the Union Government to enforce section 30, but the Court refused to entertain those petitions. There is an opinion that Ashok K. Sen, then Union Law minister, got this act made with an eye on the vote-bank, as lawyers formed a big class in the country.

Expensive Justice and the Role of the Bar

Lawyers are known to make the client pay through their nose and have been identified with the affluent. Their obsession with money is revealed in a story associated with eminent American lawyer Rufus Choate (1 October 1799–13 July 1859.) He had instructed his clerks never to accept a new client without a minimum retainer of $100. Please note, it was in the first half of the nineteenth century. Once it so happened that his clerk informed him that a new client had left only $75 as the retainer. Choate reprimanded his clerk that his actions were 'very unprofessional and against the rules of the office'. The clerk replied, 'but I took all the man had'. Then Choate said, '[T]hat entirely alters the case—to take all a man has is quite professional.'[8] In the present era, American lawyers hit headlines and bring ignominy to the profession for the exorbitant fees of tort cases where they generally get a third of a tort settlement, which amounts to several millions of dollars in many cases. Besides, some lawyers defraud their clients, take money from their trust accounts, or are involved in laundering illegal drug money.[9] In India also, lawyers have been found to be involved in money laundering. The Enforcement Directorate attached properties worth Rs 45 crore belonging to Delhi-based advocate Rohit Tandon in a money laundering case.[10] He allegedly deposited demonetized currency notes of Rs 1,000 and 500 in various accounts of shell companies and issued demand drafts in the names of beneficiaries which were subsequently cancelled (currency notes of Rs 1,000 and 500 were cancelled on 8 November 2016). Some lawyers have been notorious for getting the title of the land and properties of their clients transferred in their names.

The bench and the bar are the two pillars of the judiciary. In fact, the bar is the provenance of the bench. So, improvement in the bench is inconceivable without improving the bar. It is also a fact that judges cannot be dissolute unless lawyers tend to be so, as in most cases, it is the lawyers who act as the conduit for judges. A corrupt bar cannot perform its adjudicatory role of adjudging the bench either. There are also instances when advocates accompany judges who go on LTC (Leave Travel Concession) with their families and bear their expenditure, giving it all trappings of a picaresque story.

---

[8] A. Chroust, 'The Legal Profession in Ancient Athens', *Notre Dame Lawyer*, vol. 29, no. 339 (1953–4): 350–8; Stan Ross, *The Joke's on Lawyers* (Delhi: Universal law Publishing Co. Pvt. Ltd, First Indian Reprint 2002), p. 16.

[9] Ross, *The joke's on Lawyers*, pp. 25–6.

[10] 'ED Attaches Assets of Lawyer, Banker Accused of Laundering', *Times of India*, New Delhi, 14 February 2017.

The judiciary as the justice delivery institution is crumbling under the load of corruption and procedural rigmarole and it appears that whole institution exists for judges, lawyers, and the few affluent and influential litigants who can hijack the judicial process for their vested interests, and justice is lost in the labyrinth of legalese, legal legerdemain, and la-di-da style. The situation is not much different in the US as described by Albert P. Blaustein and co-authors, 'The powerful position of the legal profession with respect to membership in American legislative bodies, Jones observes, is a striking demonstration of De Tocqueville's thesis that "the government of democracy is favorable to the political powers of lawyers".'[11]

In July 1992, Sir Anthony Mason, chief justice of Australia, defined the role of the bar while addressing the English, Scottish, and Australian Bar like this:

> Unless the bar dedicates itself to the ideal of the public service, it forfeits its claim to treatment as profession in true sense of the term. Dedication to public service demands not only attainment of a high standard of professional skill but also faithful performance of duty to client and court and willingness to make professional service available to public … if the bar is to enjoy public trust and confidence, it must re-assert its dedication to its traditional ideals in a tangible way…. At a time when the cost of justice is a burning issue and the level of costs impedes access to justice, practices which are anti-competitive can only be justified if they are shown to serve public interest. I should affirm unhesitatingly very strong view that the existence of a viable, independent bar is an indispensable element of our system of justice.[12]

Justice Nelson of the US Supreme Court described the relation between advocate and client in these words:

> There are few of the business relations of life involving a higher trust and confidence than that of attorney and client, or, generally speaking, one more honorably and faithfully discharged; few more anxiously guarded by the law, or governed by sterner principles of morality and justice; and it is the duty of the court to administer them in a corresponding spirit, and to be watchful and industrious, to see that confidence thus reposed shall not be used to the detriment or prejudice of the rights of the party bestowing it.[13]

---

[11] Albert P. Blaustein and Charles O. Porter with Charles T. Duncan, *The American Lawyer: A Summary of the Survey of the Legal Profession* (Chicago: The University of Chicago Press, 1954), p. 97.

[12] *Commonwealth law Bulletin*, vol. XIX, no. 2 (April 1993).

[13] *Stockton v. Ford* (1850), 52 U.S. 232, 247.

In *Bushman* v. *State Bar*,[14] the Supreme Court of California[15] was asked to decide on the issue of demand for excess fees coupled with misrepresentation and an attempt to solicit work. Finding Attorney Bushman guilty, the court held that the fee charged by Bushman was so exorbitant and wholly disproportionate to the services rendered as to shock the conscience. It said:

> It is settled that gross overcharge of a fee by an attorney may warrant discipline. The test is whether the fee is 'so exorbitant and wholly disproportionate to the services performed as to shock the conscience'. (*Herrscher* v. *State Bar* (1935) 4 Cal. 2d 399, 401-402 [49 P.2d 832], quoting from *Goldstone* v. *State Bar* (1931) 214 Cal. 490, 498 [6 P.2d 513, 80 A.L.R. 701]). In Herrscher this court stated that most cases warranting discipline on this ground involve an element of fraud or overreaching by the attorney, so that the fee charged, under the circumstances, constituted a practical appropriation of the client's funds.[16]

The court referred to the observation of the same court in *Recht* v. *State Bar*,[17] that the right to practise law 'is not a license to mulct the unfortunate' [3b]. The court clearly said that his course of conduct with regard to the fee, contained an element of fraud or overreaching warranting disciplinary action.

Canon No. 12 of the American Bar Association Canon of Professional Ethics clearly prescribes: 'In fixing fees it should never be forgotten that profession is a branch of the administration of justice and not a mere money-getting trade'.

The Indian Bar—Crassly Commercial

The Indian bar is well-nigh divorced from the ideal of public service and the cost of litigation is almost prohibitive for the common man. One case runs into several generations and the litigant is forced to sell his house, land, or even cloth to pay lawyers. The Supreme Court of India is hardly a court for Indians where only the filthy rich can afford to pay the fees of lawyers. The practice of charging exorbitant fees began immediately after the Supreme Court was set up in Calcutta in 1774. The lawyers at the Supreme Court charged fees two to five times as high as those in England, which was reflected in their pompous and lordly lifestyle. They opposed any attempts by the court

---

[14] 11 Cal. 3d 558.
[15] L.A. No. 30212. Supreme Court of California, 24 May 1974.
[16] 4 Cal. 2d at p. 403.
[17] (1933) 218 Cal. 352, 355 [23 P.2d 273].

to regulate them. However, no Indian lawyer was allowed to practice before it until the middle of the nineteenth century.

In India, fighting litigation means inviting one's own perdition. The poor cannot afford to hire lawyers even in sub-divisional and district courts, and fighting a case in the high court and the Supreme Court is prohibitive even for the well-to-do. The Law Commission of India recognized this problem and in 1958, it made recommendation for State legal aid and stressed on the right to assignment of counsel at government expense: 'Unless some provision is made for assisting the poor man for payment of court-fees and lawyer's fees and other incidental costs of litigation, he/she is denied equality in the opportunity to seek justice.'[18] Again, in 1969, the Law Commission, in its 41st Report, recommended that representation by a lawyer should be made available at government expenses in all cases tried by a court of sessions.[19] The Commission again, in its 48th Report, emphasized for making such a provision for all accused who were unable to hire the service of a lawyer for want of means. The Supreme Court also brought the right to free legal aid within the sweep of fair, just, and reasonable procedure under Article 21, for such accused who cannot afford a lawyer because of poverty, indigence, or incommunicado situation.[20] In *Hussainara Khatoon* v. *State of Bihar*,[21] the Court was quite forthright that it was not possible to reach the benefits of the legal process to the poor, to protect them against injustice and to secure to them their constitutional and statutory rights unless there was a nationwide legal service programme to provide free legal services to them, and tersely commented: 'Today, unfortunately, in our country the poor are priced out of the judicial system with the result that they are losing faith in the capacity of our legal system to bring about changes in their life conditions and to deliver justice to them'.[22]

Taking serious note of the growing commercialization of the legal profession, the Court deplored the vanishing trend of serving the society.[23] In *Indian Council of Legal Aid and Advice v. Bar Council of India*,[24] the Supreme Court ruled that it was obligatory on an advocate to maintain dignity and purity of the legal profession. Several lawyers defend the astronomical fee structure

[18] 'Reform of Judicial Administration', *Fourteenth Report*, vol. 1, p. 487.

[19] Vol. 1, paras 24, 34–8.

[20] *M. H. Hoskot* v. *State of Maharashtra* (1978) 3 SCC 544: AIR (1978) SC 1548.

[21] AIR (1979) SC 1369.

[22] AIR 1979 SC 1369, 1375.

[23] *Tahil Ram Issardas Sadarangani* v. *Ramchand Issardas* (1993) Supp 3 SCC 253.

[24] (1995) 1 SCC 732: AIR (1995) SC 691.

shamelessly, and unabashedly argue that it is a market economy in which any-one is free to hire anyone; if someone engages a particular lawyer, they must pay according to his/her stature or go for someone else. Besides, they claim that they pay income tax which hurts them badly. Abhishek Manu Singhvi, senior advocate, argued in this manner in an interview to the author.[25] In 2011, a big MNC showed Rs 2360 million as its legal expenditure, as it fought a case in the Supreme Court questioning the changes made to law to introduce retrospective taxation rules. Those rules, which were back dated to 1962, were designed to require taxes to be paid retrospectively. It reportedly paid the lead counsel Rs 1 crore (10 millions) per day. If money is the only attractant for lawyers, then the justice system will always be skewed in favour of moneybags who can pay the astronomical amount demanded by the really 'talented professionals in robes!'

Unlike in the inquisitorial system, in the adversary system, the judge plays the role of an umpire for the most part, listening to arguments of both sides. They then draw their inferences and adjudicate. It requires evenness of foot-ing for both parties, in the absence of which the financially weak, unable to hire an expensive lawyer is sure to keel over. V.R. Krishna Iyer has very rightly commented:

> The Indian advocate should never be the 'learned' call girl of Money Power or of the political power of the hour, but be fighting the battle for the Disabled Human Sector. Governments have come and gone, public moral weight-lifters, revolutionary sloganeers and other brands of *mareechas* have had their innings. Hopes have proved dupes in the human rights' area, what with the happen-ings in Tihar and Bihar, even Kerala and Bengal. Let the human rights vocal-ists at the bar see beyond political and economic detinus [*sic*]. Let lawyers spare some tears for tortured prisoners, raped or robbed women, burnt brides, bonded labour, suppressed *harijans* and *girijans* pavement dwellers, the waifs and strays, the exploited, the destitute and disabled brothers and sisters dying in the heat and in the cold- the silent martyrs of social injustice whom society has declared non-persons. Advocates, as judicial decisions attest, have done their duty by India (Private) Limited! The hour is near to do your duty by India (Public) Unlimited!.... Ask yourselves, who are 'We, the People of India?' A people-conscious, people-oriented, professional patriotism alone will make the bar the bar of liberty, not pre-independence anecdotage or post-independence dotage. If Freedom is what Freedom does, the Indian bar must cease to be a conspiracy against the laity, but become a sensitive collective which will strike

---

[25] Telecast in the programme 'Tete-a-tete' on DD News on 19 December 2011.

for Right against Might, for Law and Justice based on Fuller's inspiration: 'Be you ever so high, the law is above you!'[26]

Actually, since India had no tradition of legal profession, fees was exorbitant right from the beginning. England had a different tradition where clergymen used to function as lawyers in the ecclesiastical court. For them, it was a service. The gown worn by lawyers was the dress of the clergyman. It had a pouch at the back and the client dropped some guineas in it. The practice continued even after the king's court was set up and the professional class of barristers came up. The practice degenerated in course of time, and though they could not charge their fees directly, solicitors settled it before bringing clients to them. However, barristers could not sue any client for the non-payment of their fees. Even now they cannot sue, but they can complain to the Law Society against the solicitor who has not paid the fees. Thus, eventually they got the right to demand fees. The degeneration in the profession can be gauged from the fact that by the 1870s, the Law Society established itself as an effective trade union. Solicitors were never bound by this tradition.

In England, a lawyer is free to get enrolled both as a barrister as well as a solicitor, but one has to take a license every year whether one wishes to practice as a barrister or as a solicitor that year. Solicitors did not enjoy social respectability, but in the second half of the nineteenth century, they earned financial prosperity and social prestige. Abel-Smith and Robert Stevens have written about the rise of the status of solicitors:

Even as late as 1860, solicitors were generally regarded by the upper classes as tradesmen, who, if they visited a barrister's house, entered by the back door. But the situation changed rapidly. The solicitors' preliminary examination introduced in 1860 with the aim of excluding entrants who were not gentlemen helped to alter the character of the profession. By 1881 it was claimed that solicitors were 'now largely recruited from the public schools, and that 16 per cent of those who passed the final examinations were graduates of Oxford or Cambridge. Not only social status but also power was gradually gained by the junior branch of the profession. In 1851 there were eight solicitors in the House of Commons; in 1881 there were seventeen. By the Edwardian era no one better symbolized the prosperity and respectability of middle class England than the family solicitor. Meanwhile, as far as professional relations went,

[26] V.R. Krishna Iyer, 'Law, Justice and the Bar', in *Law versus Justice* (New Delhi: Deep and Deep Publications, 1983), pp. 164–6.

it was perhaps symbolic that Britain entered the First World War with a barrister Prime Minister and ended it led by a solicitor. The 'locust years' between the War merely confirmed the earlier trends.[27]

The same English barristers who came to India to practice before the Supreme Court did not follow the ethics prevalent in their own country and earned two to five times what their colleagues did back home. Litigation in India became so expensive and long-winding running into decades or generations that it became a common belief that getting embroiled in a litigation meant moving towards perdition. During the British rule, Indian lawyers earned much more than their British counterpart and law was the most remunerative profession. M.K. Gandhi was astounded at the fabulous fee structure of lawyers in Bihar and Bengal when he came to Bihar to see the plight of indigo planters in 1917: 'The figures of the fees they charged and the standard of a barrister's fees in Bengal and Bihar staggered me. "We gave Rs. 10,000 to so and so for his opinion", I was told. Nothing less than four figures in any case.'[28] M.K. Gandhi has made caustic remarks about the exorbitant fee structure of lawyers in India:

> The economic drain that the law courts cause has at no time been considered. And yet it is not a trifle. Every institution founded under the present system is run on a most extravagant scale. Law courts are probably the most extravagantly run. I have some knowledge of the scale in England, a fair knowledge of the Indian and an intimate knowledge of the South African. I have no hesitation in saying that the Indian is comparatively the most extravagant and bears no relation to the general economic condition of the people. The best South African lawyers—and they are lawyers of great ability—dare not charge the fees the lawyers in India do. Fifteen guineas is almost a top fee for legal opinion. Several thousand rupees have been known to have been charged in India. There is something sinful in a system in which it is possible for a lawyer to earn from fifty thousand to one lakh rupees per month. Legal practice is not—ought not to be—a speculative business. The best legal talent must be available to the poorest at reasonable rates.[29]

[27] Abel-Smith and Robert Stevens, 'The Solicitors Consolidate: Status and Monopolies', in *Lawyers and the Courts: A Sociological Study of the English Legal System* (London: Heinemann, 1967), p. 187.

[28] M.K. Gandhi, *An Autobiography or the Story of My Experiments with Truth* (Ahmedabad: Navjivan Publishing House, 2011), p. 375.

[29] *Young India*, 6 October 1920. M.K. Gandhi, *The Law and the Lawyers*, complied by S.B. Kher (Ahmedabad: Navjivan Publishing House, 2011), pp. 124–5.

Jawaharlal Nehru was also pained to see how avaricious lawyers were who fleeced even freedom fighters and victims of the monstrous injustice of the British government:

A defence committee was formed for the Meerut accused, of which my father was chairman.... Money, was not easy to collect ... and lawyers would only sell their services for a full pound of somebody's flesh. We had some eminent lawyers on our Committee ... but it was not possible for them to sit down in Meerut for months at a time. The other lawyers whom we approached seemed to look upon the case as a means of making as much money as possible.

Apart from the Meerut Case I have been connected with some other defence committees—in M. N. Roy's case and others. On each occasion I have marveled at the cupidity of men of my own profession. My first big shock came during the Punjab martial law trials in 1919 when a very eminent leader of the profession insisted on his full fee-from the victims of Martial Law, one of them even a fellow-lawyer and many of these people had to borrow money or sell property to pay him. My later experiences were even more painful. We had to collect money, often in coppers from poorest workers, and pay out fat cheques to lawyers.[30]

B. Sen has written that when he was assisting senior advocate, P.R. Das in the Supreme Court, who had come over from Patna to argue the Bihar and UP Zamindari abolition cases,[31] Das mentioned a particular sum as his (Sen's) fee to the client which was so high that he was astonished, as it was completely disproportionate to his standing at the Bar: 'I whispered to him that the fee was too high. He turned to me and said, "No, that is your fee. You are from the Privy Council Bar".'[32] Indian lawyers have one more feather in their caps—they not only charge for appearance, but also for non-appearance, ensuring that the opposite party does not get any good advocates.

However, the greatest leaders of India were lawyers only who gave up their lucrative practices to serve the nation. That spirit should not die down. When the first historic all-India conference was held on 28 December 1885 in which the Indian National Congress was founded, 39 of the 72 delegates

[30] Jawaharlal Nehru, *An Autobiography* (New Delhi: Penguin Books India, 2004), p. 199.

[31] *State of Bihar* v. *Maharajadhiraj Kameshwar Singh*, AIR (1952) SC 252: (1951) SCR 889; *Raja Suriyapal Singh* v. *The State of Uttar Pradesh* (1951) SCR 1056.

[32] B. Sen, *Six Decades of Law, Politics & Diplomacy: Some Reminiscences and Reflections* (New Delhi: Universal Law Publishing Co., 2010), p. 56.

who attended it were lawyers. The Parliament and the State Legislatures were initially packed with overwhelming number of lawyers. Lawyers did raise their voice when the arrogant executive sought to trample people's freedoms, and constitutional values were at stake, be it the supersession of judges or the imposition of the internal emergency in June 1975.

In the Supreme Court, fees were quite reasonable due to the self-imposed restrictions of Setalvad. Till the early 1970s, he charged Rs 1040 for SLP (*katchi* fees) and Rs 1680 for arguments (*pakki* fees) per day. Once a big business magnate, who had lost in district court as well as in high court, moved the Supreme Court. Since his case was weak, most of the senior advocates could not find any substantial point to challenge the decision of the high court. Setalvad was approached and he accepted the brief. He got the case admitted and finally won it. The industrialist client got the relief of nearly Rs 70 lakh in the early 1970s. The grateful client wanted to meet him, but he refused. On the request of the advocate-on-record, he gave him an appointment for one minute. The client gave him a blank cheque, requesting him to fill up any amount that he wished. Setalvad flew into a rage and adjured him not to do such a thing again.[33] If some senior counsel tried to charge more, it was resisted by the bar. Ashok Sen was the first to break this self-imposed code.

Esha Saha of *Live Law* has enumerated different heads under which senior advocates charge money—retainer fee (a fixed amount that a client pays in advance to a senior counsel to secure his/her service and in a way ensures that the best legal mind is not available to the adversary), reading fee, conference fee (conference with the client to understand the case, which is charged on hourly basis; it is charged from the second conference, and there are some examples of counsel charging for conference in car, flight, and court corridor), settlement of brief charges (fee charged for vetting the brief already prepared by an advocate, legal opinion/consultation (fee charged for giving oral or written opinions; this is a good practice area for government law officers), and appearance fee. She has written that law is the most sought after and money spinning career in the US, but even the lawyers from the US are astonished to hear about the fees charged by star lawyers in our country.[34] Charging money for non-appearance, euphemistically called retainership, is the most abominable and indefensible by any logic.

[33] Justice (Retd.) Dalveer Bhandari, judge of the ICJ, The Hague, narrated this story to the author on 3 January 2013 in New Delhi at his residence.

[34] Esha Saha, 'Senior Counsel Fee: How Much is Too Much', http://www.livelaw. in/senior-counsel-fee-how-much-is-too-much/ (last accessed on 5 July 2014).

High Fees Skews Justice

Adversarial litigation system makes the litigation so expensive, and thus one-sided, that it completely throttles the fundamental values of fair and equal access to justice. Big corporate companies or affluent litigants can delay or even completely frustrate the conclusion of litigation by deploying shenanigans such as overburdening plaintiffs with documents in discovery, challenging every step of the pre-trial process and then arguing every point during trial. There are case studies of excessive adversarialism in which lawyers ensure that the other side goes broke and the process is turned upside down. It will be pertinent to cite the following case study:

> Lawyers for a large multinational fast food chain routinely issue defamation writs against anyone who criticizes the company on issues like its environmental responsibility, its labour standards and attitudes towards union representation of its workers, the healthiness of its products, misleading and deceptive advertising, and advertising aimed at children. Most protestors faced with a defamation writ from the company agree to apologise and withdraw their protest activities. When two protestors in England decide to defend the writ, the company's lawyers spend four years on interlocutory applications aiming to have the protestors' defence struck out before the case be heard on its merits. Then they spend a further 314 trial days (a record for the longest trial of any kind in English legal history at that time) and 10 million pounds on a trial in which the company is represented by a large team of barristers and solicitors, while the protestors represent themselves. The company is successful in relation to about half of the statements it alleged were defamatory. Later the defendants were successful in the European Court of Human Rights where they argued that they did not have a fair trial because they lacked legal aid, and that the outcome was a disproportionate interference with their right to freedom of expression.[35]

Legal Language, Legalese, and Prolix Draft

Lawyers are known for confusing even the best minds. They use a kind of language that is abstruse, recondite, and periphrastic. Actually, this

[35] Based on the McLibel' Case: at first instance- *McDonald's Corporation* v. *Steel* (1997) EWHC QB 366 (Unreported, Bell J, 19 June 1997); on appeal- *Steel* v. *McDonald's Corporation* (1999) ECWA Civ 1144 (Unreported, Pill and may LJJ, Keene J, 31 March 1999); at the European Court of Human Rights—*Steel and Morris* v. *The United Kingdom*, no. 68416/01 (2005) ECHR 103 (15 February 2005). Christine Parker and Adrian Evans, *Inside Lawyers' Ethics* (New Delhi: Cambridge University Press, 2007), p. 67.

is a problem with most professions, more so with the legal. Brenda Danet argues:

> [o]ne of the consequences of the complex division of labour in modern societies is the tendency for occupational specialities to develop their own communication codes. We frequently speak of these codes as 'argot', 'cant' or jargon.... 'Cant' may be the most negative term; it was first used to denote the secret language of gypsies and thieves in the fifteenth century. Occupational jargons are functional insofar as they facilitate communication about difficult technical matters but dysfunctional if they create undesirable barriers between members of the group and outsiders.[36]

Lawyers make draft that is verbose, repetitive, and circumlocutory. Obsolete Latin and foreign words are still used without any rhyme or reason as these words and phrases have equivalents in English. Some of the frequently used phrases are: *a fortiorari* (all the more so), *ab initio* (from the beginning), *ad hoc* (for this purpose), *de facto* (in fact) *de jure* (in law), *ejusdem generis* (of the same kind), *inter alia* (among other things), *ipso facto* (by the mere fact), *obiter dictum* (an observation made in the judgement which is not binding), *ratio decidendi* (the principle of law decided in the case and which is binding) and *stare decisis* (principles are authoritative and binding), and so on. Even in English, the terms of Old English, which are obsolete, are used like 'The petitioner most respectfully sheweth'. Modern legal English is still a mixture of Latin, Old English, and Norman French notwithstanding the fact that there were moves in the eighteenth century for conducting legal proceedings in English. Some common words have a different meaning for lawyers. Certain honorifics are prefixed ad nauseam like 'Hon'ble' with judge or court or 'his lordship' in the plaint, and certain expressions bordering on blandishments like 'his honour/lordship was most graciously pleased to pass this order' are frequently used. Nothing seems to have changed in this regard in the last three-four centuries. David Pannick has this to write:

> Legal language delights in unnecessary repetition: *the truth, the whole truth, and nothing but the truth ... to have and to hold ... his last will testament ... null and void ...* it revels in clichés that are generally avoided in ordinary speech: *rack and ruin ... part and parcel ... safe and sound ...* lawyers use language as a protective shell, designed to insulate them from the consequences of their word or actions: *without prejudice ... in my submission ... it would seem ... the*

---

[36] Quoted by Kathy Laster, 'Language and Law', in *Law as Culture* (Delhi: Universal Law Publishing Co. Pvt. Ltd, First Indian Reprint, 2009), p. 244.

alleged … if any … the language of the law welcomes the euphemism. It uses it for a variety of purposes including ceremony, obfuscation, and the avoidance of what might otherwise be distasteful.

All these linguistic devices help the lawyer to communicate in a tongue that cannot be understood by others. The legal profession is well aware that, in Bentham's words, 'the power of the lawyer is in the uncertainty of the law'.[37]

Statutes, often drafted by lawyers, are more often than not incomprehensible not only to the common man, but even to scholars. The footnote to Part III of Schedule One of the National Insurance Act, 1946 (UK) exemplifies it vividly. It reads: 'For the purpose of this part of the Schedule, a person over pensionable age, not being an insured person, shall be treated as an employed person if he would be an insured person were he under pensionable age and would be an employed person were he an insured person'. Footnotes are added to clear ambiguity. But what does it do? Another example from the Banking Act of 1979 (UK): 'Any reference in these regulations to a regulation is a reference to a regulation contained in these regulations'.[38]

It may be pertinent to cite the following proclamation issued by Sir George Arthur (1784–1854) when he was lieutenant-governor of Van Dieman's Land (Tasmania):

> And I do herby strictly command and order all Aborigines immediately to retire and depart from, and for no reason, and on no pretence, save as hereinafter provided, to re-enter such settled districts, or any portions of land cultivated and occupied by any person whomsoever, on pain of forcible expulsion therefrom, and such consequences as may be necessarily attendant on it.[39]

Michéle M. Asprey has written,

> unfortunately, this meant nothing to the Aboriginal people, who could not read it. They kept on returning to the 'settled districts' and kept on suffering the 'pain of forcible expulsion', which was probably considerable, as

---

[37] David Pannick, 'Mysticism', in *Judges* (New York: Oxford University Press, 1988), pp. 151–2.

[38] Quoted by Tom Bingham, 'Rule of Law', http://www.independent.co.uk/arts-entertainment/books/features/the-rule-of-law-by-tom-bingham-1880966.html (last accessed on 14 May 2014).

[39] Quoted in R. Hughes, *The Fatal Shore* (London: Collins Havill, 1987), p. 419. Michéle M. Asprey, *Plain Language for Lawyers* (New Delhi: Universal Law Publishing Co., First Indian Reprint 2011), p. 91.

well as 'such consequences as may be necessarily attendant', which no doubt included death.

The proclamation did not do anything but give the authorities an excuse to punish the Aboriginal people for breaking the law they couldn't probably have understood.[40]

Sometimes, even judges use bombastic language to make ostentation of their learning but end up writing judgments which are verbose and the least comprehensible. The following quote from Circuit judge Ralph Anderson, of South Carolina, testifies to it:

This evidentiary record consisting of a four-day trial is gargantuan, elephantine and Brobdingnagian.... It would be hebetudinous and obtuse to fail to be cognizant of the adverse consequences of a ruling in this case. However, a decision by this court should not be infected with pusillanimity and timidity. The karma of this case must not be aleatory or adventitious, but a pellucid and transpicious analysis of the law and facts.... With certitude and intrepidity and, hopefully, with some degree of sagacity and sapience and perspicaciousness, this court disposes of the relevant and germane issues. Autochthonously, this court bifurcates the issues for decisional purposes. The primigenial issue is whether a new trial should be granted. The court comes to the infrangible, ineluctable and adamantine conclusion that defendant's motion for a new trial absolutely must be denied. The French phrase 'pas du tout' is applied in rejecting the defendant's argument.... I find defendant's degree of culpability to be magnitudinous and megatherine.[41]

Lord Justice Cumming-Bruce acknowledged the unintelligibility of a decision that 'parts of this judgment I am afraid are still drafted in a kind of legal jargon which may late have to be translated into English, and I hope it is intelligible'.[42]

Franz Kafka presents a picture of advocates and the draft they make in *The Trial*. The traveller tells Joseph K,

let me tell you that my petition turned out later to be quite worthless. I even had a look at one of them, thanks to the kindness of a Court official. It was very learned but it said nothing of any consequence. Crammed with Latin in the first place, which I don't understand, and then whole pages of general appeal

---

[40] Asprey, *Plain Language for Lawyers*, p. 91.

[41] Stan Ross, 'Technicians, Inhuman, Boring, Pompous', in *The Joke's on Lawyers*, p. 73.

[42] *O'Brien* v. *Sim-Chem Ltd* (1980) 1 WLR 734, 737.

to the Court, then flattering references to particular officials, who were not actually named but were easy enough for any one versed in these matters to recognize, then some self-praise for the Advocate himself, in the course of which he addressed the court with a crawling humility, ending up with an analysis of various cases from ancient times that were supposed to resemble mine.[43]

Lawrence M. Friedman has also made a searing attack on the verbosity and vagueness of the language that lawyers use:

> Hardly anyone admires the way lawyers handle language. Good professional writing is not common; a judge like Oliver Wendell Holmes, Jr., for example, known for his pungent style, is very much the exception. The code Napoleon is said to be French style at its best. Stendhal, according to one story, sharpened his style by reading from its text. On the whole, however, lawyer-language is unloved. People indict it for a number of linguistic crimes. It is tricky, deceptive, unlovely, incomprehensible. Two sins are worth some brief comment. The first is vagueness—diffuse, windy language, whose meaning cannot be grasped; the second is verbosity, which also leads to poor communication.
>
> Vagueness is common enough in legal writing. Sometimes it is quite deliberate. It may make sense to draft a statute vaguely; empty phrases can compromise or paper over, irreconcilable differences, like the language of a diplomatic communiqué.[44]

Actually, it is the tendency among ordinary human beings to show off their erudition. The easiest way to do so is to make the writing abstruse with highfalutin and alien words couched in complex sentences. This tendency is more pronounced in case of professionals who have to establish that their area of learning is too recondite for others to tread in. Brevity is the soul of wit, as the adage goes, and brevity is a direct product of clarity. Brevity in the professional writing, particularly legal writing, is missing because lawyers themselves lack clarity and in fact, they do not prefer clarity as the mist of confusion supplies them oxygen to survive. General words have different meanings in the legal world. For example, 'distress' is a common word which means suffering, worry, and so on, but in the legal language, if someone says that they exercise 'distress' over someone, it means they seize the person's goods to realize the debt owed to them.

---

[43] Franz Kafka, *The Trial* (Penguin Modern Classics, 1974), Kindle, pp. 195–6.

[44] Lawrence M. Friedman, *Law and Society: An Introduction* (Stanford, California: Prentice-Hall Foundations of Modern Sociology Series, Stanford University, 1977), pp. 89–90.

One basic reason for the prolix draft is that for a long time, legal fees were calculated on the number of pages. In order to increase the number of pages, lawyers began leaving wide margins and blank spaces. It acquired such an odious dimension that efforts were made to curb the malpractice by specifying the number of words each folio. The effort failed to check prolixity. Besides, using redundant words and regurgitating the same facts and law again and again was also meant to make the draft longer. Though the system of payment per pages disappeared in due course, the atavistic practice remained instinct.[45]

Movement for Plain Language

Realizing the need of plain language, a movement spread around the world for making statutes, laws, bylaws, legal documents, and so on, simple and comprehensible. The movement that began in the 1970s in the US, soon spread to Canada, the UK, the European Community, New Zealand, Australia, Sweden, Denmark, South Africa, and even India. Tracing the genesis of this movement, Michele M. Asprey writes:

> The Plain language began in the 1970s as a part of the consumer movement when various corporations were prompted to explore the benefits of plain language in their consumer documents. Its growth coincided with an era of demystification of (and disenchantment with) the professions. It was a time of increasing interest by linguists and others in the *process* of communication. But even so, plain language soon entered the mainstream of business and the law, quickly gaining legitimacy as lawyers and clients began to understand its advantages.[46]

In the US, the first document which adopted the plain language is the consumer loan note, launched on 1 January 1975 by First National City Bank (now Citibank). It led to heavy reduction in the number of suits the bank had to file against consumers to collect its debts. In Australia and Canada also, the banking and insurance companies were the first to move to plain language. In the US, in 1969, President Nixon ordered that daily government journal, the *Federal Register*, be written in 'language which is readily understandable by the layman'.[47] Sweden took the lead in plain language. As early as 1713,

---

[45] Laster, 'Language and Law', p. 251.

[46] Asprey, *Plain Language for Lawyers*.

[47] Special message to the Congress on Consumer Protection, 30 October 1969. Asprey, *Plain Language for Lawyers*, p. 66.

King Charles XII issued this ordinance: 'His majesty the King requires that the Royal Chancellery in all written documents endeavour to write in clear, plain Swedish and not to use, as far as possible, foreign words.'[48]

In 1976, the Swedish government appointed a linguist to the Cabinet Office to modernize legal language. In 1978, President Jimmy Carter issued a similar order that 'regulations should be as simple and clear as possible'.[49] In the UK, the Renton Committee in its report, published on 7 May 1975, pointed to the convoluted drafting in British statutes and recommended the explanatory material. It led to rewriting of some laws. Similarly, its Civil Procedure Rules was also reformed in 1999 in the light of the Report of Lord Justice Woolf, called 'Access to Justice'. A word like *subpoena* was replaced by *witness summon*. In 1993, the European Council of Ministers passed a resolution in the European Union spelling out how legislation should be drafted: 'The wording of the act should be clear, simple, concise and unambiguous, unnecessary abbreviations, "Community jargon" and excessively long sentences should be avoided'.[50]

Laws in India are verbose and incomprehensible as they were enacted a la Britain. Nani A. Palkhivala has written:

As regards the drafting of statutes, we have unfortunately adopted the British model which is far worse than its European counterparts. For instance, the British law of copyright runs to 92 pages. The French law covering the same area, and printed in similar type-size, could be contained in 20 pages and the Swedish in only 13 pages. Even shorn of those provisions for which there is no equivalent in the laws of other countries, the British law could take up about 70 pages—more than three times the French and five times the Swedish.

Referring to a certain statute, Lord Reid said that he found it impossible 'to discover or even surmise what the draftsman can have had in mind'. Commenting on the language in which different acts of Parliament were couched, various authorities have expressed their deep dissatisfaction. 'Laxity or ambiguity of expression', was the verdict of the Statute Law Commissioners in 1835.... 'Verbose and tautologous', was the comment of the Master of the Rolls in 1834. 'That chaos of verbal darkness', was how Lord Justice McKinnon described a British statute in 1944.[51]

---

[48] Asprey, *Plain Language for Lawyers*, p. 66.
[49] US Executive Order 12044, 23 March 1978. Asprey, *Plain Language for Lawyers*.
[50] Asprey, *Plain Language for Lawyers*, p. 76.
[51] Nani A. Palkhivala, 'Truth and Service of All', in *We the People*, pp. 352–3.

Of late, the Supreme Court of India also took the initiative to simplify the law. Its Project Committee prepared a set of Restatement of Indian Law covering three different legal subjects—Legislative Privilege, Contempt of Court, and Public Interest Litigation.[52] On 11 October 2011, the then CJI S.H. Kapadia released it in New Delhi. The Committee was headed by its judge, Justice R.V. Raveendran (since retired). Another volume came out in 2012, but there has been no progress since then.

Unethical Practices

The expose by NDTV telecast on 30 May 2007, showing unethical practice of trying to win over prosecution witness by prominent lawyers, only confirms the age-old belief about lawyers. What R.K. Anand, a prominent lawyer and former MP, did is not a case of borderline deviation, but the most reprehensible attempt to affect the course of justice. He was found guilty of criminal contempt of court for colluding with the special public prosecutor for suborning prosecution witness in criminal trial and was barred from practicing before the Delhi High Court and courts below it for four months.[53] It concerned a criminal trial in which the grandson of a former admiral was accused of causing death of six people, including three policemen, by rash and negligent driving. He crashed through a police check post while driving a black BMW car in an inebriated condition. The Supreme Court listed the malpractices of advocates and upheld the punishment awarded to Anand:

> [I]n a given case a direction disallowing an advocate who is convicted of criminal contempt from appearing in court may not only be a measure to maintain the dignity and orderly functioning of the courts but may become necessary for the self protection of the court and for preservation of the purity of court proceedings. Let us, for example, take the case where an advocate is shown to have accepted money in the name of a judge or on the pretext of influencing him; or where an advocate is found tampering with the court's record; or where an advocate is found actively taking part in faking court orders (fake bail orders are not unknown in several High Courts!); or where an advocate has made it into a practice to browbeat and abuse judges and on that basis has earned the reputation to get a case transferred from an 'inconvenient' court; or where an advocate is found to be in the habit of sending unfounded and unsubstantiated allegation petitions against judicial officers and judges to the superior courts.

---

[52] Published by Indian Law Institute, New Delhi, 2011.
[53] *R.K. Anand* v. *Registrar, Delhi High Court* (2009) 8 SCC 106.

Unfortunately these examples are not from imagination. These things are happening more frequently than we care to acknowledge … In such a situation the court does not only have the right but it also has the obligation cast upon it to protect itself and save the purity of its proceedings from being polluted in any way….[54]

Lawyer Somnath Bharti, who subsequently became the Law minister of Delhi in the Aam Aadmi Party (AAP) government in December 2013, was indicted by a Patiala House court in August 2013 for 'tampering with evidence'. CBI Special judge hauled up Bharti and his client Pawan Kumar—facing prosecution on corruption charges—after the CBI accused them of influencing a prosecution witness by speaking to him on phone and discussing the case. 'The conduct of the accused Pawan Kumar and his advocate (Bharti) is not only highly objectionable, unethical but also amounts to tampering with evidence', observed the judge in her order cancelling Kumar's bail on the ground that he misused his liberty.[55] Kumar was facing prosecution by the CBI since 2006 in separate cases for his alleged acts of omission and commission while he worked with the State Bank of Mysore. In one of the cases, testimony of B.S. Diwakar, a prosecution witness, was recorded in court. During his cross-examination, Kumar through his lawyer Bharti, submitted that he wanted to confront Diwakar with an audio conversation which he wanted to place in the court. A baffled court then came to know that he/his advocate had a telephonic conversation with Diwakar in which he (Diwakar) controverted what he testified in the court. Kumar recorded the conversation and Bharti argued that his client should be allowed to place the audio tapes on record to confront the witness and bring out the truth. Kumar challenged his indictment up to the Supreme Court but was not absolved. Bharti, nevertheless, continued to claim that he had done nothing ignoble as his intention was to bring out the truth. However, Bar Council of India Rules under Section 49(1)(c) of the Advocates Act, 1961 lays down: 'An advocate shall not in any way communicate or negotiate upon the subject matter of controversy with any party represented by an advocate except through that advocate'.

These are only some of the examples. Advocates indulge in many more reprehensible practices. Many a time, advocates of the two parties strike a deal between themselves and both take money from their clients in the name of paying the judge with a promise that the money will be returned if the party

---

[54] *R.K. Anand* v. *Registrar, Delhi High Court* (2009) 8 SCC 106, para 143.
[55] *Times of India*, New Delhi, 15 January 2013.

gets an adverse order. One of the contestants is bound to win. The money of the loser is returned saying that the party which won paid more, and the remaining money is distributed between the two advocates. Many advocates work as touts for senior lawyers and charge a hefty commission from the fees charged by the senior counsel. It can be unravelled easily if one does a sting operation on lawyers.

However, the Bar Council, in all its wisdom, gave Anand a long time to reply. If 11 MPs could be expelled after conducting thorough probe in less than two weeks in 2005, why can't the Bar Council take an expeditious decision? Though the Bar Council has not been very firm and quick in cases of misconduct against lawyers, on some occasions it has taken action and recorded facts which suggest how low advocates stoop. In *H.G. Kulkarni and others* v. *B.B. Subedar*, the Disciplinary Committee of the BCI has recorded:

> *Advocate obtained signature of complainant on some blank forms, blank papers and blank cheques, and withdrew amounts from his bank account without his knowledge, which he repaid back after complaint to the bank. Also received excess amount as fee and court fee for filing cross-Appeal or cross objection in court, which he did not file, and charged the fees on a percentage basis contingent upon the result of the case.*[56]

The respondent-advocate had withdrawn Rs 2,95,766.25 from the account of the first complainant by playing fraud. The said amount was credited to the account of the respondent on 29 August 1988, and then using the blank cheque signed by the first complainant, the respondent took an amount of Rs 2,11,615 from the bank.

The Supreme Court has also commented copiously on the despicable conduct of lawyers. Condemning the callous and indifferent attitude of some advocates, the Supreme Court stressed on the need to improve the quality of service.[57] It criticized advocates attending court with firearms and browbeating, or pressurizing judicial officers or authorities calling such conduct unbecoming to the legal profession which undermines the rule of law,[58]

---

[56] D.C. Appeal No. 40 of 1996, Ram Chandra Jha (ed.), *Selected Judgements on Professional Ethics*, Vol. 1, Second Edition (New Delhi: Bar Council of India Trust, 2012), p. 425.

[57] Sanjiv Datta, Deputy Secretary, Ministry of Information and Broadcasting, *In Re* (1995) 3 SCC 619.

[58] *U.P. State Tax Service Association* v. *Taxation Bar Association, Agra* (1995) 5 SCC 716.

it exhorted that an advocate should not show disrespect, overbear, and overawe the court.[59] The Court lamented the unprofessional conduct of advocates to retain briefs and yet not appear in court, which is not occasional because of personal inconvenience but has become a regular feature.[60] In *P.D. Gupta* v. *Ram Murti and Another*,[61] the Supreme Court found that the advocate purchased property from the client, which was subject matter of dispute between the parties. The Court observed:

> A lawyer owes a duty to be fair not only to his client but to the court as well as to the opposite party in the conduct of the case. Administration of justice is a stream which has to be kept pure and clean. It has to be kept unpolluted, administration of justice is not something which concerns the Bench only. It concerns the Bar as well. Bar is the principal ground for recruiting Judges. No one should be able to raise a finger about the conduct of lawyer. While conducting the case he functions as officer of the court.[62]

Advocates have been punished for betraying the confidence of the clients, breach of trust, financial misappropriation, suppression of material facts, taking undue advantage of one's position, misuse of signed documents and forgery, purchase of property of the client in dispute, contingent fees, contempt of court, duty to the court, physical assault, and some other kinds of misconduct.[63] What has come to light is the tip of the iceberg.

Role of Law Officers of Government

In 2013, the role of Attorney-General, Goolam E. Vahanvati came under scanner for his role in country's biggest scandal of the time—the fraudulent allocation of 2G cellular spectrum. On 27 February, he made history of sorts by becoming the first attorney-general who appeared before a CBI special court in Delhi's Patiala House and stood in the witness box, refuting allegations about his role in the scam. Sushil Kumar, the defence counsel for the prime accused, former communications minister Andhimuthu Raja, peppered Vahanvati with questions suggesting that he, as the then solicitor-general, had given legal imprimatur to the policy under which the allocations

---

[59] Vinay Chandra Mishra, *In Re* (1995) 2 SCC 584.
[60] *Mahabir Prasad Singh* v. *Jacks Aviation Pvt. Ltd* (1991) 1 SCC 37).
[61] (1997) 7 SCC 147: AIR (1998) SC 283.
[62] (1997) 7 SCC 147: AIR (1998) SC 283, para 16.
[63] Ram Chandra Jha (ed.), *Selected Judgements on Professional Ethics*, Vols. 1 and 2, Second Edition (New Delhi: Bar Council of India Trust, 2012).

were made. As Vahanvati denied allegations, Raja, at one point, interjected loudly inside the courtroom, exclaiming, 'he is telling all the lies and I am the one going to jail'.[64]

Again, the role of Vahanvati and that of the then Additional Solicitor General Harin Raval, in misleading the Supreme Court in the Coalgate investigation case, raised serious questions about the role of lawyers as officers of the court who are supposed to assist in arriving at justice. Raval was forced to quit after it became evident that he lied to the Court on 12 March that the 8 March status report of the CBI into the coal scam had not been shared by the political executive. Before quitting, Raval dashed off a letter to Vahanvati accusing him of influencing the CBI investigation and making him a scapegoat.[65] In his damning latter, Raval pointed out that the attorney-general was present at the meeting with the Union Law Minister, Ashwani Kumar. Vahanvati, appearing for the Centre before a bench headed by Justice R.M. Lodha, admitted in the Court that he was present in the said meeting but he never saw the draft (report).[66] The CBI, in its affidavit submitted in the SC on 6 May, confirmed that Vahanvati was present in the meeting held by the law minister and instrumental in the changes made in the draft report, but he had denied that he had any knowledge about it. It amounts to nothing short of perjury.

The participation of the attorney-general in the meeting with the Law minister is quite disturbing. He was the top law officer of the government which was in the dock in the concerned case. So, how could he vet the report of the agency which is investigating the alleged irregularities? The attorney-general for India is a constitutional post created under Article 76 of the Constitution. He enjoys an exalted position and is one of the only two constitutional functionaries who can address the Parliament without being its member—the other one being the comptroller and auditor general. The Constitution provides that a person to be appointed as attorney-general should be 'qualified to be appointed a Judge of the Supreme Court'. So, he is supposed to be fearless like a judge and must give only the correct advice to the government, the court, and the Parliament like the conscience keeper of the country. Vahanvati is also accused of indiscretion because he continued to give opinions, or appear in cases involving Anil Ambani and his companies

[64] 'Inside Man: The Convenient Opinions of Attorney General Goolam Vahanvati', *The Caravan*, New Delhi, May 2013, p. 24.

[65] 'ASG Raval Blames Vahanvati for Interference', *The Hindu*, New Delhi, 30 April 2013; 'Law Officers Spar over Coalgate', *Hindustan Times*, New Delhi, 30 April 2013.

[66] 'AG Sat, Heard but Saw Nothing', *The Pioneer*, New Delhi, 1 May 2013.

despite being his close friend. Activist advocate Prashant Bhushan said, 'Vahanvati told me himself that he is close friend of Anil Ambani…. That, itself, is a conflict of interest.'[67]

In England, the office of the attorney-general is regarded a political office as s/he is a member of the council of ministers also. Still, as the top law officer of the Crown, s/he enjoys a considerable degree of independence. In India, it is a non-political post, but the tradition goes that the attorney-general resigns with the change of the government. However, there are examples when the law officer did not resign with the change of government. H.M. Seervai is one such example who remained advocate-general for 17 years in Maharashtra. T.R. Andhyarujina has written:

> Governments came and went but Seervai did not feel it necessary to resign with the installation of a new government nor did any new government ask for his resignation…. He refused to defend those policies of the government which he felt were unconscionable, and against his convictions. He refused the government brief when it sought to ban the teaching of English in Anglo-Indian schools, believing that the policy was wrong. He did not think it right to defend the erection of a 'martyrs' memorial' in Bombay in honour of states [*sic*] formed on the basis of languages.[68]

Justice M. Hidayatullah has also made the position clear:

> In Adi Pheroz Gandhi v. H. M. Seervai (1971 SC 385), there was a difference of opinion in the Bench mainly because of a decision of Lord Denning M. R., which we in the majority thought could not apply in India, because the Advocate-General and Attorney-General do not represent either the State or the Governor or the President, as the case may be, in the same way as the Attorney-General does in England and some of the colonies. There the Attorney-General represents the Queen in all cases in his discretion and thus has an interest. The Advocate-General in India is heard more or less as an amicus curiae and has no other interest.[69]

[67] 'Inside Man: The Convenient Opinions of Attorney General Goolam Vahanvati', *The Caravan*, New Delhi, May 2013, p. 29.

[68] T.R. Andhyarujina, 'H. M. Seervai: A Man of Character, Courage and Commitment', in *Constitutional Perspectives: Essays in Honour and memory of H. M. Seervai*, edited by Venkat Iyer (New Delhi: Universal Law Publishing Co. Ltd, 2001), pp. 6–7; Madhav Godbole, 'Judicial Reforms Nowhere in Sight', in *The Judiciary and the Governance in India* (New Delhi: Rupa and Co., 2009), p. 482.

[69] Justice M. Hidayatullah, *My Own Boswell* (New Delhi: Universal Law Publishing Co. Ltd, 2015), p. 257.

However, taking a contrary stand in *B.P. Singhal* v. *Union of India*,[70] a five-judge Constitution Bench of the Supreme Court justified the change of attorney-general on the ground of loss of confidence:

> For withdrawal of pleasure in the case of a Minister or an Attorney General, loss of confidence may be a relevant ground. The ideology of the Minister or Attorney General being out of sync with the policies or ideologies of the Government may also be a ground. On the other hand, for withdrawal of pleasure in the case of a Governor, loss of confidence or the Governor's views being out of sync with that the Union Government will not be grounds for withdrawal of the pleasure. The reasons for withdrawal are wider in the case of Ministers and Attorney-General, when compared to Governors. As a result, the judicial review of withdrawal of pleasure, is limited in the case of a Governor whereas virtually nil in the case of a Minister or an Attorney General.[71]

This is uncanny as the Court has ruled differently in case of governor, but the attorney-general has been equated with minister, diminishing the impartiality of the constitutional post.

Setalvad, the first attorney-general, observed a high standard of ethics and never called on any minister except the then Prime Minister Jawaharlal Nehru, then Home Minister Sardar Vallabhbhai Patel, and then Education Minister Abul Kalam Azad. Other ministers, including the law minister, came to his chamber. But there was a fall in the standard after him. Niren De used to call on even the private secretary to the prime minister. He took a servile position in the infamous Habeas Corpus case[72] during the Emergency that there is no right to life. Now, we see the attorney-general frequently meeting the law minster in the latter's chamber. In protocol, the law minister is senior to the attorney-general, but ideally the client comes to the lawyer. Even Setalvad was not totally right by making exceptions in cases of Nehru, Patel, and Azad. When Soli Sorabjee was appointed attorney-general in 1989 by the National Front Government headed by V.P. Singh, he made an alarming statement that his role was not that of a hatchet-man of the government.[73] Perhaps he made the statement as V.P. Singh had ridden to power with a promise to cleanse the system. The previous government had been mired in scams like Bofors, and Sorabjee wanted to forewarn that he would not be a party to any cover-ups

---

[70] 7 May 2010.

[71] 7 May 2010, para 48.

[72] *A. D. M. Jabalpur* v. *Shivkant Shukla* (1976) 2 SCC 521: AIR (1976) SC 1207.

[73] 'Raju Ramachandran, Serving GoI, Not the Law', *Economic Times*, New Delhi, 1 May 2013.

even if skeletons tumbled out of the incumbent government's cupboard. When he became attorney-general for the second time in 1998 in the NDA government headed by Atal Bihari Vajpayee, he took a position contrary to the one taken by the government in the case pertaining to the educational institutions run by the minorities.[74]

About the role of the government counsel, the Supreme Court has observed:

> A lawyer is a responsible officer of the court. It is his duty as the officer of the court to assist the court in a properly prepared manner. That is the sacrosanct role assigned to an advocate. As far as the counsel for the state is concerned, it can be decidedly stated that he has a higher responsibility.... He is expected to have higher standard of conduct … it is because he has access to public records and is also obliged to protect the public interest. That apart, he has a moral responsibility to the court. When these values corrode, one can say 'things fall apart'.[75]

Impartiality is expected of public prosecutors. They may be representing the state, but they are not supposed to chime in with the police as their first and foremost duty is to uphold justice. The Supreme Court defined their role as: 'The court has a responsibility and a stake in the administration of criminal justice and so has the Public Prosecutor., its 'Minister of Justice'. Both have a duty to protect the administration of criminal justice against possible abuse or misuse by the executive by resort to provisions of Section 361 Criminal Procedure Code'.[76]

Criminal Acts of Lawyers

Lawyers have been indulging in several unethical practices about which there are hardly any complaints. On the basis of personal experience, I can authentically say that lawyers are intimidating customers of private mobile operators and private banks for payments of arrears, which are often inflated and settlement of accounts which are generally manipulated, and would often say that they were calling from the warrant section of some court which does not exist. The numbers from which these calls are made are that of lawyers and any thorough investigation will expose the whole racket. Lawyers commit criminal offences and use their robes to ward off penal action. When the Lucknow Bench of the Allahabad High Court directed the CBI to investigate cases

[74] 'Raju Ramachandran, Serving GoI, Not the Law'.
[75] *State of Rajasthan* v. *Surendra Mohnot* (2014) 14 SCC 77, paras 31 to 33.
[76] *Rajender Kumar Jain* v. *State* (1980) 3 SCC 435, para 15.

in which lawyers are accused but they have not been named, it found that around 80 lawyers were guilty of criminal offences and arrested two of them. Lawyers of Lucknow struck work against the police action in Lucknow.[77] In 2013, Delhi Police arrested an advocate, Baljeet Singh Sehrawat, who took a contract for Rs 5 crores for the murder of Deepak Bhardwaj, Bahujan Samaj Party (BSP) leader and real estate tycoon.[78] In *Himmat Ali Khan* v. *Ishwar Prasad Arya*,[79] the Supreme Court directed to remove the name of the advocate, Ishwar Prasad Arya, from the State Roll of Advocates for ever. The advocate had assaulted his opponent with a knife in the court room and he was sentenced to rigorous imprisonment for a period of three years under Section 307 of the IPC. He also forged a letter signed by deputy secretary, Ministry of Home, Uttar Pradesh, which said that the governor had been pleased to suspend the conviction of the accused advocate under Article 161 of the Constitution. The State Bar Council (SBC) of Uttar Pradesh debarred him from practicing for three years but the Bar Council of India (BCI) set aside the order and acquitted him. The Supreme Court reversed the judgement of the BCI.

An advocate in Delhi was found to have links with terror outfit. It came to light when his name was recommended by the collegium of the Delhi High Court for appointment as a high court judge and the Supreme Court collegium endorsed it and forwarded it to the government. It was the Intelligence Bureau which rang the alarm bell that the lawyer had links with a terrorist organization.[80] Lawyers, the officers of the court, unleashed violence, and assaulted students, teachers, and journalists inside and outside Patiala House courts in New Delhi on 15 February 2016 when Kanhaiya Kumar, then president of the Jawaharlal Nehru University Students' Union was being taken to court after his arrest in a sedition case. They created mayhem in the court complex again two days later, heckling journalists and kicking Kanhaiya, prompting the Supreme Court to ask officials to ensure safety of the accused.[81] It raised a serious question mark on the role and function

---

[77] *Dainik Jagran*, New Delhi, Rashtriya Sanskaran, 27 May 2010.

[78] 'Son, Lawyer Arrested for Bhardwaj's Murder', *The Statesman*, New Delhi, 10 April 2013.

[79] Civil Appeal No. 4240 0f 1986, judgement dated 28 January 1997.

[80] 'Advocate with Links to Terror Outfit Almost Became a High Court Judge', *Times of India*, New Delhi, 1 July 2013.

[81] 'Lawyers Turn Lawless Again', *Hindustan Times*, New Delhi, 18 February 2016; 'Cops Give Goons a Free Hand, Again', *Times of India*, New Delhi, 18 February 2016.

of advocates. Barely five days earlier, on 10 February, lawyers in Lucknow resorted to arson and violence during a protest march against the murder of advocate Shravan Kumar Verma. An advocate was openly flaunting a gun.[82] One wonders if the society is heading back to the old ordeal system!

In Pakistan, in January 2011, young lawyers created mob scenes to express solidarity with Malik Mumtaz Hussain Qadri, the self-confessed assassin of Governor Salman Taseer who was awarded death sentence by the court. Lawyers showered rose petals on Qadri, a member of an elite police group assigned to guard the governor, and threatened the life of the judge who sentenced him to death.[83] Taseer was brutally slain because he mustered courage to state publicly that a blasphemy law was being used to discriminate against religious minorities.

No wonder, in the US, they are called 'paid thugs' and this image is reflected in a widely used bumper sticker: 'MY LAWYER CAN BEAT UP YOUR LAWYER'. In fact, such an incident did take place in the US in the nineteenth century when a lawyer killed another lawyer. Thomas Hart Benton (1782–1858) was the most influential Missouri politician during his tenure as a senator. He practiced law and often argued cases against Charles Lucas, a competing attorney. During a heated argument in court in 1817, Benton felt that Lucas had slighted him. Infuriated, he challenged Lucas to a duel, and the two met on Bloody Island near St Louis. Luckily the duel ended without any serious injuries to either, but Benton was not satisfied and asked for another duel. In the second duel, Benton killed Lucas with a gunshot that pierced his heart.

There are countless jokes on lawyers. An incident that took place in 1993 in California, US, suggests how lawyers are perceived and how scared they are of jokes about them. A distraught former client appeared at a San Francisco law firm of Petit and Martin and shot all those who were to be seen there. In a few minutes, nine people, including the shooter, were dead. A number of those shot, happened to be lawyers. About a week after the horrid incident, then president of the State Bar of California Harvey Saferstein called a news conference and requested the public to stop cracking lawyer jokes: 'There is

[82] Sudhanshu Ranjan, 'Not Just JNU: With Lawyers Acting as Goons, Time for SC to Step In', 18 February 2016, http://www.hindustantimes.com/analysis/not-just-jnu-with-lawyers-acting-as-goons-time-for-sc-to-step-in/story-Tb4CT0AF0adijwmTIN72uI.html (last accessed on 12 march 2017).

[83] 'Lawyers' Support for Taseer's Assassin Worries Pak', 11 January 2011, http://www.ndtv.com/article/world/lawyers-support-for-taseer-s-assassin-worries-pak-78533 (last accessed on 22 November 2014).

a point at which jokes and humour are acceptable and a point at which they become nothing more than hate speech ... [I call on] all Americans to stop the lawyer-bashing that has been going on, particularly by national, commercial sponsors that sometimes can ignite violence and aggression toward lawyers.'[84]

In Australia also, they are portrayed in similar colours. Former Labour Queensland Attorney General Dean Macmillan Wells, said that they were developing a 'legal-warrior caste', and added, 'The Wall Street sue-litigate-liquidate-terminate mentality is just not forward thinking; these black letter lawyers are the only professional group who are licensed to inflict pain-hip-pocket pain on other people'.[85]

Still, legal profession survives and the number of litigation keeps on rising. But it does not mean that people are getting justice, and so they are flocking to courts. What do the people do if they are left with no option? Crime is another option, and the growth of terrorism bears testimony to the fact that justice is the rarest of rare commodity. Injustice provides mother's milk to terrorism. The question arises: are lawyers required?

Utter Failure of the Bar Council

The Advocates Act, 1961 created an autonomous regulator—Bar Council at the national level (BCI) and SBC for each state. First, advocates elect members of the SBC, who in turn elect one member from each state for the BCI. Before the promulgation of this act, the high court in each state was vested with the disciplinary jurisdiction over advocates. Now, SBC is empowered to take disciplinary action against any advocate for misconduct, and can suspend or even cancel one's license. The BCI is the appellate authority against the decisions of the SBC, and the Supreme Court is the final appellate court. However, the experience shows that the regulator has miserably failed to ensure that lawyers observe the ethics formulated by it. Thousands of complaints are pending against advocates regarding their misconduct, but hardly any action is taken. These complaints are only a small fraction of incidents of actual misconduct, as most clients misled or hoodwinked by their lawyers, tolerate complaisantly and hardly complain. If all cases of misconduct are reported and the regulator sincerely acts on them, more than half of the practicing advocates will be struck off the roll. Unfortunately, the Bar Council

---

[84] T. Overton, 'Lawyers, Light Bulbs and Dead Snakes: The Lawyer Joke as Societal Text', *UCLA Law Review*, vol. 42, no. 1069 (1995): 1073.

[85] Ross, *The Jokes on Lawyers*, p. 5.

prefers to keep its eyes shut as it is an elected body and does not want to antagonize lawyers who are the voters. On December 2010, Rajendra Rana, member, BCI, was arrested by the CBI for allegedly accepting graft in lieu of granting recognition to a Ghaziabad-based private law college. Lawyers of Delhi immediately swung into action and stayed away from work in protest against the 'high-handedness' of the CBI.[86]

The Law Commission of India undertook an exercise to find effective regulatory mechanism to save litigants from trouble due to unruly conduct of lawyers who proceed to strikes at the drop of a hat. The Commission undertook the study of the Advocates Act, 1961, when the Supreme Court in *Mahipal Singh Rana* v. *State of UP*[87] asked it to go into all relevant aspects relating to legal profession in consultation with all concerned, and send their comments not later than 31 August 2016. The Court lamented that despite direction of the high court as long back as more than 10 years, no action was taken by the Bar Council, and so, it was exercising it appellate jurisdiction under the Advocates Act, 1961, in view of the failure of the statutory obligation of the Bar Council of the state of Uttar Pradesh as well as the BCI in case of proved misconduct of an advocate who was found guilty of threatening a civil judge. It stressed on the need to overhaul the Advocates Act to restore people's faith in the regulatory body. The Court suspended the license of appellant Rana for five years.

However, it is also true that the apex court took such a drastic step only because it involved a judge. Though lawyers need severe disciplining, it is also true that many a time, the higher courts initiate disciplinary action against lawyers. In 2016, the Madras High Court introduced crucial changes to Section 34 of the Advocates Act arrogating to itself powers of the Bar Council, penalizing lawyers for attempting to 'browbeat' judges, or giving complaints to superiors about them. It bequeathed the power to the court to debar a lawyer from legal practice lifelong and debar them as an interim measure even before inquiry.[88] It was an administrative order which was put in abeyance after the intervention of the BCI.

Though Section 34 gives certain powers to courts, it does not go to the extent of debarring lawyers from legal practice which is the exclusive domain of the Bar Council. Section 49(1)(c) read: 'An advocate ... shall not be servile and whenever there is proper ground for serious complaint

---

[86] *Indian Express*, New Delhi, 23 December 2010.

[87] Criminal Appeal No. 63 of 2006, decided on 5 July 2016.

[88] N.G.R. Prasad, D. Nagasaila, and V. Suresh, 'Do not Browbeat Lawyers', *The Hindu*, Perspective, 3 June 2016.

against a judicial officer, it shall be his right and duty to submit his griev-
ance to proper authorities.' So reporting the misconduct of a judge to the
superior authorities is not browbeating, rather, it is his duty. More so, lawyers are the only ones who observe the functioning of the court closely and
constantly, and so, in a position to know the truth. Moreover, an honest
and forthright lawyer may blurt out the truth without pulling punches to
the disliking of the judge who may take it as browbeating. The order of the
high court is also in sharp conflict with the United Nations 'Basic Principles
on the Role of Lawyers' which lay down certain minimum guarantees for
the functioning of lawyers.

However, it is also a sad fact that lawyers brazen it out in matters of professional ethics. The SBC, as well as the BCI, is enjoined under Sections 6(1)
and 7(1) of the Advocates Act 'to conduct seminars and organize talks on legal
topics by eminent jurists and publish journals and papers of legal interest'.
But the regulator has totally abdicated its duty of maintaining the academic
brilliance of the bar and seldom organizes any seminar on issues relating
to the administration of justice as its priorities are different. Such activities
would have definitely helped contain the rot in the profession as participants
share their experience and offer suggestions to repristinate the glory of the
profession.

Right of Defence

The success or brilliance of a lawyer is measured in terms of his/her capacity
to win the weakest case or get acquitted the most notorious criminal. S/he can
defend the most abominable crime on the ground that everyone has a right
to defence in an adversarial system, and that a lawyer knows nothing about
the crime personally and his/her knowledge of a case is based on documents.
Describing England of the fourteenth century, G.M. Trevelyan writes how
lawyers saved criminals:

> In most of the counties of England the King's writ ran, though it was often
> evaded or defied. Murderers and thieves, when not in service of some great
> lord, were often obliged to fly to the greenwood, or to take sanctuary and then
> forswear the realm. Sometimes they were actually arrested and brought into
> court. Even then they slipped through the meshes of law by pleading their
> 'clergy' or by some other lawyer's trick.[89]

[89]   G.M. Trevelyan, *English Social History* (London: Longmans, 1944), p. 18.

However, the right to defence does not mean that a lawyer must accept a brief even if he is convinced that his client has committed the crime. Professionally, a lawyer should never ask the client whether he has actually committed the crime because if he confesses to his guilt then the lawyer should advise him to plead guilty or else refuse his case. After hearing from the horse's mouth about the commission of the offence, he will not be able to do justice either to the client or to himself and assist the court in arriving at justice as the officer of the court. The then CJI Harilal J. Kania, defined the role of lawyer in these words:

> One of the main objects of the (Bar) Association is to maintain a high standard of professional conduct. In my opinion, that conduct consists in following three cardinal principles, viz., (1) Be true to yourself; (2) Be true to your client; and (3) Be true to the Court.... After collecting all the material and relevant facts from your client you must remember that while in the conduct of a litigation you are the mouthpiece of the client, no one has a right to ask you to do a thing which is wrong in law. No law in the technical or the moral sense of the word compels you to act against your conscience.... You owe a duty to the Court to put the facts correctly and honestly and not with a view to misguide or mislead.... Never try to mislead the Court by propounding a proposition of law, which you know is wrong. It is your duty to help the Court in arriving at a just conclusion according to the law of the land. Lack of appreciation of this code has been more frequently noticed recently.[90]

If in 1949, Justice Kania felt that professional ethics were being violated frequently, one can imagine the state of affairs at present with abject degeneration in moral values all around. Even M.K. Gandhi felt that lawyers are not interested in conciliation; rather they provoke litigation. According to him, a true lawyer is one who puts truth and service in the first place. Albert P. Blaustein and co-authors have described the American lawyer like this, 'He (lawyer) has been unhappily described as one who gets other two men to strip for a fight and then takes their clothes. And the cause he serves with such diligence is constantly met with carping criticism and complaint.'[91] In the US, lawyers contributed their skill and might to continue the barbaric system of discrimination against African-Americans. In the southern states, leaders of the White community would intimidate, persecute, and publicly hang innocent African-Americans. However, there was no dearth of advocates

---

[90] Address by the Hon'ble Sir Harilal J. Kania, CJI at the Diamond Jubilee Celebration of the Madras Advocates' Association held on 17 April 1949, AIR (1949) vol. 36, Journal Section, pp. 22–3.

[91] Blaustein and Porter with Duncan, *The American Lawyer*, p. 1.

who were ever ready to defend such abominable and racist acts they sincerely believed in the superiority of the Whites.

Lawyers use technicalities as a ruse to defend the most dreaded criminals knowing full well that their clients are guilty and mislead the court. Like the orators of ancient Greece, as mentioned above, most defence lawyers vouch for the innocence of their clients and use their ratiocinative faculty to falsify the truth. Trollope presents a quaint picture of the techniques used by lawyers:

> To turn a witness to good account, he must be badgered this way and that till he is nearly mad; he must be made a laughing-stock for the court; his very truths must be turned into falsehoods, so that he may be falsely shamed; he must be accused of all manner of villainy, threatened with all manner of punishment; he must be made to feel that he has no friend near him, that the world is all against him; he must be confounded till he forget his right hand from his left, till his mind be turned into chaos, and his heart into water; and then let him give his evidence. What will fall from his lips when in this wretched collapse must be of special value, for the best talents of practised forensic heroes are daily used to bring it about; and no member of the Humane Society interferes to protect the wretch. Some sorts of torture are as it were tacitly allowed even among humane people. Eels are skinned alive, and witnesses are sacrificed, and no one's blood curdles at the sight, no soft heart is sickened at the cruelty.[92]

The question is, can a lawyer refuse to defend an accused or a defendant? Though bar associations cannot pass any resolutions asking their members not to take up cases of certain classes of accused like those charged with terrorism or rape, and so on, individual lawyers, in my opinion, can definitely refuse to accept the brief if s/he is convinced that the client (accused/defendant/petitioner) should not be defended. It is argued that everyone is innocent until proved guilty, and that everyone should be given the benefit of doubt, and so must be defended. Lawyers argue that refusing to defend someone amounts to pre-judging. Fali S. Nariman invited international animadversion when he accepted to work as the lead advocate for UCC in the civil litigation arising out of the Bhopal gas tragedy. Pauline Comeau made a swingeing indictment of Nariman: They were once human rights activists. Now, no one is really sure.

> Highly respected Indian lawyer and human rights activist Fali Nariman, accepted the job as lead counsel for union Carbide in the case against the

---

[92] Quoted in J. Krank, *Courts on Trial* (New Jersey: Princeton University Press, 1949), p. 82; Ross, *The Joke's on Lawyers*, p. 14.

Indian government over the 1984 Bhopal incident in which 2,500 people died (according to government figures) and almost 200,00 disabled. The case was characterized by endless delaying tactics introduced by the company, and ended with what many described as an inadequate $ 470 million settlement.

Nariman continues to serve as an executive committee member of the ICJ.

Examples such as Nariman … are troublesome, some say, because they continue to be players in both worlds.

When asked, these activists argue that they have done nothing wrong in taking up their new positions. Friends say Nariman argues that lawyers have the right to represent any client, a view shared by another ICJ executive: 'It's not like he is doing anything evil'.

Others disagree, human rights activists have a degree of credibility bestowed on them once they are recognized as part of the human rights community, says Dias (Clarence Dias). Such respectability comes with responsibilities and is a much sought-after commodity that must be guarded.

For example, Nariman's hiring allowed Union carbide to cash in on the lawyer's human rights credentials. This in turn lent an aura of respectability to court proceedings and gave the impression that crass legal antics would not play a part in the outcome. In fact, repeated attempts to delay proceedings were key elements of carbide's court-room strategy.

Dias says the human rights community should push for an international code of ethics that would govern the conduct of human rights lawyers as one way of responding to the issue.[93]

Nariman, in his reply, proffered the same hackneyed argument that lawyers cannot pre-judge guilt:

It precludes the person charged with infringing the human rights of another (such as one accused of murder) the right to be defended by a 'lawyer of his choice'—in my country, a guaranteed constitutional right. Even if a human rights lawyer were to take the risk of pre-judging guilt, how would he do it? By reading newspaper reports? By conducting a mini trial of his own? Judging guilt or innocence is a difficult business. The case arising out of the assassination of Mrs. Indira Gandhi is an instance in point: three persons were accused of conspiracy to murder and put on trial; the public were convinced that they were as guilty as hell…. All the three were convicted by the trial court and sentenced to death. The high court … upheld the conviction and sentence. But, on further appeal to the Supreme Court, the judges there found no evidence

[93] Pauline Comeau, 'Fallen Angels?', *Tribune des Droits Humains* (*Human Rights Tribune*) (Winter 1992). Fali S. Nariman, 'The Bhopal Case', in *Before Memory Fades: An Autobiography* (New Delhi: Hay House India, 2010), pp. 208–9.

worth the name against one of the accused (Balbir Singh)—and he was acquitted! Would you have characterized your lawyer-cum-human-rights-activist as
'violator' if he had taken up Balbir Singh's case from the start?[94]

Nariman very ingeniously gives the example of Balbir Singh who was acquitted. Of course, the acquittal by the apex court should testify to his innocence.
It is no body's brief that a person accused of murder or any other heinous
crime should never be defended. Sometimes, doubts persist even after the
Supreme Court pronounces someone guilty, as happened with Kehar Singh,
another accused in Indira Gandhi's assassination case. Many jurists and eminent persons condemned the execution of Kehar Singh as a case of judicial
assassination. Seervai critiqued the judgment:

> The case against Kehar Singh was based on circumstantial evidence, and in
> *Palvinder Kaur* the law governing cases of circumstantial evidence was laid
> down by 3 judges of our Sup. Ct., and reaffirmed in a number of Sup. Ct. deci-
> sions. On the law so laid down, Kehar Singh would have had to be acquitted.
> The judgments of the three judges show that they were obviously unaware of
> these Sup. Ct. decisions which decisions (sic) were binding on them.[95]

Veteran socialist leader Minoo Masani wrote: 'I refer to the execution of
Satwant Singh and Kehar Singh, the first of whom was undoubtedly guilty of
murder and the second was just as clearly innocent. Kehar Singh's execution
amounts to judicial murder, since it is based on a miscarriage of justice on the
part of the courts of law'.[96]

V.M. Tarkunde, a former judge of the Bombay High Court and human
rights activist commented, 'the evidence against him was so meagre that it
would not support, as the saying goes, the hanging of even a dog'.[97]

Going by Nariman's argument, the lawyers who defended Satwant Singh
and Kehar Singh in this case defended murderers as their convictions were
upheld by the Supreme Court! So will be true of other cases in which the
accused is finally convicted. Lawyers do not and should not pre-judge, but if
s/he is convinced about the guilt of the accused then s/he is free to refuse to
work for one. Not only Balbir Singh, but there are countless such cases also in
which even the final pronouncements by the Supreme Court failed to dispel

[94] Nariman, 'The Bhopal Case', pp. 209–10.

[95] H.M. Seervai, *Constitutional Law of India*, Vol. 2, Fourth Edition (Bombay:
N.M. Tripathi Pvt. Ltd, 1993), pp. 1206–7.

[96] *The Statesman*, 22 January 1989.

[97] Amnesty International, 'India, The Death Penalty', October 1989.

doubts. One such case is that of Devender Pal Singh Bhullar for carrying out a terror attack in Delhi in 1993 in which nine bystanders were killed and Congress leader Maninderjeet Singh Bitta was grievously injured. The trial court sentenced him to death and the High Court upheld it. A three-judge bench of the Supreme Court also confirmed it but gave a fractured decision. While Arijit Pasayat and B.N. Agrawal, JJ, upheld the capital punishment, the presiding judge, Justice M.B. Shah, gave his dissent and acquitted him on the ground that the prosecution case depended solely on the confessional statement.[98] The review petition was also rejected by the same bench with Justice Shah dissenting.[99]

Therefore, one can always surmise whether the claims of the client are true or not. Certain grandiloquent principle should not be used as a casuistry to defend an abominable act in the name of the right to defence. Nariman himself refused to work as the *amicus curiae* in the Delhi High Court in an appeal against a single judge bench of the same court upholding the order of the CIC that judges of the Supreme Court should declare their assets.[100] He said that he was biased as he was of the firm opinion that judges should make a public declaration of their assets, and so, could not be a friend of the court. Why was he biased? Did he not pre-judge when he refused to assist the court as the *amicus curiae*? No. He was within his rights to do so, but it contradicts the ratiocination put forward by him in defence of UCC. Moreover, so far as having the counsel of one's choice is concerned, it is already restricted—even though it is a constitutional right—because of the exorbitant fee structure of lawyers. In how many cases would Nariman sacrifice his fees? He has himself admitted how lawyers use their acumen and extract huge money:

> The 1961 (Advocates) Act was enacted at a time when, following the British pattern, the role of the Indian lawyer was conceived as that of an adversarial combatant in court, with the judge sitting as umpire, upholding the scales even. The judge never descended into the dust of conflict to sort things out; he only decided which lawyer performed better. For more years than I can imagine, we have been using our skills not in a profession but in a game, in which the more skillful (which also tends to become the more costly) will invariably win! In India, we have perfected a poor substitute for what the great legal

[98] *Devender Pal Singh* v. *State (NCT of Delhi)* (2000) 5 SCC 234.

[99] *Devender Pal Singh Bhullar* v. *State (NCT of Delhi)*, Review Petition (Crl.) 497 of 2002.

[100] Sudhanshu Ranjan, 'Nyaya evam soochna ka adhikar', *Dainik Hindustan*, 24 January 2009.

theorist Dean Roscoe Pound described as the 'sporting theory of justice', the basic premise of which is that 'truth will prevail in the clash of zealous adversaries'. In the new millennium, we must leave behind as a relic of the past this 'sporting theory of justice'.[101]

While defending the UCC, was Nariman using his skill in a game and charging huge fees? Lawyers must not forget the advice that Abraham Lincoln gave to one of his law practice clients:

> Yes, we can doubtless gain your case for you; we can set a whole neighbourhood at loggerheads; we can distress a widowed mother and her six fatherless children and thereby get you six hundred dollars to which you seem to have a legal claim, but which rightfully belongs, it appears to me, as much to the woman and her children as it does to you. You must remember that some things legally right are not morally right. We shall not take your case, but will give you a little advice for which we will charge you nothing. You seem to be sprightly energetic man; we would advise you to try your hand at making six hundred dollars in some other way.[102]

Rape in the Courts

The way defence counsel cross-examines the rape survivor makes her undergo the trauma once again, perhaps more excruciatingly. During the anti-rape campaign in the early 1980s in the wake of the acquittal of two policemen, who were charged with raping a 16-year-old poor tribal girl in the police custody, a slogan was coined: 'She was raped twice, first by the police, and then by the courts'. She had been branded as a liar as there were no marks of injury on her body. Flavina Agnes has described the trial of the rape of an eight-year-old who lived in a lower class tenement by a neighbour, a 26-year-old man:

> During the trial, the child was cross-examined by a reputed criminal lawyer over three court dates, where her parents and she had to travel a distance of two hours each way. The busy lawyer either came late or pleaded his inability to complete the cross-examination as he had other matters to attend to. The court gave in to his request, disregarding the hardship being caused to the family of meagre means. The trial was in the designated Special Court constituted under

[101] Fali S. Nariman, *India's Legal System: Can It Be Saved?* (New Delhi: Penguin Books India, 2006), p. 120.

[102] David Luban, *Lawyers and Justice: An Ethical Study* (Princeton: Princeton University Press, 1988), p. 174; Parker and Evans, *Inside Lawyers' Ethics*, p. 30.

the Protection of Children from Sexual Offences (POCSO) Act, 2012, which stipulates special child-friendly trial procedures.

Throughout her deposition, the child, of a small build, was precariously perched on the ledge of the witness box, so that the presiding judge could see her and listen to her scared and muffled voice….

The Sakshi Guidelines (2004) stipulate that in cases concerning children, the defence lawyer must first submit the question in writing to the judge, and the judge, at his/her discretion, ask only those questions which are relevant to the incident. But these guidelines are seldom followed.[103]

Eminent criminal advocate Jethmalani, is in the habit of assassinating the character of rape victims. Defending Asaram Bapu, godman (nay conman), accused in a rape case, in the Rajasthan High Court, Jethmalani told the court that the girl who accused the godman of sexual assault was afflicted with a chronic disease which 'draws a woman to a man'. The People's Union for Civil Liberties and other groups said that Jethmalani's assertions violated the law, as stating the sexual history of victims in rape and sexual assault cases was not permitted. 'Indulging in character assassination of a woman in rape cases, and in this incident involving a minor, shows the low level to which even senior lawyers of Mr. Jethmalani's stature can stoop in order to influence the court'.[104]

Illegal for Bar Associations to Pass Resolutions to Not Defend an Accused

However, it is true that it is illegal as well immoral for bar associations to pass any resolution debarring its members from defending a particular individual or class of individuals. In 2006, the Kashmir High Court Bar Association passed a resolution that none of its members should defend those accused in sex-scandal case. The Supreme Court took strong exception to it. Hearing a petition from 13 accused who were seeking transfer of their case outside the state, a bench comprising Justice Y.K. Sabharwal and Justice C.K. Thakker quipped, 'with this type of resolution, how can proceedings go on in the court in Jammu and Kashmir? You can't be a law unto yourself'.[105]

[103] Flavina Agnes, 'For a Victim-Centric Approach', *The Hindu*, 18 September 2014.

[104] 'PUCL Protests Jethmalani's "Sickening" Argument', *The Hindu*, 18 September 2013.

[105] 'SC Slams J&K Bar Association for Denying Legal Aid to Accused', *Indian Express*, New Delhi, 29 August 2006.

Again, the Supreme Court decried this trend of passing resolutions and held it illegal in *A.S. Mohammed Rafi* v. *State of Tamil Nadu*.[106] In this case, the Madras High Court, on the basis of the recommendations made by Justice (retd) K.P. Sivasubramaniam, Commission of Inquiry, awarded a compensation of Rs 50,000 to advocate A.S. Mohammed Rafi who was allegedly assaulted by policemen during a clash with them. Both the lawyers and women police constables involved in the fracas had lodged counter criminal cases. The Bar Association of Coimbatore had also passed a resolution that no member of the Coimbatore Bar will defend the accused policemen in the criminal case against them. Not satisfied with the quantum of compensation, Rafi moved the apex court for a higher amount. Though the apex court enhanced the compensation to Rs 1.50 lakh as advised by *amicus curiae* Altaf Ahmed, it, however, pulled no punches in expressing displeasure at the manner in which the bar associations have been frequently passing resolutions asking advocates not to appear for certain persons. The Court clearly held:

In our opinion, such resolutions are wholly illegal, against all traditions of the bar, and against professional ethics. Every person, however, wicked, depraved, vile, degenerate, perverted, loathsome, execrable, vicious or repulsive he may be regarded by society has a right to be defended in a court of law and correspondingly it is the duty of the lawyer to defend him.[107]

The Court gave the example that when the great revolutionary writer, Thomas Paine was jailed and tried for treason in England in 1792 for writing his famous pamphlet 'The Rights of Man' in defence of the French Revolution, the great advocate, Thomas Erskine (1750–1823) was briefed to defend him. Erskine, who was holding the office of the attorney general for the Prince of Wales, was warned that if he accepted the brief, he would be dismissed from office. Undeterred, Erskine displayed guts to accept the brief and was dismissed from office. The Court quoted his immortal words:

From the moment that any advocate can be permitted to say that he will or will not stand between the Crown and the subject arraigned in court where he daily sits to practise, from that moment the liberties of England are at an end. If the advocate refuses to defend from what he may think of the charge or of the defence, he assumes the character of the Judge; nay he assumes it before the hour of the judgment; and in proportion to his rank

---

[106] (2011) 1 SCC 688.

[107] *A.S. Mohammed Rafi* v. *State of Tamil Nadu* (2011) 1 SCC 688, para 16.

and reputation puts the heavy influence of perhaps a mistaken opinion into the scale against the accused in whose favour the benevolent principles of English law make all assumptions, and which commands the very Judge to be his Counsel.[108]

The Supreme Court further cited the examples of how Indian lawyers defended revolutionaries during the Indian freedom movement and the accused in the Indian National Army (INA) trials. These are resplendent examples which show how gutsy lawyers have been who do not cave in under any pressure. But the examples are not apt as the issue involved defending people who had incurred the wrath of the powers that be because of their revolutionary activities, not inveterate criminals who commit abominable crimes. In the INA trial, Bhoolabhai Desai defended three soldiers—Shanawaz Khan, Gurbaksh Singh Dhillon, and Prem Kumar Sahgal—who were accused of treason against the country during the Second World War. The trial began in October 1945 at Red Fort in Delhi in which Desai was part of the 17 member defence team. But it is wrong to say that Desai defended traitors who betrayed their country. Desai was fired by patriotic zeal, not by mercenary consideration. He did not charge a single farthing from the accused and even bore the expenditure incurred on his journey and stay himself. In fact, Desai was of the view that these soldiers joined hands with Japan in the national interest as they wanted to dismantle the British yoke with help of Japan. Even Jawaharlal Nehru was part of the defence team and one day went to the court in advocate's robe. It was a symbolic gesture to show that the entire country stood by the accused. It was the pressure of the nationalist leadership that forced the court to exonerate them besides the persuasive arguments of Desai, otherwise they would have been awarded death sentence as happened in cases of treason.

Here the question is whether lawyers should defend criminals if they are convinced about their criminality. However, the court has aptly cited the instances of Neuremberg trial in which the Nazi accused of killing innocent Jews were defended or the legendary American lawyer Clarence Darrow (1857–1930) who defended every accused no matter how abhorrent or loathsome the crime may be. Most American lawyers would refuse to work for such ruthless, repulsive criminals but Darrow accepted the brief on the ground that everyone had a right of defence. By doing so, he earned the sobriquet of 'Attorney for the Damned'.

---

[108] *A.S. Mohammed Rafi* v. *State of Tamil Nadu* (2011) 1 SCC 688, para 19.

It is definitely unethical for any bar associations to pass any resolution but individual lawyers can always refuse briefs. N.A. Palkhivala refused to work for the then Prime Minister Indira Gandhi and returned her file when she imposed the internal emergency on 25 June 1975. Palkhivala was her counsel in her election case in the Supreme Court.

There are case studies when a lawyer faces serious dilemma and cannot invoke the doctrine of the right of defence. In January 2001, in Australia, a newspaper reported that a leading Melbourne criminal barrister had been asked to represent suspected war criminal Konrad Kalejs in a hearing to determine whether he should be extradited to Latvia to face prosecution over deaths of tens of thousands of Jews and others during the Second World War. The concerned barrister was a Queens Counsel as well as a civil rights advocate who was also prominent in the Jewish community and well-known for representing a variety of high-profile criminal accused. The barrister was, reportedly, born in Russia; his parents fled to Germany when he was six weeks old and later settled in Israel but again migrated to Australia. In 1997, he was quoted as telling *Herald Sun* that elderly Jews living in Melbourne would be having sleepless nights knowing Kalejs was walking free in Melbourne.[109] Kalejs was 87 at the time of extradition proceedings. He confuted the allegation that he ever served in a death squad in a Latvian war camp where an estimated 20,000 to 30,000 Jews, Gypsies, Red Army Soldiers, and others were executed. However, earlier Kalejs had been deported from the US, Canada, and Britain as he was found to have been involved in war crimes. His defence against extradition was his health problems which included legal blindness, dementia, and prostate cancer. Jewish leaders averred that it was just an alibi to escape extradition and consequently trial, but is often a false pretence. The legal process could easily have dragged on for 18 months, had Kalejs decided to fight it. The question arose: should the barrister defend him, and if so, how might he proceed?[110]

Defending Justice, Not Clients

Actually, it is assumed in the adversary legal system that a lawyer's only commitment is to advance the interest of the client with utmost zeal. The reasoning may be that the other side will try to controvert each and every point adduced with searing ferocity and put forth its own arguments with equal

---

[109] 'Leading QC may Defend Kaleijs', *The Age* (Melbourne) 23 January 2001.
[110] Parker and Evans, *Inside Lawyers' Ethics*, pp. 1–2.

zeal, unlike the inquisitorial system in which all parties are parties to the inquest. Christine Parker and Adrian Evans have written:

> Adversarial advocacy combines the 'principle of partisanship' and the 'principle of non-accountability'. The principle of partisanship means that the lawyer should do all for the client that the client would do for themselves, if the client had the knowledge of the lawyer…. The principle of non-accountability … says that the lawyer is not morally responsible for either the means or the ends of representation, provided both are lawful. If the lawyer was morally responsible, it is said, the lawyer may not be willing to act zealously to represent the client's interests.
>
> This approach is most clearly justified in the case of trial lawyers, especially criminal defence advocates who must vigorously assert the rights of the accused against the superior power and resources of the state. By corollary, the adversarial advocate approach is least justifiable if applied to a criminal prosecutor who represents the state against the accused. It is well accepted that prosecutors should act as 'ministers of justice', pay elaborate attention to fairness and candour and only present to the court those facts that they believe to be well grounded…. Historically, the adversarial advocate approach was essentially liberal, motivating lawyers to pursue client interests primarily against the power of the state. It was dependent on a conception of the rule of law which puts the courts between citizens and against the government, and required lawyers independent of the state and available to help those who want to use the law to challenge or defend themselves against the government. However, the adversarial advocate approach has extended beyond representing client interests against other private interests and in any situation where a lawyer is necessary.[111]

Lawyers definitely need to be independent of the state so that they are able to withstand pressures when corrupt regimes subvert people's rights. Lord Brougham's defence of Queen Caroline before the House of Lords when King George IV was trying to dissolve his marriage with Caroline of Brunswick by alleging that she had committed adultery is referred to as the ideal in defence. George married her in 1795 when he was still the Prince of Wales. They separated after the birth of their only child Princess Charlotte of Wales. Caroline subsequently went to live abroad and it was rumoured that she had a torrid affair with her head servant Bartolomeo Pergami. In 1820, George ascended the throne and Caroline returned and asserted her rights as queen consort of Great Britain and Ireland. George IV wanted divorce, and since it was not possible unless one of the parties was guilty of adultery, the king

---

[111] Parker and Evans, *Inside Lawyers' Ethics*, pp. 14–15.

got the Pains and Penalties Bill, 1820 introduced into the Parliament, which, if passed, would declare Caroline to have committed adultery leading to the grant of divorce. It was well known that the king had not been faithful himself. The attorney general for England and Wales, Sir Robert Gifford, led the prosecution case which began on 19 August 1820. Gifford submitted that Caroline and Pergami had lived like lovers for five years since November 1814 and had, in fact, shared a bedroom, and were seen in each other's presence arm-in-arm, and were heard kissing. He went on to give salacious details that she changed clothes in his presence. The defence began on 3 October with an electrifying speech by Brougham which is considered as one of the most powerful orations ever. Brougham threatened to divulge secrets of George's own life even if it went against the national interest, if it was the only way to ensure justice for his client:

> [A]n advocate, in discharge of his duty, knows but one person in all the world, and that person is his client. To save that client by all means and expedients, and at all hazards and costs to other persons, and, amongst them, to himself, is his first and only duty; and in performing this duty he must not regard the alarm, the torments, the destruction which he may bring upon others. Separating the duty of a patriot from that of an advocate, he must go on reckless of consequences, though it should be his unhappy fate to involve his country in confusion.[112]

Lawyers have been used in the past to draft unjust laws which they implemented as prosecutors, judges, and even defence counsel, as happened in South Africa during apartheid, the USSR under Stalin, and Nazi Germany. About apartheid in South Africa, David Dyzenhaus, who started his career as a lecturer in law in South Africa and migrated to Canada and settled there, has written how the legal fraternity comprising lawyers, judges, and law academics subverted the rule of law:

> [T]he courtroom is a 'political theatre' but that does not make it the 'theatre of politics'. There is a distinction between law and politics, which is the distinction we have already encountered between the state and government, or the state as an ideal and the state in practice. At the moment that a court accepts jurisdiction over a controversy between government and an individual, government is demoted—it loses its claim to be the exclusive representative of the state. At the same time, the individual is promoted into a public role, to one with an equal claim to represent the state. The court, then, in deciding between

---

[112] Parker and Evans, *Inside Lawyers' Ethics*, p. 15.

these claims articulates a vision of what the state is and publicly draws the line between law and politics…. Now South Africa under apartheid was not a functioning democracy, though the courts had a kind of formal independence and were engaged in the reciprocal relationship of legitimacy with political institutions which Kahn describes. The enforced divide between racial groups in the service of white supremacy meant that it was impossible to develop an 'informal tradition of norms and expectations … around political and legal institutions common to most South Africans.[113]

However, there was a small section of lawyers, judges, and law teachers who resisted apartheid. Abram Louis Fischer was one such exception who as a lawyer fought against apartheid and defended Nelson Mandela, Walter Sisulu, and 18 other African National Congress leaders who participated in the Defiance Campaign. Born in a prominent Afrikaans family, son of Ulrich Fischer, who became a highly-respected Free State Judge, Bram (as he was popularly called) became a vocal nationalist. He, along with his wife, became member of the Communist Party of South Africa. In 1953, he was banned under the Suppression of Communism Act from most gatherings and from the Congress of Democrats. Subsequently, there were raids on his house and chambers, but it did not affect the flow of briefs coming to him and he enjoyed the reputation of an outstanding counsel. Because of his defence of Mandela and involvement with anti-apartheid activists, on 23 September 1964, he was arrested for contravening the Suppression of Communism Act. He escaped but was recaptured and tried on far more serious charges, including sabotage. He was awarded life term. He paid heavily for his conviction but did everything at his command to uphold the rule of law.

The threats of terrorism, trans-national crime, and tax-evasion put a tremendous pressure on the criminal justice system even in mature democracies as the government has to curb it with an iron hand. Parker and Evans have rightly analysed the dilemma faced by lawyers:

Ethical challenges for lawyers in these situations are numerous. For example, should criminal defence lawyers comply with government requirements that they get security clearances before *defending* people accused on security-related charges? The 'torture memos' emerging from the United States indicate the pressure government and military lawyers were under to come up with ways to justify practices that would otherwise be seen as human rights abuses: for example those which occurred at Iraq's Abu Ghraib prison, indefinite detention

[113] David Duzenhaus, *Judging the Judges, Judging Ourselves: Truth, Reconciliation and the Apartheid Legal Order* (Oxford: Hart Publishing, 2003), p. 172.

in Guantanamo Bay, torture and 'rendition' (moving prisoners to countries where they could be tortured).[114]

Conversation between the Advocate and the Client Is Privileged

It is true that the personal knowledge of the lawyer is privileged which cannot be disclosed, much less used in prosecution. Section 126 of the Indian Evidence Act, 1872, enjoins an advocate not to divulge any communication made to him in the course and for the purpose of his employment as an advocate without the express consent of the client. The contents or condition of any document which he has come to know in course of his professional employment or any advice given are not to be shared by him with anyone. This obligation continues even after his employment has ceased. Further, under Section 127, the same obligation extends to interpreters and clerks or servants of the advocate as well. The BCI has framed rules under Section 49 of the Advocates Act, 1961, which define the standard of professional conduct and etiquette to be observed by lawyers. An advocate is under a statutory duty not to abuse or take advantage of the confidence reposed in him by his client.[115] It has also been provided that an advocate shall not commit a breach of obligations imposed by Section 126 of the Indian Evidence Act, 1872, directly or indirectly. The right to privacy has been granted to the client so that s/he may share all information and thought with the advocate freely.

Statutory Right of the Accused

Article 22(1) of the Constitution reads: 'No person who is arrested shall be detained in custody without being informed, as soon as may be, of the grounds for such arrest nor shall he be denied the right to consult, and to be defended, by a legal practitioner of his choice'. Section 303, Cr. P.C guarantees such a right. While interpreting Article 20(3) which guarantees the right against self-incrimination, the Supreme Court laid down that the police must inform the accused that he has a right to call a lawyer before answering to any of their questions.[116] The Sixth Amendment to the US Constitution provides, 'In all criminal prosecutions the accused shall enjoy the right ... to have the assistance of counsel for his defence'.

---

[114] Parker and Evans, *Inside Lawyers' Ethics*, p. 98.
[115] Rule 24, The Bar Council of India Rules, Part VI, p. 5.
[116] *Nandini Satpathy* v. *P.L. Dani* (1978) 2 SCC 424: AIR (1978) SC 1025.

M.K. Gandhi, the Greatest Lawyer

M.K. Gandhi practiced as a lawyer for about 20 years before giving it up in order to devote himself heart and soul to the public service. He never took up any false cases. He has written:

> I never resorted to untruth in my profession, and that a large part of my legal practice was in the interest of public work, for which I charged nothing beyond out-of-pocket expenses, and these too I sometimes met myself....
>
> As a student, I had heard that the lawyer's profession was a liar's profession. But this did not influence me, as I had no intention of earning either position or money by lying.
>
> My principle was put to test many a time in South Africa. Often I knew that my opponents had tutored their witnesses, and if I only encouraged my client or his witnesses to lie, we could win the case. But I always resisted the temptation. I remember only one occasion when, after having won a case, I suspected that my client had deceived me. In my heart of hearts I always wished that I should win only if my client's case was right....
>
> I warned every new client at the outset that he should not expect me to take up a false case or to coach the witnesses, with the result that I built up such a reputation that no false cases used to come to me. Indeed some of my clients would keep their clean cases for me, and take the doubtful ones elsewhere.
>
> There was one case which proved a severe trial.... The award was entirely in favour of my client, but the arbitrators had inadvertently committed an error in calculation which, however small, was serious, in as much as an entry which ought to have been on the debit side was made on the credit side. The opponents had opposed the award on other grounds. I was junior counsel for my client. When the senior counsel became aware of the error, he was of opinion that our client was not bound to admit it. He was clearly of the opinion that no counsel was bound to admit anything that went against his client's interest. I said we ought to admit the error.[117]

Ultimately, the senior counsel refused to argue on the condition that the error must be admitted, but Gandhi agreed only on this condition after the client gave his consent. For him, facts meant truth which he realized while preparing for Sheth Dada Abdulla's case for which he had gone to South Africa. He has written, 'facts mean truth, and once we adhere to truth, the law comes to our aid naturally'.[118] Truth remained the passion with him and it was the only touchstone on which he tested his duty towards his client and

[117] Gandhi, *An Autobiography*, pp. 332–3.
[118] Gandhi, *An Autobiography*, p. 123.

the court. J.U. Uppal has written that according to him the greatest wrong a lawyer could commit in the process of law was to be a party to the miscarriage of justice.[119]

He also promoted reconciliation between the litigating parties giving a damn to the monetary loss—something unimaginable for lawyers! While pursuing Abdulla's case, he realized that the suit, if allowed to continue, would ruin the plaintiff as well as the defendant who were near relatives and both belonged to the same city. Dada Abdulla had filed a suit against Tyeb Sheth claiming 40,000 pounds which arose out of business transactions and was full of intricacies of accounts. He successfully persuaded both parties to go in for arbitration. The arbitrator ruled in Dada Abdulla's favour awarding him 37,000 pounds and costs. However, it was impossible for Tyeb Sheth to pay down the whole amount. Gandhi then persuaded Dada Abdulla to allow Tyeb Sheth to pay the money in easy instalments spread over a several years. According to Gandhi:

> The lawyer's fees were so rapidly mounting up that they were enough to devour all the resources of the clients, big merchants as they were. The case occupied so much of their attention that they had no time left for any other work. In the meantime mutual ill-will was steadily increasing. I became disgusted with the profession. As lawyers the counsel of both sides were bound to take up points of law in support of their own clients. I also saw for the first time that the winning party never recovers all the costs incurred ... I realized that the true function of a lawyer was to unite parties riven asunder. The lesson was so indelibly burnt into me that a large part of my time during the twenty years of my practice as a lawyer was occupied in bringing about private compromises of hundreds of cases. I lost nothing thereby—not even money, certainly not my soul.[120]

The Law Council of Australia's *Model Rules* also makes it clear where an advocate knows that the client, or one of his/her witnesses, has perjured himself/herself, or has tendered evidence that is not true, the lawyer must advise the client that the falsehood must be rectified or else s/he will recuse herself/himself from the case, and seek the client's permission to inform the court of the correction. If the client refuses to give permission, the lawyer cannot continue to act, even if it means withdrawing representation in the middle of

---

[119] J.U. Uppal, *Gandhi Ordained in South Africa* (New Delhi: Publications Division, 1995), p. 88.

[120] Gandhi, *An Autobiography*, pp. 123–4.

the trial.[121] However, the same rule prevents the advocate from informing the court of lie or falsification. The rule strikes a balance by allowing the lawyer to preserve client confidentiality and at the same time giving him/her the liberty to withdraw gracefully and not be party to the dishonesty. *Model Rule* 14.1 states: 'A practitioner must not knowingly make a misleading statement to a court. A practitioner must take all necessary steps to correct any misleading statement made by the practitioner to the court as soon as possible after that practitioner becomes aware that the statement was misleading'.

No Right to Strike

Lawyers, who wax eloquent about the right of defence, go on strike at the drop of a hat, caring little about their clients. The practice is rampant notwithstanding the pronouncement of the Supreme Court in several cases that under no circumstances they should strike or boycott courts. In *Harish Uppal* v. *Union of India*,[122] the Supreme Court clearly held that lawyers should never resort to strike or boycott the court. It clarified that on rare occasions when any association of lawyers, including statutory Bar Councils, deem it imperative to call upon advocates to abstain from appearing in courts, it should be left to individual members of that association to be free to appear without fear or hindrance or any other coercive step. The Court further clarified that it would not preclude other forms of protests by practicing lawyers such as wearing of armbands which in no way interrupt or disrupt the court proceedings or adversely affect the interest of the litigant. Any such form of protest shall not however be insulting to the court or to the profession. The Court also said that though the BCI is empowered to penalize advocates for the breach of discipline or ethics, high courts could also frame rules, under Section 34(1) of the Advocates Act, 1961, and take action against lawyers with respect to their conduct before the court. However, this power has hardly been invoked to chasten lawyers who indulge in illegal and unethical activities.

The Supreme Court dealt with the issue in *Common Cause* v. *Union of India*[123] and ruled that it is unprofessional for a lawyer to go on strike or boycott the court, bar associations should not permit meetings calling for such strikes or boycotts, it is obligatory for the State and National Bar Councils to take actions against striking bar associations and sponsors of boycotts, the courts must hear matters posted before them undeterred by boycotts, and it is

---

[121] *Model Rule* 15.1.

[122] Writ Petition (Civil) 132 of 1988, decided on 17 December 2002.

[123] AIR (2005) SC 4442.

only in the rarest of rare cases that abstention from the court may be justified, such as dignity, integrity, and independence of the bar and bench, and that must be decided by the presiding judge, and even this should be confined to one day. Such platitudes are repeated in judgments after judgments which remain on paper and observed more in breach. However, so far as the boycott of the court is concerned, it is my personal view that it is justified in the extreme case if the judge concerned is depraved beyond any doubt. The continuation of such a judge sullies the reputation of the institution and shakes the trust of the people.

Lawyers Not Allowed in Some Tribunals

There are certain tribunals where lawyers are not allowed, and the litigating parties appear in person. One of these is senior citizen tribunal, where neglected parents file petitions for 'maintenance' from their wards under the maintenance and Welfare of Parents and Senior Citizens Act, 2007. The Act bars lawyers from appearing before it, but the BCI has been strongly pushing for allowing lawyers in it. In the national consultation called by the Union Ministry of Social Justice and Empowerment, NGOs and state governments opposed any tweaking of the law to allow lawyers.[124] However, the BCI has still been pushing for it. Lawyers must not be allowed in this tribunal, otherwise it will be another battlefield between family members with no hope for any relief and reconciliation as lawyers will only delay, derail, and despoil.

Role of Lawyers in ADR

Apart from litigation in the court, lawyers also negotiate on behalf of clients outside the court to settle a dispute by way of mediation/conciliation which is a mode of ADR. The question: should lawyers be allowed in the mediation, and if yes, what ethics are they required to follow? Ideally, lawyers should not be allowed in the ADR process, otherwise, ADR loses its very spirit and purpose as the same adversary process is adopted by lawyers. Now the situation has come to such a pass that besides litigating lawyers, there are increasing numbers of lawyers practicing as ADR facilitators, such as mediators, arbitrators, and sometimes even acting as ombudsman. So, now it is said that when lawyers use negotiation to settle disputes, it is not divorced from litigation.

---

[124] 'States Oppose Lawyers in Senior Citizen Tribunals', *Times of India*, New Delhi, 1 September 2010.

Marc Galanter has coined the term *litigotiation*, which means strategic pursuit of a settlement through mobilizing the court process.[125] Carrie Menkel Meadow has written that some lawyers (and clients) use ADR processes, such as court-ordered mediation, as 'just another stop in the "litigotiation" game', another 'opportunity for the manipulation of rules, time, information and ultimately, money'.[126] One experienced mediation practitioner in Australia has this to write:

> Regrettably, many litigators use ADR as an adversarial tool to gain an advantage in the litigation rather than to resolve it. Such parties unashamedly use ADR as a fishing expedition. It can take many forms ... a party can use the process to weed out weaknesses in the opponent's case. It can be used to test the demeanour or frailty of material witnesses or decision makers. It can be used for fact-finding and accumulating undisclosed information that may not have been available through interlocutory processes such as discovery or interrogatories.... It may be used to test an opponent's susceptibility to admissions or to ascertain how vigorously a point of law will be contested or conceded....
>
> There may be several other reasons why a party would use ADR process for an ulterior purpose. If there is a power imbalance, a financially stronger party may use the process and its accompanying expense for the purpose of draining the funds of a poorer litigant. ADR may be used as a delaying tactic.[127]

* * *

Lawyers are rated by their success in turning the justice system upside down in which the most crooked wins and the most inveterate criminals are acquitted. They forget that as officers of the court, it is their bounden duty to assist in arriving at justice, not to protect the client at the cost of justice and truth. Clients cannot approach a senior advocate directly; s/he can be approached only through an advocate, as a senior advocate represents justice. M.K. Gandhi was the ideal lawyer who always upheld the truth. In the words of Pyarelal, 'Gandhiji learnt to regard law not as an intellectual legerdemain to

---

[125] Marc Galanter, 'Words of Deals: Using Negotiations to Teach about Legal Process', *Journal of Legal Education*, vol. 34, no. 268 (1984): 268. Christine Parker and Adrian Evans, 'Ethics in Negotiation and Alternative Dispute Resolution', in *Inside Lawyers' Ethics*, p. 122.

[126] Carrie Menkel Meadow quoted in Sourdin, 'Alternative Dispute Resolution', in *Inside Lawyers' Ethics*, p. 127.

[127] Grant Dearlove, 'Court-Ordered ADR: Sanctions for the Recalcitrant Lawyer and Party', *Australian Dispute Resolution Journal* vol. 11, no. 12 (2000): 14–16.

make black appear white and white black, but as "codified ethics". The profession of law became to him the means to enthrone justice, not to "entangle justice" in the net of law'.[128] But lawyers are known for doing exactly the same as Jonathan Swift lampooned them that lawyers are 'a society of men … bred up from their youth in the art of proving by words multiplied for the purpose that white is black, and black is white, according as they are paid'.[129] Actually, they appear to be in the palm of their clients' hands and many a time behave life scofflaws. Lawyers prefer to call themselves counsel, which means that they would give truthful and sincere opinion. David Pannick rightly comments:

> Barristers prefer to be called *counsel*. This suggests that they act as a friend or confidant rather than in mere professional capacity. For similar reasons, when appearing in court on behalf of a client …, the barrister is paid a fee for the first day and a *refresher* (a term which implies a physical necessity for what is, after all, a financial transaction) for each subsequent day. Barristers leave the negotiation of such fees to their *clerks*, as their office managers like to be known. To explain why they feel obliged to represent rogues and scoundrels, barristers tend to refer to the *cab-rank principle*. This is serious defamation of the ethics of taxi-drivers.[130]

Cab-rank principle means that a taxi-driver has to carry the passenger who comes first, irrespective of the distance s/he wants to cover or whether it is short or long. The driver cannot refuse to a short distance passenger that he would take a long ride, otherwise his licence will be cancelled. Lawyers are known for using all the emphasis at their command to derail the course of justice. So, it is said about them that they bang facts when they are strong on facts but weak on law, bang law when they are strong on law but weak on facts, and bang the table when they are weak on both.

Lawyers are not only advocates but also human beings. So, they owe a duty to the society as responsible citizens first, and then a professional duty to the client. The reasoning that in the adversary legal system, an advocate only puts forward the best defence of the client, and the advocate must do for the client what the client would have done for himself/herself is not tenable. According to it, the lawyer's partisanship does not besmirch his/her character as s/he is not accountable to anyone.

---

[128] Pyarelal, *Mahatma Gandhi—The early Phase*, Vol. I, p. 313.
[129] *Gulliver's Travels: A Voyage to the Houyhnhnms* (1726) Ch. 5.
[130] Pannick, 'Mysticism', p. 152.

Lawyer's astronomical fee structure is the biggest discrimination against the poor who can hardly afford any lawyer, much less a leading one. This fee structure is in a crying need of being regulated. M.K. Gandhi wrote:

> I am strongly of opinion that lawyers and doctors should not be able to charge any fees but they should be paid a certain fixed sum by the state and the public should receive their services free.... The poor will be untaxed but the rich and the poor will have then the same amount of attention and skill. Today the best legal talents and the best medical advice are unobtainable by the poor.[131]

Lawyers can be social engineers as well as crooks. As social engineers, they have made sterling contribution to the society. They have used their skill and knowledge of law to combat various social maladies, as happened during the freedom movement in India when lawyers fought for the independence of the country as well as against many social ills. Similarly, Civil Rights Era, a golden period in American history, was led by lawyers, like Charles Hamilton Houston, who creatively used their knowledge of law to address the problems of inveterate inequality and discrimination that plagued the American society. Waris Husain has written:

> Mr. Houston once said that 'lawyers are either social engineers or parasites on their society', and his use of such strong language was an expression of the urgent battle that was taking place for equality at the time. Pakistan's minorities are experiencing a similar tumultuous period, and the lawyers of the nation include both social engineers and parasites. This is a fact one must remember before they make statements assessing the credibility or ideology of the 'Lawyers' or 'Judiciary' overall.
>
> Before delving into this analogy, I suggest that a 'parasite' is not intended as a derogatory term for the conservative cadre of lawyers in discriminatory societies who wish to maintain the status quo. Nature has provided parasites in almost every ecosystem, and any damage done by the organism isn't done with malice, but is merely a characteristic of the parasite. Namely, since the parasite feeds off the body it is attached to, political or otherwise, it weakens it from striving and evolving with the environment.
>
> Parasites are especially dangerous for when a political body is undergoing stress, and it can be argued that Pakistan is certainly in such a position. When looked at the pattern discrimination against religious minorities, like Ahmedis and Shias, ethnic minorities like Balochis or Pashtuns, or women, it is clear

---

[131] *The Collected Works of Mahatma Gandhi*, Publications Division, Government of India, Vol. XXXVI, p. 84.

that Pakistan's political body is in a crisis state. Yet, while such crude injustice takes place violating the central precepts of equality protected by the constitution, there are those lawyers who use the law to continue these discriminatory practices.[132]

In the USA, lawyers had their roles in aggravating injustices against Blacks. When the Supreme Court ruled in 1876 that African-Americans were to live as equals but separate from Whites, lawyers helped draft Jim Crow laws. Under it, Blacks could not be served food in the same room of a restaurant as Whites, they were required to use separate water fountains and bathrooms, and they could be debarred from serving on a jury or voting. For Roscoe Pound also, lawyers are social engineers and in that role only they would be the problem solvers.[133]

---

[132] Waris Husain, 'Are Lawyers Social Engineers or Social Parasites?', 11 October 2011, http://www.dawn.com/news/665419/are-lawyers-social-engineers-or-social-parasites (last accessed on 22 November 2014).

[133] Roscoe Pond, 'The Lawyer as a Social Engineer', http://heinonline.org/HOL/LandingPage?handle=hein.journals/emlj3&div=35&id=&page= (last accessed on 22 November 2014).

My Lord or Your Excellency

When Bismarck was the Prussian ambassador at the court of Alexander II in the 1860s, one day he looked out of a window at the Peterhof palace and was amazed to see a sentry on duty in the middle of a lawn. He inquired from the Czar why the man was there. The Czar asked his aide-de-camp, who did not know. The aide-de-camp sent for the officer in command who did not know either. The general commanding troops at Peterhof was summoned. The general informed him that it was in accordance with the ancient custom. 'What was the origin of the custom?', put in Bismarck.

'I do not recollect at present', answered the general.

'Investigate and report the result', ordered Alexander.

The investigation that took three days revealed that the soldier was posted there by an order put on the books 80 years ago! For one morning in spring, Catherine the great had looked on that lawn and seen the first flower thrusting above the frozen soil. She ordered a sentry to be posted to prevent anyone from picking the flower. In the 1860s, there was still a sentry on the lawn—a memorial to a flower, and to Catherine, who had earned the cognomen of 'Great'.

Such is the fear of antagonizing the high and mighty that several hangovers of the past continue to persist without any rhyme and reason and the supine favour-seekers uphold them without any compunction, lest they lose what they have been getting. One such ludicrous practice is the mode of address-ing VIPs and prefixing honorifics with their names. Traditionally 'Majesty', 'Excellency', and 'Highness' were used for different categories of people. Excellency is used for ambassadors, governors, and Roman Catholic bishops, and archbishops. Majesty is used only for the king or queen, while Highness is used for the members of the royal family.

Historically speaking, kings have been portrayed as ones with divine sanction to rule and so, they have been addressed by various high-sounding titles. In Egypt, when King Senusrest I of the Middle Kingdom period died, Sehetepibre, who had served under him, wanted to make a public display of his adulation and loyalty to the king. On his funerary Stela, Sehetepibre sang a hymn in which he named the king as the equivalent to the gods:

The King is Ka.
His utterance is abundance.
The one whom he brought up will be somebody.
He is khnum for all limbs.
The begetter of the begotten.
He is the Bastet who protects the Two Lands.
The one who praises him will be protected by his arm.
He is Sekhmet against those who disobey his orders.

Since the beginnings of the kingship and royal titulary in Egypt, the king was perceived to be connected to the Egyptian deities. Surprisingly, 'pharaoh', the most popular title of the Egyptian king, does not have an Egyptian genesis. Egyptians did not call their king 'pharaoh' until very late in their history, and began using it only when non-Egyptians took up the word. 'Pharaoh' is a Hebrew pronunciation of the Egyptian word, *per-aa*, meaning Great House, and was used as a label for the king himself around 1450 BCE. But the title word for the king was *nisu*, as can be seen for example in the Offering Formula, or *hetep di* nisu. Egyptians attached a lot of importance to names which represented aspects of a person or personality, and often more than one name was required to accomplish this. From around 2500 BCE, the king was adorned with up to five names. The five royal titles consist of four names, which the king assumed on the day of his accession, along with a fifth name, given to him at birth. Three of the names indicate the king's role as god, while the remaining two emphasize the perceived division of Egypt into two lands, both under his control.

In Russia, *Tsar* is the traditional title for a monarch. *Tsar* has its genesis in the Roman word 'Caesar'. Peter the Great was the first Russian ruler who did away with this title to call himself 'emperor'. As the Russian empire expanded, so did the title of the king. Nicholas II of Russia, the last tsar, held a title that was as large and unwieldy as the Russian Empire itself:

Emperor and autocrat of all Russia; Tsar of Moscow. Kiev, Vladimir, Novgorod,
Kazan, Astrakhan, Poland, Siberia, the Tauric Chersonese and Georgia; Lord of
Pskov; Grand Prince of Smolensk, Lithuania, Volhynia, Podolia, and Finland:

Prince of Estonia, Livonia, Courland and Semigalia, Semogatia, Belostok, Karelia, Tver, Yugria, Perm, Viatka, Bulgaria and other lands, Lord and Grand prince of Nizhnyi Novgorod and Chernigov; Ruler of Riazan, Polotsk, Rostov, Yaroslavl', Belo-Ozero, Udoria, Obdoria, Kondia, Vitebsk, Mstislavl, and all the Northen Lands; Lord and Sovereign of th iverian, Kartalinian and karbadinian lands and of the American Provinces; Hereditary Lord and Suzerain of the Circassian Prices and Highland Princes and others; Lord of Turkestand; Heir to the throne of Norway; Duke of Schleswig-Holstein, Stormarn, the Dithmarschen and Oldenburg.

In England, royal titles have been conferred even by acts of parliament. The Royal Titles Act of 1876 (39 and 40 Vict., c. 10) was an Act of the Parliament of the United Kingdom which officially recognized Queen Victoria as the 'Empress of India'. She assumed this title in 1876 under the encouragement of Prime Minister Benjamin Disraeli. The long title of the Act is 'An Act to enable Her most Gracious Majesty to make an addition to the Royal Style and titles appertaining to the imperial Crown of the United Kingdom and its Dependencies.'

Since India was a subject nation, Indians did not have the privilege of using such honorifics. Still, during the freedom movement, honorifics were used for towering leaders. Jawaharlal Nehru has written:

I introduced in our A.I.C.C. office a practice of addressing all our members by their names only, without any prefixes or suffixes, honorific titles and the like. There are so many of these in India—Mahatma, Maulana, Pandit, Shaikh, Syed, Munshi, Muoulvi, and latterly Sriyut and Shri, and, of course, Mr. and Esquire—and they are so abundantly and often unnecessarily used that I wanted to set a good example. But I was not to have my way. Mohamad Ali sent me a frantic telegram directing me 'as president' to revert to our old practice and, in particular, always to address Gandhiji as Mahatma.[1]

He further writes:

The high-sounding and pompous words and titles that were often used for all those prominent in the national movement, were picked out by my wife and sisters and others and bandied about irreverently. I was addressed as *Bharat Bhushan*—'Jewel of India'; *Tyagamurti*—'O Embodiment of Sacrifice'; and this light-hearted treatment soothed me, and the tension of those solemn public gatherings, where I had to remain on my best behavior, gradually relaxed. Even

---

[1] Jawaharlal Nehru, *An Autobiography* (New Delhi: Penguin Books, 2004), pp. 125–6.

my little daughter joined me in the game. Only my mother insisted on taking me seriously, and she never wholly approved of any sarcasm or raillery at the expense of her darling boy.[2]

When India attained independence, every citizen was considered equal and to bolster the spirit of democracy, a circular was issued abolishing the use of 'Excellency' for anyone. But damn circular! Instead of discarding the practice, it is almost mandatory to prefix 'His Excellency' (H.E.) with president, vice-president, and governor if being addressed in the third person. Even the letters issued by their own offices refer to them as H.E. Pranab Mukherjee became the first president to do away with the honorific 'His Excellency' immediately after assuming office in July 2012. He addressed the fourth convocation of Lalit Narayan Mithila University, Darbhanga on 3 October 2012. The format of the invitation card proposed to be printed was sent to the president's office for approval. As usual, the honorific 'His Excellency' was prefixed before his name and 'Honourable' before 'President'. His office wrote back that these honorifics should be deleted and it should be only 'Shri Pranab Mukherjee, President of India'.[3] It was also made clear that no bigger chair should be kept for the president; all chairs on the dais would be of equal size. The gesture shown by President Pranab Mukherjee to do away with the honorifics suggests that the Indian democracy is coming of age.

C. Subramanian has been the only governor so far who parted with this practice. Within a month of his assuming the office of the governor of Maharashtra in February 1990, he made it clear that he was genuinely embarrassed by being addressed as 'Your Excellency'. Thereafter, he was referred to as the Honourable Governor. In Goa, he again sent such a message by not wearing his black convocation robe. The Madhya Pradesh government created a history of sort when it restored royal title for its minister Yashodhara Raje, a scion of the Scindia family. On 19 October 2006, the state government slipped out an official gazette notification that 'Srimati' Yashodhara Raje Scindia would henceforth be addressed as 'Shrimant' Yashodhara Raje Scindia. However, the Indian National Congress took a decision in June 2009 to drop the royal titles of its leaders who were former kings but were still referred to as 'Maharaja' or 'Shrimant'. Still, a road in New Delhi named after Madhavrao Scindia has the prefix 'Shrimant' (Shrimant Madhavrao Scindia Marg).

---

[2] Nehru, *An Autobiography*, pp. 218–19.

[3] 'President Pranab Mukherjee Prefers "Sri" to "His Excellency"', *Times of India*, New Delhi, 2 October 2013.

Another ludicrous practice still in vogue is the mode of addressing the judges of the Supreme Court and the high courts as 'My Lord', reminding one of the colonial period. When India was under the yoke of imperialism, the practice of addressing the judges of the Privy Council, who happened to be the members of the Judicial Committee of the House of Lords, as 'My Lord', trickled down to our high courts, as had become the practice in the British High Court. In fact, in England, since justice was delivered by the king or the queen through the king's benches, it is the king who was addressed as 'My Lord', therefore, judges presiding over the king's or queen's benches were addressed as 'My Lord'.

It may be mentioned that lordship is a reminder of the aristocratic, feudal British society of distant past where family background, and not the merit, counted. The House of Lords has its origin to the Curia Regis (Great Council) created in AD 1215, in which all barons were members. When Edward III started inducting common men into the Great Council, aristocrats objected to it, and, therefore, a 'commonality' had to be created which grew into the House of Commons. In the fourteenth century, the Great Council was divided into the House of Lords and the House of Commons. The House of Lords comprised three strata of aristocrats—Duke, Earl, and Viscount who were addressed as 'My lord'. Knights, who formed the lowest rung of aristocracy, were addressed as 'Sir'. The membership of the House of Lords was hereditary and a lord was succeeded by his eldest son. The king was also empowered to increase the number of peerage at the recommendation of the prime minister. For the first time, Pitt the younger increased the number in the second half of eighteenth century to pass a bill.

It is not only the mode of addressing judges; feudalism is glaring in the ambience of the court. Lawyers acquiesced into it and learnt the knack of what may be called crude flattery or blandishment. David Pannick describes this tendency in these words:

Barristers *make submissions* rather than present arguments. They introduce these arguments with an obsequious *May it please your Lordship*, when 'Hello, good morning judge' would do. The fictional Sir Cyril Tart QC does not stretch credibility too far when he opens a case before Justice Squirrel with the words, 'If your Lordship pleases—as, may I add, your Lordship habitually does'. The barrister presents his arguments *with respect, with great respect*, or on difficult occasions, *with the greatest of respect*. The degree of respect voiced is, of course, in inverse proportion to the willingness indicated by the judge to agree with the arguments being advanced. Little has changed in these matters since the seventeenth century. After making his maiden appearance in court as a barrister, the future Lord Chancellor Cowper wrote to his wife to say that bystanders found fault with his performance only in that 'I did not interweave what I said with civil expressions enough to his Lordship, as "may it please your Lordship" and "I am humbly to move your Lordship" and the like'.[4]

When India ushered in freedom, it was expected that the scars of colonialism would be obliterated sooner rather than later. In this very spirit, the Supreme Court issued a circular in the early 1950s of the last century that judges of superior courts would be addressed as 'Sir' or 'Mr. Judge', and not as 'My Lord'. It also said that 'Honorable' would be used for the court, not for the judge. But it was not to be, as neither judges were ready to adapt themselves to the new democratic mores, nor were lawyers prepared to risk their practice. It has also become almost mandatory to use 'Honourable' for the judge. The nameplates carry this honorific, and in some cases the judges themselves use it with their names even in private correspondence. In the Socialist Republic of India, since justice is imparted by common men, not king, judges should not be addressed even as 'Your Honour', much less 'My Lord'.

What we have not been able to achieve even after several decades of independence is what the nascent Republic of South Africa did in one stroke. The country witnessed its first multi-racial democratic elections in April 1994. In October 1994, the Constitutional Court was created, which is now the highest court of the country. It look a decision before its first sitting in March 1995 that judges of the Constitutional Court would not be addressed as 'My Lord' or 'Your Honour' but as 'Mr. Justice so and so' and it is being followed there. Actually 'Lord' means God, for example, Lord Rama, Lord Buddha, and so on. Some judges feel that this mode of address casts a huge burden of responsibility on them to be totally impartial like God. However, godliness is not reflected in their conduct and behaviour.

Moreover, the whole style of judges smacks of feudalism—when the judge gets up, peons must remove the chair immediately, when the judge moves the security will, accompany him/her whistling and commanding others to keep the way clear. In ancient India, kings also functioned as judges, as the administration of justice was considered a divine duty. But as judges, their appearance and demeanour were different. As kings, they put on the crown and royal robes and sat on the throne while participating in the *Rajyasabha* or Darbar, and discharging their executive functions. But while acting as judges, they dispensed with such expensive attire and were required to enter the court hall in 'a simple dress' and 'with a pleasant demeanour'.

[4] David Pannick, *Judge* (Oxford: Oxford University Press, 1988), p. 153.

B.R. Agarwal comments: 'The elaborate paraphernalia which we see in the courts today seems to have been introduced by Muslim rulers and further elaborated by the British who were fond of pomp and show.'[5]

From the seventeenth century onwards, the idea of equality gained currency which was reflected in the writings of political thinkers and some political movements. The Levellers, a radical movement that originated in Cromwell's army, emphasized that privilege was the root cause of all evil, and that all citizens ought to be treated as political equals, and rejected political privilege based on birth or on professional monopolies.[6] However, in India, there is a recent trend of using Hon'ble for ministers, MPs, and MLAs, but only God knows how many of them really deserve it.

The concept of equality may be charming but only when inferiors look to superiors and superiors fume when the underclass claims parity with them. The streak of authoritarianism is too pronounced in persons vested with authority. However, due to compulsions of politics in a democracy, ministers and legislators are forced to impersonate as equals before the public, but judges are reluctant to adapt themselves and cast off the veneer of feudalism even for the sake of tokenism.

[5] 'Our Judiciary', NBT, p. 12.
[6] See Dorothy Pickles, *Democracy* (London: Muthen and Co. Ltd., 1971, p. 44.

Index

About the Author

Sudhanshu Ranjan is a veteran journalist. He has been associated with Doordarshan for more than 30 years.